NO MEXICANS, WOMEN, OR DOGS ALLOWED

NO MEXICANS, WOMEN, OR DOGS ALLOWED

The Rise of the Mexican American
Civil Rights Movement

CYNTHIA E. OROZCO

UNIVERSITY OF TEXAS PRESS, AUSTIN

Fifth paperback printing, 2012

Requests for permission to reproduce material from this work should be sent to:
Permissions
University of Texas Press
P.O. Box 7819
Austin, TX 78713–7819
utpress.utexas.edu/rp-form

LIBRARY OF CONGRESS CATALOGING-IN-PUBLICATION DATA

Orozco, Cynthia.
No Mexicans, women, or dogs allowed : the rise of the Mexican American civil rights movement / Cynthia E. Orozco. — 1st ed.
    p.   cm.
Includes bibliographical references and index.
ISBN 978-0-292-72132-6 (pbk. : alk. paper)
1. Mexican Americans—Civil rights—History—20th century.   2. League of United Latin American Citizens—History.   3. Order of Sons of America—History.   4. Civil rights movements—United States—History—20th century.
5. Mexican Americans—Civil rights—Texas—History—20th century.
6. Civil rights movements—Texas—History—20th century.   7. Mexican Americans—Texas—Social conditions—20th century.   8. Mexican American women—Texas—Social conditions—20th century.   I. Title.
E184.M50775 2009
973'.0468720764—dc22

                                                              2009020110

doi:10.7560/721098

CONTENTS

ACKNOWLEDGMENTS

This book is about the origins of the most important U.S. civil rights organization for people of Mexican descent. Mexican American men founded the League of United Latin American Citizens (LULAC) in Corpus Christi, Texas, in 1929. I began this book in a Chicano history class with Professor Víctor Nelson Cisneros at the University of Texas at Austin in 1978.

I grew up in Cuero, Texas, a town of European Americans, Mexican Americans, Mexicans, and African Americans. Cuero lies at the pinnacle of historical sites associated with Texas independence and anti-Mexican sentiment—Gonzales, Goliad, and San Antonio. Thirty miles from Gonzales, we heard the refrain "Come and take it"; thirty miles from Goliad (La Bahía), we learned of the massacre; and seventy miles from San Antonio, we were instructed to "Remember the Alamo."

In the 1960s and 1970s de jure racial segregation and de facto segregation were in effect according to race—"white," "Mexican," and "black." Slavery had thrived in Cuero, and a third of the population was African American in 1900. My neighborhood consisted of Mexican Americans, whites, and African Americans, including the son of a slave.

When my Mexican immigrant parents moved from South Texas to Cuero in the 1950s they found extensive racial discrimination. In the 1920s my mother immigrated from Nuevo León, Mexico, to Mercedes, Texas, where a schoolteacher whipped her hands with a rubber hose because she spoke Spanish. She has self-identified mostly as a Mexican American, while my father died with a Mexican identity, rejecting U.S. citizenship and refusing to learn English. He remained what U.S. Immigration and Customs Enforcement calls a "resident alien." They found the schools, hospitals, cemeteries, and theater segregated. A Mexican school existed in Cuero, but in 1940 the city's LULAC chapter and LULAC lawyers from San Antonio shut it down. My parents were initially refused a home loan because of race. My sister told me that when we were kids, white kids pelted us with peaches because we were "greasers." Schools taught us to be ashamed of being "Mexican." At the same time, Mexican Americans were also prejudiced toward Mexicans: a Mexican American even beat up my immigrant dad.

In the 1970s my mother cofounded a LULAC chapter in Cuero. During my undergraduate years (1976–1978) toward the end of the Chicano movement I never told self-proclaimed Chicanos that my mother was a "LULACer" because Chicano movement activists despised LULAC as "middle-class assimilationists." But my family was working-class, and my parents were proud of their Mexican heritage. My father was a Mexican citizen, and I grew up in a tricultural home. This tricultural world I grew up in—American, Mexican American, and Mexican—was similar to the context in which LULAC operated in the 1920s.

I thank two women for making the heart of this research possible. Señora Adela Sloss-Vento of Edinburg, Texas, shared her collection with me. Likewise, the wife of Alonso S. Perales, Marta Engracia Pérez de Perales, let me use her husband's papers. These collections are still not in any library. I thank Señora Sloss-Vento's son, Dr. Arnoldo Vento, for an interview about his mother. Enrique Sáenz and Ed Idar Jr., who both have passed away, permitted interviews about J. Luz Sáenz and Eduardo Idar Sr., respectively. Dr. Carmen Tafolla provided documents about James Tafolla Sr.

I thank all the scholars who helped me. Nelson Cisneros saw a historian in me when I was a college sophomore writing a twenty-page research paper. Michael Stoff and Ricardo Romo supervised my senior honors thesis. Professors Arnoldo Vento, José Limón, Emilio Zamora, and Juan Rodríguez encouraged my scholarship, as did then graduate students Estevan Flores and Devón Peña. Professor Limón gave me a copy of the Order Sons of America (Orden Hijos de América) 1922 constitution, and Professor Zamora lent me an interview he conducted with LULAC founder John Solís. Professor Rodríguez also shared J. Luz Sáenz' writings. At the University of California at Los Angeles (UCLA), Professors Juan Gómez-Quiñones, Norris Hundley, and Kathryn Kish Sklar mentored me. I also thank UCLA Professors Joyce Appleby, Stanley Coben, James Wilkie, George Sánchez, Raymond Rocco, Leobardo Estrada, and Richard Chabrán. My thanks go also to Professor

Arnoldo De León, Devón Peña, research assistants Virginia Adams, Mayra Lucero, and Kathleen Kennedy, and indexer Nick J. Bravo.

The following institutions provided research and travel funds: UCLA Institute of American Cultures; UCLA Program on Mexico; National Women's Studies Association; National Hispanic Scholarship Fund; UCLA History Department; Tomás Rivera program funded by the Pew Manuscript Completion Project (then University of Texas at San Antonio [UTSA] Provost Ray Garza and University of Texas at Austin [UT Austin] Vice Provost Ricardo Romo); UT Austin Mexican American Studies Center; University of New Mexico (UNM) Center for Regional Studies (Director Tobías Durán); UNM Southwest Hispanic Research Institute; UNM Chicano Studies; and UNM Department of History. The Ford Foundation provided dissertation and postdoctoral fellowships. I conducted research for Chapter 4 as a research associate at the Texas State Historical Association. In 1996 the association published *The New Handbook of Texas*, a six-volume encyclopedia on Texas history in which several biographies first appeared.

I thank the staff at the following institutions: the Nettie Lee Benson Latin American Collection and the Center for American History at UT Austin; Houston Metropolitan Research Center; Lorenzo De Zavala Texas State Library; Bancroft Library at the University of California at Berkeley; Texas A&M University at Kingsville South Texas Archives; Institute of Texan Cultures of San Antonio; San Antonio Public Library; and Corpus Christi Public Library. At the Benson Latin American Collection I thank Roberto Urzúa, Elvira Chavira (who built the foundation of the LULAC Archive), Gilda Baeza, and Margo Gutiérrez. Rare Books and Manuscripts Reading Room staff members included Wanda Turnley, Carmen Sacomani, Jamie Purcell, Anne Jordan, Jane Garner, María Flores, Michael Hironymous, Helen Clements, and Russell Thomas.

The following people helped locate photographs: Eva Sáenz, Rose Garza, Luz María Prieto, and Luis Wilmot; David Mycune of the Hidalgo Historical Collection in Edinburg, Texas; Dean Gilberto Hinojosa of Incarnate Word; Thomas Kreneck; Cecilia A. Hunter at Texas A&M in Kingsville and Grace Charles at Texas A&M in Corpus Christi. The following activists permitted interviews: John Solís, M. C. Gonzáles, Adelaida Garza, Carolina and Louis Wilmot, and María Hernández. Emma Tenayuca's correspondence to me also proved valuable. I thank photographer Mark Jones and cartographer Molly O'Halloran.

Throughout my research I have maintained some connection with LULAC. I have been able to help LULAC members learn more about its origins than the organization has been able to help me with my research. Nevertheless, the national, state, and local councils have been instructive. National President Ruben Bonilla of Corpus Christi, Texas, opened his files to me before there was a LULAC Archive at the Benson Latin American Collection at UT Austin in 1980. Alicia Corral of the Professional Women's Council of Los Angeles provided assistance in attending and presenting at national LULAC conventions. Attending these conventions and more recently being a LULACer from 1999 to 2003 in Ruidoso, New Mexico, provided an ethnographic opportunity in LULAC.

Finally, I would like to thank my family. My father, Primitivo, died before this book was completed, but he expressed pride in my work. My mother, a community leader, writer, and orator, has always supported my education and work. Their hard work allowed all six Orozco children to graduate from college when college became somewhat more accessible to La Raza in the 1970s. My sister Sylvia facilitated the completion of this project, and Irma, a professional translator, served as my translator. I also thank my husband, Leo Martínez. My marriage has given me insight into the role of women in politics. Finally, I thank my cherished "son," Buddy—now allowed into dog heaven.

NO MEXICANS, WOMEN, OR DOGS ALLOWED

Introduction

LULAC, I SALUTE YOU

Friends, I'd like to tell you
What happened in Corpus
Some men got together
And formed LULAC
They were few in numbers
But they had a lot of courage.
They were tired of seeing their people
Suffer such pain.
Garza and his friends
Men of devotion.
But in their hearts
They felt a revolution.

       —EUSEBIO "CHEVO" MORALES,
       LULAC MEMBER, 1987

The League of United Latin American Citizens (LULAC) is the oldest Mexican American civil rights organization in the United States and celebrated its eightieth anniversary in 2009.[1] With several thousand members today, it is one of the largest Latino voluntary associations. Mexican American men founded LULAC on February 17, 1929, in Corpus Christi, Texas, when the Corpus Christi chapter of the Order Sons of America (OSA), the Order Knights of America (OKA) of San Antonio, and the League of Latin American Citizens (LLAC) of South Texas united.[2] (Mexican American women could not join until 1933.) The oldest, largest, and most important of these groups was the OSA, founded in San Antonio in 1921. It had seven chapters in South Texas by 1929.

LULAC's original purpose was to "develop within the members of our race the best, purest, and most perfect type of a true and loyal citizen of the United States" and to "eradicate from our body politic all intents and tendencies to establish discrimination among our fellow-citizens on account of race, religion or social position as being contrary to the true spirit of Democracy, our Constitution and Laws."[3] These goals, anticipated earlier in the founding of the OSA, ushered in a new political era among Mexican-origin people in the United States.[4]

Both the OSA and LULAC reflected the aspirations of a nascent Mexican American male middle class committed to combating racism as an obstacle to community empowerment. Unlike other Mexican-descent organizations in the 1920s, the OSA and LULAC found inspiration in the United States more than in Mexico.[5] Their members were among the first to assert a Mexican American identity and claim their U.S. citizenship by arguing that they possessed the rights accorded them by the U.S. Constitution.[6] At the same time they believed their U.S. citizenship obligated them to serve their nation, the United States. This U.S. patriotism prompted Chicano movement scholars of the 1970s to refer to the OSA and LULAC as examples of the "politics of accommodation" or "adaptation."[7]

Unlike most organizations in the Mexican-descent community at the time, the OSA and LULAC emphasized U.S. citizenship. In 1927 at a convention in Harlingen, Texas, Mexican immigrants—the conference majority—walked out of the meeting when it was argued that only U.S. citizens could join the association. Mexican Americans there—U.S. citizens—went on to found LLAC and two years later founded LULAC.

In this study I place the rise of the OSA and LULAC organizations within their proper historical context, the Mexican American civil rights movement in Texas. I stress context because most scholars who have written about the league were Chicano movement activists and have judged LULAC by Chicano movement or Chicano nationalist standards of the late 1960s and early 1970s.[8] Until only recently, many historians expected LULAC to mirror the Chicano movement organizations of the late 1960s and early 1970s. They failed to address LULAC within the context of the 1920s.

These historians abhorred what they thought the league represented—middle-class interests, assimilation, and political accommodation. Instead, they focused on the working class, the maintenance of "Mexican culture," and resistance to exploitation and political domination.[9] It is now clear that the Chicano movement idealized, romanticized, and essentialized La Raza and the working class. Scholars expressed limited, static, and ahistorical notions of "Mexican culture" and did not fully comprehend the meaning or spectrum of resistance to racism. Consequently, until recently LULAC has been demonized by most scholars and activists.

Chicano scholars were especially critical of the identity that they believed LULAC members chose.[10] The Chicano movement rejected the identity of "Mexican American" and "American" and criticized LULAC for embracing these identities. Likewise, those who self-identified as "Chicano" idealized the identity of "Mexican" and romanticized the indigenous, especially the Aztec. Chicanos were also critical of LULAC's adoption of English as its official language in its first constitution.[11]

Chicano political scientists began to write about LULAC in the 1970s.[12] Armando Navarro described the league as "middle class Mexican Americans" who organized "petite-bourgeoisie patriotic service clubs dedicated to assimilation into the Anglo culture."[13] Alfredo Cuellar wrote that the OSA and LULAC advocated the "politics of adaptation" and that "the politicization of Mexican Americans" did not occur until after World War II.[14]

The 1980s witnessed a more benign treatment of LULAC. The decade produced a new political climate with significant gains made by the Southwest Voter Registration and Education Project and the Mexican American Legal Defense and Education Fund, mainstream organizations like LULAC that pursued legal challenges and voting as means to improve the Latina/o condition. Their success prompted Chicano scholars to rethink their views of earlier civil rights organizations.[15] LULAC President Rubén Bonilla's administrations of the late 1970s and 1980s also convinced LULAC critics that the association was capable of progressive social change. By 1989 political scientist Carlos Muñoz Jr. noted that LULAC had "re-surfaced as the leading national Mexican American political organization."[16]

Yet, the Chicano nationalist interpretation lingered through the 1990s and continues even to this day. In 1985 Chicano movement activist and Raza Unida founder José Ángel Gutiérrez referred to "the LULAC example of assimilationist thought."[17] Navarro continues to espouse this interpretation.[18] Now, scholars in whiteness studies are misreading the league, rendering a neo–Chicano movement interpretation of LULAC.[19]

Moving in the right direction is historian Craig A. Kaplowitz, who has been critical of Chicano movement interpretations of LULAC and has suggested that LULAC, along with the American GI Forum, proved to be at the forefront of Mexican American civil rights in Texas.[20] He focuses on LULAC and its interface with national policy. While in his study Kaplowitz does an excellent job of addressing the league's ties to U.S. presidential politics and national policy, his concept of "national" is limited. LULAC's concept of La Raza as a nation as well as its multinational and transnational identities must also be understood. LULAC has recognized and imagined a Raza nation and acted accordingly.

A scholar who has changed his earlier views is political scientist Benjamín Márquez, the most important scholar of LULAC. While his LULAC: *The Evolution of a Mexican American Political Organization* (1993) was influenced by the Chicano movement, in his more recent writings he has utilized new research on social movement theory and provided a more balanced treatment of the league.[21] Here I give more attention to his older work because this interpretation continues to wield significant influence.

THEORETICAL APPROACHES

Histories of LULAC date back to 1930, starting with the work of political scientist Oliver Douglas Weeks. Following cursory studies of the league in the 1970s, new conceptual tools appeared after 1980. Scholars have applied the following conceptual tools: political generation, class and consciousness, incentive theory, and whiteness.

Weeks used ethnographic research to conduct his study.[22] In 1929 the National Advisory Board of Social Sciences commissioned University of Texas professor Weeks to attend the founding convention and write "The League of United Latin American Citizens: A Texas-Mexican Civic Organization." But he gave scant attention to civil rights struggles of South Texas associations that dated back to 1921 and preceded LULAC. Likewise, though he mentioned the Harlingen convention of 1927—the first attempt at unification by the various associations—he did not address what happened there or explain the event's significance. All research before 1980 relied on Weeks.

Mario T. García's 1989 *Mexican Americans: Leadership, Ideology, and Identity* was the first study of LULAC by a professional historian and the first to apply the political generation model. He defined a "political generation" as "a group of human beings who have undergone the same basic historical experiences during their formative years," and he considered 1930 to 1960 as one.[23] He saw LULAC as the first organizational sign of the "Mexican American generation." But he ignored the 1910s and 1920s as part of his gen-

erational analysis and only briefly mentioned the emergence of the OSA and LULAC. Generational models can be useful, but the heterogeneity of the Raza community must be considered as well; immigrants and women did not fit into this model. Nor does it account for regional differences in the United States or the spectrum of political ideologies. Thus the model of a political generation can be complicated by citizenship, gender, region, and political ideology.[24]

Using the concepts of class, culture, and consciousness in his intellectual history of San Antonio in the 1930s, historian Richard A. García offered a second framework to study LULAC. *Rise of the Mexican American Middle Class* presents a nuanced portrait of the league, though García too recognized a "Mexican American generation of the 1930s." He saw 1929 as a turning point in the evolution of Mexican American politics and thus focused on the 1930s. He asked, "Why and how were the 1930s the period in which consciousness changed from Mexican to Mexican American?"[25] But he ignored the 1920s.

One of Richard García's contributions was in making a distinction between the Mexican American middle class and the Mexican middle class. He showed that such identity formation is often relational.[26] In other words, a Mexican American identity was created in relation to or as compared to a Mexican immigrant identity in Texas. He highlighted ideologues Alonso S. Perales and M. C. Gonzáles, with great attention to class, culture, and consciousness. García's approach can be applied to the 1920s.

Political scientist Benjamín Márquez applied a third framework—incentive theory—while still adhering to a Chicano movement interpretation. His *LULAC: The Evolution of a Mexican American Political Organization* surveys league history from the 1920s to the 1990s. He argues that LULAC can be understood by looking at individual self-interest. This study is marred by an overarching incentive theory that historical evidence does not uphold.

Historian Neil Foley suggests a fourth conceptual tool, referring to "whiteness," to understand LULAC. Whiteness studies emerged in the 1990s. Foley argues that LULAC did not aspire to Mexicanness and that the league made a Faustian pact (a devil's deal) with whites to be included in the category of "white" as part of their political strategy. He concludes, "LULAC members had tried just about everything they could to prove how Americanized they were: they spoke English, voted, used the court systems, got elected to office, actively opposed Mexican immigration, and excluded Mexican citizens from membership in LULAC," mistakenly equating democratic ideals with European Americans.[27] Foley contends that by "choosing the Caucasian option," Mexican Americans "forged White racial identities that were constructed on the backs of blacks."[28] "Whiteness" has some usefulness in the study of LULAC, but focusing on "Americanness," "Mexican Americanness," and "Mexicanness" is more appropriate, especially in the 1920s. Moreover, it is important to study racial formation and identity formation by insiders and outsiders.

LIMITATIONS OF PREVIOUS STUDIES

Previous studies have been flawed as they relate to class, identity, immigration, citizenship, social movements, biography, periodization, and methodology. First, scholars have called LULAC "middle class" but have rarely addressed its meaning. Class in the Mexican-descent community in the 1920s has been misunderstood. The middle class in the Mexican-origin community is not the same as the European American middle class. Scholar Mario Barrera has called this group a "colonized middle class," and I concur.[29] Yet, this middle class was privileged as compared to the Mexican-origin working class. Moreover, there was a Mexican American middle class and a Mexican immigrant middle class.

Second, previous studies misrepresented the league's ethnic or national identity. Critics in early studies scoffed at LULAC because its members called it "Latin American,"[30] and critics assumed this was a play at whiteness rather than a pan-American identity. Early scholars placed uneven emphasis on the group's identification with the United States.[31] Similarly, historian F. Arturo Rosales introduced another conceptual tool—shifting ethnic consciousness—but used it only to refer to a change from Mexicanness to Mexican Americanness.[32] He did not see any other kinds of shifting consciousness. Moreover, consciousness or identity can be ethnic, national, transnational, multinational, or some mixture.

Not enough attention has been placed on the multiple, shifting, intersecting, and contradictory identities that LULAC has had. Early Chicano scholarship was inconsiderate of multiple identities. Today, Chicana/o cultural studies, a new field of inquiry since the late 1990s, suggests the need to understand various identity constructions. These multiple identities arise from changing historical circumstances and specific situations and contexts. These identities are created in relation to others and have even constituted political strategy.[33] Moreover, identity, naming, and labeling are not necessarily permanent—they can be temporary, flexible, and negotiable.

Earlier studies made identity formation synonymous with the process

of Mexican Americanization, which it is not. Historian George J. Sánchez' *Becoming Mexican American* focuses on the social and cultural aspects of becoming Mexican Americanized in Los Angeles in the 1930s.[34] However, there was another, competing, and even more dominant identity in Los Angeles in the 1930s—a Mexican identity that Sánchez has ignored.[35] Likewise, in Texas in the 1910s, 1920s, and 1930s, the competing identity of Mexicanness was especially strong.[36] In addition to Mexican Americanization as identity formation as studied by Sánchez, I am interested in the politics of U.S. citizenship, a topic Sánchez has not addressed.

Third, social scientists have misunderstood the OSA and the league's relations with Mexican immigrants. They have seen the OSA and LULAC as exclusionary and almost anti-Mexican. Historian David Gregory Gutiérrez notes in *Walls and Mirrors* that the relationship between Mexican Americans and Mexican immigrants across history has been ignored.[37] He mentions the league's policies toward immigrants but does not explain how the Mexican immigrant middle class and Mexican immigrant working class indeed helped to define LULAC's politics. Mexican immigrants have historically been a group by which LULAC has defined itself.

Gutiérrez mentions the Harlingen convention of 1927, one of the first known clashes between Mexican Americans and Mexicans and a significant chapter in the history of LULAC, but he does not discuss it as a defining event, as I argue it was. LULAC's relations with immigrants are more complex than Gutiérrez suggests; LULAC's concepts of community, nation, and identity must be examined. Its strategy of Raza political empowerment was especially important.

A fourth limitation with previous studies involves citizenship, which many authors ignore but which has garnered more attention since the late 1990s.[38] Ronald Beiner's *Theorizing Citizenship* points to its multiple meanings.[39] I use it here to mean both a legal or official status designed by nation-states and to designate desirable "civic" behavior or agency. But I will call citizenship as legal status "national citizenship" and citizenship as desirable civic behavior "social citizenship." Recently, "cultural citizenship" and "regional citizenship" have been introduced as further ways to fully understand immigrants' lives, practices, activism, and participation in the United States.[40] South African feminists have called for the "(un)thinking" of citizenship.[41] However, these ideals did not apply in the 1920s. Both national and social citizenship have been intertwined with race, class, and gender and help explain Mexican American civic activism as exhibited by the OSA and LULAC.

Fifth, previous studies have not considered using social movement theory to study the league and have not conceptualized the "Mexican American civil rights movement."[42] Chicano historiography is finally acknowledging this concept, though most still believe it emerged after World War II despite numerous historians having documented LULAC's civil rights struggles in the 1930s. In 1987 historian and sociologist David Montejano stated that although La Raza initiated civil rights "struggles" in Texas in the 1910s and 1920s, a civil rights movement did not come to fruition there until after 1945.[43] Thus, the OSA and LULAC have been excluded as organizations in the Mexican American civil rights movement. With the exception of Julie Leininger Pycior's research on the San Antonio OSA council, the significant activity of the OSA in the 1920s has heretofore gone undocumented.[44]

Historians of the twentieth-century Chicano experience have examined many aspects of the Mexican American civil rights movement.[45] The four-hour documentary *Chicano!: The History of the Mexican American Civil Rights Movement* introduced the phrase "Mexican American civil rights movement" to the general public.[46] Historian F. Arturo Rosales' book accompanying the series did not discuss the concept of the Mexican American civil rights movement, though he used it in his title.[47]

Sixth, previous OSA and LULAC studies have not considered genders. Most Mexican American civil rights studies have not gendered men and have excluded women. Since the 1990s women have constituted half if not more of LULAC membership. And while Chicano scholars have typically been critical of LULAC, they have yet to criticize men's privileged place in it or women's subordination within the league. Sources on women are plentiful but have simply been ignored or have not been seen through a gendered lens.[48] Women's places in the organizations and movement have yet to be understood.[49]

Masculinities, genders, and homosocialities have been ignored in most studies of Chicano political associations. Homosociality is defined by historian Carroll Smith-Rosenberg as social relations among members of the same gender.[50] Homosociality among Chicanas has received much attention but not homosociality among Chicano men. The field of men's studies arose in the 1980s, but the study of gendered Chicano men is now emerging.[51]

I am especially interested in the role fraternity, brotherhood, and manhood played in organizing the OSA and LULAC. Historians have assumed that because men founded LULAC, gender as a tool of analysis is of use only when women became members in 1933. Men in the OSA and LULAC, however, lived gendered lives and had various gender ideologies about men's and women's political participation.

A seventh limitation involves periodization. My study focuses on the period 1910–1930, and I argue that the events and historical processes of this era are crucial in understanding the OSA and LULAC. Scholars have referred to the "Mexican American mind," a "Mexican American generation," and the "rise of the Mexican American middle class" as phenomena of the 1930s, pointing to the founding of LULAC in 1929 as evidence.[52]

However, it is the 1910s and 1920s that explain the emergence of the OSA in 1921 and LULAC in 1929. The ideological currents of the 1910s and 1920s require attention, as do the experiences of OSA and LULAC founders and members.[53] These currents emanated from Mexico, Texas, and the United States and influenced OSA and LULAC activists. Moreover, I will examine World War I's impact on the emerging civil rights movement.[54] The Progressive Era, with its emphasis on reform, order, and assimilation, and the 1920s, which gave rise to greater class inequities, also serve as the broader context. The recent research of Mae M. Ngai on the making of "illegal aliens" in the 1920s sheds light as well on the transformation of racial identities and citizenship in that decade.[55]

An eighth limitation involves methodology. Many studies chronicle organizational activities and significant events but pay scant attention to organizational ideology and structure over time. In addition, studies have made little use of membership lists, constitutions, or minutes to carefully assess who joined or even to assess the associations' politics over time. Early studies gave only brief attention to historical actors, usually focusing on one or two male leaders while ignoring rank-and-file members and women.[56] In this study I focus on a wide range of leadership, I touch on membership, and I address nonmembers—many who were women.

Finally, my book differs from previous accounts that have simply defined the OSA and LULAC as accommodationist. I place both organizations within the context of the 1920s and consequently within the framework of resistance to European American domination. More often than not, academics have focused on the internalized racism of OSA and LULAC members;[57] I chose instead to look at their hybridity and resistance. They operated within the context of a new era, new politics, new identities, new nationalisms, and new gender relations—in short, as Mexican American middle-class men resisting European American domination. Thus, the study of the OSA and LULAC requires a reconsideration of class, culture, consciousness, ethnicity, immigration, nation, citizenship, social movements, genders, and periodization.

WHAT'S IN A NAME

The question of identity is crucial to this study, and readers must understand the politics of naming before proceeding. Identities, by both insiders and outsiders, are important. In this study I pay attention to how outsiders (non-Raza) named the Mexican-origin community through racial formation and racialization. Likewise, I pay attention to how insiders (La Raza) named themselves and defined themselves through self-identity, class formation, community formation, nationalism, and citizenship.

Two concepts are critical in understanding racial identity—racial formation and racialization. Scholars Michael Omi and Howard Winant define "racial formation" as the "process by which social, economic, and political forces determine the content and importance of racial categories, and by which they are in turn shaped by racial meanings."[58] In the 1920s "whites," "Mexicans," "Mexican Americans," "México Texanos," "Americans," and "La Raza" were common identities. The 1920s brought a new era in how Mexican-origin people were being imagined, defined, and constructed both by whites and on their own. In this study I will explain how the meaning of "Mexican" changed from the 1910s to the 1920s and will address how a Mexican race was constructed. I will also explain how "Mexican" became synonymous with "immigrant."

Racialization is "the extension of racial meaning to a previously racially unclassified relationship, social practice, or group."[59] Understanding "Mexican" as a racialized imaginary is key to this study. As the "Mexican race" and "Mexicans" were being defined in a different way, a new paradigm—"the Mexican problem"—emerged as a means European Americans created to racialize and subordinate La Raza. The OSA and LULAC were a response to "the Mexican problem." Hereafter in this study when I employ the term "Mexican" in quotes, I do so to denote racialization—racist and essentialized European American perceptions of La Raza.

The labeling of La Raza as a homogeneous Mexican problem was synonymous with European Americans' appropriation of Americanness for themselves. While the early 1910s saw the dominant society defining "American" in a typically WASP way, the Americanization movement of the late 1910s formalized this effort. Yet around the same time, World War I raised new questions and possibilities associated with Americanness. How would La Raza define itself during the war? Would its constituents claim their Americanness as American citizens? Would they claim their future with the United States if they were Mexican immigrants living in the United States? And

would white Americans accept Raza veterans as equals? So in this study I
seek to understand how La Raza was defined by outsiders as "other," "other
than American," and "un-American."

I further seek to understand and explain self-identity and community
formation. Self-reference and identity are both historically specific, reflecting a particular time in history. Variables of citizenship, class, birthplace,
residence, language use, education, and color have influenced ethnic, racial,
and national identity. Social, cultural, political, and ideological differences
continue to exist within the Mexican-origin community.[60] Class, citizenship, and gender have had their effects as well on identity within the Raza
community.

Self-referents among La Raza in the 1920s included "México Texano" as
used in Spanish. If translated—which was rare—it was translated among La
Raza as "Mexican Texan," not "Texas Mexican."[61] Members of this group
were typically born in the United States, and/or their life experience was
largely within Texas. México Texanos were U.S. citizens who identified with
Texas as a state, with a regional culture, and with the United States. "México
Texano" accurately reflected the cultural milieu in which OSA and LULAC
members lived. They operated in Mexican, México Texano, and European
American worlds. "México Texano" preceded the term "Mexican American"
and seems to have been in vogue between the 1880s and 1920s. It represented
the hybridity of many in La Raza who lived in Texas—part Mexican, part
Texan.

The term "Mexican American" was barely emerging in the 1920s and
would not become common until the 1960s. It will be used here as synonymous with "México Texano." Still, the emergence of "Mexican American"
represents a shift from a Spanish to an English cultural milieu and a shift by
México Texanos from a regional identity to a national identity as well as the
hybridity of La Raza.

"La Raza" was another popular self-referent in the 1920s. Its use here is
not my attempt at pan-Latino or pan-American nationalism. Nor is it bio-
logical determinism. Rather, it reflects usage by the people being studied
who identified a community based on race, nationality, and multinational-
ism or transnationalism. Historian Elliot Young argues that there was an
"artificial unity" around the term, but I am interested in how La Raza used
it to constitute a community and nation, whether imagined or real.[62]

While acknowledging the multiplicity and impermanence of identities, I
use specific terms in specific ways herein. I reject the labeling of the entire
community as "Mexican" or "Mexican American." I use "Mexican-origin"

and "Mexican-descent" to denote a common group distinct from European Americans. I will use "European American" as synonymous with "white" and "American." "Mexican" without quotation marks will designate those born in Mexico whose life experience was largely there and who were citizens there, while, as mentioned earlier, "Mexican" in quotes will designate the racialized imaginary. "México Texano" is a self-referent by Texans of Mexican descent, and "La Raza" is a self-referent used here by both Mexican Americans and Mexicans.

BOOK ORGANIZATION

The book is divided into three parts. Part One addresses the historical context giving rise to the OSA and LULAC. Chapter 1 explores La Raza's social, economic, and political status from 1910 to 1930. I examine South Texas as a distinct region, economy, and society in the diverse settings of urban San Antonio, semi-urban Corpus Christi, rural Alice, and the Lower Rio Grande Valley. The OSA and LULAC emerged during the region's transformation from a rural ranching and farming society to a modern urban society based on agribusiness. Urbanization, immigration, and education gave rise to the México Texano male middle class as part of changing class formation. This new class arose in the context of racial segregation and the racialization of "Mexicans" as "the Mexican problem." The lack of an independent female Mexican American middle class will also be addressed.

In Chapter 2 I analyze the social and ideological origins of the OSA and LULAC by focusing on significant events and ideological currents in the 1910s and 1920s. A shift emerged then in ethnic and national identity or consciousness from México Texano to Mexican American. This change was evident in ideological currents emanating from the Mexican Revolution, the Plan de San Diego, World War I, Progressivism, the Americanization movement, Mexican immigration, federal immigration policies, and "the Mexican problem." New policies and practices of national and social citizenship arose. These events and currents in the United States, Texas, and Mexico influenced the thinking of the emerging male middle class.

Part Two addresses movement leaders and organizers, their activities in the 1920s, the significant events of the Harlingen convention of 1927, and the founding of LULAC in 1929. The emergence of the OSA and the Mexican American civil rights movement is the subject of Chapter 3, in which I discuss how La Raza strategized its resistance against racial oppression. Politics by Mexicans and Mexican Americans are described. I address the role of the Mexican consulate in the political empowerment and disempowerment of La Raza, and I document significant civil rights activism by the OSA and others in San Antonio, Corpus Christi, and Alice throughout the 1920s. I consider class, gender, and citizenship in organizational life.

Chapter 4 provides the first collective biography of the LULAC leadership. In LULAC circles, several of these men are considered founders or founding fathers. But LULAC identified only a few founders, and most are unknown to academics and the general public. I profile the lives of eleven men, with attention to how class and race shaped them and examine what each thought about women's participation in politics. It would be essentialist and inaccurate to simply characterize these men as patriarchal or macho. Attitudes toward Mexican immigrants or Mexican immigration are also considered.

The Harlingen convention of 1927, at which México Texanos excluded Mexicans from their organization, is discussed in Chapter 5. The convention spotlighted conflict between México Texanos and Mexicans over the issues of citizenship, nationhood, identity, and political empowerment. In the chapter I examine México Texano ideologies of citizenship and why and how they believed their political destiny differed from that of Mexicans. I explore the Mexican consulate's relationship to México Texanos and discern differences between Mexicans and México Texanos. How México Texanos defined community and nation is addressed, as is the hybridity of México Texanos, since they fought narrowly defined categories and communities of "American" and "Mexican." I address the issues of citizenship and gender: Was the exclusion of immigrants from what would become LULAC the best strategy for the political empowerment of La Raza? Was women's exclusion the best strategy?

In Chapter 6 I chronicle the founding of LULAC and examine why LULAC and not the OSA became the premier organization. How Mexicans, México Texanos, and European Americans received LULAC's formation is addressed. I compare the 1922 OSA constitution and the 1929 LULAC constitution to measure shifts in ethnic, national, and class identities from the 1910s to 1929. This is the first study of the 1922 OSA constitution and the most detailed analysis of the 1929 constitution.

Part Three concerns theory and methodology, particularly in relation to social movements and gender. Chapter 7 touches on social movement theory. I discuss Márquez' early work and provide an alternative framework in understanding the LULAC organization and members' incentives to join. I assess the usefulness of social movement theory as applied to 1920s Mexican American civil rights activism.

In Chapter 8 I raise questions about methodology in the study of women in OSA and LULAC politics. I question the analytical categories social scientists have used to describe women's supposed exclusion. I ask how we define "political," "activist," "auxiliary," "leader," and "women citizens." Women's marital status, motherhood and its impact on organizational politics, public activism, and social movements are addressed. I address Raza women's empowerment through ladies auxiliaries and Ladies LULAC chapters. I analyze gender as an organizing principle by women and ask whether difference, segregation, or feminist strategy on the part of women explains this separatism.

Finally, I assess how women constructed themselves in their autobiographical narratives and history. How did they define community, citizen, and nation? Focus is placed on Adela Sloss, Adelaida Garza, and Carolina de Luna. The biographies and autobiographical narratives of two other women—Emma Tenayuca and Maria L. de Hernández—raise additional questions about Raza empowerment and whether LULAC chose the best path for the political empowerment of La Raza and women.

PART ONE

SOCIETY AND IDEOLOGY

The Mexican Colony
of South Texas

ONE

> *The horizon of life for the Mexican American, especially
> in Texas, was dark and dreary. The skies, during the
> early twenties were menacing; the clouds were fraught
> with racial discrimination, threats, and economic
> slavery. . . . Strong tributaries constantly flowing into a
> river of hate and disdain; almost reaching flood propor-
> tions were the public signs along the public highways in
> front of restaurants: "No Mexicans Allowed." So there
> were no movies, no barbershops, no swimming pools,
> no jury service, no buying of real estate, no voting, no
> public office.* —M. C. GONZÁLES, LULAC NEWS, 1974

This story begins in South Texas. In the 1910s and 1920s industrialization, urbanization, and the rise of agribusiness fostered the region's integration into the state and nation, encouraging European American migrants and Mexican immigrants to move there. This affected racial arrangements, class composition and formation, and La Raza's identity formation. Out of this cauldron of social and economic ferment emerged a Mexican American civil rights movement.

This chapter addresses the social, demographic, and economic development of South Texas and the status of the Mexican-origin community. Urban San Antonio, semi-urban Corpus Christi, rural Alice, and the Lower

Texas map (lower left) and detail showing South Texas–Mexico border region. Courtesy Molly O'Halloran Inc.

Rio Grande Valley (the Valley), an agricultural region, are discussed. It also addresses the rise of the Mexican American middle class and the formation of the "Mexican race" in the context of heightened racial violence and segregation in the 1910s and 1920s.

South Texas encompasses the state south of San Antonio, north of the Rio Grande, and east of the Gulf of Mexico.[1] Today it includes the cities San Antonio, Corpus Christi, Laredo; towns like Alice; and the Rio Grande

Valley. A homeland to indigenous peoples, Spain colonized this far northern frontier of its vast conquered territories in the Americas. Here, Spaniards, Indians, and racially mixed people established missions, *pueblos* and *villas* (towns), *ranchos* (ranches), and *presidios* (forts). San Antonio, Nuevo Santander, and Laredo became key settlements in the 1700s, and Spanish land grants permitted landownership with ranching and farming along the Rio Grande and Nueces River.[2]

Mexico inherited this region after it won its independence in 1821. After Texas independence, the Texas republic claimed the area, including the region south of the Nueces River, but was not able to attract European American settlement until after the Civil War. After the U.S.-Mexico War of 1846–1848, most South Texas residents continued to see Mexico as their homeland. Others connected to U.S. politics and participated in the Civil War. Around 1850, approximately 18,000 persons of Mexican origin, 2,500 European Americans, and several thousand Indians lived here.[3] In the post–Civil War era, urban centers included San Antonio, Brownsville, Rio Grande City, El Paso, and Laredo, but few European Americans lived there.[4] The railroad ran through San Antonio, Alice, Eagle Pass, and Laredo in the 1870s, spurring European American control of South Texas' economic development.[5]

South Texas residents developed a distinctive border culture based on ranching and farming, the patriarchal family, the close-knit community, and proximity to Mexico.[6] Despite an incipient hybrid American and Mexican culture, most continued to identify themselves as "Mexicans," "México Texanos," and members of "La Raza."[7] Although most were citizens of the United States since 1845 or 1848, few referred to themselves as "Mexican Americans" or "American citizens" in English or Spanish. Few took pride in an "American" identity. English was mostly foreign and unspoken. For this reason, scholars have called the region part of *México de afuera*, or "Greater Mexico." South Texas was a México Texano homeland.[8]

CORPUS CHRISTI

Karankawas, Lipan Apaches, and other Indians first settled this region. Spanish and Mexican ranchers and farmers settled the Corpus Christi region in the 1760s. About seven hundred people lived there in the 1840s, and after the Civil War, it became a distribution center for South Texas and northern Mexico. The railroad arrived around 1880, leading to a population of more than ten thousand by 1910.[9]

The few Spanish land-grant owners here had lost their lands by the 1880s. The landless turned to tenancy and farm labor.[10] Nueces County produced more cotton than any other in the United States; 60 percent of the production was owned by European American absentee growers.[11] After 1910, a small number of Mexican-origin people became property owners. In 1914 only one person of Mexican descent in Nueces County owned land, but 585 did by 1929.[12]

Most of La Raza owned no property and worked as cotton pickers and were locked out of the higher-paying jobs in foundries, machine shops, creameries, cotton oil mills, and small factories. By 1932, 97 percent of the cotton pickers were of Mexican origin, having displaced African Americans by the mid-1920s.[13] Scholar Dellos Urban Buckner reported that "large numbers" of La Raza left the Valley for the Corpus Christi area, where working conditions were better.[14] Sixty-five percent of the county's migrants came from the Valley in 1929.[15]

In the midst of this agricultural boom, Corpus Christi urbanized. In 1920 European Americans outnumbered La Raza two to one, but by 1930 La Raza outnumbered whites. Nearby Kingsville experienced similar demographic change; its Raza population more than doubled from 1920 to 1930.[16] This mixed population prompted Paul S. Taylor to call Nueces County "an American Mexican frontier."[17]

SAN ANTONIO

After World War I, San Antonio also experienced urbanization and demographic change. New railroads, highways, and air routes tied the city to the nation, and during World War I the military infrastructure expanded. The petrochemical, communications, and transportation industries grew, reducing the significance of agriculture, manufacturing, and the military. The city served as a labor distribution point for La Raza, with Mexican laborers en route to Midwestern steel mills and Eastern coal mines.[18] Better transportation and communication facilitated the city's urbanization. Five railroads connected to San Antonio, and the Texas Highway Department opened in 1917. By 1924, nineteen hard-surfaced roads left San Antonio.[19]

The city's population grew from 53,321 in 1900 to 231,542 in 1930, making it the most populous Texas city for several years in the 1920s. It had the most Mexican-origin people in the nation from 1890 to 1900. In 1910 they numbered 29,480 and in 1930 82,373 (35 percent of the city's total population).[20]

LOWER RIO GRANDE VALLEY

South of Corpus Christi lies the Valley, an agricultural heartland span-ning a million acres. The Valley remained largely untouched by land de-velopment, commercial agriculture, railroads, and European American contact until 1904, when the railroad arrived.[21] As agribusiness grew in the 1920s, the population increased, new towns arose, and class structure changed. The Valley was becoming the state's most productive agricultural region.[22] Mexican-origin men prepared the land for agribusiness and picked the crops.

Commenting on changing racial and class arrangements, historian Jo-vita González called the arrival of European Americans an "American inva-sion."[23] She noted,

> For nearly two hundred years the Texas-Mexicans had lived know-ing very little and caring less of what was going on in the United States. . . . These people had lived so long in their communities that it was home to them, and home to them meant Mexico. . . . Mexican newspapers brought them news of the outside, their children were educated in Mexican schools, Spanish was the language of the peo-ple. Mexican currency was used altogether.[24]

She also called the arrival of "Americans" (whites) "a material as well as a spiritual blow to the Mexicans, particularly to the landed aristocracy."[25] She elaborated on the "Mexicanness" of the region rather than its "American-ness," noting that few schoolchildren spoke English.

New towns sprang up. By 1929 these included Harlingen (population 14,000), San Benito (12,500), McAllen (10,000), Edinburg (7,000), Mission (6,500), Mercedes (7,000), Weslaco (7,000), and Donna (6,000). Brownsville's population grew to 22,000. By 1929, three-fourths of the Valley's residents lived in towns of populations over 2,500.[26] Race relations also changed.

European Americans, many Midwesterners, now dominated Hidalgo and Cameron Counties in the Valley and nearby Zapata, Webb, and Duval Counties. Hidalgo, once 98 percent Raza, was now 54 percent Raza; Cam-eron's Raza populace fell from 88 percent to 50 percent.[27] Raza farmworkers, immigrant and native, were at the bottom of this new class order. A small México Texano middle class was emerging, and a few European American businessmen were getting rich.

ALICE

Fifty-four miles west of Corpus Christi lies the small town of Alice. It became the state's busiest cattle-shipping center after the railroad arrived in 1883. Incorporating in 1904 with a population of 887 people, it became the seat of the new county—Jim Wells—in 1911. The 1920 population was 1,180, but a minor oil boom spurred the population to 4,239 by 1931, leading the town to call itself the "Hub City of South Texas."[28]

Alice had a significant Mexican population. Spanish-language newspapers appeared, including *El Eco* in 1896, *El Cosmopolita* in 1903, and *El Latino Americano* in 1920, suggesting a literate middle-class Spanish-speaking audience. Still, Alice, like Valley towns farther south, was a "dual town," racially segregated with "Mexicans" on one side of town and European Americans on the other.[29]

DEMOGRAPHIC UPHEAVAL IN SOUTH TEXAS

South Texas experienced dramatic change between 1900 and 1930, giving Corpus Christi, San Antonio, Alice, and the Valley a modern contour with European American migrants and Mexican immigrants forging a new South Texas. The entire state saw a shift in demographics and race relations with the entry of many Mexican immigrants and small farmers of European American descent.[30]

Mexican immigrants comprised 1 percent of the population around the turn of the twentieth century but 15 percent by 1930. The Mexican Revolution (1910–1929) led many to the United States. In a sample of documented Mexicans coming to the United States in the 1910s and early 1920s, 90 percent listed no profession or skill and only 2 percent were professionals.[31]

This demographic shift paralleled national immigration policy. The Immigration Act of 1917 let 73,000 Mexican workers enter the United States to counter World War I labor shortages; immigration acts in 1921 and 1924 set further allotments. According to historian Mae M. Ngai, the 1924 act was the "first comprehensive restriction law placing numerical limits on immigration" and creating "global racial and national hierarchies."[32]

After 1924, racial ideology and thus immigration policy continued to change. Texas Congressman John Box's bill would limit the entry of all Western Hemisphere immigrants, especially Mexicans.[33] And in 1924 the government created the U.S. Border Patrol, a legal, political, and psychological border between Texas and the United States on one side and Mexico on the other. The Border Patrol institutionalized anti-Mexican sentiment, "alien" status among La Raza, and deportation. In the first five months of 1929 alone, authorities deported 2,617 Mexican "aliens" from Brownsville, Mercedes, and Hidalgo.[34] A new "other" had been created.

THE WORKING CLASS

In this new racial and class order, Mexican-origin workers became more important. One historian has noted "the re-arrangement of the population in new social classes" and found Mexican-origin labor "limited to a very few occupations."[35] Half of La Raza in 1930 worked in agriculture, mostly as farm laborers.[36]

This working-class community was subordinate to European American employers, and race, citizenship, gender, age, and language affected wages.[37] In Corpus Christi most Raza men labored in the fields. Others worked in the street and highway department, building trades, or fishing. Sociologist William Knox found that fewer than one-third of 1,282 Mexican-origin families of his study had steady or permanent jobs in San Antonio.[38] In the Valley, Mexican-origin men's wages could be eight times lower than the minimum cost of living.[39] According to one scholar, farmworkers' wages were "inadequate to maintain the Negro at his present standard of living."[40]

Few Mexican-origin women (about 15 percent in 1900) worked for wages. Knox's San Antonio survey revealed that one-sixth of those surveyed were wage earners.[41] Gender ideology suggested that women should marry, raise children, and be "protected" by men. Working outside the home was considered a disgrace; working women were seen as "a draw-back to motherhood, a handicap to the physical and moral being of the offspring, and to the general care of the home."[42]

Women often worked as domestics or in the informal sector, some as street vendors. In 1930, about 17,000 Mexican-origin women labored as domestics and 5,415 as farmworkers in Texas. In San Antonio in 1930, more than 3,000 Mexican-descent women could be found in manufacturing and mechanical industries; about 3,000 in domestic, personal service, and clerical jobs; 670 in trades; and about 200 in the professions. They also could be found in garment, candy, and cigar factories. In Corpus Christi women worked as cotton pickers, domestics, and laundresses and in fish and shrimp canneries.[43]

Minimal workforce participation by women and low wages meant Mexican-descent children had to work. "The Mexicans do not exploit their

children," observed a contemporary, "but they cannot see any use for more
than a little education when the making of a living is so hard."[44] Moreover,
growers often petitioned schools to bend truancy laws during the picking
season.[45]

Even with the financial contributions of women and children, the
Mexican-origin working class could not afford adequate housing, clothing,
or food, not to mention modern conveniences like telephones and wash-
ing machines. In 1924 only 559 Raza residences in San Antonio owned
telephones.[46] In 1929 most of La Raza lived below the poverty level, as did
40 percent of the nonfarm families in the United States.[47]

THE MÉXICO TEXANO MIDDLE CLASS

With the new economic and racial order, a small Mexican-origin middle class
emerged. U.S. citizenship, education, proficiency in English, maleness, and
a Mexican immigrant clientele that European Americans ignored or banned
from businesses allowed this group to advance.[48] It included skilled laborers,
small businessmen, and professionals, though its composition varied by lo-
cale. In San Antonio it consisted of professionals, store owners, and skilled
laborers. In Corpus Christi a professional sector did not exist; store owners
and skilled laborers were this middle class. According to Jovita González,
the middle class in Starr, Cameron, and Zapata Counties consisted of small
shopkeepers and artisans.[49] English-speaking México Texanos held an advantage over the new immigrants. English-speaking Mexican-descent men
averaged five dollars more a week than monolingual Spanish speakers. For
women, the difference between México Texanas and Mexican women was
ninety cents a week. Class differences among men were more marked.[50]

The México Texano middle class should be distinguished from the Mexican immigrant middle class that arrived during the Mexican Revolution.
A small number of middle- and even upper-class political refugees found a
haven in San Antonio, South Texas, and border towns where they became
business owners and joined native community leaders.[51] In San Antonio, for
example, exiles Ignacio and Alicia E. Lozano founded *La Prensa*, the first
statewide Spanish-language newspaper in Texas, in 1913.[52] In the 1920s José
Rómulo and Carolina Munguía, the grandparents of later Mayor Henry
Cisneros, arrived in San Antonio. Historian Richard García has estimated
that by 1929 the middle-class México Texanos and their families and the
middle-class immigrants numbered 5,000 out of a total of 80,000 members
of La Raza in San Antonio.[53]

Racialization in 1900 had intensified by 1920. European Americans saw persons of Mexican descent as "Mexicans" and commonly referred to them as "Meskins," "Messcans," or "greasers."[67] They typically imagined "Mexicans" as a homogeneous group bereft of differences by citizenship, class, language, and region. But the era witnessed a new construction of "Mexican." As waves of immigrants arrived, the "Mexican race" came to the fore.

The racialization of La Raza can be seen in U.S. Census Bureau classifications. In 1920 La Raza was considered "white," but by 1930 the official designation was "Mexican."[68] Educator Emory Bogardus contended that some "Mexicans" were conspicuously "low-grade illiterates" and wrote, "It is the latter who unfortunately furnish the stereotype that most Americans think of when the word Mexican is mentioned."[69]

This racialization also meant that European Americans appropriated the term "American" for themselves, associating "Americanness" with "whiteness." What exactly an "American" was then is not clear, even as it was being defined by proponents of an Americanization movement that began in 1915. "American" itself was often a racialized category.

Mexican Americans were racialized and excluded from the category of "American," and whites were not yet able to consider or conceptualize a people called "Mexican Americans." The name "Mexican American" was not yet part of public racial discourse. Middle-class Mexican Americans began to identify themselves as such during this era. J. Luz Sáenz, a LULAC founder, wrote a book called *Los mexico-americanos en la Gran Guerra* (Mexican Americans in the Great War); it has not been translated. In 1929 when lawyer and LULAC founder J. T. Canales testified before the U.S. congressional immigration hearing, he had to define "Mexican American" for his audience.[70] Acceptance and usage of "Mexican American" by European Americans, Mexican Americans, and Mexicans would come a generation later, perhaps as late as the 1960s.

Racialization resulted in increased segregation in the 1920s. Kathleen May Gonzáles, of French and Mexican descent, noted in her 1927 study of San Antonio that "to be able to enter into some American gathering, he [a person of Mexican descent] must at least claim to be a Spaniard."[71] Another observer noted, "There is little culture in common between the two nationalities, therefore, they have but little social relationship. Communication between the two groups is very meager."[72] In response to a questionnaire, a San Antonio resident at the time is quoted as saying, "Although there exists no social discrimination theoretically, practically Anglo-Saxon society does not mix with the Mexican society."[73] Buckner notes "a distinct class division, socially, between the English [whites] and the Mexican people" in the Valley.[74]

Racial violence was commonplace in the 1910s and peaked in 1915 with the South Texas race war. The Texas Rangers were stationed in South Texas due to the Mexican Revolution and meted out racial violence including murder.[75] Most of La Raza considered the Rangers a repressive force, referring to them as *los rinches*. In 1915 a handbill announcing the Plan de San Diego (Texas), a plot by some in La Raza to overthrow the U.S. government and end European American tyranny in South Texas, specifically mentioned Ranger repression: "The miserable Ranger bandits who patrol the tributaries of the Rio Bravo are daily committing crimes and atrocities against defenseless women, the elderly, and children of our race."[76]

The Texas Rangers became a more modern police force after 1920. In 1918 state legislator J. T. Canales of Cameron County, the only México Texano legislator in the Texas House of Representatives between 1904 and 1930, filed nineteen charges of wanton killing, flogging, torture, and assault on prisoners.[77] The investigation somewhat modernized the state police and ended the Rangers' reign of racial repression.

Another racist organization, the Ku Klux Klan (KKK), reappeared in Texas around 1920, racializing the pre-1930 political environment. In 1920 the KKK had 450,000 members in Texas, 80,000 in 1926, and 780 in 1930 after Governor Miriam Ferguson persuaded the legislature in 1926 to make it a crime to wear a hood in public. At the KKK's height, more than 500 Klan members lived in San Antonio, some of them prominent in the city's social and political circles.[78] The Klan did target "Mexicans." According to San Antonio's Mexican consul Enrique Santibáñez, the Klan posted signs banning "Mexicans" from certain areas. The presence of Mexican laborers contributed to Klan formation in Brownsville, Mercedes, Edinburg, McAllen, and other towns along the Rio Grande. KKK members lynched three Mexican Americans after World War I.[79]

Some of the racially motivated murders of the 1910s and 1920s took the form of lynchings. The number of reported lynchings varies. Historian F. Arturo Rosales found 24 between 1889 and the 1920s, while other historians claim 282.[80] During the Plan de San Diego episode (1915–1917) an estimated 300 to 5,000 persons of Mexican origin were killed, some by lynching.[81] By 1922 the *New York Times* wrote, "The killing of Mexicans [in the United States] without provocation is so common as to pass almost unnoticed."[82] La Raza found little justice in the courts.[83]

RACIAL SEGREGATION

As the numbers of Mexican immigrants and European American newcomers increased, racial segregation also increased. Racial segregation of La Raza originated in the late nineteenth century but became more widespread and institutionalized in the early twentieth century as a strategy of racialization. Racial segregation against African Americans appeared in the first Texas constitution after Reconstruction, with references to "whites" and "coloreds." The constitution did not refer to "Mexicans." In the late nineteenth century white legislators were confused as to the racial definition of Mexicans as a combination of Indians, Mexicans, and colored. There was no de jure segregation, but by the 1890s a tripartite system of segregation in the schools had emerged in some counties despite the lack of a legal basis for this action.

Residential segregation constituted the first pattern of segregation against "Mexicans." Members of La Raza often preferred to live close to one another, and discriminatory housing practices contributed to the establishment of *barrios* and *colonias*. Valley real estate companies enforced residential segregation as well. In 1927 activist and LULAC founder Alonso S. Perales denounced the discriminatory sales policies of the McAllen Real Estate Board and the Delta Development Company.[84] Jovita González lamented, "In the towns they [La Raza] see themselves segregated into their own quarters as an inferior race."[85] San Antonio had its "separate ethnic town," a "town within a city"—the segregated Mexican colony by the 1880s called "the nether world known as the 'West side.'"[86] Unless they claimed Spanish ancestry, members of La Raza could not buy homes or land outside the barrios.[87]

Segregationists represented all sectors of European American society. In 1920 ex-Governor James Ferguson wrote in *The Ferguson Forum*:

> We have a separate coach law to separate white and black, and to keep down trouble the Mexican must be separated too. We are not going to give more privilege to the Mexican than we do to the negro, who is far superior to the Mexican in every attribute that goes to make a good citizen.[88]

Here Ferguson counted "Mexicans" as a group apart, neither white nor black, but surely inferior to African Americans, who, at times, were considered "citizens."

Posted signs reading "No Mexicans Allowed" and "Whites Only" signified racial location and privilege that "Mexican" bodies were not supposed
to transgress. Authorities and individual residents determined private, local, and regional arrangements of churches, hotels, motels, restaurants,
cemeteries, housing, beauty shops, barbershops, club houses, swimming
pools, water fountains, public restrooms, theaters, prisons, and hospitals.[89]
LULAC founder M. C. Gonzáles recalled,

> In those days, from El Paso to Brownsville, all along the highways
> you would see restaurants dotted with signs: "No Mexicans Allowed"
> and we couldn't go into restaurants, swimming pools and theaters;
> we had to go to places whereas [since] they were in "little Mexico,"
> little towns separate and apart from the cities; they were the Mexican
> sections of the cities. We couldn't go to a barber shop, the movies; we
> couldn't do many things.[90]

Besides race, ethnicity, and citizenship, other factors such as class, proficiency in English, skin color, dress, appearance, age, and gender determined
discriminatory practices. For instance, Corpus Christi school authorities
permitted the children of Mexican Consul Gabriel Botello to attend the
"white" school because of his diplomatic status,[91] though social prominence
did not guarantee nondiscrimination. In 1911 a European American legislator referred to millionaire state Representative J. T. Canales as "the greaser
from Brownsville."[92]

EDUCATION

School segregation constituted another type of institutionalized racism and
racialization. Article 7, section 7 of the 1876 Texas Constitution privileged
whites through separate schools for "whites" and "coloreds," a reference to
African Americans.[93] In 1876 white Texas legislators saw La Raza as neither
white nor colored but as some peculiar racial entity. In Corpus Christi the
segregation of Mexican-origin children began in 1892 when school officials
established a "temporary" tripartite school system. Taylor notes that "practically coincident with the entry of Mexican children to the city schools, a
separate school was provided for them."[94] Four years later, 110 children attended "Mexican" schools in Corpus Christi.

After 1920 schools institutionalized segregation through permanent
school buildings. From 1922 to 1932 the number of "Mexican" school dis-

tricts in fifty-nine counties doubled from 20 to 40 and by 1942 increased to 122. In 1930, 90 percent of South Texas schools maintained separate schools for "Mexicans," some of which had the officially designated name "Mexican School."[95]

In 1927 San Antonio was "the only city of any size in Texas, outside of the border cities of Eagle Pass and Laredo, that permits the Mexicans to attend school with the native white American children in the elementary grades."[96] In 1913 authorities did not officially segregate San Antonio schools, probably because residential segregation created de facto segregation. For instance, 90 percent of the students at Navarro, González, Ruiz, Johnson, and Barclay Elementary Schools were "Mexican." In 1930 school officials tried to segregate students in South San Antonio, another "Mexican" section of town.[97]

Corpus Christi established segregation in the early twentieth century. In 1911 trustees again inquired into "the feasibility of separating the Mexican and American children in these ward schools."[98] And that year the school district constructed a two-story frame building known as the Fourth Ward Mexican School. In 1916 a principal and five European American female teachers comprised the staff. In 1919 the board named the school after segregationist Cheston Heath, who in 1914 had asked that the superintendent "be instructed to have all Mexican children go to the Mexican school,"[99] which effectively institutionalized disadvantage.

Around 1930 in Corpus Christi, Mexican-origin children accounted for $6,000 in state aid, but officials spent $2,000 on them.[100] The inequitable distribution of funds ensured a second-rate education, as educator H. T. Manuel described:

> In some cases the differences are profound: the Mexican school is any covered structure in bad condition without curtains, with old furniture, without a library, educational materials, except for old text books, without running water, primitive restrooms, with poorly prepared and poorly paid teachers. The school was in session for extremely short periods as compared to other schools in the district which are modern buildings, fully equipped with all kinds of educational materials. This is not an exception.[101]

In 1929 the Texas Educational Survey General Report concluded, "In some instances segregation has been used for the purpose of giving the Mexican children a shorter school year, inferior buildings and equipment,

3 2 Society and Ideology

and poorly paid teachers."[102] Teachers were less experienced.[103] The practice and policy of segregation enacted whiteness and Mexicanness.

Despite segregation, educational opportunities for La Raza did expand due to the changing economy. The industrial and service sectors required more educated and skilled workers. Likewise, in 1915 Progressives succeeded in obtaining a compulsory attendance law for eight- to fourteen-year-olds, although school officials ignored it when local employers needed workers.[104] Eleuterio Escobar Jr., a LULAC member, recalled, "Most of the children of school age were doing such work as grooving, plugging, and general farm and ranch duties. . . . I never saw that any of my mates ever reached the sixth grade."[105]

The number of Raza children attending public schools soared. In 1922 La Raza comprised only 1.5 percent of the school populace and six years later, by 1928, comprised 13 percent.[106] Jovita González observed, "The children of this class [workers] are doing something that their parents never accomplished, they are going to school, learning to read, to write and to speak English."[107] Indeed, this was the first bilingual generation in the state; she was one of the first Mexican Americans in Texas to publish essays in English.

Schools played the most important role in La Raza's bilingualism and biculturalism; they operated as "citizen factories."[108] Public schools introduced English to the Spanish-speaking community, and English-only was the general rule. In 1927 merchants in counties along the U.S.-Mexico border advocated teaching Spanish in elementary schools in towns of more than 5,000 population, but English-only was common.[109] By 1930 Jovita González observed that Raza schoolchildren were "the converging element of two antagonistic civilizations; they have the blood of one and have acquired the ideals of the other."[110] Indeed, a truly hybrid people—both Mexican and American—was emerging.

Although Americanizing students, the schools ensured that La Raza would obtain little education. Instead, La Raza was tracked into vocational or domestic training. San Antonio's Sidney Lanier Junior High School, predominantly comprised of Mexican-descent children, boasted the city's largest and most elaborate shop facilities.[111] Likewise, girls received lessons in sewing, cooking, and art in preparation of housewifery.

Girls received less than an adequate education. High school graduation was unusual for them. In Corpus Christi, the first male México Texano graduated in 1900, twenty-seven years after the first four European Americans.[112] Between 1920 and 1930, eleven graduated, several who were young women, including a valedictorian. Early marriage made further schooling difficult, and girls faced another obstacle if they tried to leave home for college; marriage and family were the primary goals.

Schools employed few México Texana teachers. A handful had teaching credentials from cities like Saltillo and Monterrey, Mexico. In 1929 Corpus Christi had one Mexican-origin teacher. Emilia Vela Hernández taught in Kingsville in the 1920s. The number of México Texana teachers who worked in San Antonio is unknown; in the late 1920s Jovita González taught at St. Mary's Hall, a private school, and in the 1920s and early 1930s Ester Pérez Carbajal was a prominent teacher in the city. In 1938 the Corpus Christi school district hired its second México Texana teacher, Sophia Lozano, while Brownsville hired its first and second México Texana teachers in 1925 and 1940, respectively.[113]

College graduates were few. Knox's survey of 1,282 members of La Raza in San Antonio revealed that not a single one had a degree. In 1930, of 38,000 students who attended Texas colleges, only 188 were of Mexican origin, and 34 of these were from Mexico. México Texanos and México Texanas comprised less than 1 percent of all college students. There were six times as many African Americans in college in Texas in 1930 due to the historically black colleges. In 1928–1929 there were 57 Spanish-surname undergraduates at the University of Texas at Austin, 30 from the Valley; 50 attended the Arts and Industries College in Kingsville in 1933.[114]

Graduate students and faculty were rare. Carlos E. Castañeda was born in Tamaulipas, Mexico, raised in Brownsville, and a Mexican citizen until 1936; he was a graduate student at the University of Texas at Austin in the late 1920s, as was Jovita González.[115] Castañeda may have been the only Raza professor in the state of Texas in 1930; the first México Texana joined the University of Texas at Austin faculty in the 1940s.

Thus, institutionalized racism (segregation, English-only classes, tracking, and lack of access to colleges), illiteracy, and lack of education characterized La Raza's educational experience. In 1929 only half of all Mexican-origin Texas children were in school; most completed less than four years of schooling.[116]

La Raza responded to educational neglect, monolingualism, and monoculturalism by organizing classes, schools, libraries, bookstores, and publishing houses. In Corpus Christi the Colegio Minerva was opened in 1915, and fifty students attended another private Mexican school there in 1929. In San Antonio several mutual aid societies maintained libraries. Women played a key role as teachers and in establishing schools.[117] But these efforts proved minimal. Schooling Americanized La Raza and helped to foster the development of a sector that would accept an identity as "Americans" and identify with the United States.

POLITICAL DISEMPOWERMENT

After the 1846 U.S.-Mexico War, La Raza became an ethnic minority, a people within a nation, a nation within a nation, and a transnational community all at once. After 1900 the changing economy, demographics, and racialization led to less México Texano political representation at the state, county, and local levels. México Texano state legislators were almost nonexistent. J. T. Canales was a state representative from 1905 to 1910 and from 1917 to 1920, but there were no others until Augustín Celaya served from 1933 to 1941. Voters elected John C. Hoyo and Henry B. González of San Antonio to the state legislature in 1941 and 1956, respectively. The first México Texana, Irma Rangel of Kingsville, was not elected until the 1970s.[118]

At the county level representation was meager and had declined in parts of South Texas since the 1860s. Between 1857 and 1946, only two México Texanos held political office in Nueces County. In 1929 in San Antonio only one México Texano held a city or county elective office—Alfonso Newton Jr., the sheriff. The 1914 and 1929 *Texas Almanac* revealed that in those two years there were no Spanish-surname county judges, county clerks, attorneys, treasurers, school superintendents, health officers, tax assessors, tax collectors, sheriffs, district judges, district clerks, county commissioners, city council members, or mayors in Bexar County, where San Antonio is the largest city.[119]

In Brownsville in the Valley the situation was similar. In 1876 México Texanos there controlled 48 percent of all elected offices. By 1932 they held only 5 percent of the offices. From 1912 to 1958 no México Texano served on the Commissioners Court.[120] México Texanos were constables but held no other offices. In Webb County, outside of the Valley, with Laredo as its seat, La Raza maintained more political power than did any other locality in the state in the nineteenth century; there the status of La Raza also deteriorated. In 1885 La Raza held all five positions in the county but only four of ten in 1911, two of ten in 1926, and one of fourteen in 1931.[121]

In addition to a paucity of elected representatives, La Raza had to contend with political machines and bosses. In the Valley counties of Starr and Cameron, a few México Texano landowning families like the Guerras and the Canales used family ties, patronage, and loans to boss voters.[122] In the late nineteenth century Democrats developed a color scheme to facilitate voting by illiterate voters and/or voters who read Spanish. They instructed voters to place an *x* on the ballot for their color-coded Red or Blue candidates. After 1902 Texas instituted a poll tax, and the political machine lent workers poll tax money, often subtracted from pay. This practice was declared illegal in 1912 but persisted nonetheless.[123] Political bosses arranged transportation to the polls or, if necessary, prevented voters from reaching them. On occasion they used the Texas Rangers or local strongmen to intimidate voters. The Better Government movement and Progressivism sought to end these machines.

Bosses intimidated the Raza working class and less educated. These included *vaqueros*, shepherds, artisans, small-scale landowners, and day laborers who lacked land, employment, capital, or education. For instance, in 1919 the King Ranch, the largest in Texas, politically bossed five hundred workers. Reportedly, along the border a few parents could get diplomas for their children so they might find employment in civil service jobs like deputy sheriff or street cleaner.[124] One San Antonio resident testified that La Raza voted "in order to secure employment with [the] city or county."[125] In 1919 Antonio Valdez of that city stated, "Right after this election, I was put on the police force."[126] In 1931 San Antonio city workers who voted for the administration's candidates earned a dollar.[127]

Bosses manipulated Mexican citizens. Under the 1887 Texas Constitution an "alien" could vote by declaring his intent to become a naturalized citizen.[128] Politicians like James B. Wells, a powerful figure in the state Democratic machine from the 1880s to 1920, ensured that Mexican citizens could vote. He and his allies ensured that white primaries, a mechanism to exclude African American and Raza voters in some counties after 1902, did not take shape in South Texas so Democratic machines could use Mexican immigrants. Those who were naturalized or declared their intent to naturalize could vote until Progressive reformers ended this practice in 1927.

The illegal use of Mexican citizens and Texas Rangers in Corpus Christi was highlighted in the Glasscock-Parr contested election hearing of 1919 in the state senate. Archie Parr became a senator due to votes by "alien Mexicans."[129] Bossism existed in urban San Antonio too. In 1919 Antonio Valdez testified, "I . . . went and got all of these men that I had brought in to be paid for their votes, and brought them to the polls to vote as they had been paid to do."[130] And in May 1923 the *San Antonio Light* accused the Rangers of intimidating La Raza and African Americans at the polls.[131] According to scholars John A. Booth and David R. Johnson, after 1925 Progressives in San Antonio themselves became the new bosses—making workers pay poll taxes, instructing them on how to vote, and expecting them to influence others.[132]

It was easy to manipulate La Raza. The 1924 *Guía general*, the San Antonio city directory, reported: "In the first place, we know that many Mexican residents of the city, the county, and the state in general do not know exactly whether they have to pay the poll tax or not."[133] Illiterate residents and/or Spanish-only readers knew little about voting. In 1929 Oliver Douglas Weeks, a political scientist who conducted extensive interviews in South Texas, wrote:

> Friendship and fear greatly influence them to vote. To them the vote has little or no significance except to return a favor to someone in power to whom they owe their job, money, personal attention, or something else. They recognize [him] as their local political ring leader. When voting time nears, in many cases they receive their paid poll tax receipt by mail or some other way. Some kind benefactor has paid their poll tax for them.[134]

Weeks and most European Americans contended that La Raza had little understanding of U.S. politics. Weeks wrote, "It is the common testimony of informed persons that the Mexican Americans have little or no concept of American politics."[135] La Raza's lack of political participation can be attributed to exclusionary practices, political intimidation, voter alienation, and ignorance.

Despite the systematic effort to limit and impede voting by La Raza, "political feudalism" was on the decline. By 1920 the breakdown of the ranching order and the rise of agribusiness began to free workers from paternalistic political control. Progressives introduced a new political era that emphasized an English-speaking, educated citizenry and an independent vote free of bossism. Yet, some of their reforms worked against La Raza. Laws in 1917 prohibited the use of interpreters, and a 1927 law prohibited Mexican citizens from voting. Alonso S. Perales, a LULAC founder, commented: "In some towns the system is well organized and in others it is not, but there is no room for doubt that this new bossism prevails regularly."[136] Progressives introduced new ways to manipulate La Raza.

Most European Americans apparently saw little difference between Mexican citizens and México Texano citizens, often racializing "the Mexican" voter. In 1928 a Corpus Christi resident noted that "the Mexican[s] all Vote and There [*sic*] vote is controlled by some Political leader."[137] Professor William Leonard characterized "the Mexican vote" as a "political menace." Leonard said, "These people do not desire or appreciate citizenship. They do, however, retain vestiges of the primitive man's willingness to attach themselves to followers to anyone who may have shown them a kindness."[138] Observers at the time wrote that European Americans often considered submission to authority a "Mexican" trait and "Mexicans" incapable of democracy. White newcomers to the Valley "condemned the Mexican-Americans as an ignorant people who were unfit to have a vote."[139] Little distinction was made between México Texanos and Mexicans, whether they were bossed or independent voters.

Some México Texanos exercised independent votes in a tradition of partisan participation as individuals, as members of political clubs, and as a bloc at the local and regional levels. In Corpus Christi in the 1890s a Club Republicano existed, and a Club Demócrata functioned there in the 1890s and in 1915. In 1910, J. T. Canales appealed to México Texanos to vote for gubernatorial candidate R. V. Davidson. Francisco A. Chapa of San Antonio and Amador Sánchez of Laredo, staunch Democrats, helped Oscar Colquitt win the gubernatorial Democratic primary in 1912. In 1921 some México Texanos called for a bloc vote against racist gubernatorial candidate James Ferguson.[140] Paul S. Taylor even notes that in Corpus Christi in 1929 Raza voters "control[led] the balance of power politically."[141]

Assuming most of these voters were middle-class, this group exercised an independent vote because it was free of bosses, *patrones*, and Rangers. In 1929 in Corpus Christi, México Texanos and México Texanas accounted for 21 percent of voters, though only 16 percent in the county. Of the 8,000 who paid the poll tax in 1928, about 500 were México Texanos. In 1928 in Bexar County, 50,000 persons paid their poll taxes, and about 5,000 of them were México Texanos and México Texanas.[142]

The formation of new counties in the 1910s gave La Raza the promise of more political representation at the county and town levels. These new geographical boundaries (brought on by compromises between political bosses and newcomer commercial farmers and businessmen) transformed the political order in South Texas; between 1910 and 1921, thirteen counties emerged. Included among these were Jim Wells, Brooks, Kenedy, Kleberg, Jim Hogg, and Willacy Counties.[143]

Middle-class México Texana women voters were few, though politicians occasionally courted their votes. A Corpus Christi México Texana told Taylor: "When they [European Americans] want your vote, you're an American."[144] Most politicians and México Texanos failed to treat México Texanas as "women citizens." With the exception of a few women like Eva García in Austin, México Texanas remained outside of electoral politics during the 1920s. The early 1930s saw some organizing around electoral politics by México Texanas in the Valley. In 1933 in San Antonio, a list of "committeemen" candidates revealed the name of one Spanish-surnamed woman, Adela H. Jaime, among eighteen México Texanos.[145]

Not one México Texana held public office in Bexar County or Nueces County in the 1920s.[146] European American women, on the other hand, obtained one-third of the offices of county tax assessor across the state by 1930. European American organizations devoted to impacting policy such as the state League of Women Voters or the Federation of Business and Professional Women's Clubs excluded México Texanas.

In most counties, European American men controlled the courts and police. In San Antonio, México Texanos appeared regularly on petit and grand juries, but no Texas women served on juries until 1954.[147] Before 1925 no México Texano had served on a Corpus Christi jury.

CONCLUSION

During the 1920s South Texas experienced the rise of a new Mexican American male middle class. This middle class serviced the new wave of Mexican immigrants. Despite privilege within the Raza community, this sector was still colonized. It operated in a society that privileged "Americans" over "Mexicans," "whites" over "Mexicans" and "coloreds," "American citizens" over "aliens" or "noncitizens," men over women, the middle class over the working class, and English speakers over Spanish speakers.

México Texano businesses were not represented in the finance, industrial, transportation, or communications sectors. Few México Texanos were professionals or educated; instead, most were small-business owners, skilled workers, or artisans. Businesses were mostly small stores servicing "Little Mexico"—Mexican neighborhoods.

Although some members of this first-generation male middle class benefited from public schooling that became more accessible after 1915, high school graduation was rare and college the exception. New business and work opportunities gave this group its privilege over most Raza workers and most Mexican immigrants. An independent Mexican-origin female middle-class sector did not exist; women tended to join the middle class through family ties or marriage.

Racialization in this era was brought on by demographic shifts, a new class order, and political change. As La Raza's numbers rose and social proximity between whites and La Raza increased, the dominant white society responded with racial segregation; it enacted the physical, geographical, social, and psychological "otherness" of "Mexicans" and institutionalized La Raza's colonized position in the new racialized order. European Americans created a "Mexican imaginary," racializing "Mexicans" as "other," nonwhite, and non-American.

On the other hand, there was a simultaneous and contradictory response—incorporation of La Raza into the dominant society through Americanization and assimilation. Progressive reforms such as compulsory education fostered Americanization and assimilation, and more English-speaking México Texanos emerged. The national impulse incorporated members of ethnic minorities into U.S. society. The Americanization of Mexicans vis-à-vis schooling was a new strategy to undermine La Raza's efforts to preserve ethnicity. La Raza would learn the dominant society's language, culture, and history but would still be "other" and "nonwhite." Color, physical attributes, accents, and Spanish surnames still marked "Mexican" bodies.

Changes in class and racial formation brought substantial political change. "Political feudalism" was declining, but the racialization of La Raza heightened attention to a monolithic "Mexican" voter—the Mexican American citizen-voter became invisible. Still, an active, strong, independent México Texano voter group, cognizant of the new social, political, and economic order, was emerging. This context gave birth to the Order Sons of America in 1921.

Ideological Origins
of the Movement

TWO

*All of south Texas is now overrun with a low caliber
of Mexican emigrants who are a decided blight to the
American people . . . they are not only a racial problem but a social and economic problem as well. Their
ideas are entirely un-American. They refuse to learn
and speak the English language and never will become
American citizens.*

—LETTER TO CONGRESSMAN JOHN BOX FROM
RODDIS LUMBER AND VENEER COMPANY, 1928

This chapter focuses on the 1910s and 1920s as formative decades for Mexican American consciousness amid major ideological influences and social
change in the United States, Texas, and Mexico. Signs of this shift were the
multiple identities La Raza used to name itself. By 1921 the male Mexican
American middle class began to more publicly acknowledge an "American"
identity and claim U.S. citizenship. Few, if any, Raza organizations had
done this before. The Order Sons of America (OSA) was founded in the
1920s in South Texas. Most scholars assert that a Mexican American identity
emerged here in the 1930s after LULAC was founded in 1929.[1]

This shift emanated from ideological influences generated by several
events, movements, and policies that included the Mexican Revolution beginning in 1910, the Plan de San Diego episode of 1915, the Progressive
movement of the 1910s and 1920s, the Americanization movement in the

post-1915 era, World War I, waves of Mexican immigration, the eugenics movement, and the talk of "the Mexican problem" in the 1920s. These currents altered the identity and consciousness of the México Texano middle class, giving rise to an emerging and new identity in public discourse—"Mexican American."[2]

FROM MEXICAN TO MÉXICO TEXANO AND MEXICAN AMERICAN

The México Texano middle class had to contend with three reference groups in constructing its own identity and politics—the dominant society (white European Americans), Mexican immigrants, and the Raza working class. The dominant society could not imagine La Raza as part of its community, citizenry, or nation—its members assumed that persons of Mexican origin were immigrants and thus did not consider México Texanos legitimate citizens.

Mexican Americans likewise had to construct their identity in relation to Mexican immigrants who largely identified Mexico as their nation and maintained allegiance to Mexico, resisted Americanization, and promoted Spanish monolingualism. Their nation (or imagined community) was Mexico. Their idea of community included *México de afuera*, Mexicans who lived outside Mexico's borders and espoused a transnational politic with emphasis on Mexico's politics. A small refugee middle class was the most vocal of this group. Finally, Mexican Americans had to construct their identity around the large Raza working-class community. Despite the latter's citizenship mostly as "Americans," they tended to speak only Spanish and to identify themselves as Mexican and Mexico as their nation and homeland.

Identities were already multiple in the late nineteenth century, but around the 1890s a new identity emerged, that of "México Texano." Club México Texano existed in Corpus Christi in the 1890s, but Alice journalist Casimiro Pérez felt the need to explain his usage of "México Texano" to his readers in 1892.[3] It was used to emphasize place of birth, regional identity, and a heritage in Texas and to make distinctions between immigrants and native Texanos. Calling oneself "México Texano" signified identification with Texas more than with the United States, or the "American" (white) people. Most México Texanos did not express an "American" identity or loyalty to the U.S. government despite the facts that some voted, fought in U.S. wars, and participated in civic endeavors.[4] Instead, they continued to express loyalty to Mexico but stopped short of taking residence there. By the 1910s "México Texano" was being used in political discourse, as evident in the

Primer Congreso Mexicanista of 1911, the first statewide Raza conference, and in the Plan de San Diego, a revolt planned against the U.S. government in South Texas in 1915.[5]

By the 1920s the male middle-class México Texanos who had begun to distinguish themselves from Mexicans in Texas and from Mexicans in Mexico began developing a new awareness of U.S. citizenship. Thus, the OSA's first constitution, written in 1922, referred to México Texanos as "Americans" and U.S. citizens. This signaled a shift toward a Mexican American identity. Still, members of the México Texano male middle class were identifying themselves as Mexican, México Texano, and Mexican American.[6]

This new identity reflected national, transnational, and multinational ties and thus the hybridity of México Texanos, who were staking out their national and political loyalties during the tumultuous 1910s and 1920s. By 1929 a more stable Mexican American identity was cemented. Though the dominant society had created a binary, either/or proposition for La Raza, México Texanos found a more complex reality and fashioned multiple identities revealing hybridity.

THE MEXICAN REVOLUTION

During the Mexican Revolution, a civil war that lasted from 1910 to 1929, various class and racial sectors attempted to redefine the nation's political and economic order. The revolution made Mexican immigrants and Mexican Americans consider Mexico's future.[7] México Texanos discussed Mexico's politics, distributed propaganda against the Mexican government, smuggled arms and ammunition from the United States into Mexico, and used Texas as a military base.[8] Many México Texanos expressed loyalty and political sympathies with México despite their U.S. citizenship. Spanish-language newspapers in Texas called on La Raza to defend the interests of the Mexican fatherland. Some individuals operated in a binational context, loyal to both Mexico and the United States. For instance, Francisco A. Chapa of San Antonio and Laredo ex-Mayor Amador Sánchez, both prominent Democrats in Texas electoral politics, were indicted for violating U.S. neutrality laws when they got involved in the Mexican Revolution. Likewise, Deodoro Guerra, a wealthy Democrat and boss in Starr County, reportedly helped Pancho Villa's supporters obtain supplies. Jovita Idar of Laredo cared for wounded revolutionaries in Mexico.[9]

European Americans' racialization of La Raza led them to believe La Raza was loyal to Mexico, not the United States. In 1913 European Americans in Laredo noted "reports of open displays of anti-Americanism by some members of the Mexican community." [10] White border residents anticipated a Mexican invasion and a local "Mexican" uprising after the United States invaded Vera Cruz, Mexico, in 1914. [11] And the Texas Rangers received numerous reports of "anti-American" displays throughout the 1910s. Governor James Ferguson said in 1920: "The problem with the Texas-Mexican population is that their sympathies are with Mexico, and they never extend any cooperation to our authorities but are continually aiding and abetting the lawless element overrunning our country from Mexico." [12] Ferguson could not comprehend how some México Texanos could sympathize with both Mexico and Texas. La Raza's diverse responses to the revolution confused whites.

The revolution fostered the Mexican bandit stereotype. Fear of bandits peaked in 1915 when Pancho Villa raided Columbus, New Mexico, and later when the Plan de San Diego, a plot by Mexicans and México Texanos, was discovered in San Diego, Texas. Within months authorities were referring to "bandit raids," and one historian declared that "these bandits, whatever their particular type, collectively created more fear among, presented a greater danger to, and committed more depredations against the American [white] border populace than did all the actions of various revolutionists combined." [13]

Fear of Mexican bandits extended beyond South Texas. In 1913 Rangers received reports that "the Americans [whites] living in remote places from Del Rio to Laredo were in 'constant fear' of Mexican attack." [14] In 1914 the adjutant general traveled between Austin and San Antonio to investigate reports of "heavily armed Mexicans." [15] The media exacerbated fears. In San Antonio, newspapers reported a city rampant with "bandits." Picture postcards featured "Mexican bandits" along the border. [16]

While fear of bandits raised tensions, so did the U.S. government's militarization of South Texas. Permanent military bases were established between 1911 and 1917, and President William Howard Taft ordered 30,000 troops to the Texas-Mexico border for five months. [17] Governor Oscar Colquitt sent 1,000 state militiamen to Valley towns. In 1916 the National Guard joined the U.S. Cavalry there. By 1917, 150,000 troops, mostly whites, were patrolling South Texas. The presence of the U.S. military made La Raza feel like they were experiencing an invasion. [18] Order returned to South Texas when President Woodrow Wilson recognized Carranza as Mexico's president in 1917 and ordered U.S. troops removed. [19]

Militarization affected race relations. Teacher and LULAC founder J. Luz Sáenz explained:

In 1910 when unfortunate events of the Mexican revolution burst, the effect of such calamity trespassed our frontiers and greatly embittered our already bad civil and political condition in Texas. Numerous abuses were perpetrated on members of our race such as lynchings, persecutions, etc. Time there was when international relations were very acute and in consequence worse was the animosity for those of our racial element.[20]

PLAN DE SAN DIEGO AND THE SOUTH TEXAS RACE WAR

In the midst of the Mexican Revolution, an ambitious plot by "Mexicans" to overthrow the U.S. government was discovered. Deodoro Guerra of the elite Guerra family helped uncover the plan when he assisted in the arrest of a man in 1915. The Plan de San Diego charged the United States and European Americans with racial domination and La Raza's disempowerment. Subsequent raids by La Raza convinced European Americans that a "Mexican" uprising in Texas was eminent. A hundred skirmishes, raids, and violent confrontations took place between 1915 and 1920, some of which expressed grievances against European Americans and the United States government.[21]

To preserve law and order, Governor Ferguson sought funds for more Texas Rangers from President Wilson. Plan supporters Aniceto Pizaña and Luis de la Rosa had initiated seventy-three raids targeting European American property.[22] White residents planned suppression and inflicted "summary punishment . . . upon any suspected bandits who may fall into their hands."[23] A thousand "Mexicans" would rise in arms, whites rumored.

By August 1915 the *Washington Post* reported that "every American citizen in the three southernmost counties" of Texas feared the eruption of a "racial fight."[24] In September 1915 a circular announced an uprising on September 16, Mexico's Independence Day. Texan military personnel and civilians braced for the uprising, which did not occur. However, murders and lynchings of "Mexicans" ensued.[25] Whites continued to organize conferences and vigilante committees. In October 1915 Brownsville's mayor organized a South Texas conference attended by two hundred persons. Vigilante committees compiled "black lists" of suspected raiders or collaborators and proceeded to kill, lynch, and burn homes of suspects. By October, five thousand whites were patrolling the Valley. The Texas mainstream press intensified racial tension, calling "Mexicans" "mangely wolves," "lice of the thickets," "hounds of perdition," and "devils."[26]

The "bandit" raids were frightening. One European American resident of the Valley, Dorothy Pope, recalled towns "being plagued by bandits" and "nights of hiding in corn fields or lying beside a gun along a canal waiting and watching."[27] An oldtimer explained, "They [Midwestern white newcomers] never had seen a Mexican in their lives and they look for them to have a knife in their boot-legs to cut you."[28] Hidalgo County Judge James Edwards expressed this anxiety:

A band of mounted men could easily swoop down upon any one of the numerous and populous but unprotected towns of the county, and with torch and flame, wipe it out of existence in a night, killing and massacring men, women and children while they slept. There is no need to tell you what the Mexican race is.[29]

Virginia Yeager of San Diego noted:

Well San Diego gets nervous, if this is what you are talking about, they have had some killings there, some Americans have killed the Mexicans and they would get nervous occasionally and if somebody slams a gate they get up and go to Alice and say there is an [sic] Mexican uprising and this was one of those Nervous [sic] things that spread all through the border.[30]

According to historian Evan Anders, "Hundreds of Mexican Americans fell victim to European American vigilante action, race hatred along the Rio Grande soared, and the base of support for the raids [on European Americans] grew."[31]

This South Texas race war left numerous persons of Mexican descent dead. Yeager estimated 300 to 5,000 dead. The exact number is unknown because local authorities and Rangers failed to take an official count, ignoring rotting corpses. According to a Mexican consulate, a list of names of the "assassinations" of Mexicans and México Texanos totaled 250 to 300.[32] Moreover, troops mailed a "tremendous number of postcards depicting burned and mutilated Mexican corpses which they sent back home, often with the sentiment: 'A good greaser is a dead one.'"[33]

Rangers contributed to repression. Before 1910 they were stationed across the state. During the 1910s some twenty-seven to eighty Rangers patrolled the state, with the Valley as a base of operation.[34] Historian Walter Prescott Webb explained the role of the Rangers in the South Texas race war:

The situation can be summed up by saying that after the troubles developed the Americans waged a reign of terror against the Mexicans and that many innocent Mexicans were made to suffer. . . . In the orgy of bloodshed that followed, the Texas Rangers played a prominent part, and one of which many members of the force have been heartily ashamed.[35]

J. T. Canales, a LULAC founder and Ranger ally, called the conflict a "wholesale slaughter."[36] Everyday folk bore the atrocities. Resident Cecilia Almaguer Rendón recalled Ranger and "bandit" harassment:

They sent many "rinches" as La Raza called the Rangers to the area where we lived because they thought we were helping the Mexican bandits, that we were feeding them. At that time, we were quite scared. The bandits would come around and ask for food, and if you didn't give them any they would take what was already prepared. But the bandits never came to our home because the "rinches" were nearby. . . . The "rinches" killed him [a suspected bandit] without asking him any questions. They just apprehended people and took them. We were afraid to challenge them because they were like big animals and they had guns. We had heard from others that the "rinches" had hurt some families previously by poking them with their carbines, trying to get them to tell where the men in the family were. They just looked for the men. There was no remedy but to pray to God that the "rinches" go away, that matters calmed down. That was all. After that we went to Brownsville. Many families abandoned their farms and lost their belongings. We had lots of cows, chickens, and pigs. Everything was left behind.[37]

The Rangers committed so many atrocities that Canales initiated a legislative hearing. He charged them with faulty internal investigations, unqualified personnel, political corruption, torture, and murder.[38] Even legislator William Harrison Bledshoe, a Ranger supporter, conceded that South Texas authorities "didn't consider it of enough importance down there to indict a Ranger for killing a Mexican."[39] The consequences of the Plan de San Diego conflict were far-reaching. Half of the Mexican-origin community left South Texas, many returning to Mexico.[40]

This South Texas race war made whites further question México Texanos' loyalties. J. Luz Sáenz noted that while serving in World War I an officer questioned his loyalty to the United States when he asked him about the "San Diego incident." The officer told him, "I know these greasers well. We will never get anything out of them. Once a Mexican always a Mexican." Sáenz added, "We were accepted, but during our entire military life, we felt a humiliating load of distrust on our shoulders, a kind of suspicion . . . never free to defend our national honor . . . It was 100% prejudice."[41] By 1920 a U.S. government report concluded, "Lightly spoken of as 'greasers' and regarded as bandits and professional revolutionists, rarely will you find an American [white] who is willing to give them [La Raza] credit."[42]

PROGRESSIVE ASSAULT

In addition to events in Mexico and South Texas, currents like Progressivism in U.S. society fostered change. Seeking to bring order to an increasingly industrial, bureaucratic, and modern society, reformers worked toward a stable, efficient political order. They introduced new ideas about politics, education, ethnicity, and citizenship.[43] They convinced Texas lawmakers to enact electoral reform that affected La Raza's political power in both beneficial and detrimental ways. Other reforms made school attendance compulsory, and initiated Americanization plans for La Raza students.[44]

Progressives sought to reduce the impact of the Raza electorate. In 1918, during the anti-German hysteria of World War I, German- and Spanish-language interpreters' jobs with government were terminated, and naturalized citizens could no longer receive assistance from election judges unless they had been U.S. citizens for twenty-one years.[45] Moreover, in 1927 election codes were amended to prohibit voting by the foreign-born, including those naturalized. Until then, South Texas political bosses had ensured La Raza's vote, as it was vital to winning elections in the region.

Progressives were critical of the "Mexican" voter and founded Good Government Leagues (GGLs) to get rid of "alien" voters. In fact, M. C. Gonzáles worked with the GGL in San Antonio.[46] But on occasion they also made no distinction of citizenship. In Hidalgo County the GGL sought to end boss politics like the Anderson Y. Baker Democratic machine. In 1928 reformers intimidated hundreds of Raza voters at the polls, shouting, "Don't let those Mexicans in to vote. Throw them out."[47] These actions made México Texanos stress U.S. citizenship. Progressive reform proved yet another assault on La Raza.

THE AMERICANIZATION MOVEMENT

Emerging around 1914, the Americanization movement helped define a Mexican American identity. A response to "too much" non-European immigration, its proponents labeled immigrants as a social problem and promoted English-language usage and "Americanism." It defined an "American" as patriotic English-speaking Anglo-Saxons in the United States. Four million immigrants who spoke a language other than English were a threat.[48]

Proponents defined "Americanization" vaguely. Sociologist Alfred White defined it as "the process of unifying both native and foreign born in perfect support of the principles for which America stands, namely liberty, union, democracy, and brotherhood," a definition ringing with American exceptionalism.[49] Others said it embodied the superiority of the English language, patriotism, citizenship, and antiradicalism. Former President Theodore Roosevelt propagated these themes. In 1915 he said:

> We should devote ourselves, as a preparative to preparedness,
> alike in peace and war, to secure the three elemental things: one,
> a common language, the English language; two, the increase of our
> social loyalty—citizenship absolutely undivided, a citizenship which
> acknowledges no flag except the flag of the United States and which
> emphatically repudiates all dubiety of intention or national loyalty;
> and, three, an intelligent and resolute effort for the removal of indus-
> trial and social unrest, an effort which shall aim equally to securing
> every man his rights and to make every man understand that unless
> he in good faith performs his duties, he is not entitled to any rights
> at all.[50]

The movement highlighted U.S. citizenship and patriotism. Sociologist Alfred White wrote, "As a nation the ideal of patriotism is essential to its success. Patriotism above partisanship is one of the criteria of a good citizen."[51] He added, "The obligation of citizenship must be understood and practiced." This movement, like Progressivism, stressed civic participation but was xenophobic.

Americanization efforts were widespread. Settlement homes, women's clubs, churches, schools, industrial plants, labor unions, and chambers of commerce advanced them. In San Antonio the Christian Woman's Board of Missions of the Disciples of Christ opened the Mexican Christian Institute in 1913. Bilingual México Texanas Micaela Tafolla and Clara

Cantú at the YWCA's International House and National Catholic Community House helped. In the Rio Grande Valley, home economics clubs reached out to Raza homemakers to teach home economics "American-style."[52] Local defense councils created during World War I advanced the cause.[53] In 1920 the International Reform Bureau in Washington, D.C., studied how to Americanize Mexicans, and Texas schools expanded these initiatives.

Federal and state laws promoted Americanization. The federal Espionage Act of 1917 and the sedition law of 1918 required loyalty to the federal government by U.S. citizens. Likewise, the Texas legislature passed the Hobby Loyalty Act in 1917, in the words of one advocate, to "ferret out Mexican propaganda, pro-Germanism, anti-Americanism, and to assist in winning the war."[54] During World War I, Texas banned criticism of the U.S. government, flag, officers, and uniform and questioning U.S. participation in the war, assigning punishment by fine and imprisonment.[55]

The movement promoted English as the nation's official language. Fifteen states passed laws requiring English as the sole language of instruction in the 1920s,[56] and Texas prohibited German and Spanish classes in public schools. Annie Webb Blanton, state superintendent of public schools, sought to enforce English-only rules: "If you desire to be one with us, stay, and we welcome you, but if you wish to preserve, in our state, the language and custom of another land, you have no right to do this. . . . You must go back to the country which you prize so highly."[57]

The Spanish language had been excluded from the public school curriculum since the nineteenth century in San Antonio, Corpus Christi, and Alice. In 1919 the Sam Houston School in San Antonio had a Speak English Club; its creed read:

It will make us better Americans.
It will help us to get better jobs.
It will be easier to get work.
We can understand the newspaper.
It is spoken more than any other language.
It is the language of liberty.[58]

Another group in San Antonio was called the S.S.S. (Stop Speaking Spanish) Club.[59,60] Now, not only was everyday assimilation and incorporation into the mainstream occurring, but racist notions of "Americanism" were being promoted as well.

WORLD WAR I

World War I was another event that influenced Mexican American identity.[61] Historian Carole Christian called the war the "first concerted effort by the American government and White society to promote the involvement of Hispanics in national life."[62] She saw it as an "assimilating influence" because wartime activities led to a "Mexican American consciousness" and the "Mexican American generation" of the 1930s. I argue there were two additional significant consequences of wartime participation. First, World War I highlighted citizenship. Many México Texanos asked themselves if they were citizens of the United States. Second, México Texano veterans asked themselves why, as U.S. citizens, they were treated as "noncitizens," second-class citizens, or aliens. Why did they fight for democracy abroad and find racism at home?

The Selective Service Act highlighted citizenship. In 1917 Congress required all men between the ages of twenty-one and thirty to register for duty. "Foreigners" were to register with a local agency and prove their nationality.[63] But who was a "foreigner"? Who was a "citizen"? Many Mexican Americans were unsure of their citizenship.

The war raised citizenship, patriotism, and identity issues—all complicated issues for La Raza, especially México Texanos. LULAC founder and elite J. T. Canales of Brownsville wrote, "I did not know it [that he was a U.S. citizen] until I began to study the law."[64] In 1918 the Laredo newspaper *Demócrata Fronterizo* proclaimed, "The children of Mexican citizens who are born in the United States are Americans," as if a discovery had been made.[65] Another newspaper noted that "one of the biggest mistakes made by Mexican parents is to think that at age 21 when his offspring reached legal age he could go to the Consulate and obtain his American citizenship automatically without having been born in the United States."[66] Despite the incorporation of Texas into the United States in 1845 and the Treaty of Guadalupe Hidalgo of 1848, many México Texanos were unaware of their U.S. citizenship. Adding to the confusion for South Texans was the contested status of the Nueces Strip, the area between the Nueces River and the Rio Grande, a territory claimed by both Mexico and the United States between 1836 and 1848.

Like the Mexican Revolution, World War I raised the issue of loyalty. Many European Americans contended that blood or race determined the loyalty of La Raza and that consequently they would evade the draft. At the 1919 legislative hearing on the Rangers summoned by legislator Canales, a committee member asked México Texano Ventura Sánchez "as to whether or not he himself has any 'blood' [relatives] that had gone across the Rio Grande [evaded the draft]." The committee member added that a México Texano "is unmistakably a Mexican by descent. He may be an American citizen, I hope he is and a good one, but the blood is there."[67] H. W. Baylor of San Antonio, a constituent of State Representative John C. Box, wrote in a letter to Box that "the Mexican[s] who comes from [Mexico] neaver [sic] become citizens—and I know when we entered the World War every Mexican who could left for Mexico."[68]

Shortly after the draft was announced, large numbers of Mexican-origin men fled to Mexico, fomenting the idea that in general they were draft dodgers. Mexicans and México Texanos were not sure if they would be drafted or not.[69] Among economist Paul S. Taylor's field notes on Nueces County was the following: "Mexicans leaving this country for fear of being drafted. Probably due to German propaganda. Make it clear that Mexicans positively will not be drafted."[70] On May 29, 1917, Governor James Ferguson appealed to President Wilson to "exempt all Mexicans" (those from Mexico) from registration and selection, arguing:

> A very serious situation confronts me. From a large portion of Texas come pressing reports to me that Mexican laborers are leaving the fields and going to Mexico to escape registration. The idea has gained much credence among them that they are to be conscripted and taken to France immediately. On account of a greater portion of the Mexican population being unable to understand English, it is almost impossible to explain to them the registration laws. In fact we have some difficulty explaining them to our own people [whites].[71]

Some members of La Raza did flee to Mexico; 93,000 persons returned to Mexico in 1917, while only 38,000 did so a year earlier.[72]

La Raza fled to Mexico not only to escape the draft but also to avoid the Rangers, who in some towns assisted draft boards. Virginia Yeager, an associate member of the San Diego, Texas, advisory draft board, reported, "The Mexican[s] left that country [South Texas] by thousands, not because they were afraid to go to war, they wanted to but they were afraid of the Rangers; that is the truth." She added that she "tried to get those boys [México Texanos] to go [fight in Europe] and told them they would enjoy it, that the army was not like the Rangers, that they would be better men for going."[73] Was the draft yet another Ranger roundup?

Because of immigrant flight and because of agribusiness' needs, U.S. officials initiated a campaign to persuade Mexican immigrants that they would not be drafted. Governor Ferguson asked President Wilson to proclaim "at once exempting all Mexicans from registration and selection during the year 1917."[74] U.S. Secretary of State Lansing administered the campaign; posters were placed on telephone poles, on billboards, and at train stations. Prominent México Texanos like J. T. Canales, F. A. Chapa, and local priests helped. Likewise, Canales and Chapa traveled throughout South Texas giving "loyalty speeches."[75] Canales described his work:

I went to Brownsville, and there was a great exodus of Mexicans into Mexico, and the charge was made that it was on account of the Rangers and also on account of the registration. General Morton was in charge, and he asked me to make speeches with him in my county to show to the Mexicans, to explain to them the Registration Law and show to them that Governor Ferguson had promised to put a stop to all this mistreatment of the Mexicans, and I did. It was printed and circulated, it was translated into Spanish by Colonel Forto, and my name is signed to it.[76]

Mexican immigrants and México Texanos responded to the war differently; some volunteered, were drafted, or fled to Mexico. Because the government required men to register at local agencies, some Mexicans living in Texas believed they too would be sent to Europe, and indeed, some were. México Texanos responded in several ways. The law and/or patriotism motivated many to register, while others remained uninformed. Still others claimed exemption or evaded the draft. México Texanos who did not consider themselves "Americans" ignored the draft. They did not identify as U.S. citizens because "Americans" (whites) discriminated against them, and they did not feel like Americans. In 1920 Colonel L. M. Maus, head of a national Americanization research program, explained:

Few [Mexican Americans] regard themselves as citizens of the United States, as was shown during the recent draft of the World's War. Thousands of the Mexican boys in the border states failed to return their questionnaires and when called to account by the local authorities frankly stated that they did not return them because they were not considered American citizens.[77]

Even Maus referred to these young men as "Mexicans," not "Mexican Americans."

"Mexicans" were not sure if the "No Mexicans Allowed" applied to the U.S. military. David Barkley Hernández said the San Antonio draft boards would not accept him for military service. His mother was Mexican, and he "was afraid that if they [white military authorities] found out he was of Mexican descent, they might not let him go overseas or they might have booted him out."[78] He enlisted as "David Barkley" and became the army's first person of Mexican descent to win a Congressional Medal of Honor.

Patriotism, duty, adventure, money, and a desire to escape the barrio led some México Texanos to join the two hundred thousand Texans in the military during World War I. San Diego Constable Ventura Sánchez expressed his patriotism: "We are proud of it [the Mexican heritage] but ten times more proud that we are American citizens."[79] Other México Texanos felt obligated to serve. One U.S. citizen, a man born in Mexico but reared in Rio Grande City, explained, "It don't look right for us being of Mexican descent to act in such a way [evade the draft], after living here and being in this country for so many years."[80] The song "La Guerra" expressed patriotism to the United States: "We Texanos also know how to die for a great nation."[81]

Some México Texanos were aware that fighting for the United States posed a contradiction when "Americans" treated them as inferiors. A parent from Roma told educator Jovita González:

> In spite of these things [racial discrimination] we showed our loyalty during the World War when we sent our sons to the front, and when those of us who were too old to serve in the army offered our services free of charge to the Draughting [sic] Board and war commissions.[82]

Among those veterans who would later organize the OSA and LULAC were John C. Solís and M. C. Gonzáles of San Antonio; Alonso S. Perales and J. Luz Sáenz of Alice; and Ben Garza of Corpus Christi. M. C. Gonzáles volunteered at the age of seventeen, serving as interpreter for the military attaché at the U.S. embassies in Spain and France. He had training in stenography, typing, and law. Perales served in the Army in Texas and later worked in the Department of Commerce for two and a half years. Ben Garza worked in the shipyards, while his brother Joe went to France.

Soldiers experienced both racial integration and segregation. Ben Garza's brother Joe Garza of Rockport and Corpus Christi said, "I shared a tent with three Anglos and they treated me just like everyone else. Growing up the way I did, I can't describe what this meant to me."[83] Perhaps the best evidence of how the war affected one significant group of Mexican-origin men is J. Luz Sáenz' published diary, *Los mexico-americanos en la Gran Guerra*.[84]

M. C. Gonzáles noted La Raza's sacrifice for the United States. He referred to those "who in large numbers crossed the Atlantic and whose bodies were buried with due military honors in Flanders field."[85] Indeed, México Texanos and Mexicans were among the five thousand Texans who did not return.

Military service had a profound effect on Mexican-origin veterans. According to Christian, México Texanos "became aware of opportunities in the larger society" and "became aware of the advantages of participation in American life"; veterans may have "encouraged other Hispanics to enter American life."[86] This interpretation, however, suggests that "American life" was indeed open to La Raza who merely had to take advantage of what American society offered.

In the 1920s veterans found limited opportunity and encountered closed doors. Sáenz noted, "After demobilization from service in World War I

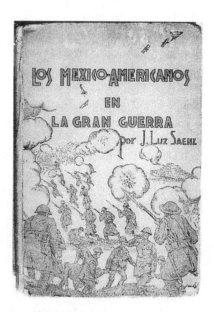

Cover of *Los Mexico-Americanos en la gran guerra*, written and published by J. Luz Sáenz, 1933. Courtesy Eva Sáenz Alvarado.

Sign painted on wall in San Antonio
reading "We Serve White's Only No
Spanish or Mexicans," 1949. Courtesy
Center for American History, University
of Texas, Russell Lee Photograph
Collection, 1935–1977.

it took only three days after we had received our Honorable Discharge to
throw us out from restaurants and deny us service as human beings."[87]
México Texano veterans found even more "No Mexicans Allowed" signs
when they returned; racial segregation was increasing. They could die in
war and work in the fields but could not return as "Americans" or "citizens."
They experienced second-class citizenship.

Lawyer Alonso S. Perales wrote about this second-class citizenship in
1919 in a letter to Nat M. Washer, president of the Americanization Committee of Bexar County. He noted that a teacher of Mexican origin, probably
J. Luz Sáenz, was hired to teach, but the proprietor of a hotel refused to accept him, explaining that his hotel did not admit Mexicans, whether citizens
or not.[88] Perales viewed these acts of discrimination as "counterproductive
to Americanization efforts."

Mexican-origin veterans expected society to recognize their contributions. One man from Roma in South Texas said, "We hoped that this would
change the Americans' attitude towards us, but to them we are still Mexicans."[89] Even the American Legion excluded Raza veterans. The American
Legion and Mexican-origin and European American merchants sponsored
a Fourth of July celebration in Falfurrias, Texas. The barbecue was a racially
integrated affair, but the dance was "for whites" only, probably because of
possible sexual interaction:

One of them [a member of la Raza] who had received a decoration for bravery, snatched it from his coat lapel, threw it on the floor and trampled it saying, "If shedding blood for you Americans does not mean any more than this, I do not want to ever wear your colors, from now on I am ashamed of having served in your army." [90]

Scholars Manuel Gamio and Paul S. Taylor spoke to México Texano veterans in the 1920s and recorded their sentiments about second-class citizenship. Gamio wrote,

As part of the American army, many México Texanos took part in the European war. It was a slap on the face every time they were humiliated when authorities or society in general acted like they didn't know their rights. We fought in the war, they said, we gave our blood to the United States and we have the right to be treated as Americans. [91]

Taylor wrote about the OSA in Corpus Christi:

There were a number of men who served in the war. Then when they came home they found that they were not served drinks at some fountains and were told that "no Mexicans were allowed." They raised the question, "What are we, Mexicans or Americans?" [92]

A member of the OSA told him:

The world war taught us a lesson. We had thought we were Mexicans. The war opened our eyes. We have American ways and think like Americans. We have not been able to convince some people [European Americans?] that there is a difference between us [and the old Mexicans]. To the average American, we are just Mexicans. [93]

M. C. Gonzáles pointed to this contradictory treatment in a 1931 essay:

In time of war we were recognized as "Americans" and many of our comrades laid their lives upon the alter [sic] of sacrifice for our country. In time of peace are the good people of our country to receive us as "Americans," or are we to step back into the role of "an alien" until another war is had? [94]

Gonzáles explained that

> this [segregation] was still going on after the first World War and
> many of us had been overseas and fought for this country and fought
> for these rights; so we thought we had a pretty good program to de-
> velop. We decided to fight.[95]

Sáenz praised Mexican American veterans' loyalty in World War I. He
and Luis Rodríguez of the *mutualista* (mutual aid association) Sociedad de
la Unión in San Antonio envisioned a monument on Main Street Plaza and
even succeeded in getting Mayor C. M. Chambers' promise to erect it. Sáenz
published a book in 1933 calling for the memorial, but it was never built. His
book proved the only lasting monument to Raza World War I veterans.[96]
Indeed, soldiering and veteran status provided an important aspect of identity formation in the making of the Mexican American male middle class.[97]
Latinas did not have this experience, as I will discuss later.

IMMIGRATION AND THE INCREASING SIGNIFICANCE OF CITIZENSHIP

Just as the war affected Mexican American consciousness, new waves of
Mexican immigration complicated it. Working-class and middle-class immigrants became reference groups to the emerging México Texano middle
class.[98] Historian David Gutiérrez notes, "Mexican immigrants themselves
felt a deep pride in their nationality and what they considered to be their
'purer' Mexicanness."[99] Immigrants promoted Mexican nationalism and
the Spanish language even as Mexican American middle-class men moved
closer toward U.S. nationalism and bilingualism.

Mexican middle-class immigrants promoted Mexican nationalism and
were vested in Mexico's politics. Members of this middle class were among
the 25,000 political refugees who arrived between 1908 and 1914 in Texas,
especially in San Antonio, El Paso, and Laredo. They sought to "develop
and instill in Mexicans in the United States and in Mexico a desire for a
sense of order, stability, and unity."[100] They wanted "to serve as the intellectual and cultural memory" of Mexico that would seek "to deter the Americanization of Mexicans in the United States," as historian Richard García
has written.[101] They were against assimilation in the United States.

This Mexican middle class advocated Mexicanness through the press, mutualistas, and *fiestas patrias* (Mexico's patriotic holidays). Ignacio and Alicia Lozano owned *La Prensa*, the only statewide Spanish-language newspaper from 1913 into the 1950s; its influence was tremendous, reaching many cities and towns in Texas and beyond. It emphasized politics in Mexico and loyalty to *la patria*, Mexico. It supported voluntary repatriation to Mexico, resistance to Americanization, and rearing children with a Mexicanist consciousness. Its philosophy clashed with the México Texano middle class who advocated for La Raza in the United States and who sought to help future generations defend themselves in U.S. society.[102] The influence of the Mexicanist press cannot be overstated; there were thirty-eight Spanish-language newspapers in Texas in the 1920s, many owned by Mexicanists.[103]

With more Mexican immigrants in the 1910 and 1920s came increased discussion of citizenship. Citizenship has been theorized in different ways but falls under two general categories described earlier: citizenship as legal status (national citizenship) and citizenship as desirable activity (social citizenship). Political scientist Will Kymlicka has found that "citizenship is intimately linked to ideas of individual entitlement on the one hand and of attachment to a particular community on the other hand."[104] While the Americanization movement highlighted social citizenship in the late 1910s, national citizenship was more important in the 1920s.

Other laws and events contributed to Mexican Americans' awareness of U.S. citizenship. Some labor unions began making distinctions among La Raza by citizenship. The American Federation of Labor (AFL) decided to organize Americans of Mexican descent, hiring Clemente Idar of Laredo as its first national organizer in Texas. Moreover, in the early 1920s federal authorities initiated the first deportation and repatriation drives against Mexicans in Texas.

U.S. immigration policies toward Mexico changed substantially between 1917 and 1930, with Mexican immigrants being further designated as undesirable "aliens." A 1917 law did not specifically focus on Mexicans, and they were largely exempted from its provisions. But nativists wanted no Mexicans and called for restrictions in 1921 and 1924, without success.

Finally in 1924 federal policy changed. The first comprehensive immigration restriction law was put in place with quotas from Mexico, casting Mexican immigrants as undesirable. And the U.S. Border Patrol was created, highlighting citizenship. Historian Mae Ngai has found that "immigration policy re-articulated the U.S.-Mexico border as a cultural and racial boundary, as a creator of illegal immigration."[105] Cultural, political, and psychological boundaries heightened around what was "American" and

"Mexican."[106] Beginning with 450 employees, the Border Patrol institutionalized the idea that Mexicans were undesirable "aliens" and a social problem.[107] Patrolman Clifford Perkins recalls:

> By the fall of 1928, the Border Patrol was functioning effectively
> enough in the San Antonio district to have reduced the number of
> illegal Mexican aliens in towns and cities located one to two hundred
> miles from the border. With more manpower available, we began
> assessing situations farther afield and discovered [that] many illegal
> entrants moving south at the onset of winter were escaping appre-
> hension by stopping short of areas where the Plan [of San Diego]
> was known to be active.[108]

Mexican immigrants were no longer simply viewed as workers or bandits:
now they were a suspect class, a class apart. The Border Patrol made Mexican Americans conscious of citizenship. Nativists had succeeded in creating
the foundation of "the Mexican problem."

CREATION OF "THE MEXICAN PROBLEM"

"The Mexican problem" was an ideological construct by whites to further
demonize La Raza. While the notion that La Raza was a detriment to U.S.
society was not new, during the 1920s a specific reference to the dilemma
was called "the Mexican problem." The new waves of immigration, restric-
tionist immigration policy, the increase in segregationist practices, pro-
assimilationist efforts, creation of the Border Patrol, and eugenics led to
this problem. Eugenics, new theories about hereditary and racial difference,
fueled the idea that there was a "Mexican race." Eugenist Charles Davenport
warned:

> The United States population could rapidly become darker in pig-
> mentation, smaller in stature, more mercurial, more attached to
> music and art, more given to crimes of larceny, kidnapping, assault,
> murder, rape and sex-immorality, and more given to burglary, drunk-
> enness, and vagrancy than were the original English settlers.[109]

This was scientific racism.[110] San Antonio resident Arthur E. Knolle wrote
state Representative John C. Box that "the Mexican will finally conquer the
American, not by force of arms, but by the slow and sure process of infiltra-

tion."[111] Immigration restrictionists utilized eugenics and its theories about a "Mexican race" in calling for an end to Mexican immigration.

"The Mexican problem" was cast as a cultural, social, political, and economic dilemma. *Saturday Evening Post*'s Kenneth L. Roberts pointed to the problem "Mexicans" posed for European American society. In 1928 a Texas Department of Education bulletin stated, "The Mexican is Texas' immigrant problem."[112] In sum, culturally, "Mexicans" refused to learn English, rejected assimilation, or were incapable of either. Socially, they were prone to criminal activity, filth, and disease. Politically, they refused to naturalize, become U.S. citizens, and participate in civic life; they did not understand politics or were prone to authoritarianism. And economically, they were laborers (not middle class) and took working-class jobs from whites.[113]

Fear of the Mexican problem was captured in a letter written to Box during immigration hearings:

All of South Texas is now overrun with a low caliber of Mexican emigrants who are a decided blight to the American people and American institutions from any and every standpoint. They are not only a racial problem but a social and economic problem as well. Their ideals are entirely Un-American. They refuse to learn and speak the English language and never will become American citizens. They are just the same old Aztec Indians now that they were 100 years ago. Worthless—despicable. Socially they are impudent, sullen and obnoxious. The white people of San Antonio have not a single park or place of amusement where they can go and enjoy themselves without the obnoxious presence of a horde of Aztec Indians calling themselves Mexicans. They have lowered the standard of wages to such an extent that a white man cannot meet their standards and compete with them any more than he could with a Chinese or Jap. Every day, the City papers are full of sensational accounts of thefts, felonious crimes, knife stabbings, automobile wrecks, etc. by Mexicans.[114]

Thus "Mexicans," especially after 1924, came to be defined as a problem, nuisance, menace, and liability to "Americans." Moreover, by 1930 the U.S. Census referred to La Raza as "Mexicans," while in 1920 they were called "White." Mexican Americans were typically included in the group called "Mexicans" and had to respond to the dominant society's racialization of La Raza as a Mexican race problem. Therefore, this social construction of

"Americanness," the "Mexican race," and "the Mexican problem" became La Raza's problem.

CONCLUSION

A Mexican American consciousness began to emerge in the 1920s as a result of ideological currents in the United States and Mexico. The Mexican Revolution fueled fears of a revolution in South Texas and resulted in militarization and racial violence. The Mexican Revolution prompted immigration waves to Texas, permanently altering the class and cultural composition of the Mexican-origin community in the United States. Mexican immigrants' reverence for Mexico made middle-class México Texanos stress their U.S. citizenship.

The Plan de San Diego and the ensuing South Texas race war made Mexican Americans' politics in the 1920s more conservative. European Americans' fear of Mexican bandits, a racially inspired revolt, and México Texanos' fear of repression affected the mindsets of both groups in the 1920s.

The Progressive and Americanization movements placed extensive attention on national and social citizenship. Progressives attacked political bossism, giving impetus to an independent México Texano sector. Reformers assaulted the "Mexican" voter and in some cases worked to disenfranchise Raza voters. This gave México Texanos cause to organize. Likewise, the Americanization movement amplified themes of U.S. patriotism, citizenship, assimilation, and English-only policies in the 1920s.

World War I had a significant impact on Mexican American consciousness. At the same time the war engendered patriotism, it raised the issue of national and social citizenship in the Mexican-origin community. The war gave some men both a racially segregated and integrated war experience, and it raised the contradictions of American democracy and racism at home. This new awareness was first expressed by men as women were socialized into domesticity; an independent México Texana middle class hardly existed, and women did not experience war in the same way men did.[115]

The 1920s saw a new era of racialization, with whites imagining and constructing "the Mexican problem." The dominant society questioned Raza's citizenship and allegiance and was unable to conceptualize Mexican Americans as U.S. citizens. Nor could the dominant society comprehend possible multiple or shifting allegiances to more than one nation.

"The Mexican problem" profoundly influenced Mexican American consciousness. Mexican American identity and politics were influenced by European Americans, Mexican middle-class immigrants, and working-class Mexican Americans and Mexican citizens. Mexican American politics coalesced in 1921 in the Order Sons of America, which supported allegiance to the United States, not Mexico. This group embraced its hybrid identity and rejected the dominant society's binary. Mexican Americans were both Mexican and American and not purely Mexican or American; indeed, a new hybrid identity and people were being forged. The Order Sons of America symbolized this new identity.

PART TWO

POLITICS

Rise of a Movement

THREE

We declare it the duty of citizens of the United States
of Mexican or Spanish extraction to use their influence
in all the fields of social, economic, and political action
to secure the fullest possible enjoyment of all rights,
privileges, and prerogatives granted to them under the
American Constitution and to accomplish this we believe
that a national organization should exist.

—ORDER SONS OF AMERICA CONSTITUTION, 1922

Historian David Montejano asserts, "There would be no vigorous or unified opposition against segregation until after World War II, when Texas veterans would organize to challenge the dramatic condition of race supremacy."[1] Eleazar Paredes contends, "It was not until World War II that the Chicano . . . emerged as his true self—a man of dignity, a man who knows his rights and will demand them, not request them."[2] Historian María Eva Flores has argued that World War II "made Mexican American men and women feel entitled to equal treatment."[3] Most scholars find that the American GI Forum, a veterans' organization, initiated true civil rights activism in Texas. Yet scholars Guadalupe San Miguel Jr., Thomas Kreneck, Mario García, Richard García, and Arnoldo De León have documented civil rights struggles in the 1930s, especially by LULAC.[4] A closer look reveals that the origins of the Mexican American civil rights movement can be found in the 1920s with the founding of the Order Sons of America by men including

World War I veterans who organized the OSA to defend La Raza. Historian Julie Leininger Pycior was the first to stress the OSA's significance.[5] The OSA inspired activism throughout the 1920s and would culminate in the founding of LULAC in 1929.

In this chapter I address struggles against racial oppression before 1929 and explain why a permanent civil rights organization did not take root until the OSA in 1921. I examine strategies of resistance by networks, mutual aid societies, and the Mexican consulate. These efforts included the Gregorio Cortéz defense network, the Primer Congreso Mexicanista, the Agrupación Protectora Mexicana, and La Liga Protectora Mexicana. After 1921 a more Mexican American politics arose. The most important was the OSA, with chapters in San Antonio, Corpus Christi, and Alice. While the OSA was successful in spreading civil rights agitation across South Texas, a split in San Antonio led to the formation of the Order Sons of Texas and the Order Knights of America. Most of these groups would rejoin in 1929 to form LULAC. As each organization is discussed here, class, gender, and citizenship will be addressed so as to explain the rise of a Mexican American male middle-class politics.

RESISTANCE TO RACIAL OPPRESSION

Mexican Consulate

La Raza protested through letter-writing campaigns, petitions, boycotts, and, in the late nineteenth century, appeals to the Mexican consulate. Mexico established consular offices in the Southwest after 1848. Fifty-one such offices existed in the United States in 1920, and by 1921 sixteen of them had been established in Texas in places like San Antonio, Corpus Christi, Laredo, and Brownsville.[6] The consulate was to maintain "friendly" relations with the United States and was prohibited from meddling in U.S. politics.[7]

La Raza appealed to the Mexican consulate to seek redress for lynching, segregation, racial discrimination, and labor exploitation. In 1922, for instance, the Mexican government protested the murder and lynching of sixty Mexicans throughout the United States. In 1926 San Antonio Consul Alejandro P. Carrillo petitioned Governor Miriam A. Ferguson to ban discrimination against Mexicans in public places.[8]

Over time, La Raza increasingly recognized the consulate's limited power in solving racial oppression. In 1928 *El Heraldo Mexicano*, a San Antonio newspaper, asserted that the consulate "has not obtained any success . . .

Therefore we believe that we ourselves ought to leave these places, mainly rural, where we cannot count on justice."[9] The consulate clashed with political refugees from Mexico who were enemies of the Mexican government. In February 1919 *La Prensa* wrote that consulates were refugees' worst enemy.[10] Moreover, the consulate had no power or authority to work on behalf of U.S. citizens who were Mexican Americans.

Mutual Aid Societies

There were a few Raza national or statewide organizations. The Alianza Hispano Americana, a national mutual aid association founded in Arizona in the 1880s, was organized in San Antonio in 1913, died a few years later, and was reactivated in 1925. There were also Masons among La Raza, including chapters in San Antonio, Corpus Christi, and Laredo. And the Orden Caballeros de Honor y los Talleres (Order Knights of Honor) had twenty-four Texas chapters in 1911. The Woodmen of the World (WOW, known as Los Leñadores del Mundo or Los Hacheros), part of a large national European American organization, was another association providing sickness and burial insurance benefits while promoting brotherhood and social life. Women participated in auxiliaries or "groves" independent of men's "camps."[11]

Mutualistas on the local level were the most important kind of organization in the community, dating back to the mid-nineteenth century. Their philosophy included fraternity, protection, patriotism, altruism, material assistance, faith, work, Mexican nationalism, and unity among La Raza.[12]

Mutualistas addressed health, employment, legal issues, immigration, education, property rights, and civil rights. They responded to insurance companies' refusals to sell policies to "Mexicans." Societies typically banned discussions of religion, politics in Mexico, and partisan politics to avoid conflict.[13]

These organizations operated in a Mexicanist cultural framework that revolved around Mexico's past, present, and future.[14] They publicized meetings in Spanish-language newspapers and held meetings in Spanish. They organized fiestas patrias with great fanfare, though on occasion they celebrated U.S. patriotic holidays too. Membership was open to both Mexicans and México Texanos; citizenship was irrelevant. Mutualistas in San Antonio maintained few ties to the "larger society" and responded to crises precipitated by racism, poverty, or natural disaster. They were limited by lack of familiarity with the English language and mainstream institutions like schools and courts.

When mutualistas addressed civil rights issues, they usually referred to them as issues of "defense" or "protection."[15] They provided protection from employers, unions, schools, courts, banks, and the police. They organized fund-raisers for legal-defense cases and collaborated with the consul.

South Texas had numerous mutualistas. Between 1915 and 1930 San Antonio had twenty-five societies with a total of more than 10,000 members. In 1920 La Sociedad de la Unión boasted more than 1,000 members, though most had about 250. La Unión, like the others, included Mexicans and México Texanos and typically consisted of skilled and common laborers. Professionals comprised less than 7 percent.[16]

Women's involvement in mutualistas was limited. In 1911 Laredo had at least six societies, none of which included women.[17] In 1915 Corpus Christi boasted at least thirteen such associations, with only a few including women.[18] In San Antonio thirteen mutualistas excluded women, while two others had women's auxiliaries, and two women-only mutualistas existed.[19] Both women and men tended to organize by gender.[20]

But by the 1920s the Sociedad Benevolencia Mexicana and Sociedad de la Unión, mutualistas founded in the nineteenth century, established auxiliaries. Even so, men monopolized leadership positions; only one woman, Luisa M. de González, presided over a San Antonio mutualista that decade. Female mutualista members were mostly homemakers or working-class women.[21] At times, men even headed the ladies auxiliaries.[22]

By the 1920s the Mexican consulates recognized that La Raza's local interests could be strengthened with a strong statewide or national association directed at Mexican citizens. During the recession of the early 1920s, the consuls organized Comisiones Honoríficos (Honorific Commissions), quasi-governmental clubs for men, and Brigadas Cruzes Azules (Blue Cross Brigades), beneficent groups for women. In the 1920s fifty-two brigades and thirty-five commissions existed. People of middle-class and working-class means joined, and U.S. citizens were permitted in both groups, though they could not vote in club elections or serve on boards.[23]

By the 1920s Mexicans and México Texanos were beginning to make distinctions by citizenship in mutualistas and other clubs. Mexican citizens organized the Orden Hijos de México (OHM) in San Antonio. Founded in 1897, it disbanded in 1914 due to the Mexican Revolution. Restricted to Mexican male citizens, the OHM sought "the intellectual and moral improvement of all Mexicans residing in San Antonio."[24] It promoted Mexican citizenship, helped Mexican citizens register property, organized patriotic holidays, and held discussions about Mexico's politics.[25]

Previous attempts to organize La Raza across Texas ignored citizenship.

Missteps in understanding help in understanding the problems La Raza had in creating a permanent statewide force. These included the informal Gregorio Cortéz defense network in 1901, the Primer Congreso Mexicanista (First Mexicanist Congress) in 1911, and the Agrupación Protectora Mexicana (Mexican Protective Association) in the 1910s, and the Liga Protectora Mexicana (Mexican Protective League) in the late 1910s. None survived.

Gregorio Cortéz Defense Network

The need for a statewide organization became apparent at the turn of the twentieth century during the Gregorio Cortéz affair. But essential elements for effective organization were missing: there were no statewide Spanish-language newspapers, few paved roads, and few cars. Local defense committees emerged in San Antonio, Houston, and Austin, often led by mutualistas, in a regional network.[26] Pablo Cruz, a pharmacist and editor of *El Regidor* in San Antonio, and F. A. Chapa, editor of *El Imparcial de Texas*, supported efforts along with other México Texano and Mexican men and women in Texas and Mexico of all classes. Women worked as translators, fund-raisers, and petitioners.[27]

Yet no lasting way to defend La Raza resulted, as teacher J. Luz Sáenz of Alice commented:

We have seen movements arise every time a catastrophe befalls us.
We've organized against abuses, barbarous lynchings, and acts of
cruelty and have seen our people excited for the reason of self-
preservation. We've seen many organizations arise—the case of
Gregorio Cortéz in 1906—our blood started flowing, but all we did
was compose and sing *corridos.*[28]

His statement that La Raza merely wrote *corridos*, ballads, was incorrect since he had limited contact with the main defense centers outside of South Texas. Moreover, conditions were not yet ripe for a statewide defense organization. Still, the Cortéz affair led to networking that would prove important later. Nicasio Idar, a printer and editor of *La Crónica* in Laredo, for instance, organized the first statewide Raza conference.

Statewide Agrupación Protectora Mexicana

A second effort at a Texas association came with the Agrupación Protectora Mexicana, which organized in response to lynchings. Devoted to "union, equality, and justice," Sáenz described its founding: "We were motivated by two brutal lynchings, one in Stockdale and the other in Rocksprings; at the San Antonio *mercado* we formed the Mexican Protective Association."[29] Founded on June 25, 1911, in San Antonio soon after thirteen-year-old Antonio Gómez was lynched, the group sought to "come out for its members in the courts where outrages are committed with them, such as cold-blooded murders, lynchings, and so forth, or the taking of their homes or crops."[30] By September 1911 chapters had been formed in twenty-five towns and cities. Leaders included Doneciano Davila and Emilio Flores and others involved in the Cortéz defense network. Sáenz presided over the Moore, Texas, chapter, and in San Antonio, activist Mauro Machado was involved. Though both would play key roles in the 1920s, the Agrupación Protectora died before 1920.[31]

Primer Congreso Mexicanista

Nicasio Idar helped organize a second group to respond to lynching. His family organized the Primer Congreso Mexicanista around Mexican Independence Day in 1911 in Laredo. Nicasio's children Jovita and Eduardo Idar Sr. may have assisted. Before the congress, Mexican Cónsul Grajeda of Laredo had called upon twenty-five men including Nicasio Idar to organize México Texanos, but the Mexican government transferred Grajeda, probably because he was overstepping his official duties.[32] This was one instance in which the Idar family witnessed the consul's inability to protect La Raza.

Around 1911 two gruesome lynchings in Texas led to mobilization. The Gómez lynching and the burning alive of Antonio Rodríguez, among other violent acts, resulted in a statewide conference. Issues included deteriorating economic conditions, the loss of Mexican culture and the Spanish language, social discrimination, educational discrimination, and the pattern of officially tolerated lynchings.[33] Letters, circulars, and newspapers advertised the statewide congress. Circulars referred to "Mexicanos," "México-Texanos," and "La Raza," suggesting their interchangeable nature in the 1910s and the minor distinction given to citizenship. Delegates came from across Texas and from Nuevo Laredo and Tamaulipas in México.

The event drew three hundred to four hundred male mutualista members. Men's associations including the Orden Caballeros de Honor and the Logia Masónica Benito Juárez (Benito Juárez Masonic Lodge) congregated at the event. These delegations ensured that the congress and any subsequent organization founded there would be male-dominated, though at least three women attended, one of whom was Jovita Idar.[34] Women were absent for a number of reasons but primarily due to gender ideology that defined women's place as the home.

The organization that resulted from the congress was called the Gran Liga (Grand League), and it was not limited to U.S. citizens or men.[35] Article II on membership noted that the association was to be formed *por mexicanos y méxico-texanos de uno o otro sexo* (by Mexicans and México Texanos of either sex); it was to labor *por la Raza y para la Raza* (by La Raza and for La Raza).[36] The constitution did not elaborate on why or how women were to participate.

Shortly after the convention, Jovita Idar formed the Liga Femenil Mexicanista (Mexicanist Feminine League), an interesting move since the Gran Liga sought to include women. Thus, women determined the nature of their own voluntarist politics. They decided to organize separately from the men, selected a name for their group, and outlined their own agenda, which reflected a distinctive women's beneficent political culture emphasizing education. They founded a school for children.[37]

The congress delegation mirrored issues of identity and citizenship, especially the minor distinction made between México Texanos and Mexicanos. Organizers invited La Raza without attention to citizenship. Mexicans from Nuevo Laredo, México, were invited as speakers and delegates. México Texanos there referred to themselves as both "México Texanos" and "Mexicans." México Texanos called those from Nuevo Laredo as well as their compatriots from Texas "Mexicans."[38] The groups recognized differences among themselves, whether legal or cultural, and no conflict resulted; the conference participants praised Mexico and "Mexicanness."[39] Delegate Gregorio E. González proclaimed, *En cada parte del mundo en que exista un Mexicano, exista [existe?] la Patria* (Wherever in the world a Mexican exists, the fatherland exists).[40]

Despite these subtle distinctions in identity with regard to Mexicanness, *congresistas* agreed that the two groups could unite in a single organization. Most delegates agreed that their political future and agenda lay in Texas, not Mexico. The proceedings reveal no discussion about politics in Mexico or about organizing with Mexicans south of the Rio Grande. One scholar claimed that participants in the congress "did not have the opportunity" to participate directly in U.S. electoral politics, but there is no evidence that the Congreso Mexicanista or the Gran Liga identified this participation as part of its political strategy. Its strategy was "mutual protection."[41]

The Congreso Mexicanista led to the organization of the Gran Liga, which resembled a mutualista. Its goal was "unification of the entire Mexican element in the United States" (*unificación de todo el elemento mexicano, en los Estados Unidos*).[42] The proposed national organization was to carry out the principles of morality, culture, instruction, and fraternity among its members; protect its members when they were treated unjustly by authorities; protect members against unlawful acts by other persons; create a fund for the organization; and prevent the exclusion of Raza children from Anglo American schools.[43] Although documents allude to legal defense, participants did not discuss lawyers, nor were civil rights mentioned.

While the congress was successful, the Gran Liga died.[44] The assembly lasted a week but allotted only one day to organizing; the logistics of establishing a permanent association did not receive enough attention. So when conventioneers left Laredo, the lack of phones, roads, and money hindered organization, and another conference failed to materialize.

Liga Protectora Mexicana in Austin

Since no statewide group survived, local groups continued to materialize. M. C. Gonzáles, a World War I veteran and a legal assistant, approached lawyers Love and Patterson in Austin in 1917 with a plan to form a legal protection society called La Liga Protectora Mexicana. By 1920, five hundred laborers and farmworkers in South Texas had joined. The league published a Texas legal handbook to help renters, common laborers, shopkeepers, and small contractors. It sponsored a column in *El Imparcial de Texas* of San Antonio from 1917 to 1921 providing information on tenant rights, school laws, adoption, and personal loans.[45] However, when Gonzáles moved to San Antonio, the league fell apart. He would later become a LULAC founder.

A statewide organization could only be sustained after World War I. *La Prensa* facilitated coverage of statewide issues beginning in 1913. The war spurred the building of highways, cars became common in the 1920s, and greater ease of transportation, like broader communication, boosted the potential for organizing. With the surge of Mexican immigration after 1920, plans were made to form a lasting association. In 1925 yet another mutualista confederation was planned, probably by immigrants, but its first meeting was never held.[46]

The male middle class, many of whom were World War I veterans, gave rise to a new initiative to organize a new kind of resistance. By 1920 this sector was emerging and included several activist lawyers such as M. C.

Gonzáles. This younger element joined seasoned activists J. T. Canales, J. Luz Sáenz, Mauro Machado, and brothers Clemente Idar and Eduardo Idar Sr. Scholar Américo Paredes found that by the 1920s, "there were no longer any thoughts of revolt; there were no new ballad heroes. The new leaders were all political leaders."[47] New leaders shifted emphasis from "mutual protection" to "civil rights" and toward a Mexican American identity.[48]

Order Sons of America in San Antonio

The first civil rights organization lasting throughout the 1920s was the Order Sons of America. In 1920 and 1921, eight friends camped and barbecued at Lorenzo Morales' ranch near Helotes, northwest of San Antonio.[49] The group included John C. Solís, a twenty-year-old wholesaler and the youngest of the group; Francisco (Frank) Leyton, a thirty-year-old saddle maker and the oldest of the group; his brother Melchor Leyton, a baker; Pablo Cruz, a printer and the son of Pablo Cruz of *El Regidor* of San Antonio; Abraham Armendáriz, another printer; Vicente Rocha, a coffee salesman; Mercy Montez, a professional boxer and ex–lightweight champion of Mexico; and Leo Longoria, his trainer.[50] Montez may have been a Mexican citizen; the others were México Texanos. Solís, Cruz, and Longoria were war veterans.[51]

From these social gatherings a new organization emerged. Solís elaborated on the discussions they had:

> We [La Raza] had lost everything including all the land, and it was all the land in our part of the country. It was no longer ours; it had passed to new owners; people who our ancestors had invited to come to Texas. For over 200 years everything in this part of the country had been ours. It been settled by our ancestors at great sacrifice. But the loss of the land was not the worst thing that was happening, we had lost all representation in the government; our educational situation was very bad . . . in fact, we had gone so far back that it was significantly pathetic.[52]

Besides land loss and exclusion from public schools, Solís recognized racial segregation:

> You would go and sit down in a restaurant that didn't have the sign ["No Mexicans Allowed"] and they would come and tell you: "We

don't serve Mexicans here." Those were the conditions we were fighting. You couldn't go to barber shops. You couldn't go to an Anglo theater.[53]

So these men decided to organize but were "turned down by hundreds of our people who were afraid that if they started this movement they would lose their jobs," Solís said.[54] He explained, "So after about a year of thinking, talking, and planning, we decided to call on the older citizens and one of the leaders of that era."[55] They invited community leaders Ramón H. Carvajal Jr., a well-read barber; James G. Tafolla Sr., district clerk in the criminal court; and Feliciano G. Flores, a deputy sheriff.[56]

On October 13, 1921, thirty-seven men gathered at Carvajal's barbershop at 1506 South Flores Street in San Antonio.[57] Others attending besides Carvajal's friends and customers were Eleuterio Escobar Jr. (a salesman for Fox Photo Company), Onécimo Fierro, and Gregorio Flores.[58] They selected Carvajal as temporary chair, but conflict arose over who would preside.[59] Tafolla Sr. and Flores each wanted to be president, a heated discussion ensued, and both men lost their tempers.[60] Melchor Leyton made a motion:

> In view of the fact that this meeting is uncontrolable [sic] and dangerous, I make a motion to let Mr. Flores and Mr. Tafolla run for president under one condition—that the one who recieves [sic] more votes for the presidency of this organization, will remain, the loser will leave this organization forever.[61]

Tafolla Sr., better educated and more influential, won the election, and despite Leyton's proposal, Flores became vice president.[62]

One hundred and fifty men attended the group's first public meeting, on November 4, 1921, at Fest Hall at 1423 South Flores Street, and selected the name Order Sons of America (OSA), or Orden Hijos de América.[63] "America" was meant to refer to the United States, not the Americas—the first sign that this association differed from other groups.[64] In English, "Sons" in the name made clear that the organization was male, while in Spanish the proposed gender composition was vague, since *hijos* means "sons" or "children." The OSA's objective was to "work for the intellectual and social progress of the Spanish speaking community residing in the United States."[65] Its purpose was "the intellectual, musical, educational and physical development of its members, by the promotion of economic and educational conditions among members and their families."[66]

The association was not organized to be a mutualista, though it had some similar characteristics. Pycior viewed the OSA as a "variation of the mutualista theme" but reported that it "lacked the traditional insurance benefits."[67] But a membership card refers to "death benefit assessments,"[68] and the 1922 ritual book provided guidelines for funeral ceremonies, which only members could attend.[69] Still, members probably did not join the group to obtain these benefits, and unlike the typical arrangement in some mutualistas, priests were not named honorary members.

Clemente Idar, James Tafolla Sr., and Ramón Carvajal Jr. wrote the constitution.[70] Idar, by then an AFL organizer, brought his pro-labor orientation to the document. The constitution stated that members were "to use their influence in all fields of social, economic, and political action in order to realize the greatest enjoyment possible of all the rights and privileges and prerogatives extended by the American constitution." The "use of political action" immediately distinguished this organization from mutualistas, which typically did not identify politics as their mission. A reference to "influence" was an acknowledgment of the dominant society's power.

At forty-five pages, the constitution had a preamble, order of business, declaration of principles, officers' stations (where each was to stand during meetings), obligations, bylaws, rules of order, and a constitution committee report. It merged elements of a mutualista, a civic group, a political association, and a labor organization into one.

OSA organizers were conscious of its place in history, as is evident in a 1927 Spanish-language OSA constitution:

The Order Sons of America . . . has been created with the specific purpose of turning the tide of events, combating the negligence and moroseness of citizens of this country of Mexican or Spanish extraction who have never had heretofore some well defined ideal as to what they intend to do in their capacity and within the bounds of their duties, rights, and prerogatives as citizens of the United States.[71]

While the authors manifested slight self-blame (or internalized racism) for La Raza's oppression, they also accepted responsibility for La Raza's condition.

The OSA selected its members considering citizenship, class, and gender.[72] It was to be composed "exclusively of citizens of the United States of Mexican or Spanish extraction, either native or naturalized."[73] Mexican citizens were excluded. This citizenship requirement reflected México Texano identity.

The 1922 constitution included a membership application form inquiring about occupation, business address, citizenship, and two sponsoring members.[74] Reference to "business" and a telephone number suggests a preference for the middle class.[75] Age, marital status, and birthplace were also mentioned. Applicants could check either "I am an American Citizen by birth . . . or naturalized . . . or I intend to become an American Citizen."[76] And gender-specific language such as "Mr." and "Brother" suggested men were preferred.[77]

Yet the authors of the constitution consciously integrated references to women. The preamble included the goal "to bring about the organization of women and children of the same racial extraction into Auxiliary Councils and Juvenile Branches." This attempt at inclusion should probably be attributed to Idar.

Despite Idar's intent to include women, albeit in an auxiliary, men did not bother to organize women, nor did Micaela Tafolla, James Tafolla Sr.'s wife.[78] Micaela was a teacher, worked with the settlement house International Institute and with Mexican-origin women in voluntary associations, and had expressed "a willingness to serve" the community. Jovita Idar, who lived in San Antonio in the 1920s, did not organize one either.[79]

OSA membership numbers ranged from 50 to 250,[80] and 600 attended the first anniversary celebration.[81] Headquarters were established in 1924 in downtown San Antonio, complete with a billiard room, further signifying a male domain. Several years later, meetings were held at the Amigos del Pueblo Hall in a barrio, probably because Tafolla Sr. simultaneously presided over the OSA and the Orden Amigos del Pueblo, a mutualista.[82]

The OSA fought race discrimination in the criminal justice system. In 1923 Juan Morales and Victor Fuentes were accused of murdering Fred Roberts, a European American resident of Corpus Christi. The OSA raised funds for the case.[83] It lobbied Governor Miriam Amanda Ferguson to pardon Sabas Castillo for an alleged crime, and it sponsored public lectures on constitutional rights and voting to develop "good" or "responsible" citizenship.[84] The OSA cooperated with the Mexican consulate, mutualistas, and European American authorities.[85]

Members discussed the peculiar position of La Raza. In an address Tafolla Sr. explained,

> We have a native land and we don't . . . in regard to the law we have rights, equal to any other, but the truth is that in reality we don't have rights. We need a Moses like the one who redeemed the oppressed Israelites of Egypt.[86]

He captured the México Texano predicament; like the Hebrews, México Texanos and Mexicans in the United States were a colonized people and nation. Yet by law México Texanos were U.S. citizens relegated to second-class citizenship.

After a few years, dissension arose within OSA ranks, giving rise to three organizations: the Order Sons of Texas, Club Protector México-Texano (México Texano Protective Club), and Order Knights of America.

Splinter Organizations in San Antonio

Defectors founded the Club Protector México-Texano. Chartered in 1921, its purpose was "educational in that it is formed for the purpose of instructing and advising the Mexican race, members of this organization, as to suffrage, citizenship, conditions and rights under the laws of the State of Texas and the United States."[87] John Solís, Frank Leyton, M. C. Gonzáles, Mauro Machado, and Raymond Muguerza joined.[88]

A second group that defected from the OSA was the Order Sons of Texas, organized by Feliciano Flores.[89] It held its first anniversary at the Gran Círculo de Obreros Hall, where Flores and attorney Alonso S. Perales discussed discrimination and the rights of "Mexican Americans."[90] Flores said the "antipathy that many Americans still feel for Mexican-Texans ought to disappear,"[91] referring to several violent attacks and the exclusion of "Mexicans" from swimming pools in Terry Wells, a town near San Antonio.[92] Perales outlined the problems of México Texanos and identified both veteran and U.S. citizenship status as a basis for asserting their rights:

> These men of Mexican descent marched to the battlefields and exposed their lives in defense of the flag with stars and stripes. Those brothers who were lucky enough to return with their lives are saddened now to see that the antipathy Americans have had toward them for almost a century continues and increases day by day but with whom they were inclined to live side by side.[93]

The OST used the same strategies as the OSA of working with European American officials and the Mexican consulate. Officials including James McAskill, Sheriff Jim Stevans, and District Judge W. McClury attended functions.[94] Shortly after the first-anniversary event, the OST held a lengthy meeting with Cónsul Alejandro Lubbert to develop antidiscrimination strategies.[95]

The OST protested segregation in schools and restaurants. Following a scathing report by *La Prensa* on the status of Mexican-origin children in Bexar County's rural schools, the OST met with the county superintendent to protest segregated schools in Converse, Texas.[96] The superintendent explained that schools were segregated because "Mexicans" were "dirty." The OST sent a commission to Devine, Texas, to address a restaurateur's refusal to serve "Mexicans." Committee members and lawyer W. S. Anthony met with the owner who had thrown out Julian Suárez, a México Texano veteran. The commission talked with the county judge, clerk, and sheriff before they pressed charges.[97] No conviction resulted.[98]

OSA Expansion into South Texas

Although the OSA could not prevent infighting and splintering in San Antonio, it expanded into South Texas. The authors of the OSA constitution planned to expand across the United States.[99] By 1923 Pearsall and Somerset, Texas, had organized chapters. J. T. Canales tried to form a chapter in Brownsville, while plans were also made to create chapters in Laredo, Eagle Pass, Del Rio, and El Paso. The campaign spread in the Valley and other parts of the state.[100] Councils were successfully formed in Pearsall, Somerset, Corpus Christi, Alice, Kingsville, Beeville, and Uvalde.

Order Sons of America in Corpus Christi

After some initial efforts, John Solís moved to Corpus Christi in 1924 to reorganize OSA Council No. 4 there.[101] Founding member Louis Wilmot, a watch repairman in Corpus Christi, explained:

> When the news came that an organization in San Antonio was fighting against similar problems as we were experiencing, we accepted their invitation to join them . . . Brother John Solís of the Sons of America extended the invitation to Corpus Christi. We then organized Council 4 of the Sons of America.[102]

They rented the Lozano Woodmen of the World Hall.[103]

Solís described considerable differences between the situations in San Antonio and Corpus Christi: "I found conditions worse that [*sic*] those in San Antonio. There [in Corpus Christi] they had a Mexican school. You couldn't eat in the Anglo restaurants. You couldn't bathe in North Beach because you were a Mexican. There were signs that said: 'No Mexicans Allowed.'"[104] Reflecting on those years, Wilmot recalled conditions that led to forming OSA in Corpus Christi: "They [European Americans] didn't want Mexicans to get ahead. They wanted us to remain as slaves."[105]

Twenty-five men joined, including Solís, Wilmot, Andrés de Luna Sr., and Ben Garza, a restaurateur.[106] Membership varied from 20 to 250, and attendance ranged from 15 to 40.[107] Meetings sometimes addressed membership nominations, secret ballots, and black-balling.[108] An attendance list juxtaposed with the 1923–1924 Corpus Christi city directory suggests that 55 members were middle-class and 2 were laborers.[109]

Three years later members discussed women's inclusion. Clemente Idar, who was either visiting or living in Corpus Christi, suggested a "Ladies Auxiliary of Council Wives and Relatives," as the constitution provided.[110] Committee member Wilmot examined the issue, but no auxiliary resulted. The minutes mention no auxiliary, and Ofelia Wilmot, Louis' wife, and Ben Garza's wife, Adelaida, told me they never belonged to an auxiliary.[111] Yet men and women explained this exclusion differently. John Solís argued, "We were starting out. We were having a hard time with men. In those days, women was [sic] alone in the house. They didn't take an interest in public affairs."[112] Referring to the necessity of travel to participate, Adelaida Garza, a wife and mother, said she was too busy caring for the home.[113]

But evidence that women were actually involved can be assessed through the minutes and oral history. A second reference to women in the minutes was on August 10, 1927, when Mrs. Stillman, Mrs. Fred Barrera, and Miss Annie Peña acted as ticket takers at a rodeo fund-raiser.[114] Interviews with women, however, tell a different story and reveal a larger role. When Corpus Christi women decided to organize, they formed a philanthropic social club. In 1926 about twenty married women and widows, including Adelaida Garza, Ofelia Wilmot, Mrs. Willie Benson, Mrs. Joe Stillman, Mrs. Chapa Garza, and Elvira Lozano, organized a club independent of the OSA, although most of their husbands were OSA members.[115]

The Alpha Club was composed of *puras señoras* (nothing but women).[116] Garza explained how they organized: "Let's go to *comadres* [godmothers]. We was all with kids." Women with the largest homes hosted the meetings; these were Mrs. Galván, Mrs. Vicente Lozano, and Adelaida Garza. Members played bingo and poker and organized familial celebrations on Christmas, New Year, and Easter. They met twice a month to play and conduct

Ofelia and Louis Wilmot, Corpus Christi activists, 1934. Courtesy Luis Wilmot.

business. In 1929 the city directory listed Ernestina Zepeda as secretary and noted meetings *en las casas de los miembros a la ocasión* (at members' houses, depending on the occasion).[117] Members initiated a Christmas project with clothing, baskets of fruit, and a tree for children; Adelaida Garza and Mrs. Stillman raised funds. They determined their own projects and decided how to help the OSA. Garza said, "We never did ask them [men], 'What can we do?' We know what we [can] do."[118] Women were especially concerned with social welfare and children, beneficent activism.

The club aided the OSA "in everything they did," Garza said. She mentioned flowers for the parade, probably a reference to Council No. 4's first-place Fourth of July parade float in 1924.[119] She concluded, "I worked hard. I worked very hard." The club lasted into the late 1930s.

Despite cooperation, the OSA and the Alpha Club were homosocial organizations. Men enjoyed male company and did not want women at meetings. Secret rituals codified by a manual complete with passwords, references to "brotherhood," and the social and cultural milieu suggest that the OSA was indeed a fraternity. Thus the OSA paralleled other fraternal orders such as the Masons, Orden Caballeros de Honor, and the Knights of Columbus.[120]

Like the San Antonio organizations, the Corpus OSA chapter focused on desegregation, particularly of a swimming pool, beach, and jury, and it fought for an improved "Mexican" school. In 1926 committee members Solís, Andrés de Luna Sr., Antonio Mireles, and Lee Campbell addressed the bathhouse issue.[121] Solís reported that the Palace Bath House excluded "Mexicans." To respond to a discriminatory act at the bathhouse against Cruz Gutiérrez' daughter, de Luna reportedly

> took some ex-service men, the blackest [of Mexican origin] I could
> find, some of whom were wounded in France and had the whitest
> record any man could have. One of them [Mireles] offered to beat
> up the proprietor and call it square, but I told him not to do it. They
> went to the bathing house and were refused.[122]

Solís said J. D. Todd, a liberal European American lawyer, advised him that "the Palace Bath House is violating the law in discriminating against people of Mexican origin." The OSA paid Todd twenty-five dollars for his counsel.[123] In 1927 another committee dealt with "discrimination on North Beach."[124]

Still another committee sought to obtain México Texano representation on grand juries in the county. It issued a petition on December 1, 1925:

> We the undersigned citizens and taxpayers of Mexican extraction of
> this county request of you that in the selection of jury commissioners
> for your court, you give due consideration to the claims of our people
> that heretofore, in rare instances, if ever, were citizens from our race,

which composed a large part, if not one-half the population of the county, selected for such services.[125]

A letter was sent to city, county, and district judges "in regards to the naming of juries of Mexican extractins [*sic*]."[126] Solís approached District Judge Wright and explained that as U.S. citizens, México Texanos were entitled to serve on juries. Wright told Solís he had not summoned any México Texano jury commissioners because México Texanos were "uninterested" and could not understand the language of the court. But Judge Wright conceded that "there should positively be no discrimination on account of race."[127] Solís then asked for the name of a white appointee sympathetic to México Texanos who would in turn name a México Texano juryman. This commissioner was W. B. Hopkins, who wrote to the OSA:

> Your order is to be commended for your desire to do your part as citizens of the county and in your efforts to assist in the enforcement of the law, and i [*sic*] for one am anxious to encourage you in such laudable undertakings, and will do all that I conscientiously can to help you carry same out. . . . I am glad to know that your organization has taken the attitude it has, and I shall do all that I can to foster such ideals.[128]

The other two white jury commission members refused to admit a México Texano but conceded when Hopkins threatened to approach the judge. The first México Texano juror in Nueces County was Vicente Lozano.[129] In my 1980 interview, Solís said they were "lucky" that the judge was receptive.[130] The OSA had to influence white men in power, so they appealed to them on the basis of U.S. citizenship, the law, and civic duty.

The OSA had less success in desegregating the Corpus Christi school system. There were four white elementary schools with twenty-three teachers.[131] The "Mexican" school was a two-story frame building with a principal and five teachers; there was no "Mexican" junior or senior high school.[132] Unable to convince school authorities to allow "Mexican" children into their schools, the OSA asked for a new building. On September 13, 1925, the OSA dedicated Chester L. Heath School, the renamed elementary school, ending its racialized name as a "Mexican school." J. T. Canales, James Tafolla Sr., music professor J. A. Pajares of San Antonio, and local white authorities spoke at the opening. The OSA even bought a piano for the school and presented it for the dedication ceremony.[133] In 1926 the OSA awarded two of the first México Texano high school graduates with wristwatches, utilizing a fifteen-dollar contribution from the Benito Juárez Camp 2126 WOW.[134]

Council 4 hired lawyer J. D. Todd to help a tenant sue a white landowner for seven hundred dollars in owed wages.[135] Again, the OSA displayed how the legal system could remedy injustices. The council displayed its patriotic and civic spirit toward the United States at city functions. It sponsored a float for the Fourth of July in 1924, and OSA members marched in white and blue uniforms in the Elks Parade in 1927.[136] When Mexican Antonio Fuentes took a moving-picture reel of the event, the council made him an honorary guest. OSA members positioned themselves to "show" European Americans and "prove" their Americanness. Council No. 4 mentored La Raza in the nearby towns of Robstown, Bishop, and Banquete and communicated with people in Victoria and Alice.[137] The minutes refer to a motion to call on J. T. Canales.[138]

The Corpus Christi OSA exhibited a commitment to statewide efforts when it established chapters in Alice, Kingsville, Beeville, and Uvalde,

Order Sons of America, Corpus Christi council in Elks parade, 1927. Courtesy Nettie Lee Benson Latin American Collection, University of Texas at Austin.

maintaining communication, offering advice, and attending meetings.[139] Kingsville was ripe for organization. On August 3, 1927, de Luna and Ernesto Meza reported that they "expect[ed] to have a council install[ed] in that place with at least 100 strong."[140] Reportedly, Mexican-descent parents there were pressuring the district to build a modern, well-equipped "Mexican" school.[141] Indeed, the OSA and Canales, not simply "Mexican parents," took on these efforts. Canales told Paul S. Taylor:

> At Kingsville at Port [the Board] of Education wanted separation and the Mexicans called me in to fight it. . . . I told the board we are demaneded [*sic*] separation[;] that we wanted our children to learn obedience and polite manners; that the American children were rough and sassy and without respect for others; that it might be regarded as necessary to develop independence and aggressiveness but that we believe that obedience was a foundation of education in which our children were safe, tough, but we wanted facilities, we were tax payers and wanted a good school ventilation and lighting equipment, etc.[;] that we were entitled to law[;] also that we wanted teachers who liked to teach Mexicans—if they don't like us don't give them to us and we got a $75,000 builiding [*sic*].[142]

Order Sons of America in Alice

The Corpus Christi OSA council helped organize Alice by distributing five hundred handbills to promote the Alice chapter.[143] The Alice chapter differed from those in San Antonio and Corpus Christi, though it had similar rituals. Minutes of the Alice OSA chapter, like those of Corpus Christi's, reveal that the secretaries had limited mastery of written English and less than a high school education. Unlike Corpus Christi's minutes in English, the Alice minutes recorded dialogue and were in English and Spanish.

The Alice minutes suggest how hard it was to organize in a racist rural setting. The first meeting was held on February 3, 1927, with Francisco Pérez as president. Forty-five men were initiated, but the membership averaged between thirteen and twenty-nine. Alice paid forty-five dollars to Council No. 4 of Corpus Christi.[144] Three members were from nearby Agua Dulce, and six honorary members, including one from San Diego, Texas.

The Alice council encountered its first problem when locating a meeting place. Organizers rented Salazar Hall, apparently a privately owned building, for an initiation ceremony but discussed a future location. A member volunteered to meet with school trustees and county commissioners; on April 5, 1927, he reported that he had asked school authorities about renting a room, but they asked him "who would be responsible for the windows." The minutes for April 5 reveal the discussion: "Prof. Powers most [*sic*] think we have a bunch of kids or a band of outlaws in our order[;] his mistake[, as] we are a true American citizens [*sic*]." Infuriated over the authorities' question, a member said whites were "treating us like a chinnese [*sic*]," perhaps ignoring his own prejudice against Chinese. He concluded that "they treate [*sic*] the Mex. people that reside in Jim Well[s] county with no consideration at all."

These April 5 minutes reveal how conscious OSA members were of race and citizenship. A member had asked Powers to join the OSA, but "he said no because this order is for Mexicans." Brother Garcia then told him "this [order] takes nothing but American Citizens." The minutes mention "the matter of taking [*sic*] to the newspaper on regard to the use of the Mex. when they write up something."[145]

The minutes for March 13, 1927, show that citizenship was addressed when prospective candidates were discussed. Brother Olivares said the chapter should see whether a prospective voter "has a good reputation so [he] would avoid troubles for the future to try to be good citizens so the community [can] be proud of our Order Sons of American [*sic*] and make a real American order." But Brother Juan G. García objected to Olivares' criteria of inclusion. He said, "His intention[s] are to receive ery [every] application made by every citizen—that want to join this organization. And he said we cannot refuse nobody[;] our doors are open for every Mexican." First vice president Brother Carlos García responded, "We have to get the very best material." Pablo T. Gonzáles agreed that they should "pick the best citizens because this organization is for the rest of the nation and that all good American citizens was [would] accept." The March 13 minutes allude to "good citizens," "every citizen," and "best citizens," but whether this signified social citizenship or national citizenship is not clear.

At the April 5, 1927, meeting the issue of citizenship led to further discussion and a debate as to whether future generations of La Raza should learn English or Spanish. Members debated the value of an "English school and a Spanish school," which led to a discussion of racism. A member reported that the European American teacher who taught the Spanish class in Alice asked, "Who would eat more. The Negro eating the watermelon or the Mexican eating the tortilla?" This discussion ended with a call for native Spanish-speaking teachers. Clearly, they valued Spanish and English.

Citizenship was indeed an intriguing matter. On one hand, the OSA constitution written in San Antonio and presumably adopted in Alice did not permit citizens of Mexico. On the other hand, the president of the Alice chapter was a Mexican citizen. Apparently, in a small town where there was a Mexican middle class, their inclusion in battles for La Raza could not be discounted.[146]

An active council, Alice OSA sponsored a successful *barbacoa* (barbecue) fund-raiser, and guests from Corpus, Brownsville, San Antonio, McAllen, La Grulla, Encino, Robstown, Edinburg, Falfurrias, Sugarland, San Diego, Del Rio, Rio Grande City, and Penitas came. Expected guests from Eagle Pass, Uvalde, and Crystal City did not arrive. County and city officials, honorary guests, an orchestra, "American Legion boys," and "fire boys and wifes" (*sic*) also attended. Sarah and Jessica Farías prepared salads.[147]

The Alice OSA members dreamed of expansion. Minutes refer to a potential membership of a thousand and to hosting a convention. The Alice council rented a hall in San Diego, and the secretary "asked the brotherhood to advertise to find new members and if possible to go to Palo Blanco, Orange Grove, and other places."[148] Despite its small size, the Alice OSA made strides in unifying La Raza, especially in South Texas.

Order Knights of America in San Antonio

As the OSA expanded throughout South Texas, the OSA council in San Antonio was splintering. There the Order Knights of America (OKA), or Orden Caballeros de América, emerged from the OSA. By 1927 the Club Protector had dissolved and left disgruntled OSA members—especially Solís and Gonzáles—outside any group.[149]

The OKA's symbolism paid homage to La Raza's European heritage. In English, "knights" suggested men, a brotherhood, and warriors, while in Spanish, *caballeros* meant "gentlemen" or "gentlemen riders"; members conceived themselves as both knights and caballeros. This reference may have been taken from fraternal lodges in the United States that emerged in the Victorian era; knights were a "staple of the fraternalists' metaphorical diet."[150] Along with knights, shields and lances were pictured on OKA newsletters, all fitting in well with the idea of defense of La Raza, a "noble" effort.

OKA members Solís, Gonzáles, and Machado along with Ramón Carvajal, Frank Leyton, and Vicente Rocha abandoned the OSA for several reasons. First, they were younger and wanted more "direct activity." Second, they were disillusioned with Tafolla Sr.'s and Flores' penchant for politics; both men were employed by elected officials who allegedly "bossed" and "voted" San Antonio voters. An unnamed leading resident of the Valley—probably Canales—told scholar Paul S. Taylor that Tafolla Sr. wanted to be constable, an elected position.[151] Third, the younger men were disenchanted with Tafolla Sr.'s monopoly of the presidency.[152] This was indeed a problem. The OSA constitution, which was revised in 1927, gave the president and the San Antonio council considerable control.

The OKA's stated purpose was

> educating its members, who are to be composed exclusively of descendants of the Mexican Race, in their rights and obligations as citizens or inhabitants of the United States, and through mutual instruction and discourse, encourage a development along intellectual, social, moral, and physical lines, and to so train them as to elevate and bring about greater progress and general advancement as such citizens and inhabitants of the United States of America.[153]

The foreword states, "All men are created equal and have an equal right to happiness," a reference to the U.S. Declaration of Independence.

Unlike the OSA constitution, the OKA's did not exclude Mexican male citizens from its membership. The OKA's objects and principles referred to its members as "citizens or *inhabitants* of the United States" (my emphasis).[154] This reflected M. C. Gonzáles' official ties to the Mexican consulate and a realization that Mexican citizens (at least the male middle class) could contribute to the cause. Carvajal Jr., Gonzáles, Solís, M. J. Morales, and Henry Cañamar filed a charter with the Texas Secretary of State.[155] About fifty men including Machado attended meetings at the Aztec Building in San Antonio.[156]

The OKA sponsored Christmas festivities for Mexican-origin children in 1927 that 2,500 people attended. Held at Cassiano Park on South Laredo on the west side, it featured Professor Rodríguez' band, candy, fruit, and toys.[157] Gonzáles reported, "That night they [the children] dreamed of a large, beautifully decorated X-mas tree, the like of which they had never before seen . . . for surely never before had the poor Mexican children on the West Side of San Antonio witnessed such a wonderful pageant."[158] Teresa Rodríguez, Beatriz Sáenz, and Antonia Pérez contributed to the event. The OKA wrote about this event in English in its newsletter, never afraid to refer to the children as "Mexican." The OKA also denounced the exclusion of La Raza from swimming pools.[159]

Beginning in November 1927 the OKA distributed 1,500 free monthly bilingual news magazines. Some essays were in English and others in Span-

Order Knights of America's Christmas celebration at Cassiano Park on the West Side in San Antonio, 1927; John Solís, sixth from the left. Courtesy Nettie Lee Benson Latin American Collection, University of Texas at Austin.

ish, suggesting that Mexican Americans and Mexicans were the targeted audience. President Ramón Carvajal appointed Henry Cañamar editor, with James Pratt and Felipe Valencia as assistants.[160] About twenty pages long, the OKA *News* featured organizational updates, essays on tenant farmers, socio-economic conditions, and the law. The newsletter praised the contributions of La Raza to the United States. It quoted William Jennings Bryan saying that during World War I "the yanks of mexican [*sic*] extraction acquitted themselves nobley [*sic*], many of them winning several decorations; while many more laid down their lives gladly, to make the world safe for Democracy!"[161]

Apparently, by the third newsletter, in January 1928, Mauro M. Machado felt a need to write "An Answer to Our Critics," a succinct paragraph about OKA philosophy:

We have associated ourselves for God and Country, and for the following purposes: To uphold and demand equal rights for the American citizens of Mexican extraction; to elevate our brothers to bring about greater progress and general advancement; to maintain law and order; to foster and perpetuate a high standard of citizenship; to preserve the memories and noble deeds of our forefathers in these United States; to inculcate a sense of individual obligation to the community, state and nation; to combat the ignorance of both the classes and the masses; to make equal rights the master of might; to promote fellowship and good-will on earth; to safeguard and transmit to posterity the principles of justice and freedom; to consecrate and sanctify our comradeship with our actions and by our devotion to mutual helpfulness; one for all and all for one.[162]

Machado seemed to be defending the more Mexican American nature of the organization yet ironically referring to "one for all and all for one," a reference to the medieval Three Musketeers.

South Texas Lecture Tour

Activism initiated by the OSA in San Antonio and South Texas began to spread even farther into the Rio Grande Valley. This effort was spearheaded by two individuals—Alonso S. Perales and J. Luz Sáenz, whose activism and employment took them to numerous towns during the 1920s. Perales had briefly joined the OST in San Antonio but was not an OSA member.[163] He expressed dissatisfaction with the San Antonio organizations—OSA, Club Protectora, OST, and OKA. Thus, in the summer of 1924 he and Sáenz initiated a series of *conferencias* (lectures) encouraging organization and traveled to Corpus Christi, Kingsville, Falfurrias, Edinburg, Mission, and Rio Grande City.[164] Flyers and Spanish-language newspapers advertised the talks and provided coverage.

Perales and Sáenz addressed education, unity, and political action. "Education," Perales said, "facilitates economic progress and from economic progress, social evolution results." Furthermore, he defined political activity as the vote. "The vote is our voice in government," he said, concluding that unity provides strength.[165] At the time, the two were not aware that several years later La Raza would finally come together to discuss uniting all the disparate organizations.

Their work represented the last efforts before a major gathering was held in Harlingen, in the Valley, in 1927. Thus, from 1921 to 1927 significant organizational work took place in South Texas. This was a new chapter in the history of La Raza.

CONCLUSION

La Raza had employed numerous defense strategies against racism before 1920, but the various defense networks and organizations could not survive before then due to limited transportation and communication systems.[166] Over time La Raza realized the changing nature of national citizenship. Citizenship affected the Mexican consulate's authority, defining the limitations of this office. The consulate accordingly organized the Comisiones Honoríficos for men and Cruz Azul brigades for women. México Texanos became increasingly aware of national citizenship and México Texano versus Mexican politics. Although La Raza made little distinction regarding citizenship in 1911, by 1920 citizenship had become a major organizing principle. The OSA in San Antonio allowed only Mexican Americans, and the Comisiones Honoríficos allowed only Mexican citizens. Yet the OSA in Alice permitted Mexican citizens, suggesting that unity for La Raza was more important there. Likewise, the OKA allowed "inhabitants" who were not necessarily U.S. citizens to join.

By the 1920s La Raza began more systematically addressing the glaring disparities in civic status and legal treatment by tackling racialization, desegregation of public schools and public accommodations, and the racist administration of justice. The OSA ushered in a new kind of resistance to racial oppression, including fighting for the right of México Texano men to serve on juries. It took up the case of individual Mexican-origin workers exploited by white employers. Contrary to one assessment that the OSA waged "class-specific protests" for "the rights of the respectable educated Mexicans," desegregation was a "race-specific protest" that cut across class, citizenship, and gender lines within La Raza.[167]

These male organizations, in turn, extended lesser-than citizenship status to México Texanas, that is, to women. The OSA constitution permitted women's auxiliaries, but no one organized any. The political and fraternal culture of the OSA kept women out. Mostly men found comfort around barbecues, barbershops, and billiards. When the OSA organized new chapters, apparently no women were contacted, and meetings were probably held at businesses owned by men.

Further evidence of the OSA's fraternal nature is the provision in its constitution for women to join in auxiliaries, probably at the behest of profeminist Clemente Idar, but the typical OSA man did not invite women to form any. Despite exclusion, women organized their own voluntary associations. They did not organize civil rights associations in the 1920s, though women married to OSA members did support civil rights efforts and raise money. In San Antonio the wives of OSA or OKA members did not form auxiliaries or clubs. Corpus Christi women founded the Alpha Club, a social and beneficent society. The women's primary motivation was to serve their husbands, families, and the collective family of La Raza.

The Mexican American civil rights movement first emerged in the 1920s, not the 1930s or 1940s. Many in the Mexican American male middle class were World War I veterans, and as a class these men developed a political consciousness of U.S. citizenship. The OSA splintered but nonetheless waged seven years of civil rights activism in San Antonio, four years in Corpus Christi, two years in Alice, and months or years in other towns. Resistance appeared not only in urban San Antonio, semi-urban Corpus, and rural Alice but throughout the Valley, where orator Perales and Sáenz prepared others for future organization. This activism culminated in a major convention in Harlingen in 1927 that promoted a goal of organizational unity.

Founding Fathers

FOUR

*[The México Texano community] is part of Mother
Earth, it is in its bosom, deep down in its heart, precious metals, gold, silver, diamond, oil, in fact, precious
friendship, golden deeds, diamond-spirited citizens, but
those things are not apparent on the surface as yet . . . In
seeking for the treasure we will encounter hard strata
of solid rock. . . . The reward for our labor is not to be
expected within the first few hundred feet of drilling into
the heart of men, but after we have spent much labor,
thought, energy, time, money.*

—M. C. GONZÁLES, 1930

The public, even among La Raza, knows little about the leaders of the Mexican American civil rights movement in Texas, especially those who led the
effort that resulted in the founding of LULAC. Until recently, historians
had little interest in them since they allegedly acquiesced to racial oppression or middle-class interests. Activists and scholars of the 1970s called these
men *vendidos* (sell-outs) and "accommodationists"; as late as the 1990s, political scientist Benjamín Márquez saw LULACers as self-interested middle-
class men.[1] Leadership is important because leaders are "architects of organization, ideology, and mobilization. They influenced others and invested
labor, thought, energy, time, and money."[2]

Historians have recognized only a few LULAC leaders. Richard García wrote about lawyers and ideologues Alonso S. Perales and Manuel C. Gonzáles; Emilio Zamora wrote about J. Luz Sáenz; and Richard Ribb has written an excellent study of J. T. Canales. But there is still no published biography of any of these leaders, and with no group profile, their collective contributions are still unknown.[3]

In 1931 Adela Sloss wrote *La Prensa* about Alonso Perales' key role in LU-LAC.[4] The league began documenting the history of its leadership with the founding of *LULAC News* in August 1931. This topic became more pertinent in 1937 after the first president, Ben Garza, died. However, the question of exactly who founded LULAC created controversy early on. In 1937 Alonso S. Perales wrote "El verdadero origen de la Liga de Ciudadanos Unidos Latino Americanos" (The True Origins of LULAC), listing leaders he believed significant. He wrote this to counteract discussions and writings that referred to Garza as "the" founder of LULAC. Members began thinking about LULAC's past. In 1939 the national LULAC organization named Andrés de Luna Sr. national custodian of records. His letter to Mauro M. Machado of San Antonio signaled the controversy over the founding fathers:

> I was gone [going to] ask you, Manuel Gonzáles, Solís and may be
> [maybe] a few others to come and bring all records or old letters to
> write . . . the real history of the league before we pass away, because
> if we don't we will also pass into oblivion, and some of this envidiosos
> [these jealous ones] will take the whole credit.[5]

The February 1940 issue of *LULAC News*, the official news magazine, was dedicated to the league's history and included the essay "History of LULAC." An unsigned article, probably written by de Luna, called Gonzáles, Mauro M. Machado, John C. Solís, Ben Garza, Andrés de Luna Sr., Canales, and Perales the founding fathers.[6]

Official histories written later generally recognized the national presidents and the first slate of national officers, Ben Garza (president), Andrés de Luna (secretary), and Louis Wilmot (treasurer), as the leaders. And in the 1970s a small feud developed between the Corpus Christi and San Antonio LULAC chapters and Adela Sloss-Vento as to who was the real "father" of LULAC—Ben Garza or Alonso S. Perales.[7]

Using manuscripts, autobiographies, correspondence, essays, books, newspapers, newsletters, and oral histories, in this chapter I present the first collective biography of the leaders of this Mexican American civil rights movement. They appear here together for the first time.[8] Moreover, these stories demonstrate complexities and enrich our knowledge of 1920s activists. In writing these biographies, I considered the following variables: citizenship, generation, class, education, employment history, war experience, and organizational membership. In addition, I address each individual's perspectives on race or ethnicity, class, immigration, and women's political participation. Color and appearance of these leaders are also mentioned because looks have mattered. I interviewed two leaders and considered others' opinions of these leaders.

I have identified eleven leaders or founding fathers.[9] Most of them left written records, but documents alone did not determine my selection. John C. Solís left no archive and was not a president in the 1920s, but oral histories speak to his significance. Mauro Machado left no archive, but Andrés de Luna considered him key to the founding, and I believe de Luna.[10] Moreover, Machado's activism dates back to the 1910s, and I believe he was key to mobilization.

Despite the patriarchal restraints on women's lives, a few women exercised leadership in gender-defined ways, as I will discuss later. Today, most people believe that women's exclusion is explained by machismo in the 1920s.[11] However, the men exhibited a spectrum of thought on women's political participation and inclusion. If a male leader was married, I asked if his wife participated in civic affairs. Did the leader support women's suffrage and organizational activism? Did religion influence his perspective on women's activism?

The founding fathers included attorney J. T. Canales, teacher J. Luz Sáenz, labor organizer Clemente Idar, journalist Eduardo Idar Sr., wholesaler and furniture store manager John Solís, lawyers Alonso S. Perales and Manuel C. Gonzáles, district clerk employee James Tafolla Sr., restaurateur Ben Garza, baker Andrés de Luna Sr., and clerk Mauro M. Machado.

JOSÉ TOMÁS CANALES

José Tomás (J. T.) Canales was born on a ranch in Nueces County, Texas, on March 7, 1877. His mother was a descendant of José Salvador de la Garza, the recipient of the Espíritu Santo Spanish land grant that occupied most of what is now Cameron County. Canales was also a descendant of Juan Cortina, a nineteenth-century rebel against European American authority, whom he considered a hero. His mother's family owned extensive holdings of ranch land in Nueces County at the time of Canales' birth. At the turn of the twentieth century the family owned more than four thousand head of cattle, and by 1930 the family had interests in cotton, banking, and commerce and owned thirty thousand acres.[12] In a testimony before Congress in 1930, Canales identified himself as a Chamber of Commerce representative and businessman. He saw Spanish land grants and the Treaty of Guadalupe Hidalgo as historical reference points, signals that he was conscious of his Spanish and Mexican heritage.[13]

Canales attended private and public schools in Mexico, Nueces County, and Austin. From 1890 to 1892 he enrolled in the Texas Business College in Austin. After participating in a cattle drive, he moved to Kansas, where he lived with the D. F. Wallace family and completed high school. He was a Catholic who converted to Protestantism. In 1896 he began his studies at the University of Michigan; three years later he received a law degree and became the school's the first Latino graduate.[14] As Ribb has noted, Canales was the most educated Texano in the state, and few white Texans matched his education. From 1900 to 1903 he practiced law in Corpus Christi and Laredo before moving to Brownsville, where he worked in the county assessor's office. From 1912 to 1914 he served as superintendent of the Cameron County public schools; there he stressed English in the classroom.

He was connected to political machines controlled by the King family and James B. Wells. Canales served five terms as a state legislator between 1905 and 1920 for the district spanning Cameron, Hidalgo, Starr, and Zapata Counties and later Willacy County. As a Progressive he supported women's suffrage and corporate reform. In 1910 on the House floor he was called "the greaser from Brownsville," despite his stature and light skin. During World War I, he belonged to the "Four-Minute Men," a cadre of orators who supported the war; he urged México Texanos to stay in the United States.[15] In 1918 he led a campaign to reform the Texas Rangers and filed nineteen charges against them. In retaliation, the Texas Rangers threatened him in Brownsville and Austin, and a fellow legislator verbally harassed him for his stand.[16]

Canales harbored some racialized ideas about "Americans" and "Mexicans," particularly laborers. He told social scientist Paul S. Taylor, "The superiority of race is not a question of color but one of industry and effi[ci]ency[,] the ability to do more work or [on] less food." As to "race pride," Canales said, "I told my people that they should be proud of their race, the Latin Race, [as it has] produced the greatest music, art, portrait; the Anglo-Saxon[,] the greatest government [insistent on dispensing] Justice." He told Taylor, "What we want to develop is Mexicans of wealth and education not co[n] stables."[17] In a *LULAC News* column Canales described racial supremacy

José Tomás (J. T.) Canales, lawyer, state representative, Texas
Rangers reformer, LULAC founder, and major author of
LULAC constitution, 1919. Courtesy South Texas Archives,
James C. Jernigan Library, Texas A&M University at Kingsville.

as tied to class in the minds of "Our Anglo-Saxon brethren, who have heretofore believed in race superiority because they possess more wealth and
more land than their less fortunate brothers of Latin extraction."[18]

Canales wielded much influence over México Texano voters as a political
boss organizing the Raza vote.[19] He was a conservative Democrat.[20] His correspondence reveals that he was paternalistic and caustic. He married Anne
Wheeler of Houston, a European American, in 1910; they adopted her niece.
His wife was not involved in civil rights work. He voted in favor of women's
suffrage and argued for México Texana inclusion in Parent-Teacher Associations. Canales became the fourth LULAC national president. The most

established politician in México Texano society, he was a respected, seasoned veteran and the wealthiest, oldest, and best educated. A devout man, he believed that "to have different races is a plan of God. God will take care of that [discrimination?]."[21] Beyond egotism, Canales shared credit for the founding of LULAC, although he was the major author of the LULAC constitution. Canales died on March 30, 1976.

JOSÉ DE LA LUZ SÁENZ

José de la Luz Sáenz (known as J. Luz Sáenz) was born on May 17, 1888, to Chrispina and Rosalio Sáenz in Realitos, Texas.[22] His father was a railroad worker, bookkeeper, ranchworker, and shepherd; his mother was a homemaker.[23] After his mother died Petra Ramos became his stepmother, and the family moved to Mexico and then returned to Alice, Texas, in 1900. He started school at age twelve and graduated from Alice High School in 1908, the first Mexican American to do so. He taught in the public schools for eight years before the war and attended summer school at the University of Texas at Austin, Southwest Texas Teachers College in San Marcos, Texas Arts and Industrial College in Kingsville, and Westmoreland College in San Antonio in the 1920s.[24] In 1917 he married María Petra Esparza, a descendant of the Esparzas who fought at the Alamo in 1836. They had seven children. She raised the children while he worked as a teacher and participated in civil rights work.

In the 1910s Sáenz witnessed what he referred to as "the birth of the short term, badly equipped, neglected shacks and the undemocratic segregated schools for Mexican children."[25] In his own words, he sought to "open the school doors for the workers' children." An educator who wore eyeglasses, he cultivated an intellectual demeanor and was called "El Profesor." He saw his efforts as "hard battles for the intellectual advancement of our people." He taught in Jourdanton, New Braunfels, and Kingsville and on several occasions either quit or was fired because he refused to keep quiet about La Raza's condition or because whites feared he would incite mobilization. For instance, in 1930, when he was employed in La Jolla, Texas, administrators fired him when he refused to speak out in favor of a political candidate.[26] "Persecuted," he "had to go to other places in search of work."[27]

Sáenz supported the work of mutualistas. In the 1910s he presided over the Agrupación Protectora Mexicana in Moore, Texas, and wrote for Spanish-language newspapers. Early on, he wrote and spoke from the historical context that "the Indians were the first inhabitants of this land. Then

José de la (J.) Luz Sáenz, teacher and LULAC founder, 1908. Courtesy Eva Sáenz Alvarado.

came the Spaniards and still later the mestizos or Mexicans."[28] He, more than other leaders, recognized La Raza as a cultural, racial, and historical hybrid that embraced multiple identities. He was a formidable orator.

Sáenz volunteered for military duty in World War I because of his loyalty to the United States and his wish to counter accusations that La Raza was disloyal. Still, during his military service, Sáenz endured the epithet "greaser." He served as a private in the Army intelligence section and then spent eighteen months as a soldier on the lines in the bloodiest battle at Verdun, France, where 70,000 died. He traveled to England, Belgium, Luxembourg, and Germany.[29] He was about thirty years old as a soldier and kept a diary during his duty. In it he wrote, "My country's call took me from where I was, teaching the children of my people, and placed me where I could defend their honor, their racial pride, where I could assure them a happier future."[30] He served as a private and taught Mexican nationals in his company to read and write.

In 1924 he obtained a promise to honor World War I veterans from the San Antonio mayor that nonetheless did not materialize. In 1933 Sáenz published his diary, letters, and commentary in *Los méxico-americanos en La Gran Guerra y su contingente en pro de la democracia, la humanidad y la justicia*, which, in his words, "voiced the feelings of an important racial element so far neglected, much mal-treated, and worst misrepresented to the world."[31]

Sáenz saw himself as a "warrior" fighting two fronts. He listed his "hobby" as "free lance writer for magazines and newspapers in defense of people of Mexican extraction and their children."[32] He wrote, "I fought battles there [in Dittlinger, Texas] until I convinced county officials to pay the teacher for the schooling of our children. . . . Now that I wear the uniform of a warrior I have the hope of winning other battles that will bring justice to our people." He predicted, "This war for you and for me will not end when we finish with the Germans . . . For us the worse war will remain." He concluded, "Our happiness would never be complete without the removal of that hateful historical and social prejudice against our people in Texas."[33]

Civil rights activist Adela Sloss remembered the educator as "more mature, demonstrating experience, calm, and courage" and commented on his "indomitable faith and amazing bravery." She explained, "At times he had to come to the town where I lived, and for several different reasons he would arrive walking. He always came with some matter dealing with our cause, be it to write in newspapers, to write to congressmen, or to unite the people in order to discuss various matters dealing with our cause."[34] Similarly, Perales wrote that Sáenz "really work[ed] untiringly and with no self-interest."[35]

In the 1930s Sáenz served as an official Ladies LULAC organizer. Around 1948 he completed his bachelor's and master's degrees at Sul Ross University.[36] In 1950 he received a contract for a book tentatively titled *Mysterious Realism*, but before it was published Sáenz died of complications from surgery, on April 12, 1953.[37] Sáenz took due credit for his activism when he wrote in a 1950 publicity questionnaire, "I originated the League of United Latin American Citizens."

MAURO M. MACHADO

On January 15, 1897, Mauro Machado was born in Benavides in Duval County to Albino R. Machado and Epigmenia Perea. He was reared in San Antonio. He attended Navarro School and San Fernando Catholic College. As a teenager, Machado belonged to the Agrupación Protectora Mexicana in 1912–1913 and was a "constant companion" of Emilio Flores, its key or-

Mauro M. Machado, clerk and LULAC founder, *LULAC News* cover, May 1933. Courtesy Center for American History, University of Texas.

ganizer.[38] He met J. Luz Sáenz at that time. Machado was also a member of the OSA, El Club Protector México-Texano, and several fraternal societies, as well as a cofounder and the first president of the Order Knights of America. He attended the Harlingen convention of 1927, and "from there on he labored continuously for the union of all three organizations."[39] He would later become the first president of LULAC Council No. 2 and the fifth national LULAC president.

Machado's significance seems to be in his hard work in making contacts throughout South Texas in the 1920s. According to *LULAC News*, "He knew leaders in practically every community in our great Southwest . . . knew them by their first names. That was the secret of his success. That is why he will forever stand high as the Organizer for LULAC."[40] In the 1930s he served as president of Council No. 2 of San Antonio, which organized a "Flying Squadron" to develop LULAC councils in other towns throughout Texas. That decade it was estimated Machado was responsible for forming 85 percent of the LULAC councils, and in 1939 the national LULAC president called him the "hardest working LULACker."[41] He also managed a girls' LULAC basketball team in 1932, perhaps suggesting respect for girls. While *LULAC News* commented on his 1930s activism, I believe his contacts in the 1910s helped him organize in the 1920s as well.[42]

CLEMENTE M. IDAR AND EDUARDO IDAR SR.

Clemente M. Idar was born to Nicasio and Jovita Idar, both U.S. citizens, on November 11, 1893, in Laredo.[43] The family had a newspaper and printing business and was involved in local civic and political affairs. Clemente Idar attended the Methodist-run Lydia Patterson Institute until the fifth grade but otherwise educated himself by reading books and newspapers and by mastering vocabulary lists. He joined his family in Laredo in publishing *La Crónica*, an activist newspaper in which he condemned "barbarous acts of cruelty and savagery committed against Mexicans[,] burning them alive, lynching them without just cause."[44] Since he had three fingers cut off while working on a printing press, he saw no action in World War I. Clemente Idar worked in Laredo on the city labor board to prevent strikes and labor disruptions.[45] He married Laura Hernández in 1913, and she raised their six children at home.

Clemente Idar was a strong advocate of women's rights, and he encouraged women to participate in civic life. A man of vision, he advised Leonor Villegas de Magnon to organize the Cruz Blanca—Mexico's Red Cross—

Clemente Idar, American Federation of
Labor organizer and LULAC founder,
1928. Courtesy Institute of Texan
Cultures, University of Texas, donated
by A. Ike Idar.

into a national and international corps during the Mexican Revolution.
Scholar Clara Lomas has revealed what Idar told Villegas:

> You have a great future. You have found a path filled with good
> fortune. . . . Use the tact and talent of great women. . . . You should
> reply [to Mexico's President Carranza] making it clear that you are
> one of the future leaders of the Republic. . . . Request authorization
> from the First Chief to create brigades of the Cruz Blanca through-
> out the entire country. . . . Thereby . . . you will have established in
> Mexico a charitable institution as a vivid testimony of your revolu-
> tionary work.[46]

He would prove to be the greatest advocate of women's activism. The family's Methodist background may explain his profeminist inclinations.

In 1918 Idar began organizing and chartering AFL locals in Laredo. In
1919 he moved with his family to San Antonio, and AFL founder Samuel
Gompers hired him as the first Mexican American organizer in the United

States. There Idar organized both Mexicans and Mexican Americans; during the 1921 recession, however, Idar helped plan a repatriation program for fifty thousand Mexicans in Texas. In 1926 the AFL sent him to Los Angeles to survey the status of Mexican workers. A Mason, he also worked with mutualistas and labor associations.[47]

Recognized as an eloquent orator, his missing fingers must have impressed workers. Villegas de Magnon noted of one of Idar's "brilliant" speeches that "he could sway the multitudes in English or Spanish."[48] In the early 1930s President Franklin Delano Roosevelt asked him to serve as U.S. Secretary of Labor, but Idar declined due to poor health; he died of diabetes on January 27, 1934. Of all the leaders, he was most intimately connected to organized labor.

Eduardo Idar Sr., Clemente's younger brother, was born on July 27, 1887.[49] He attended school for eight years and was largely self-educated. He worked as a printer's apprentice and for *La Crónica*. From 1913 to 1916 he was an auditor in Laredo. He married Irene Guerra in 1917, and they had three children. Also in 1917 he founded the newspaper *Evolución*, in which he supported U.S. entry into World War I and La Raza's participation in the

Eduardo Idar Sr., journalist and LULAC
founder, circa 1920s. Courtesy Institute
of Texan Cultures, University of Texas,
donated by A. Ike Idar.

service. That year he wrote that the Spanish-language press in Texas should initiate a campaign of public instruction among its readers, thereby revealing that his community included Mexicans and the working class. Eduardo Idar Sr. advocated for women's rights.

A Mason and an orator, Eduardo Idar Sr. believed in mutualism and a moral code. In 1922 he headed a library organized by comrade Simón Domínguez.[50] In 1926 he started another newspaper, *Las Noticias*, which had a circulation of two thousand. Canales called Eduardo Idar Sr. "an eloquent intellectual supporter of LULAC."[51] He died on March 13, 1947, of a heart attack resulting from diabetes. His son Ed Idar Jr. continued the family tradition of activism and during the 1950s became a major force in the American GI Forum.

As México Texanos living right on the border, the brothers Clemente Idar and Ed Idar Sr. and their families were particularly in tune with the issue of citizenship. Both men were middle-class activist journalists politicizing La Raza, and both have been slighted in discussions of leadership.

MANUEL C. GONZÁLES

Manuel Carbajal (M. C.) Gonzáles was born on October 22, 1900, in Hidalgo County to María Luisa Carbajal and Ruperto Gonzáles as the youngest of seven children. He was a descendant of José María Jesús Carbajal, who had supported Texas independence, advocated an independent republic in northern Mexico/South Texas, and sided with Mexico during the 1846 Mexican American War. José María Jesús Carbajal was governor of Tamaulipas and lived in Hidalgo County.[52] M. C.'s father, born in Mexico, worked as a ranch hand, and his mother worked as a laundress and homemaker. His father died when M. C. was twelve, and the family moved to San Antonio. As a working-class boy, he worked for Western Union as a messenger and at the age of thirteen and fourteen made deliveries for Chapa's Drugstore. Francisco Chapa was a *político* with ties to several Texas governors and the Democratic Party, giving Gonzáles an ear for politics early in life and valuable mentorship from an activist of an earlier generation. A voracious reader, Gonzáles graduated from Lanier High School and attended Nixon Clay Commercial School in Austin, where he learned stenography and typing.[53] He worked for the district court in Hidalgo County, and as secretary to the law firm of Patterson and Love in Austin in 1917 he helped found the Liga Protectora Mexicana, which served Mexican-origin workers.[54] In 1921 he founded

Manuel (M. C.) Gonzáles, lawyer and LULAC founder, circa 1930. Courtesy Nettie Lee Benson Latin American Collection, University of Texas at Austin, and courtesy Melisa Gonzáles.

the Asociación Jurídica Mexicana (Mexican Legal Association), a legal aid society.

In 1918 Gonzáles joined the Army and became secretary to the military attaché at the U.S. embassies in Spain and France. Then he worked as a secretary to Senator Harry B. Howes of St. Louis, Missouri, and briefly attended St. Louis University's law school. He studied at the University of Texas at Austin and passed the bar in 1924.

Gonzáles remained cognizant of his working-class origins. He told a journalist,

> I was born poor, reared poor, and for the most part my childhood
> was spent with poor people of my Mexican race, and I became
> acutely aware of the exploitation that [Mexicans] were constantly
> victims of; of the suffering they underwent, of the constant humilia-
> tions and suffering they underwent.[55]

He saw himself as a defender of La Raza.

When Gonzáles returned to San Antonio, he got involved with the Better Government League, reformers who believed in Progressivism, which was fighting the political machine. He founded the newspaper *El Luchador*.[56] In 1928 he wrote the San Antonio Mexican Chamber of Commerce's constitution and from 1926 to 1958 worked as a legal advisor for the Mexican consulate.

Historian Richard García interviewed Gonzáles and captured his essence when he described Gonzáles as "a handsome, scholarly, aristocratic-looking man whose urbanity, fragility, gentleness, and intellectual ability affected everyone."[57] But he was fragile only in his last years. An attractive man, his well-tailored suits gave him stature; labor activist Emma Tenayuca fondly recalled his good looks.[58] Canales called Gonzáles "an intelligent, smart, and smooth speaker."[59]

In command of the law as well as the English and Spanish languages, Gonzáles was an effective and even poetic writer. He wrote, "We are builders of a better race. . . . when all is understood . . . we shall leave less of wrong behind. And more of what is good."[60] He married Cornelia Blank, a European American, and they had one daughter. Cornelia belonged to the Pan American Round Table, a women's club, and participated with the short-lived LULAC auxiliary in San Antonio in 1931.[61] They divorced and in 1959 he remarried, this time to Rose Olga Solís (John Solís' daughter), with whom he had four children. He became the third national LULAC president and died of natural causes on June 12, 1986. Gonzáles was a major leader in the 1920s, but only his 1930s activism has been highlighted. I had the pleasure of interviewing him twice.[62]

JOHN C. SOLÍS

John C. Solís was born on January 1, 1901, in San Antonio as the second of nine children of Juan M. Solís and Francisca Flores, both Mexican citizens.[63] His father worked as a motel cook, and his mother worked at home. At fourteen Solís quit school to help the family by working at odd jobs and later as a professional baseball umpire. Despite being underage, he volunteered to serve in World War I, joining the National Guard. After the war Solís worked at a wholesale house in San Antonio from 1922 to 1924 and then the Laguna Fishing Company in Corpus Christi. In the late 1920s Eleuterio Escobar Jr. hired him to manage his furniture store in San Antonio, where he worked until 1937.[64]

In the late 1920s, Solís told Paul Taylor, "The biggest drawback which the Texas-Mexicans face is that no matter how we behave or what we do or how long we have been here we are still 'Mexicans.'"[65] Solís' first name was John because his parents did not want him to suffer as a "Mexican." Solís left only one essay concerning his involvement in LULAC. He cited an ancestral right to the land: "For over 200 years everything in this part of the country had been ours . . . it had been settled by our ancestors at great sacrifice. They brought civilization to these parts . . . education, religion, art, culture, and all of these were our heritage."[66]

A humble and sincere leader whom Tenayuca called "a man of courage," Solís did not draw attention to himself. In his essay on the early days of the OSA and LULAC, "LULAC Milestones," he rarely used the identifier "I." Instead of writing "I reorganized the Corpus Christi council," he wrote "which the writer had organized in 1925." Yet, reminiscing after forty years of civic labor, he wrote about his activism, "That is why this humble person says to you now, as I have said many times before, that for what you have done for my people in the past, for what you are doing for my people in the present, and for what you will do for my people in the future, I thank you from the bottom of my heart."[67]

Solís stressed the collective, not individuals:

Through these many years, hundreds and even thousands of men, women and young people, Americans of Latin extraction, particu-

John Solís (third row from bottom, second from left), furniture salesman and LULAC founder, 1929. Courtesy Nettie Lee Benson Latin American Collection, University of Texas.

larly of Mexican origin, have given of their time and money; some have made great sacrifices to make these contributions to the cause. We wish we had the space to name them all.[68]

He stressed the many, not the few; women and youth, not just men; the cause, not individuals; "we," not "me"; and giving, not leading.

In 1934 he married actress Amparo Villalongín; they had three children. Later in life he obtained a master's degree in business administration at St. Mary's University in San Antonio and attended the University of Houston. From 1974 to 1982 he worked for U.S. Congressman Abraham (Chick) Kazen. Solís was a Mason. He died of natural causes on July 6, 1984. Today Solís is remembered by LULAC in San Antonio. I was fortunate to interview him.[69]

JAMES TAFOLLA SR.

Born in Texas around 1872, Santiago Tafolla Jr. went by the name James Tafolla Sr., although he was the son of the Reverend Santiago Tafolla Sr. and Anastacia Salinas.[70] His father, born in New Mexico, was orphaned, ran away from home, and was taken in by a Georgia man; he fought in the Civil War for the Confederacy and later settled in Texas, becoming a justice of the peace in Bandera, where he received 165 acres due to his military service. He then became a Methodist preacher in Laredo and San Diego, Texas. The elder Tafolla penned an autobiography in 1908 that remains unpublished.

A third-generation American, James Tafolla Sr. traveled from town to town with his parents, eventually settling in San Antonio. He worked in the district clerk's office in the criminal court as an official interpreter.[71] His light skin and stout build facilitated his entry into the courthouse. Active in mutualistas, he was an officer of the Orden Amigos del Pueblo and the Cruz Azul's first vice president in the 1920s.[72]

Based on an interview with James Tafolla Sr., Mexican anthropologist Manuel Gamio wrote the following in his field notes:

> He says he feels like a Mexican. But he is an American citizen. He respects this country but he says man's law has determined that his nationality is American, not his sentiments. Mexicans dislike Tejanos but things are changing and there is greater understanding. Americans are more inclined to recognize the Tejanos' merits.[73]

James Tafolla Sr. (at podium), employee at district clerk's office and OSA president, here probably at a mutualista event, circa 1920. Courtesy Dr. Carmen Tafolla.

Tafolla expressed his hybrid Mexican and American backgrounds.

He married Micaela Jiménez, a caseworker and teacher affiliated with the International Institute of the YWCA, where she taught Spanish and English. There is no evidence she was active with the OSA or LULAC. Despite his wife's career outside the home, Santiago harbored patriarchal ideas about women's place in society. In a 1939 essay titled "Motherhood" he noted, "The mother is the Goddess of the home. The ideal mother is the mother that loves her home and loves the companionship of her children." He criticized women "in high social circles" who were

> constantly training their children to live without them, in order to be able to attend all social functions. . . . The real mother, the ideal mother, shuns most social functions and is devoted to her home and children. . . . Such mothers are the admiration of our land . . . the mother of good citizens; God bless our land with such mothers.[74]

In 1947 Tafolla died of a heart attack. He proved to be an obstacle to unification of the organizations that split from the Order Sons of America in the late 1920s. Nevertheless, he played an important role throughout the 1920s. His son James Tafolla Jr., born in 1898, became an attorney and national LULAC president in 1935–1936.[75]

ALONSO S. PERALES

Alonso S. Perales was born on October 17, 1898, to Susana Sandoval and Nicolás Perales in Alice, Texas. Orphaned at age six, he worked as a child.[76] Still, he graduated from high school and from Draughn's Business College in Corpus Christi. He was drafted into the Army during World War I and received an honorable discharge in 1920. He then took the civil service exam and moved to Washington, D.C., where he worked for a year and a half

Alonso S. Perales, lawyer, LULAC founder, and major author
of the LULAC constitution, 1948. Courtesy Nettie Lee
Benson Latin American Collection, University of Texas, and
courtesy Raymond Perales.

at the U.S. Bureau of Standards, Department of Commerce. He received a
bachelor of arts degree from the George Washington University and a law
degree in 1926.

Perales began contemplating La Raza's condition in 1919 and was especially bothered by La Raza's defamation. In 1923 he wrote the *Washington
Post* to complain about the film *Bad Man*, which portrayed Mexicans as bandits. At some point he worked for the Latin American Affairs Office.[77] In the
1920s he began a career as a U.S. diplomat; he participated in thirteen diplomatic missions in the Dominican Republic, Cuba, Nicaragua, and other
Latin American countries. This experience gave him both an "American"
and Latin American consciousness. In referring to one racist portrayal of
La Raza, he called it "an insult to the official representatives of the Mexican
government and all the other Hispano American diplomatic staff members
living in Washington who, although they are not Mexicans, resent as much
as we do the outrages inferred to our race by virtue of the ties of blood and
language that connect us."[78]

Skilled at documentation and a master of the media, Perales wrote two
books, *Are We Good Neighbors?* and his two-volume *En defensa de mi raza*
(In Defense of My Race). In the latter book he concludes with the essay "El
verdadero origen" on the origins of LULAC:

> It is my belief that I have fully demonstrated (with no interest beyond
> that of stating the facts as they are for the information of those inter-
> ested in knowing the truth) that the present writer was the INITI-
> ATOR OF THE IDEA AND MAIN FOUNDER [his emphasis]
> of our present-day LEAGUE OF UNITED LATIN AMERICAN
> CITIZENS.[79]

He also named Canales, Garza, and Sáenz as key players. A man with some
ego, he proclaimed himself to be the "main founder" although during the
1930 congressional testimony mentioned earlier he testified, "I am one of
the founders" of LULAC.[80]

En defensa de mi raza was his battle cry. Perales was concerned with de-
bunking the idea of the "Mexican race's" inferiority. At the 1930 hearing he
declared, "Being a Mexican by blood, and being just as proud of my racial
extraction as I am of my American citizenship, I feel it is my duty to deny
most emphatically that the Mexican race is inferior to any other race."[81] In
his testimony he asked, "Why have we not produced outstanding men in

Texas?" and answered, "racial prejudice . . . attempts have been made to keep us down."[82] Perales tended to stress La Raza's role in its own racial uplifting. In his book he argues, "We need more leaders and men who will give luster and prestige to our race."[83] He failed to see women as leaders or "women citizens" despite his collaboration with women such as María L. Hernández and the young Adela Sloss.

Richard A. Garcia writes that Perales, trained as a lawyer, asserted that "the law, the U.S. constitution, and citizenship gave the Mexican Americans de facto and de jure equality" and that La Raza needed to "emulate our Anglo fellow citizens" with regard to civic duty and patriotism.[84] Perales was known as a magnificent orator. Sloss recalled his "distinguished appearance and [that he] spoke with great enthusiasm of our problems."[85] In 1942 an unknown author wrote a *calavera*, a Day of the Dead poem, about him:[86]

> From the beginning
> A symbol of correction
> with powerful words
> said with conviction
> A Tejano patriot
> who defended the Mexicano
> in any given moment
> He was a mover and man of ideas
> A powerful man, a 100%
> in the court, in a fight.

Professor Gilbert R. Cruz, a Texano who taught history in Arizona, heard Perales speak during the late 1940s. He recalled:

Perales represented a new generation of articulate professionals, emerging middle class business men and battle scarred veterans proud of their bicultural heritage. He possessed an impressive speaking voice that thundered with conviction. His capacity to use both languages with enormous facility and skill captivated his audience. I swelled with pride upon hearing his voice. So did everyone else. . . . He projected immense loyalty to the institutions that were paramount in the lives of his people, notably the extended family, role of the Ancient Church, and the grandeur of his culture. There was no question about his moral courage. He spoke with almost a deep religious feeling of purpose. Perales was tough, driven and endowed with an optimism to combat an adversary basking in triumphal boasting.[87]

Perales was a lifelong Democrat. In 1922 he married middle-class México Texana Marta Engracia Pérez, with whom he had already corresponded for six years. They adopted three children much later.[88] She did not involve herself in the women's activism of the 1920s but was a member of the interracial Pan American Round Table.[89] Marta ran a bookstore. According to their daughter, Marta was a student of piano and opera who preferred to play the piano and sing to her husband at the end of the day.[90] A devout Catholic, Perales died on May 9, 1960.

ANDRÉS DE LUNA SR.

Andrés de Luna Sr. was born in 1888 and educated in Webb County grammar schools by a tutor. In 1924 he worked at a bakery and opened his own in 1930. He became a notary public. He married Carolina Barrera, and they had one son. Carolina was extensively involved in 1920s and 1930s activism.

As secretary of the Order Sons of America, de Luna recorded most of the Corpus Christi OSA's minutes. He could write in English, but his grammar was limited.[91] One descendant has suggested that Carolina did most of his secretarial work. Andrés de Luna Sr. presided over the OSA one year and acted as LULAC's national secretary in 1929.[92] In the 1930s he served as custodian of the records for nine years. He (and perhaps Carolina) should be credited with writing the first official LULAC history; Corpus Christi's council issued the first such history in *LULAC News* in 1940. In 1930 he served as secretary of the local Woodmen of the World. In 1940 he became the first México Texano to serve as election judge in Nueces County.

During their interview, de Luna told Paul S. Taylor about the bathhouse incident described earlier: "About 1924 there was discrimination at the Palace Bathing house against Mexicans. They discriminated against Cruz Gutiérrez' daughter. It is all right to discriminate against the individual but not against the race." After the OSA obtained some concessions, de Luna concluded, "There is still some discrimination but it isn't against all Mexicans."[93] de Luna said service in World War I had significance, skin color had meaning, and negotiation—not violence—solved problems.

de Luna died on December 11, 1956. His obituary called him simply a charter member of LULAC, but his role as national secretary and

Andrés de Luna Sr., baker, LULAC founder, and LULAC historian, 1940. Courtesy Nettie Lee Benson Latin American Collection, University of Texas.

national historian made him significant.[94] de Luna is remembered only in Corpus Christi.

BERNARDO F. GARZA

Bernardo F. (Ben) Garza was born in 1892 in Brownsville to Bernardo and María de Jesús Flores de la Garza, both of Mexico.[95] After his father died in

Bernardo F. (Ben) Garza Sr., restaurateur, LULAC founder,
and first LULAC president, 1930. Courtesy Ben Garza Jr.

1908 Ben helped his mother support the family of seven in Rockport, near
Corpus Christi. He completed the sixth grade, apparently the highest grade
in the Mexican school. He then waited tables. Later he worked on a ship
construction crew in Rockport to contribute to the war effort and helped
his brother become the first México Texano graduate from Rockport High
School.

Garza then moved to Corpus Christi and opened the Metropolitan Café
with three co-owners. As one observer noted, "He was the owner of a restaurant in a very respectable part of town in the Anglo-American section.
People looked up to him because of that situation."[96] Frequented by European American businessmen, the middle class, and city leaders, the down-

town restaurant seated seven hundred. Garza called it "one of the leading restaurants" in the city. Apparently buying out his co-owners, he finished paying for his restaurant shortly before his death.[97] An entrepreneur, by 1926 he also entered the real estate business.

Garza was a sincere servant of the needy and a philanthropist. When Perales suggested he serve as the first president of LULAC, he responded, "My intentions are good, but I know that I lack the education to be at the front of such an organization. Nevertheless, I am always willing to put the shoulder to the wheel and see it go through." Perales considered him "intelligent, energetic, honest, and sincere."[98] Indeed, his testimony before Congress in 1930 reveals an articulate, smart man concerned with the welfare of workers, immigrants, and business.

Involved in good works and able to cross racial boundaries despite his limited education, Garza served as president of the Corpus Christi Chamber of Commerce and as a board member of the Salvation Army. In 1926 he presided over the local Woodmen of the World chapter and in 1928 headed the Corpus Christi campaign for Mexican presidential candidate José Vasconcelos through the Vasconcelos for President Club, revealing a connection to mutualistas and Mexico's politics.[99] In 1928 Garza moved to Arizona in hopes of curing his tuberculosis, then returned to Corpus Christi. Popular and successful, he was often encouraged to run for political office when he lived in Corpus Christi, as he acknowledged: "Many gentlemen of Anglo-Saxon origin have approached me and requested me to offer myself for that office, because they know I would have the Mexicans solidly on my side."[100]

When Garza died of pneumonia in Corpus Christi on February 21, 1937, City Hall doors closed. A *LULAC News* headline in March captured his spirit: "Ben Garza Spent Life in Hard Work and Activity for Civic Betterment." City leaders dedicated a park in his honor, and he was eulogized by LULAC members. A personable and generous man, he became well known after his death. He was married to Adelaida Carrilles, a homemaker, and they had five children.[101] Despite Adelaida's homemaker status, she was directly connected to the OSA and LULAC and helped initiate the Alpha Club. Because Ben Garza was the first national president of LULAC he has been called the "father" of the league. In truth, he was but one founder. LULAC member Leopoldo Castañon suggested the value of league members: "After having succeeded in their respective careers, [those men] have not forgotten their people and have taken it unto themselves to work, and fight if necessary, for the upliftment and betterment of our race."[102]

CONCLUSION

México Texano civil rights movement leaders constituted a diverse group but shared some experiences. Most were born in the United States to parents who were either immigrants or U.S. citizens, some of whose families lived in Texas for generations. Living during an era of lynching, these leaders experienced racial subordination and second-class citizenship despite their U.S. citizenship. They were racialized as "Mexicans."

Most were born into working-class families; Canales, a member of the upper class, was an exception, as were Tafolla and the Idar brothers, all of middle-class upbringing. Most of the founders thus had firsthand experience with poverty and hard work. Some took on family responsibilities at an early age, instilling in them a strong work ethic and greater appreciation for education. All had regular contact with workers and immigrants.

These activists have been generalized as middle-class, but this categorization does not fully address their origins. Nor does it account for the formation of a consciousness rooted initially in working-class life. As adults they did not have a working-class worldview. Clemente Idar was a labor organizer, and the OSA's constitution reflected working-class interests. Still, this cadre of leaders included professionals, small-business owners, and skilled laborers.

With regard to education, all had some public schooling. About a third graduated from college. Lawyers Canales, Gonzáles, Perales, and Sáenz were powerful orators and writers. All had more education than the average OSA or LULAC member or the average Mexican American and much more than the average Mexican in Texas.[103] Public schooling in "citizen factories" fostered their Americanization. They could read and write some English, but not all were proficient in speaking or writing English. All could read Spanish. All were bilingual, although Eduardo Idar Sr., who spent most of his life in Laredo, seems to have been Spanish-dominant. Culturally, the leadership was México Texano and Mexican American, although Canales, Gonzáles, Perales, James Tafolla Sr., Sáenz, and Solís had all lived outside of Texas in European American and European worlds during World War I. Living in Washington, D.C., Perales had greater exposure to a Latin American consciousness and was a patriotic U.S. diplomat.

Participation in World War I also translated into American patriotism. Most were World War I veterans who experienced both integration and segregation during the war and found racism and second-class citizenship upon their return.[104] A battle on the home front was just beginning.

These leaders assumed multiple ethnic and national identities. While scholars have suggested that they stressed their "American" identities, they were in fact Americans. Moreover, they took pride in their Indian, Spanish, Mexican, Mexican American, México Texano, and Latin American identities and negotiated these when necessary. Each individual chose his own respective identity but typically referred to himself as México Texano, Mexican American, or Mexican. Like other México Texanos, they resented the loss of a homeland to European American domination.

Despite the racism they encountered, these activists experienced upward mobility that fueled their optimism. Most of them were self-employed and hence did not suffer from the whims of European American employers. Because they were financially independent they could take risks that others could not or would not dare. Some were active in mutual aid societies and the Masons. They saw no contradictions in promoting mutuality and cooperating with Mexican immigrants in other organizations. Garza even participated in the politics of Mexico.

Several leaders saw themselves as defenders and warriors. Sáenz, Gonzáles, and Perales especially used these male military motifs and saw themselves leading the charge against discrimination. They were strategists and soldiers fighting the war against racism, knights defending La Raza's honor.

With regard to gender politics, the leaders exhibited diversity. Not all were married; Solís, for instance, was single until 1934. Some had wives who were involved with the OSA or LULAC; these included Adelaida Garza, Carolina de Luna, and Cornelia Gonzáles. Perales, Canales, Sáenz, and the Idars were married, but their wives were not involved in related organizational work. Perales' wife was more involved with the Pan American Round Table. Micaela Tafolla had her own interests in settlement-house work.

Male leaders had different ideologies about women's participation in activism and politics. Tafolla seemed to hold the most conservative thinking on the subject, even as his wife was active outside the home; Perales and Canales were moderates; J. Luz Sáenz was progressive; and Clemente Idar was profeminist. However, as we saw, a conservative position on the question of women's participation in the OSA was enacted, and only in the early 1930s was a more progressive position taken. So in the 1920s leaders of this Mexican American civil rights movement were men who saw themselves as builders of a "better race," shielding La Raza, and soldiering in the war against racism.

The Harlingen
Convention of 1927

FIVE   *No Mexicans Allowed*

*The heated debate at Harlingen was whether or not we
were going to work together with Mexican citizens or
work exclusively for Mexican Americans. That created
friction, dissension, and it broke up the meeting.*
—M. C. GONZÁLES, 1979

In the midst of an emerging Mexican American civil rights movement, the
next key event was a convention billed as a "pro-Raza" effort held in Harlingen in South Texas in 1927. The objective was to provide an organizational
solution to the problems La Raza faced and unite all the disparate associations originally associated with the Order Sons of America. But instead of
unity, division surfaced. This time the division was over the question of
citizenship. Harlingen conventioneers decided that U.S. citizenship should
determine membership of the proposed association.

In this chapter I examine the politics of citizenship and especially the
events before, during, and after the conference that highlight the debates
about inclusion. Conference organizers said two questions would be addressed there: Should both Mexican Americans and Mexicans be members
of a future organization? And which existing organization among those already connected to the OSA should lead the charge?

I also address how México Texano leaders, Mexican leaders, and various Spanish-language and English-language newspapers remembered and
reported conference events years and decades later. Each explains why they
supported or condemned the exclusion of Mexicans.

Finally, I address the increasing significance of citizenship and México Texano hybridity so as to explain the exclusion. Tied to these questions were the following issues: How would a civil rights movement take shape? Who belonged to the Raza community and defined its membership? How would La Raza achieve empowerment in the United States as opposed to Mexico? What role would class play? What role would Mexican immigrants in the United States play in this empowerment? What role would women play? What role would the Mexican consulate play? What significance would citizenship have as a political strategy for the empowerment of La Raza? And how would México Texano hybridity and a unique position vis-à-vis citizenship, nation, community, and race shape responses?

THE HARLINGEN CONVENTION

The Harlingen convention of 1927 was the second major statewide attempt to unite the various Mexican-origin organizations following the Primer Congreso Mexicanista in 1911. Like the Congreso Mexicanista, organizers invited Mexicans and México Texanos to the event; but unlike those at the Congreso Mexicanista, participants in Harlingen decided that Mexican citizens living in the United States could not join their organizational efforts. According to several México Texano leaders, only Mexican Americans could provide leadership and solutions to the unique problems facing Mexican Americans in the broader Mexican-origin community.

In 1921 OSA founders had envisioned a united front. But by 1927 the OSA, the Order Sons of Texas, Club Protector México-Texano, and Order Knights of America were duplicating efforts and minimizing potential influence in San Antonio. OSA chapters had been established throughout South Texas but not yet in the Valley. Communication between OSA chapters was limited, and no state convention had been held. So in 1927 México Texano activists began to discuss a merger of all these disparate groups.

In July 1927 Alonso S. Perales, J. Luz Sáenz, J. T. Canales, and other South Texas community representatives formed the Comité Provisional Organizador Pro-Raza (Provisional Pro-Raza Committee), in which Perales acted as president and Felipe Herrera of Harlingen as secretary.[1] According to *La Prensa*, Herrera initiated a unity campaign on July 10 referred to as "la Asociación Pro-Patria" (the Pro-Fatherland Association).[2] Was *patria* (fatherland, country) a reference to Mexico? Or was it a reference to the nation of La Raza, a nation within the United States?

Membership of the association consisted of México Texanos and Mexicans. At least one member, M. Flores Villar, was a Mexican citizen, but Mexicans were probably outnumbered on the committee. One newspaper described committee members as "people with status in the political and commercial spheres of this region."[3] Representatives came from Mercedes, Weslaco, Brownsville, Edinburg, Mission, San Benito, Donna, Raymondville, and Harlingen, all from the Valley.[4]

According to Perales, dissension soon arose within the committee: one faction favored a single organization embodying both México Texanos and Mexicans, while the other wanted two separate associations to address distinct needs and goals of each citizen group.[5] Perales favored two organizations and suggested a conference to resolve the matter; Harlingen was the site selected.

The Corpus Christi OSA invited Perales, Sáenz, and Herrera to discuss the forthcoming convention.[6] John Solís (OKA) sent a telegram to the Corpus Christi group around July 20, apparently asking if several OKA representatives might attend.[7] M. C. Gonzáles (OKA) attended the Corpus Christi meeting on July 27. On July 31 Andrés de Luna Sr., Ben Garza, Eulalio Marín (Corpus Christi OSA), and several other committee members met with Perales.[8] Gonzáles, Solís, and Mauro M. Machado, a joint member of the OSA and OKA, also met with the group.[9] They tried to dissuade Perales from forming yet another organization to prevent further disunity, but to no avail;[10] he suggested they send delegates to the conference to offer solutions.[11] So each organization selected its convention delegates: Gonzáles and Machado (OKA), Clemente Idar and Teodoro Góngora (Corpus Christi OSA), and James Tafolla Sr. and Ramón Carvajal (San Antonio OSA).[12]

Organizers reported the upcoming event to English-language newspapers. Several of these newspapers made reference to "Mexicans" being active, and others seemed puzzled over the idea of "Americans of Mexican Descent," placing the phrase in quotes. The *Houston Chronicle*'s headline read, "Mexicans to Meet at San Benito to Form Association"; the *Brownsville Herald* used the headline "Mexicans to Form Society." The *McAllen Daily Press* headline read, "Will Organize 'American of Mexican Descent' Society." The *San Antonio Express* reported "Texas Mexicans Are to Organize Protective Association to Be Formed at Harlingen" and "Spanish-Speaking Residents Meet for Organization."[13]

The conference attracted more interest from the Spanish-language press. *La Prensa* (San Antonio), *El Cronista del Valle* (Brownsville), *La Avispa* (Del Rio), *El Comercio* (Harlingen), and *México en el Valle* (Mission) announced the meeting. Newspaper coverage ran from August 5 through 17, 1927. On

August 5 *La Prensa* announced the gathering as one at which México Texanos would unite but not with Mexicans. Herrera traveled to San Antonio to garner support and perhaps influence preconference press coverage
apparently biased toward the formation of a México Texano association.[14]
The headline in *El Cronista* on August 12 referred to "Una gran convención
de mexicanos en Harlingen, Texas" (A Large Convention of Mexicans in
Harlingen, Texas). *La Avispa*'s headline on August 6 read, "Se organiza una
importante asociación de méxico-americanos y mexicanos" (An Important
Association of Mexican Americans and Mexicans Is Organized); according
to its journalists, unity was forthcoming. In contrast, *El Comercio* warned its
readers of potential antagonists who advocated for the division of Mexicans
and México Texanos.[15]

Spanish-language flyers announced a convention open to mutualistas
and all persons of Mexican descent. Organizers sent official invitations to
associations.[16] Tafolla Sr. and Carvajal were commissioned to invite other
organizational representatives to serve as delegates.[17] The conference call
was made to "all persons," but the political culture of the times defined this
to include only men. *El Comercio* anticipated male conventioneers, referring
to "Sres. Delegados" (Gentlemen Delegates).[18]

The organizers clearly stated the conference's purpose; the program
would address eight items, two that were particularly significant.[19] First,
"Would the organization to be formed be composed of Mexican Americans
and Mexican citizens or just Mexican Americans?" Second, "Into which existing organization would the others merge?"[20] The manner in which the
committee posed the first question showed preference for a México Texano
membership, since no mention was made of an organization solely of Mexican
citizens. The phrasing of the second issue suggested the acceptance of an
existing organization, likely of Mexican American origin. No major Mexi-
can-only organizations such as the Comisiones Honoríficos were involved.

Controversy over these two issues began before the conference started.
On August 10 Mexican citizen Carlos Basañez Rocha, director of *México en
el Valle* newspaper, asked Perales about the proposed organization's constit-
uency.[21] Perales replied:

> The type of organization that the initiators of this movement pro-
> pose to found is a strong entity which will sincerely and persistently
> labor by all means for the well being of the Mexican Americans
> and when possible, of the Mexican citizens residing in this country,
> especially in Texas. The success of this organization will depend on

the type of men that lead it. Consequently, the first thing we will do is elect as leaders a nucleus of honorable, energetic, and intelligent men. The question whether the proposed organization should be integrated by Mexican American citizens and Mexican citizens will be resolved in this convention by a majority of votes.[22]

Perales' concern for México Texanos first, as well as his faith in a cadre of leaders, was evident. The interests and needs of Mexicans would be addressed "when possible." Nevertheless, he stated that democracy should be allowed to take its course.

México en el Valle of Mission and *El Comercio* of Harlingen responded with a Mexican perspective. On August 12 in an editorial in *El Comercio*, Z. Vela Ramírez, a teacher at a private Mexican school in Kingsville, argued for unity to tackle problems afflicting "la Raza Mexicana."[23] Likewise, Flores Villar, associated with *México en el Valle*, warned conventioneers:

Do not come with false prejudices of alliances that will impede the triumphant march of our ideals. As you enter the gateway to the Valley, we want you to lay aside all of the aggressive weapons which some ill-intentioned people may have given you, and to exchange them for the ideals of unity and harmony that we so much need these days.[24]

Flores Villar predicted dissension among conference participants, and his reference to "ill-intentioned people" seems to have been a reference to Perales and several members of the committee. Unity, Flores Villar instructed, must prevail, perhaps assuming or imagining that La Raza was unified or at least that Mexican and Mexican American men would cooperate.

Another article in *El Comercio* provided detailed suggestions by T. Fraga, a representative of "AHUEHETE" No. 2364, Woodmen of the World of Laredo, for organization. He recommended a monetary fund, defense and education committees, a weekly publication, a statistics and employment committee, an executive finance committee, and inexpensive dues.[25]

On August 14 México Texano and Mexican men from across Texas gathered at the Harlingen Auditorium. There is no evidence that women (wives, relatives, friends, and compatriots) were invited or attended. Nevertheless, Adela Sloss, a 1927 graduate of San Juan High School, had a keen interest in the event; she kept clippings and other documents about it though she did not attend.

Some men traveled from as far as Fort Worth and Houston to attend. Estimates of those attending range from two hundred to five hundred. *La Prensa* reported two hundred delegates, but whether these were actually delegates or participants is unclear. In 1979 M. C. Gonzáles recalled five hundred in attendance.[26] With the exception of several orators, a list of attendees is not available. Most were probably leaders in mutualistas and middle class; a few journalists were present. What is clear is that Mexican citizens were the majority, perhaps representing various mutualistas from throughout the state or perhaps more numerous because they feared possible exclusion.

The first order of business was the selection of a presiding officer and a secretary; Perales and Sáenz were elected, respectively. Then conventioneers decided to extend voting privileges to all in attendance, not just delegates.[27] This ensured that Mexicans, not México Texanos, were now the majority of voters, probably an unforeseen development on the part of Mexican Americans.

The next agenda item was membership for the proposed organization. On this point, Perales, Clemente Idar, Eduardo Idar Sr., and Canales argued for the exclusion of Mexicans.[28] They offered sympathy to their Mexican "brethren" but argued that progress could be more quickly realized through a México Texano association. Apparently, organizers did not designate speakers to advocate any Mexican perspective. *La Prensa*, *El Cronista*, *El Comercio*, and *México en el Valle* did not mention any Mexican speakers.

The meeting seems to have included an agenda among the preselected orators.[29] Dialogue—often heated—ensued between the orators and the predominant Mexican audience. According to San Antonio OSA and OKA member Eleuterio Escobar Jr., "This point [the membership issue] caused very heated discussions that lasted all morning."[30] México Texanos sought to preserve their organizational vision, one that dated back to 1921. Disagreements eventually led to a "Mexican walkout" by 75 percent of those in attendance.[31] A few México Texanos may have walked out also. Only a few México Texanos from Corpus Christi, San Antonio, Brownsville, and possibly Alice remained in the auditorium.[32] Did México Texanos outnumber Mexicans at the convention? In 1931 Sáenz wrote, "Many immediately abandoned the hall without waiting to see the final result."[33]

M. C. Gonzáles explained the walkout to me:

We [México Texanos] told them [Mexicans], "We will not join with you." Regardless of how big you [are]—you can't force us to be part

of you, so you form your organization, and we'll quit. You can out-
vote us, but we won't be a part of it. So they just quit; they couldn't
do it without us.[34]

México Texanos tried to convince Mexicans to support a political organization of México Texanos, agreeing to their own exclusion. Mexican citizens
did in fact need México Texanos' English-language skills, their privileged
acculturated status, and their U.S. citizenship—all of which gave access to
the dominant society.

Protestors did not leave simply because of rational objections. Escobar
and Gonzáles said Mexicans were insulted and hurt. Perhaps some México
Texanos felt that way too. The controversy was just beginning.

NEWSPAPER COVERAGE AND RECOLLECTIONS
OF THE CONVENTION

Convention minutes are not available, but newspapers, published essays,
manuscripts, and oral histories offer insight into the event and its after-
math. México Texano conventioneers explained what happened there, and
English-language and Spanish-language newspapers provided Mexican and
México Texano perspectives of the exclusion. The *Mission Enterprise* offered
this account:

> There were in the hall a large number of persons not American citi-
> zens, and Mr. Canales insisted that as the purpose of the organiza-
> tion was to be exclusively of Americans of Latin descent the Mexican
> citizens present be not allowed to participate. The suggestion created
> an argument and there seemed no disposition to exclude the non-
> citizens (that is, Mexican citizens). There was a chorus of seconding
> voices to Mr. Canales' motion, and it was the determining action that
> the Mexicans not American citizens be excluded from the meeting.[35]

When the "non-citizens" had withdrawn, the newspaper reported, the
meeting was reorganized.[36] It is interesting to note that the paper referred
to Mexicans as "non-citizens." According to this account, Canales played
the key role in excluding Mexican citizens. It is unclear if there was only a
motion for exclusion and not a vote.

Spanish-language newspapers provided contradictory accounts of the
meeting, some taking a México Texano perspective and others a Mexican

perspective. *El Cronista* of Brownsville described the events from a México Texano perspective:

> After long, brilliant, and heated deliberations, the question was put up to a vote. By a majority of votes, it was decided that this organization should be composed exclusively of American citizens of Mexican descent. Some Mexican citizens left disgusted and saying that they had been deceived, but this attitude is unjust because in the invitation and in the program which was circulated, it was clearly advertised that the question of citizenship would be resolved by a majority of votes in the cited convention.[37]

According to this report, those in favor of a México Texano association outnumbered those in favor of a united front. After the convention, Perales sent this newspaper a similar report that explained voting procedures.[38] This Brownsville newspaper seemed to side with Canales and Perales—México Texanos.

While *La Prensa* was a Mexicanist voice, the Lozano family publishers accepted and validated México Texano political strategies without criticism:

> Canales . . . resolved the question saying that what was to be done was to form a group that would work in the political arena, and for this reason, it should be formed only by the American citizens of Mexican origin. This motivated the Mexicans to leave the assembly who had responded considering that an association of México-Texanos and Mexicans could be formed to work in favor of the interests of "la raza" in things in which there was no justice for either element.[39]

Canales seems to have announced that the proposed organization's character and strategy was to be Mexican American. Mexicans, he argued, could not participate in "politics." Perales may have influenced the San Antonio newspaper.

In contrast, editorials in *El Comercio* of Harlingen and *México en el Valle* of Mission, newspapers apparently controlled by Mexicans, hinted at political manipulation and alienation. *El Comercio*'s commentary took an acerbic tone in describing Canales' speech as

> proposing at the same time that this organization should be integrated by Mexican Americans exclusively, since Mexicans from

MEXICO are a PITIFUL LOT who come to this country in great caravans to retard the Mexican Americans' work for unity, Mexican Americans that should be at the Anglo-Saxon's level. [Emphasis theirs; translation by a México Texano][40]

After this editorial, Perales wrote Canales that he recalled his reference to Mexicans as "poor destitutes," a sympathetic reference, not a derogatory one.[41] Assessing Canales' class bias, somewhat racialized thinking about Mexicans, and personality as revealed in his correspondence, I believe he called Mexicans a "pitiful lot."[42] Or was something lost in translation?

Mexican perspectives on the exclusion are known only through México Texano commentary and a few articles in the Mexican press located in the Adela Sloss-Vento and Alonso S. Perales papers. This, then, is the extent of our knowledge of Mexicanist interpretations of the events at the Harlingen convention.

MÉXICO TEXANO LEADERS' ACCOUNTS

Besides newspaper accounts, several México Texano conventioneers' perspectives have been documented. Across the decades in his writing and through oral histories, M. C. Gonzáles has commented the most about the exclusion. Canales, OSA member Eleuterio Escobar Jr., Perales, Sáenz, and Eduardo Idar Sr. also left accounts.

M. C. Gonzáles' Account

Gonzáles explained the exclusion by addressing the broader issue of Raza empowerment; he did so in 1931 in the first issues of *LULAC News:*

> The Mexican citizen[s] can at least call upon their government [Mexico] for protection through the many conveniently located Consular offices, and in cases of grave [in]justice appeal may be had through diplomatic channels, but we citizens of the United States of Mexican extraction, we are helpless, unless we join hands and work under the banner of LULAC.[43]

Actually, there were consular offices and a few diplomatic options available to Mexican citizens, though most were ineffective. Conversely, Gonzáles listed rights and privileges only available to Mexican Americans:

The Mexican citizen, he being an alien and not having the right to vote and participate in the administration of governmental affairs, not being able to sit on juries, hold public office, cannot complain when those privileges granted by the [U.S.] Constitution are not given to them.[44]

In a 1967 interview Gonzáles again recalled the conflict between Mexican Americans and Mexicans:

We had quite a gathering. . . . There was a very disconcerting issue and that was the proposition that in Texas we had quite a large number of Spanish-speaking people but a large percentage of them were citizens of Mexico who had lived here for many, many years and naturally wanted to be respected and acknowledged and recognized that we who are natives of Texas are naturalized Americans as the case may be, should not carry the burden. We felt that we should not carry the burden because these citizens of Mexico were very ably represented by the Mexican Consulate. They had the government of Mexico to look after them whereas we had nothing. We didn't have the proper leadership; we didn't have the trained men nor numerical strength; we did not have the financial background, we did not have any guidelines.[45]

Gonzáles reiterated some of the problems México Texanos had in terms of leadership, education, demographics, money, and plan of action. He concluded, "We decided to go ahead and segregate ourselves from the citizens of Mexico."[46]

Gonzáles elaborated further on the exclusion in 1979 when he told me, "When you tell them, 'We don't want you.' They said, 'Well, to hell with you!'"[47] He added a legalistic perspective based on the issue of citizenship:

It had nothing to do with Mexico, that we were not Mexican citizens, that we were citizens of this country. That this country protected us under the constitution of the United States and of the states. And that only citizens of this state and of this nation could assert certain rights as citizens, especially the right to vote and the right to serve on juries, the right to be a notary public or public official.[48]

And he explained the Mexican position:

Your papa and your mama and my papa were born in Mexico. And we were all living here and we were all Mexicans with *sangre mexicana*. And whatever they [whites] were doing to us, was a disgrace to the race which was the culture and background of our forefathers. Why shouldn't I join you in that fight?[49]

He was referring to a community tied by blood, culture, Mexican heritage, race, territorial location in the United States, and racism against La Raza. Mexicans, he suggested, said race needed to be the basis for organization, not citizenship.

Besides believing citizenship to be primary and the strategy for the empowerment of La Raza, México Texano leaders organizing the event also seemed to ensure that their position would be chosen. The OKA and the Corpus Christi OSA foresaw the problem of a minority voice at the convention and had devised a plan in case the vote did not go in their favor. Gonzáles said, "We took a separate vote, we had an agreement with those who were citizens of the United States, that we would secede, and meet in Corpus Christi."[50] Gonzáles concluded: "We decided to go ahead and segregate ourselves from the citizens of Mexico."[51] Gonzáles' accounts give us the most insight into México Texano leaders' reasons for excluding Mexicans.

J. T. Canales' Account

Canales left recollections of the event but remembered it differently. He suggested that México Texanos were on both sides of the question, with Gonzáles favoring Mexican inclusion and Eduardo Idar Sr. favoring Mexican exclusion. In a letter to a LULAC friend in 1960, Canales recalled:

At said meeting, when I arrived the question was whether the movement was to be composed solely of American citizens, or would the citizens of Mexico be included. The late Eduardo Idar of Laredo was speaking for the former, and Mr. Manuel C. Gonzales of San Antonio, who claimed to represent the Mexican consul at said city, led the debate for the latter. After some discussion, I was recognized and, after explaining why it was not prudent to expose our good fellows of Spanish descent, moved that said organization be restricted to American citizens, and this motion carried by an overwhelming vote. Mr. Gonzáles and his Mexican citizens retired from the building.[52]

Canales acknowledges his key role at the conference. He reported that a motion was made for exclusion and that a vote was taken on the motion. He clarified the role that Eduardo Idar and Gonzáles played. I believe Eduardo Idar wanted a México Texano organization only and that Gonzáles favored having both.

Eleuterio Escobar Jr.'s Account

México Texano Eleuterio Escobar Jr. of San Antonio recalled the positions of various leaders. He belonged to two of the San Antonio organizations and attended the convention. He wrote in his unpublished autobiography:

> Some of the delegates thought that the new organizations should be formed of American Citizens, but on the other hand it was an embarrassment and sadness to eliminate some members who were not American citizens, but at the same time were very active in this struggle. They were not American citizens, but their children were, and they too like Mexican Americans felt the taste of oppression abussion [*sic*] and tyranny that was applied by our Texas High Officials.[53]

Escobar Jr. commented that Mexican citizens *were* involved in the struggle for the empowerment of La Raza. Moreover, the children of Mexican immigrants born in the United States were U.S. citizens, further complicating the equation. And European Americans typically treated Mexican Americans and Mexicans alike.

MEXICAN CRITICS OF THE EXCLUSION

Mexicans also left records of the exclusion. The controversy did not end when Mexicans—and possibly some México Texanos—walked out. Indeed, the press covered the controversy and fueled the dialogue. Perhaps the most critical response came from *México en el Valle* of Mission, though only a few translated excerpts from this newspaper have been found. Flores Villar wrote in *México en el Valle* on September 10: "An insult . . . instead of saying . . . 'We are Mexicans by race [México Texanos proclaim] I am an American!'"[54] Carlos Basañez Rocha of *México en el Valle* accused Perales of two irregularities.[55] He said that at one point Perales argued to include both groups and that on another occasion he argued for an exclusively Mexican American organization. He charged Perales with permitting voting irregularities, specifically that the membership (citizenship) question was voted on twice.

Perales refuted these charges in a personal letter.[56] On August 27 *México en el Valle* directed additional criticism at Perales' handling of the proceedings. Perales responded by explaining that before the citizenship vote was taken, another was taken to determine who could vote—delegates or all participants. Basañez Rocha had confused this vote with the membership question, Perales told him. He referred him to Sáenz, the convention's acting secretary, and asked the journalist to correct his account.[57]

Meanwhile, Perales wrote Sáenz,

So, then, I hope that you will examine the acts and that when he asks you for a report (or before, if you judge it convenient or prudent) that you tell him that I expressed my opinion only once, and that was that the organization should remain comprised of Mexican American citizens. Also tell him that this matter of citizenship was submitted to a vote only once, which was when it was resolved by majority, that the society be of Texas Mexicans.[58]

Perales told Sáenz how to answer Basañez Rocha's inquiry, perhaps either repeating fact or swaying him toward how the letter might be written. He told Sáenz that if Basañez Rocha did not retract his statement, he might charge the journalist with libel. Moreover, he added, "if he does not retract immediately, I am going to send him very far [to Mexico?]; maybe Lic. Canales will help me, because he [Basañez Rocha] unjustly insulted him by saying he said something which he did not."[59] Perales would not tolerate public criticism.

Perales wrote Canales about *México en el Valle*'s criticism the next day. He referred him to the August 19 and 27, 1927, issues of *México en el Valle* in which Flores Villar had attacked Canales: "Immediate steps to obtain a retraction" should be taken, said Perales, "or else sue them for libel and have their sheet discontinued."[60] He added that Basañez Rocha had written similar accusations about himself: "He too has been attacking me pretty hard but I intend to scare the life out of him before long. We must make these guys kneel before us publicly and ask us to forgive them."[61]

Flores Villar and Basañez Rocha continued to criticize México Texano leaders. On September 10 Flores Villar wrote in *México en el Valle*:

[A]s an insult much to the Mexican race, we find some renegades who, instead of saying with pride "We are Mexicans," by race, state (without seeing for a moment in the mirror their bronze color and their totally Indian aspect, the origin of their Race and not their Nationality), quite proudly "I am American!"[62]

To Flores Villar, "race" and nationality were primary, citizenship secondary. To him, the fact that Mexican Americans were U.S. citizens was irrelevant; instead, it was race that mattered. Basañez Rocha attacked México Texanos who spoke about racial pride but who did not espouse Mexican nationalism:

It isn't necessary to spell out what happened when the warped intentions of these spokesman became public; these spokesmen who wanted gifts and public offices claimed to work toward the building of the future by means of a trick based on blessed principles, worthy of better company. And as always happens to those who seek personal gain or a warped end, they were the tricksters but claimed to be the trick by appearing before the public conscience, in a ridiculous comparison, as the new redeemers and suffering Christ.[63]

The "trick" Basañez Rocha implied apparently was Mexican Americans' espousal of pro-Raza tenets and Raza nationalism. But their intentions were not warped, nor did they seek personal gain. Moreover, they espoused Raza nationalism, not Mexican nationalism.

Perales found it politically expedient to answer criticism directed at him and other México Texano activists. So from September 7 through September 13, 1927, he published his extended essay titled "La evolución de la raza mexicana" in *La Prensa* of San Antonio, comparing the distinctive political evolution of Mexican Americans versus Mexicans in the United States.[64] In this treatise on Mexican American citizenship and Raza empowerment at the time, he proposed education, organization, and the vote as key components. He postulated two distinct sectors within the Raza community, Mexican Americans and Mexicans in the United States. He acknowledged more differences than similarities and recognized México Texanos' privilege over Mexicans vis-à-vis U.S. citizenship. He did not recognize binational, multinational, or transnational politics by these two sectors and foresaw La Raza's assimilation into the United States over time.

Perales addressed the Harlingen convention and his intent to form a strong Mexican American organization.[65] He said that when asked whether both Mexican Americans and Mexicans could collaborate, he answered yes, but only as two groups with different standards, each preserving its national identity. The two would then cooperate in intellectual, economic, and social arenas.[66] His peers disagreed with him, he explained, so he then proposed a convention to resolve the citizenship question. He said, "Thus I, not wanting to cast myself as an egotist, dictator, or imperialist, proposed that we convoke the leaders of our race in Texas and discuss the [citizenship] issue there."[67]

Perales mentioned Mexican criticism of México Texanos' reports of the convention proceedings: "For example, they said that the citizenship question was put to [a] vote twice—that the first time, those that wanted both elements won by 'a clear majority.'"[68]

Besides the essay in *La Prensa*, Perales found a second way to respond to the criticism. At the Harlingen convention a new organization was formed; it was called the Mexican American Citizens League. A chapter of that organization, the Mexican American Citizens League of McAllen, took the initiative to suppress criticism.[69] On September 27 its president, Deodoro Guerra, probably Canales' friend, directed a request to the Immigration Service in Brownsville and to a special investigator in the U.S. Department of Justice:

> Naturally, one of our major tenets is: One Hundred Percent loyalty and devotion to our flag and our institution. We felt just pride in stating openly that we are American citizens when anyone happens to ask and we most strongly question the right of an alien to criticize us, to insult us, and to brand us.
>
> Such doctrines of M. Flores Villar and Carlos Basañez Rocha thwart the labor of the Mexican American League, hamper the Americanization work of other similar organization[s] and strike at the very foundations of our great Republic, inasmuch as these men are preaching that Race comes first and Nationality second.
>
> I trust that our Government will see its way clear to heed our protest and order the said Mexican citizens, M. Flores Villar of Harlingen, and Carlos Basañez Rocha of Mission, to either cease in their un-American and pernicious activities immediately or else leave the country.[70]

Guerra appealed to the language of the dominant society—the ideology of 100 percent Americanism, suggesting that "alien" Mexican citizens needed deportation. Guerra sought to silence critics.

Corpus Christi OSA Council No. 4 joined the Mexican American Citizens League and thus joined Perales' side in this dispute. Andrés de Luna Sr., secretary of the OSA council, wrote Guerra explaining his council's position:

[A]fter a lengthy discussion this Order agreed to support your attitude in that case in any way, shape or form, that you see fit to bring that newspaper to at least give an apology for the attacks and insults to our nationality; it is a pity that the parties involved in this case are of our race, but nevertheless it will teach them and some others a good lesson for the future progress of our people in Texas.[71]

de Luna also saw the future of La Raza in Texas. Besides this letter of support, he wrote to the immigration officer in Brownsville: "We highly commend the attitude taken by the McAllen league, and trust that our Government will not overlook their protest or the insults of our nationality." It was signed, "For Our Country, Andrés De Luna."[72]

The fate of Basañez Rocha and M. Flores Villar is undocumented, but regardless of what happened to the two critics, La Raza continued to criticize México Texano leaders. According to one México Texano activist, this criticism also came from "average" México Texanos. An unnamed Corpus Christi OSA member, perhaps Andrés de Luna Sr., told social scientist Paul S. Taylor:

The average non-political American of Latin descent calls us [the members of OSA] "renegade." He says, "You are Mexicans, not Americans." Mexican citizens even in their press attack us. We are called renegades and anti-Mexicans. We call them visitors. They tell us, who are trying to tell them [Mexicans in Texas] to be more loyal to the US, "But your forefathers are all of Mexican origin and you should continue to be Mexican." We say he is a visitor and it is none of his business.[73]

This comment suggests that the "average," "nonpolitical" México Texano was Mexicanist in orientation and was critical of an emerging Mexican American identity and politics. Among Mexican citizens it was unclear who was a visitor and who would become a permanent "alien resident" or naturalized citizen. Too many Mexicans' futures were tied to labor needs; they could not stake permanency in the United States. Mexican Americans, on the other hand, were home and here to stay. Like Eduardo Idar Sr., this OSA member criticized the complacent and those who had not claimed a permanent stake in the United States. Disagreements about identity, citizenship, nationalism, and the role of immigrants would continue.

CRITIQUE OF THE MEXICAN CONSULATE

If the question of inclusion was not already complicated, yet another controversy arose—the role of the Mexican consulate and his role in the empowerment of La Raza. There was discussion as to why the Mexican consul in San Antonio, Alejandro Carrillo, sent a consular representative to Harlingen who happened to be M. C. Gonzáles.

To some México Texano leaders, this role compromised Gonzáles' position on citizenship. Eduardo Idar Sr. and Perales, who were more adamant about keeping the consul out of México Texano issues, criticized the consul and Gonzáles. According to Eduardo Idar Sr.'s Laredo newspaper *Las Noticias*, Gonzáles read a letter from the consul at the convention:

> [I]n his expressive letter he [the Mexican consul] sent his congratulations and apologies for not being present, because the Institution in formation had a determined civic character in the United States, which was correct and [for this acknowledgment] he was to be thanked. Naturally this did not mean that the conventioneers' beliefs should be subjected to Lic. Gonzáles, his representative, who[,] seeing that what he intended to undoubtedly do, opted to retire [from the meeting], which caused regret yet did not minimally interrupt the proceedings.[74]

Idar then argued that the consul tried to interfere in Mexican American affairs and sought to incite Mexican citizens against a México Texano organization. He said Gonzáles stuck with the México Texano position, but Idar believed that Gonzáles nonetheless had encouraged Basañez Rocha's criticism of Perales and Canales.[75]

Perales contended that Gonzáles favored an organization of México Texanos and Mexicans and supported Basañez Rocha. He expressed this in a note to San Antonio OSA members Machado and Rubén Lozano as well as Clemente Idar:

> CB Rocha, a political refugee, publisher of a small newspaper at Mission, has been attacking Mr. JT. Canales and me thru the columns of his sheet, and MC. Gonzáles, of San Antonio, is supporting him, as

you will see from the copy of his telegram. I am merely bringing this matter to your attention so that you understand my attitude in my future dealings with MC. Gonzáles.[76]

On September 12 Clemente Idar protested Gonzáles' alleged actions to the Mexican consular officials. Eduardo Idar Sr. telegrammed suggestions to Perales. On September 23 Perales wrote Eduardo Idar Sr.:

Rocha also attacked your brother Clemente quite strongly thru the columns of his sheet. I am merely bringing this matter to your attention so that you may thoroughly understand my attitude in my future dealings with MC. Gonzáles. The Mexican American Citizens League, McAllen, has already taken some very drastic action with reference to the publication.[77]

On October 5 Eduardo Idar Sr. defended Perales, Canales, and his brother Clemente and criticized Basañez Rocha, Flores Villar, Gonzáles, and the Mexican consul. He fended for Canales, who descended from a *familia respetabilísima* (much-respected family). Moreover, he argued that Canales had placed his own life in danger when he denounced the Rangers' assassination of Mexicans in 1919, thereby insinuating that Canales was not anti-Mexican. In contrast, he described Basañez Rocha as a political refugee residing in Mission and one who was *haciendo méritos* (making points) to return to Mexico. Eduardo Idar Sr. went on to identify the consul as the true culprit:

It is not strange that the consulates try to control the Mexican organizations which are founded in the United States to utilize them in their political, anti-clerical propaganda and to exclude from them refugee elements but what seems unlikely is that the Consulate General of San Antonio, Texas, was displeased because he could not obtain the control of the México Texanos, who in this form have nothing to do with Mexico's politics.[78]

This was a Mexican American critique of the consulate's role in the United States. While Perales and the Idars believed Gonzáles supported the Mexican critics, Gonzáles stated in 1967 and 1979 that he did indeed favor the México Texano position. Gonzáles further suggested that the consul saw the proposed organization as yet another tool to protect the Mexican citizen: "Certainly, it was in his interest and to see to it that Mexican citizens could join us. Because he needed all the help he could get from whatever source to protect the rights of Mexicans."[79]

Gonzáles did ultimately take a México Texano position. At the same time, through his work with the consul and in his work with LULAC after 1929, he had a more Mexicanist, transnational, and inclusive approach than Perales. It was his job to report on how the Mexican consulate saw the proposed organization. I believe he saw advantages to both positions.

TWO EXPLANATIONS OF THE EXCLUSION

Regardless of their intent, the actions taken by México Texano leaders' actions remained unclear to both Mexican citizens and Mexican Americans. México Texano leaders justified the Mexican exclusion in the press for more than two years; criticism must have been widespread. Perales and Eduardo Idar Sr. sought to explain the exclusion.

Alonso Perales' Explanation

Perales sought to explain the exclusion of Mexican citizens from the organization in his two-part essay "La evolución de la Raza Mexicana" in September 1927 and in "La unificación de los méxico americanos" two years later, in September 1929, after LULAC was founded in February 1929. It is no coincidence that in 1927 Perales spoke of "la Raza Mexicana," and by 1929 he addressed the more specific Mexican American unity. Nonetheless, even after 1929, Perales would continue to refer to "La Raza."

Five arguments were central to Perales' discussion: (1) improvement would fall upon the Mexican American due to "his" U.S. citizenship before it would reach the Mexican citizen, a foreigner and immigrant; (2) the two groups demonstrated two distinct tendencies—Americanist and Mexicanist; (3) "brotherly" ties would be broken if both groups were admitted to one organization; (4) citizenship and thus the vote was the tool for improvement for Mexican Americans; and (5) Mexican citizens could not legally vote, and if they did, they would become "men" without a country.

Perales concluded that if racism ceased, Mexican Americans would be the primary benefactors. He quoted O. R. Vázquez, a Mexican residing in New York, who wrote to *La Prensa* in May 1929:

Our [Mexican citizens' in the United States] welfare and our progress would be the same as the Europeans who are also immigrants of this country if we, like them, received help and protection from those of our race. Unfortunately, Mexicans who were born here and have lived under North American dominion find themselves placed in a low political, social, and economic level. . . . They don't guide us, teach us the language, [or] these customs and laws. If they don't have opportunities in politics, business, and jobs, naturally we won't have them either. If they are insulted, segregated, and abused, so will we, those who immigrate from Mexico, be censured and denied contact with other races.[80]

He recognized that in the United States, Mexican Americans were privileged over Mexican citizens by virtue of their national citizenship.

His second argument was that Mexicans and Mexican Americans had distinct identities:

In the first place, the tendency of the Mexican American is Americanist. That is, even though we are not trying to Americanize the citizens of Mexico, they want to develop among the members of our race who already are American citizens by birth or by naturalization. The Mexican citizen doesn't have to become Americanized. There are several reasons. On the one hand is his nationalistic sentiment, and on the other is the lack of a favorable environment, as Messrs. Vásquez, Maus, and Handman have aptly declared.[81]

Perales recognized that Mexican Americans were subject to "Americanist" tendencies by virtue of being born Americans or naturalizing as U.S. citizens. Yet he did not recognize class, education, region, or gender as factors in their degree of Americanization. Moreover, he did not acknowledge Americanization as a generational process. Nor did he acknowledge the Mexicanist orientation of most Mexican Americans and their lack of U.S. nationalism. And for Perales, Mexicans had no intention of becoming Americanized because of their Mexican nationalism and because the advantages of U.S. citizenship were few, as racism was so marked.

He argued that Mexican citizens rejected "Americanization." He referred to the San Antonio Board of Education's Americanization program for Mexican children in 1924. Project director Dr. Jerome Rhodes said he received few applications for the Americanization project.[82]

Similarly, Mexican citizens criticized this plan in the *San Antonio Light*, as quoted in Perales:

Why the intent to Americanize the children of Mexican parents when there is no effort in Mexico to Mexicanize the Americans? The Mexican father will not send his children to schools in which Americanization is enforced. He knows that although they have been an American citizen in name he is not accepted as such by the American people.[83]

Perales also quoted Renato Cantú Lara, Mexican consul in San Antonio at the time:

The Mexican will not Americanize. He has lived a long time in Mexico, and he has learned Mexican thought and ideals; thus it would be difficult for him to become Americanized, knowing he is not a typical American. His blood, ideas, and thoughts are different, and ultimately he sees that people don't completely accept him as an American. As far as Americanizing adults, this is nonsense because almost all of them have lived too long in Mexico, and their Mexican sentiments are so nationalist that American education would not change them.[84]

Cantú Lara noted that applicants for U.S. citizenship were few. So not only did Mexicans not Americanize, they also did not (or could not) become American citizens. Thus, Perales cited European American authorities, Mexican officials, and Mexican citizens themselves to present his case about Americanization. He gave little attention to the factors that impeded Americanization—racism, xenophobia, and segregation. And he did not acknowledge the generational nature of Americanization as it related to La Raza.

Perales' third argument was that Mexican Americans and Mexicans could not organize jointly. If they cooperated in one organization, constant opposition (due to their distinct tendencies) would result. Mexican Americans would push for Americanization, while the Mexicans would endorse Mexican nationalism, creating constant opposition. But Mexicans and Mexican Americans did cooperate in mutualistas. He noted that Mexican Americans were not "prepared to guide or assist the newly arrived alien in learning the English language or in understanding American laws and customs," as they understood little themselves.[85] He believed Mexican Americans knew little themselves.

He argued that an inclusive membership would fragment around election time. He stated that México Texanos might influence Mexican citizens to vote in the United States, causing Mexicans to lose their citizenship in Mexico. Further, illegal voters could receive a two- to five-year sentence in the penitentiary, and consequently Mexicans could not obtain U.S. citizenship. *Hombres sin patria* (men without a country) would be the result. But México Texano voters were limited, and few encouraged illegal activities.

So, only Mexican Americans could utilize the vote in a conscious and intelligent manner to improve their lot, Perales states in another installment of his newspaper series:

> When we the American citizens of some state, county, or city, have reason to believe that we are governed by public servants who harbor racial prejudices, who are incompetent, dishonest, unjust, and good for nothing, we have no one to blame but ourselves. The remedy effectively is the voting booth.[86]

The vote was indeed one tool of political empowerment not available to Mexican citizens and less of an option for working-class México Texanos.

Perales subscribed to liberal democratic ideology. He blamed the injustices of the system on elected officials who allowed or practiced corruption and/or injustice. He thereby placed a direct blame on voters who elected corrupt politicians. The ballot would allow for intelligent and conscious voting if social citizenship was undertaken. The ballot could then place men in office who were more responsive to the needs of La Raza. Perales evidently had little concept of the woman citizen or the female public official. And he did not readily acknowledge social citizenship on the part of Mexicans.

He argued that it was time Mexican Americans were represented in all areas of government. Consequently, with new office holders, improvement for Mexican Americans would result and then, and only then, for Mexican citizens. How this improvement would come about he did not say.

México Texano leaders argued that Mexicans had several existing organizational vehicles at their disposal. Shortly after the Harlingen convention, Perales wrote, *Ahora solo falta que los ciudadanos mexicanos formen también una fuerte organización* (Now all we need is for Mexican citizens to form a strong organization too). But he did not speak to México Texanos' ability or responsibility to form this organization. He did not mention any strong statewide Mexican association but considered Hijos de México, a male middle-class club based in San Antonio, the proper vehicle for Mexicans' empowerment in the United States.

Eduardo Idar Sr.'s Explanation

Eduardo Idar Sr. helped explain México Texano strategy. Central to his arguments were that: (1) Mexican Americans could not accept Mexican citizens as their spokespersons; (2) Mexicans already had recourse through the Mexican consulates and affiliated organizations, Comisiones Honoríficos and Brigadas Cruz Azul; (3) Mexicans sometimes posed a political problem for an independent Mexican American vote; and (4) Mexican Americans could not risk making either the U.S. government or the Mexican government an enemy.

Idar contended that México Texanos had to control their own destiny, one distinct from Mexican citizens in the United States and in Mexico. In his assessment, there were some Mexicans who could and would cooperate with Mexican Americans on pro-Raza issues. Residency in the United States for several years gave Mexicans the right to both cooperate with and criticize México Texano activists:

> If prestigious Mexicans, truly respectable, of pure background, who
> might have lived among us for many years and identified with us,
> out of the affection we have inspired in them gave us intelligent and
> constructive suggestions, well justified within the strictest loyalty,
> which naturally we would not disregard, we would like to have their
> assistance and obtain their advice, [and] even request it; but when it
> comes from individuals of no standing at all among us, who arrived
> only yesterday in this country, we cannot tolerate associating with
> them whatsoever.[87]

His "individuals of no standing" was not a reference to working-class immigrants; he was speaking to critics unfamiliar with the Mexican American predicament. Referring to Harlingen conventioneers, he said:

> There were highly respectable persons there by any measure . . .
> [T]hese persons have not taken it upon themselves to attack us,
> [rather,] they have left us to work for the common ideals of race and
> the legitimate aspirations of a truly general orientation.[88]

Idar concluded, "We ask only that the foreign elements not antagonize us and that they not mess with our future activities."[89]

For Idar, Mexicans could appeal to the consulate, but Mexican Americans could not. He was vehement about México Texanos working independently of the consul; he was familiar with at least three instances when the consul was powerless or an obstacle to Mexican American progress. Consul Grajeda was transferred for his attempt to involve himself in political organizing in 1911. On another occasion, the Mexican consul in Laredo reported that there was no discrimination in Texas, although in July 1911 *La Crónica* reported that the Mexican consuls were slow in entering the Antonio Gómez lynching case.[90] Even Eduardo Idar Sr. realized that Mexicans really had little recourse through the consul and that an appeal to the consul was more theory than fact.

Idar added that if the consuls subjected México Texanos to their whims, the latter would have to submit to antireligious propaganda, defend Mexican presidents like Álvaro Obregón, and attack the United States for its nasty tricks.[91] The Mexican American, Idar argued, had a unique relationship with Mexico.

Like Perales, Idar was opposed to the opportunity that Mexican citizens might lend political bosses:

> If there are foreign elements who indirectly participate in the electoral contest corrupting the vote of Mexican Americans so they can gain influence and money, unmistakably the occasion will arise in which we would have to go against them, as undoubtedly we would go against politicians who, being citizens of this country, use our vote without respecting our moral and social interests.[92]

Idar argued that Mexican Americans, however, could not oppose the Mexican or U.S. government. *Los México-Texanos como grupo organizado no son ni pueden ser enemigos* (As an organized group, México Texanos are not and cannot be enemies).[93] He contended that if Mexican Americans were critical of the U.S. government, their citizenship would be questioned. Mexican Americans, he held, could not afford to be enemies of either government, since they had distinct goals and a fixed citizenship.

Finally, Idar argued that Mexican organizations like the Comisiones Honoríficos for men and Cruz Azul brigades for women already provided an organizational base for Mexicans in the United States. In contrast to Perales, Idar recognized the need to organize a broader community that included women and the working class.

POST-1929 COMMENTARY ON THE EXCLUSION

Mexican Americans' predicament and the exclusion of Mexicans were still being discussed in 1931. Reflecting on the 1927 Harlingen congress in 1931, J. Luz Sáenz called it a "big skirmish" and remarked on "the facility with which many of our racial brothers were scandalized when they witnessed our first clash of opinions in the first skirmish of our social evolution."[94]

Adolph A. Garza of San Antonio wrote an essay delineating how México Texano historical interests and identity diverged from Mexico. He said "Texanos" fought for Texas independence "because of the oppression of Mexico." He added that if national origin accounted for loyalty to Mexico, "then we believe in a new, strange, unprecedent[ed,] and unnatural phenomenon of governmental science."[95] If such were the case, then Mexicans should be loyal to Spain and all "Americans" to England.

Garza argued that Mexican Americans had a "peculiar position" because of their heritage and relationship to Mexico. As he saw the problem: "You don't belong to Mexico, and the Anglo-Saxon will not accept you socially, politically." He continued, "We are proud of being a member of that race which reached the heighth [sic] of civilization amid the jungles of the Western Hemisphere," but "we have different customs, different methods." He added, "We will fight, if necessary, if any one dares to say anything about the 'Mescan,' and will be as eager to protest if some people will talk of our beloved country," perhaps referring to Mexico.[96] Whether this is the last published discussion of the exclusion of Mexicans is unknown. What is known is that Garza and México Texano leaders expressed their peculiar condition—they were México Texanos and thus hybrids.

MÉXICO TEXANO HYBRIDITY

México Texanos fit into the narrow social constructions of neither "Mexican" nor "American." At the same time, they were both American and Mexican. Keen to capture this peculiar condition was Mexican anthropologist Manuel Gamio, who conducted ethnographic work in Texas. His "Relaciones entre mexicanos, méxico-texanos y americanos" (Relations Between Mexicans, México Texanos, and Americans), written in the 1920s, is the best discussion of the topic. He described "the" México Texano:

> The Texas Mexican, who has Mexican blood and American sentiments, in my opinion is a hybrid product; he loves the United States

but especially Texas, because he was born here, he pledges to the American flag because they taught it to him in school, he feels like an integral part of this great country, and so he feels superior to men of his race who come from Mexico.[97]

If Mexican Americans felt superior to Mexicans, it was because they were schooled in the dominant society's schools and internalized Americans' sense of superiority.

Whether Gamio accurately portrayed the working-class México Texanos/as is questionable, but he did capture the essence of the México Texano middle class. He had interviewed James Tafolla Sr. and his wife, Micaela. Gamio described the way Tafolla Sr. had explained his identity: "He says he feels like a Mexican; but he is an American citizen. He respects this country [the United States,] but man's law has decreed that his nationality is American, not his sentiments."[98] Nevertheless, Tafolla Sr. identified himself as a Mexican American and not as a Mexican. And according to Gamio's interview transcript, Tafolla Sr. said, "The Mexican resents the Tejano." Although Gamio recognized differences between Mexicans and México Texanos, he also said these differences were superficial, thereby stressing commonalities, possibly meaning race.

Hybridity was recognized with the group identity of México Texanos. As early as 1911 Eduardo's father, Nicasio, wrote in *La Crónica* that the impacts of public schooling on La Raza included the loss of the Spanish language and Mexican history and culture:

With the deepest sorrow, we have seen Mexican professors teaching English to children of his race, without taking into consideration the mother language, that with each passing day, is forgotten and, with each day, suffers alterations and changes that materially hurt the eardrum of any Mexican, even those with a limited knowledge of Cervantes. If, in the American school that our children attend, they learn Washington's biography instead of Hidalgo's and instead of Juarez' glorious acts, Lincoln's feats, although noble and just, are taught, this child will not know the glories of his native country, nor will he love it, and he will look at this father's countrymen with indifference.[99]

Educator William John Knox of San Antonio remarked on the deliberate process, aided by material incentives, of Americanizing children of Mexican descent. And, Knox said, there were a large number of young American-Mexicans who are alive to every issue before the American people and ready to stand for this country against any other. They are, of course, courteously silent about Mexico and her ideals and are slow to pass criticism.[100]

México Texanos, hybrids, decided they could use their U.S. citizenship as strategy in the empowerment of La Raza.

CITIZENSHIP, NATION, RACE

Was the exclusion of Mexican immigrants by Mexican Americans the best strategy for the empowerment of La Raza?[101] Contrary to some interpretations, México Texano activists did not simply blame racism on immigrants, nor was their relationship with immigrants simply defined by European Americans' anti-Mexican sentiment. Instead, they referred to the Raza community as their own.

In deciding that only U.S. citizens or naturalized immigrants could join their organization, México Texanos asserted that citizenship mattered because the laws said so.[102] Citizenship is a status conferred by a nation that stipulates rights and obligations. It can define the right to vote, eligibility for political office, and service on juries.

In contrast, Chicano studies scholar Renato Rosaldo has referred to "cultural citizenship," suggesting that membership in a society makes one a citizen. Membership encompasses how one contributes to and participates as a resident, worker, consumer, and soldier. Rosaldo suggests that "cultural citizenship attends, not only to dominant exclusions and marginalizations, but also to subordinate aspirations for and definitions of enfranchisement."[103] The agency, interests, and perspectives of cultural citizens are considered.

But in the 1920s European American society appropriated the term "citizen" and treated Mexican Americans as second-class citizens and Mexican immigrants as noncitizens. This was especially true after the creation of the Border Patrol in 1924. Moreover, white society did not acknowledge cultural citizenship among La Raza.

How did Mexican immigrants fit into the question of citizenship, nationhood, and nationalism? Mexicans in the United States constituted a diverse group that included individuals born in Mexico or to one Mexican American parent, political refugees, immigrant workers, and children. Workers could be temporary sojourners, circular migrants who came to the United States to work on a regular basis, or they could be permanent residents.

However, with subsequent generations, many Mexicans "temporarily" living in the United States became permanent and Americanized. Likewise, their children were U.S. citizens, attended public schools, and became Americanized.

To which nation or nations did Mexicans in the United States belong? To which nation did they express loyalty and nationalism? In the 1920s Mexican citizens expressed a wide range of opinions toward naturalization, Americanization, U.S. racism, and the U.S. government. Overall, they preferred Mexican nationalism over U.S. nationalism, rejected U.S. naturalization, and shunned Americanization.

At the same time, the Mexican government did not treat Mexican immigrants as its own, either. Immigrants in the United States, predominantly of the working class, were of little concern to Mexico. And given its unequal relationship with the United States, Mexico could do little to protect its citizens abroad. Mexican consuls had little power. Mexican immigrants imagined Mexico as their nation but had no political representation or voice in Mexico, even though they believed they had a home there.

Thus Mexican Americans began to make distinctions regarding citizenship for several reasons. Mexican Americans themselves were a hybrid—part Mexican and part American. Many saw U.S. citizenship as a strategy for the political empowerment of La Raza. Mexican Americans had to appeal to whites in power. In an era when cultural pluralism was nonexistent and English-only rules and assimilation were stated policy, national citizenship was a basis for racial justice. John Solís explained of the 1920s and 1930s:

> At that time we didn't want to say we were Mexican . . . not because
> we were ashamed—every LULAC [member] is very proud of his
> Mexican heritage—but we wanted to get away from the Mexi-
> can because everywhere you could see signs saying "No Mexicans
> Allowed."[104]

Who could speak for and on behalf of La Raza? Those with the best chance of being effective were middle-class, English-speaking Mexican American men.

Had México Texanos permitted Mexicans, how many would have participated? Would they have acquiesced to bilingualism, or would they have asserted Spanish only? And what of their Mexican nationalism? Was it rooted in political realities or nostalgic and idealized? Were México Texanos simply asking Mexicans to take note of immigrants' current or future political conditions?

Was there another, alternative organization to the various México Texano groups, more Mexicanist in nature, to which Mexicans would have submitted? Or was México Texanos' U.S. nationalism offensive to Mexicans? And would México Texano organizations have survived if they had had Mexican members? Would these Mexican citizens have been subject to deportation? What of their children born in Mexico or the United States?

Undocumented immigrants could not plan or predict permanent residency in the United States. Immigrants were not always here to stay. They could not claim permanent residency, with unpredictable employment and possible deportation from the Immigration and Naturalization Service. Undocumented immigrants could not always stake out a future. Immigration laws change, as do the economy and attitudes toward immigration.

In the 1920s México Texanos were in no position to argue for expanding U.S. voting rights, binational voting rights, or dual citizenship for Mexican immigrants. They themselves were treated as second-class citizens and a class apart. In 1939 Communist Emma Tenayuca and her husband, Homer Brooks, of San Antonio argued that the "denial of voting rights to the foreign born mean disenfranchisement of nearly half of the adult Mexican population."[105] They added that the poll tax and migratory labor also led to significant disenfranchisement. Tenayuca and Brooks estimated that of 120,000 Raza in San Antonio, only 8,000 were eligible to vote. Even a Mexican American Communist believed voting was empowerment.

Tenayuca and Brooks recognized the efficacy of the concept of La Raza. They acknowledged La Raza as an "oppressed national group,"[106] and staked out La Raza's political future in the United States, as did Perales and Eduardo Idar Sr. Tenayuca and Brooks wrote that "the solution to the problem of the Mexicans and Spanish Americans lies in the Southwest and not in Mexico."[107] They noted that "their economic (and hence, their political) interests are welded to those of the Anglo-American people of the Southwest."[108]

Tenayuca and Brooks asked whether excluding Mexican immigrants actually was the equivalent of excluding the working class. In 1981, reflecting on LULAC's (and OSA's) role in the twentieth century, Tenayuca wrote, "This type of activity is fine, and must be applauded, but what about the hundreds of thousands of Mexicans brought in during the 20s for the development of agriculture in the southwest?"[109] The Mexican American working class was also excluded. The typical Mexican American had a Mexicanist orientation, could not speak English, and could not or did not join the league. The dilemma was to find an organizational solution to La Raza's plight as an oppressed people with a significant immigrant population whose citizenship was Mexican.

The dominant society treated both Mexican Americans and Mexican immigrants as nationless people. Shunned by the United States and Mexico, they constituted a third political entity, neither U.S. nor Mexican. Did they constitute a nation by themselves? Yes. They utilized the concept of "La Raza" to capture the fluidity of this group that could exist in the United States or Mexico, without border constraints.

The concept of La Raza was useful. Acknowledging its prevalent use in the early twentieth century, historian Elliot Young has argued that La Raza was an idealized concept and not a homogeneous community with one vision—class was a major contradiction within it. But so was citizenship and gender. La Raza was an "imagined community" in which citizenship, class, and gender differences were subordinate. It could be simply a useful transnational concept.

La Raza was an oppressed people within the United States but could also refer to the people in Mexico or other Latin American countries. La Raza in the United States was conscious of its colonized status. OSA President James Tafolla Sr. noted, *Tenemos patria pero no la tenemos* (We have a country but we don't have one).[110] In 1910 *La Crónica* had called Mexicans "condemned to be the Jews of the American continent," damned to an eternal wandering across the Americas.[111] Anthropologist Gamio suggested that Mexicans considered Mexican Americans *hombres sin patria*. Most Mexican immigrants claimed Mexico as their homeland, but in reality, they too were homeless and in a similar peculiar predicament. Mexican immigrants were like Mexican Americans—men and women without a country or nation. These are difficult questions still unanswered in the twenty-first century.

CONCLUSION

The Harlingen convention excluded Mexican citizens from the organization formed there. Although México Texano leaders invited Mexicans to attend the conference, most had not intended an association including both groups. Though the Spanish-language press announced that participants would decide membership composition, Mexican American leaders controlled the event.

Several factors ensured a México Texano organization. Mexican Americans were elected acting president and secretary. Only México Texanos were speakers, and some may have even spoken some English to the Mexican majority. There may have been errors in parliamentary procedure or voting irregularities and/or lack of familiarity with procedures. Finally, some Mexican Americans had a contingency plan for secession if the majority opinion had not gone their way.

México Texanos furthered their interests when they countered or suppressed several Mexican critics. But there was no conspiracy against Mexican compatriots. Rather, the dominant Mexican American civic associations were already hybrids—more México Texano than Mexican.

The Harlingen convention highlights shifting identity. At the Primer Congreso Mexicanista of 1911, racism was identified as the problem, and "unity" between México Texanos and Mexican immigrants was the solution. At Harlingen, racism was still identified as the problem, but now an organized Mexican American male middle class was identified as the leadership. Besides, organization, education, U.S. citizenship, and the vote were now tools for political empowerment. The México Texano male middle class would use liberalism to fight its battles. Maleness continued to serve as an organizing principle. The Mexican American woman citizen, though able to vote since 1920, was ignored.

The convention highlighted the question of community, citizenship, nation, and homeland. México Texanos affirmed their U.S. citizenship and their political future in the United States. Mexican Americans staked out their home in the United States while arguing that Mexican immigrants had an uncertain future there. They decided who would act on behalf of La Raza in the United States. They would wait for some other organization to work on behalf of immigrant-specific interests.[112]

The Harlingen convention was a historic clash between Mexican immigrants and middle-class Mexican Americans. Despite official exclusion, Mexican immigrants would be central to Raza empowerment. And Mexican Americans would utilize their U.S. citizenship to promote the interests of La Raza, especially in desegregationist efforts that benefited all of La Raza.

It was a political irony that México Texanos excluded Mexicans in order to be pro-Raza. Mexican Americans privileged U.S. national citizenship, while Mexicans at Harlingen privileged race and Raza nationalism.[113] Still, Mexican Americans did not abandon the concept or community of La Raza; they maintained some political and moral commitment to compatriots and ethnic, racial, national unity.

Despite agreement on México Texano's own "Mexican problem," unity among Mexican American organizations was still not realized in Harlingen. Ironically, no unified México Texano association resulted, either.

LULAC's Founding

SIX

*We shall destroy any attempt to create racial prejudices
against our people, and any infamous stigma which may
be cast upon them, and we shall demand for them the
respect and prerogatives which the Constitution grants
to us all.* —LULAC CONSTITUTION, 1929

The Order Sons of America, the Order Sons of Texas, and the Order Knights
of America did not unite at Harlingen. After the convention "settled" the
citizenship question, yet another organization was founded there—the
League of Latin American Citizens (LLAC). Activists were frustrated with
further duplication and consequently over the next two years tried to merge
these four associations. In February 1929 the four groups would finally unite
in an association that would eventually be known as the League of United
Latin American Citizens (LULAC).

In this chapter I chronicle the events that led to the founding of LULAC.
While the narrative shows that leadership prevented an earlier México Texano merger, it also shows the proactive role several leaders played in bringing a new vision to the merger. LLAC and LULAC were not like the OSA
or OKA. A new cadre of leaders brought new strategies vis-à-vis race, class,
gender, and citizenship to empower La Raza. Thus in this chapter I will not
only describe the rise of the league, I will also compare and contrast how
the OSA and LULAC differed by examining their constitutions. Finally, I
address how and why LULAC became a permanent fixture in U.S. history.

EFFORTS TOWARD A MÉXICO TEXANO MERGER

Discussions about a merger began before the Harlingen convention. All except the OSA in San Antonio and Tafolla Sr. wanted to unite. Unity talks were held by the Corpus Christi OSA, the OKA, and Sáenz and Perales, who especially wanted to form a new organization.[1] They discussed "which organization should lead the fight and what name it should have."[2] According to OKA member Eleuterio Escobar Jr., they agreed it was

> a good idea to consolidate all these organizations into one to give more strength to the cause because their main efforts were to tear up the oppressors' chains which we had been carrying for over 100 years by segregation in Texas of Mexican Americans in schools, restaurants and park[s and] swimming pools.[3]

Tafolla Sr. insisted they select the name Order Sons of America, "first, because the name was very adequate, second, because it was formed before the others, and it was the pioneer."[4] Likewise, OKA members offered the name Order Knights of America because "they were the originators of the idea to consolidate all organizations into one."[5] But no merger happened before Harlingen.

A possible merger was discussed at Harlingen. Escobar Jr. recalled "the big guns" (Canales, Perales, Clemente Idar, James Tafolla Sr., Eduardo Idar Sr., and M. C. Gonzáles) addressing this issue.[6] Tafolla advocated for all the associations to subordinate themselves to the OSA.[7] He explained this view to Eduardo Idar Sr.:

> Who is it that cannot get together, those who remain loyal to their Order, or those who desert and organize another similar organization? Then again, in all frankness, after the Harlingen Convention, still another organization has arisen called the "LEAGUE OF LATIN-AMERICAN CITIZENS," and this right in the face of our offer at the Convention that our doors were wide-open for them to come in and join us; yet, the statement has been made repeatedly that they only organized to find out and to show us that they could organize; in other words, to show that they did not care to get together, unless they could have their own way.[8]

Tafolla proved to be an obstacle to the merger even after Harlingen.

LEAGUE OF LATIN AMERICAN CITIZENS

Since leaders could not agree that all groups should subordinate themselves under the OSA, a fourth organization was founded at Harlingen. But there was so much conflict at that convention that members left without selecting a name for the new association.[9] Perales headed this group,[10] and two weeks later he "provisionally called it the Latin American Citizens."[11] A month later the group was headquartered in McAllen and was known as the Mexican American Citizens League;[12] by November Perales was calling it "League of American Citizens of Latin Descent."[13] When the organization's manual was printed, its official name was League of Latin American Citizens.[14]

This association was the first to use "League," "Latin American," and "Citizens" in its name. Perhaps the name referred to the "Latin League," Latin-speaking nations conquered and absorbed into the Roman Empire, just as Mexican Americans had been conquered by the United States and European Americans.[15] Alonso Perales probably came up with the name. The use of "Latin American" may have represented Perales' diplomatic activities for the United States in Latin America. Also, in 1920 the newspaper *El Latino-Americano* was being published in Alice and edited by Casimiro Pérez Álvarez, later Perales' father-in-law.

Scholars have considered "Latin" a euphemism for "Mexican," and indeed it was. But "Mexican American" was not the final choice for the organization, either. Both "Mexican" and "Mexican American" would have reminded activists of the Harlingen debacle. Yet "Latin American" referred to Mexican Americans' connections to Mexico and nations south, though still not implying an invitation for Mexican citizens, Latinos such as Puerto Ricans and Cuban Americans, or Latin Americans to join. The use of "Citizens" was a way for México Texanos to assert 100 percent U.S. citizenship and a reminder to Mexican immigrants that they were not eligible to join.

When LLAC was founded, Harlingen conventioneers passed a resolution promoting a merger with the OSA and all others:

> Resolved that the chair shall appoint a committee consisting of one delegate from each of the towns here represented, of which the [committee] chair shall be the chairman, and that this committee shall have full and plenary powers from this assembly to study the Constitution and By-Laws of the Order Sons of America and make suggestions tending toward their amendment, if they see fit to amend their Constitution, and communicate with a committee from the Order

South Texas map showing Order Sons of America and League of Latin American Citizens councils, 1920s. Courtesy Molly O'Halloran Inc.

Sons of America with equal powers, to the end that this organization (the LAC) may be incorporated into the Order Sons of America.[16]

LLAC organizers sought to unite México Texanos in South Texas, so the Lower Rio Grande Valley was targeted first. LLAC spread "like wildfire in the Valley country" into Harlingen, Brownsville, Mercedes, Weslaco, Mission,

Edinburg, La Grulla, Encino, and Penitas.[17] It also spread to Laredo and to Gulf and La Salle in Matagorda County.[18]

LLAC locals' activities are mostly unrecorded, though Eduardo Idar Sr. reported on the Laredo chapter's struggle with the local political "ring," as he described it to Perales:

> [T]he local "Ring" is fighting us very strong and persistently and yet with the fact that we are not taking a hand in local matters but they do not want us under any circumstances to hold a civic organization permanently amoung [*sic*] our people.[19]

He wrote that he was reorganizing the chapter and added,

> I am including you [on] an invitation we are printing to send to all of our deserters, which are a strong majority in our League . . . lots of our boys had deserted because they were anxious to fight the "ring" while others were afraid and they also deserted.[20]

Besides Eduardo Idar Sr., LLAC's key leaders were Perales, Canales, Sáenz, and Deodoro Guerra of McAllen.[21] In 1927 recent high school graduate Adela Sloss wrote Perales of her interest in his activism, but he did not invite her to join the league. He only remarked, "Please accept my thanks for your encouraging remarks with reference to our Organization—The League of American Citizens of Latin Descent."[22] Mexican citizens and women were not permitted to join.

There were some similarities between LLAC and the OSA. Like the OSA's, the LLAC membership application asked about occupation, citizenship, naturalization, and voting patterns. Similar rituals included the Pledge of Allegiance, Washington's Prayer, and singing the songs "America," the "Star-Spangled Banner," and "The Eyes of Texas Are Upon You."[23] Unlike the OSA, LLAC had an umbrella structure with a "president general" (state chair).[24]

In September 1927 Perales appointed a committee to study the OSA constitution so as to seek a merger.[25] Canales and Eduardo Idar were committee members. Likewise, Perales asked the Corpus Christi OSA to suggest revisions; the council's minutes reported that "they answer[ed] the best they could."[26] Shortly before Perales' request, Tafolla Sr. had written Corpus Christi, as had a "Brother Morales," probably Andrew Morales, of San Antonio, who "urged the members to stick together to SOA" (Sons of America) and appealed to Corpus Christi not to secede from the parent OSA in San

Antonio.[27] On October 10 Tafolla Sr. wrote to Perales, "Unless the changes or suggestions that your committee might offer are very radical, I see no reason why we could not be united under one banner."[28] Tafolla was hoping the OSA would remain dominant and its name be preserved.

By early November the Corpus Christi OSA was contemplating merging into LLAC, sometimes also called the Latin American Citizens League (LACL). On November 2 the minutes stated, "Answer Perales letter and tell him to write Tafolla again—Dave Barrera reported that he was not decided."[29] At that meeting, "Brother Idar," probably Clemente, "recommended to amalgam[at]e with LACL."[30]

But by mid-November it was clear that Perales did not plan to merge with the OSA. On November 19, in an effort to promote unity, Eduardo Idar submitted organizational suggestions to Canales, Perales, Tafolla Sr., and Ben Garza, president of the Corpus Christi OSA. He recommended that Canales serve as general president; Perales and Tafolla Sr. as honorary presidents; Clemente Idar as general organizer; and Vela of Laredo, Ben Garza of Corpus Christi, and Eleuterio Escobar Jr. of San Antonio as district organizers. Eduardo volunteered to serve as chief of Spanish newspaper propaganda.[31] He suggested *La Prensa* as the communications medium to publicize information for "Mexican immigrants as well as American citizens in regard to the US Constitution, immigration laws, etc."[32] Interestingly, Mexican immigrants were still in the minds of some leaders. Eduardo Idar obviously saw conflict between Perales and Tafolla.

But Perales and Canales refused to submit to the OSA, seeing fundamental problems with its constitution and its leader.[33] They disliked Tafolla Sr.'s boss style and charged him with using the OSA to further personal political ambition.[34] They questioned the association's effectiveness. Perales suggested that what was needed was an active association, "not an organization to IMPRESS the politicians and public officials with the sole objective of obtaining favors and seats in City Hall and the Court House."[35] They had hoped to end excessive presidential power,[36] and they wanted to delete mutualista tenets and other impractical articles.[37] They wanted more influence.

By December the conflict between Perales and Tafolla was evident. On December 14 Eduardo Idar wrote Tafolla Sr. that "the matter stands between you and Mr. Perales, you two are the head of both of our Institutions and you must meet the other half way. We, the others are simple, subordinate elements, we will agree if you two agree."[38] Clearly there was deference to Perales and Tafolla Sr., although Eduardo Idar was himself an established leader. Tafolla Sr. responded to Idar:

But remember, Mr. Idar, that the fault is not with the SONS of AMERICA. Our Order was the first one to organize, and since its origin, others have arisen, with the same principles, with the same ideals, with [the] same purposes, and yet, KNOWING that there was already such an organization in existence.[39]

Tafolla Sr. added that LLAC "did not care to get together, unless they could have their own way." He concluded, "Our patience has been worn out waiting for the so-called amendments to be sent in by the Committee of the League."[40] The commission suggested revisions to the OSA constitution, among them that presidents be elected annually so different men in various towns might serve, but Tafolla Sr. refused to listen.[41]

By 1928 prospects for a merger looked dim. There were eight LLAC councils, at least four active OSA chapters, and the OKA, all without an umbrella group.[42] Merger attempts slowed down because Perales spent most of the year in Washington, D.C.; Havana, Cuba; and Nicaragua.[43] Ben Garza, Corpus Christi president, left for Tucson in 1928 for treatment of his tuberculosis. No merger was in sight.[44]

ORDER KNIGHTS OF AMERICA FACILITATION OF THE MERGER

Finally in 1928 Perales sought another strategy for unification by bypassing the OSA of San Antonio (and Tafolla Sr.) and convincing the Corpus the Christi OSA and OKA to join LLAC. In April Perales asked Garza to persuade the groups to do so; he told Garza that he could be president.[45] Garza declined the offer, noting that Perales, (Clemente?) Idar, or Canales were more intelligent and better educated.[46] Later, Perales suggested to Garza that the Corpus Christi chapter call itself "Sons of America council, League of Latin-American Citizens."[47]

A breakthrough occurred around June 1928. Mauro M. Machado wrote Perales and reported that the OKA was ready to join LLAC provided that the Corpus Christi OSA also merged.[48] But Garza was still not convinced that his group should abandon the OSA. On August 22 he explained to Perales the obstacles his council faced in a possible merger with LLAC:

The hardest part is when it comes to merging the Sons of America without the consent of the President General. . . . [W]e could desert the Order and join yours, but we have already established such a good reputation in this town, we hate to lose what we have already accomplished. Besides, we would lose all the near councils that we established.[49]

So in late August, OKA representatives stepped up unification efforts. They traveled to Corpus Christi; there both parties decided that Eulalio Marín, editor of *El Paladín*, should press for unification. *El Paladín* did so on August 31.[50] Marín called for the formation of

> [o]nly one big and strong [organization], it is time for us to sacrifice some our ideas and all of our selfishness and admit our errors. . . .
> Let's form a new race at the border of these two great and powerful nations [Mexico and the United States] and we shall continue being Americans, so we can comply religiously with our duty and Mexicans when it comes to getting our rights, most especially in South Texas.[51]

Marín's initiative was a call for a new organization, a "new race." Garza observed, "But, to my surprise, after I sent newspapers to everyone that I thought would take part in the discussion, nobody has answered our suggestions."[52] So the Corpus Christi OSA and the OKA agreed to merge even if LLAC and the San Antonio OSA refused.

Perales received the initiative while in Nicaragua and reacted by telling Garza. "Frankly speaking, I am somewhat disappointed to learn that the Corpus Christi Council of the Order Sons of America and the Order Knights of America have not yet joined the League of Latin American Citizens."[53] The OSA's only option, he added, was to join LLAC.

Garza finally took other steps toward a merger. In December he and fellow Corpus Christi OSA members traveled to San Antonio. According to Tafolla Sr., "At that meeting it was decided to call the Convention, but rather disagreeable incidents arose at that meeting."[54] An OKA member reported events to Perales:

> Thanks to the advice from you, the progressive bunch of men headed by our old pal Ben Garza, took "the bridle in their teeth" and came down here and told our friend the President General to resign or they would quit the Order! . . . He pleaded with the Corpus boys for one more chance, but they just simply "burned him up."[55]

There in San Antonio it was decided that five delegates from the four organizations (San Antonio OSA, Corpus Christi OSA, OKA, and LLAC) should form a Ways and Means Committee to plan consolidation. More-over, those who had left the San Antonio OSA (OKA members and ex-OSA members in the city) would join this effort. The organizers scheduled the second Sunday in January 1929 as the day to unite.[56]

OKA members made it known that the name of the proposed new group was irrelevant to them as long as they united. However, they made it clear to Corpus Christi that "we also have objections in consolidating with any-thing Jim Tafolla may lead."[57] When word reached the Alice OSA chapter that a new association was in the making, Francisco Pérez of Alice expressed concern. He wrote Professor Carlos E. Castañeda, "Societies are pretending to hold a convention to see whether it is possible to consolidate into one."[58] The proposed January 13, 1929, meeting did not occur, most likely because Perales was in Washington, D.C.[59]

Another reason the conference did not take place is that, according to Tafolla Sr.,

one of the members of this Council [the San Antonio OSA] made a motion to rescind the action taken at that [December] meeting and to not call a Convention. . . . [W]e should not allow any man or set of men from the outside to dictate to us as to what we should do or should not do.[60]

But according to Corpus Christi member Andrés de Luna Sr.,

Tafolla promised that he would *study the case* and would make his decision known in the least time possible. Such decision was awaited and in view of the fact that it did not arrive the commission decided to write. . . . [T]hen sirs, . . . it is a pity to say it . . . Sr. Tafolla . . . replied saying that in a meeting of that chapter the foundation of an-other organization was not approved.[61]

Around February 7 Perales attended a Corpus Christi OSA meeting at which it was "agreed right there to sever their connection with the Order Sons of America."[62] Members voted unanimously to withdraw from the par-ent OSA and scheduled a convention "for the purpose of uniting all Latin American organizations."[63] The next day they mailed back their charter, and as concerned activists they issued an invitation to congregate signed as "Ex OSA, formerly OSA." By February 11, Pérez of Alice had been notified that the "Ex-Sons of America" were hosting a statewide convention on February 17.[64]

A week before the convention Perales convinced Canales that a merger with the OSA and OKA was a good idea. Canales was allegedly reluctant to recognize the work of the two groups, but Perales claimed that he himself was "perfectly determined to make any concessions which may be necessary to bring about the end desired, namely our unification."[65] Unity was near.

LULAC'S FOUNDING, FEBRUARY 1929

Two hundred fifty persons reportedly made reservations to attend the Corpus Christi convention.[66] At one o'clock on a cold, rainy Sunday about 175 people gathered at Salón Obreros y Obreras on the corner of Carrizo and Lipan Streets.[67] Delegations from the ex-OSA chapter of Corpus Christi, the Alice OSA, the OKA, and the Brownsville, McAllen, Encino, and La Grulla chapters of LLAC attended with delegates present.[68] The San Antonio OSA refused to send delegates.[69] According to convention observer and political scientist Oliver Douglas Weeks, 25 delegates and 150 other participants were present.[70]

Ben Garza called the meeting to order and was selected presiding officer. Conventioneers chose M. C. Gonzáles as secretary.[71] Proceedings were conducted in both English and Spanish.[72] Louis Wilmot of Corpus Christi sang the opening hymn; John C. Solís read Washington's Prayer. Then Andrés de Luna Sr. explained that the Corpus Christi chapter quit the OSA because it had

> resolved to unify all the Chapters of our Order and to invite some other organizations of identical aims in order to work for the unification of all and form a single organization more solid, which should give more practical results to the development of the noble cause of justice for which we have been fighting.[73]

When deliberations began, no one spoke against the merger, and "admirable decorum was maintained and a remarkable spirit of harmony prevailed."[74] Those speaking in favor of unity included, in this order: Perales, Sáenz, Marín, Canales, and Gonzáles. Tafolla Sr. attended the event but remained unusually silent, and either he was not a designated speaker or no one bothered to record his statements.

Perales pressed for unity:

> [N]ever as now will we have a better opportunity of uniting ourselves and in a harmonious union of force and patriotism to claim

our rights and prerogatives which will be the only things that we will bequeath to our children.

He ended his speech with the declaration "I vote for unification," to which there was prolonged applause.[75]

Sáenz gave a most dramatic speech, alluding to his sense of duty as a Mexican American soldier:

> It is [now] time that we unite or on the contrary we shall be lost, and not only we, but—what is sadder—our descendants. Separated we shall be no more than dispersed forces easy to overcome.
>
> For centuries generations of our ancestors lived here watering this land with the sweat of their honest toil contributing to the development of which today it is so proud. . . . And now not only in peace but in war we have taken up arms in its defense, and when we have returned with the scar or wound or the grief of having left in the fields over there across the sea hundreds of our dead brothers, we have met with the fact that all our forces were lost in the abyss or inocuous [*sic*] racial prejudice, and we continue being the same.[76]

Canales made what some described as an "eloquent" speech. He explained that some OSA members "worked for themselves" instead of "fighting for the good of the rest." He added, "I take the liberty of asking that this union serve only to dignify individuals for their honorable activities and not for their dirty politics," a reference to Tafolla Sr.[77]

Gonzáles spoke last in favor of unity, though he reminded conventioneers of Harlingen. He informed the audience that he worked for the Mexican consulate, and in recommending the union he "did not wish to offend the Mexican citizens."[78] After these rousing speeches, Marín moved for unification; Pablo Rocha seconded.

To solidify the merger conventioneers selected a commission composed of two representatives from each existing organization to select a name and to provide a "basis of operation."[79] The commission included Perales and Canales (LLAC), Machado and Solís (OKA), Marín and de Luna (ex–Corpus Christi OSA), and Fortino Treviño (Alice OSA).[80] The San Antonio OSA did not join the organization being formed. With James Tafolla Sr. eliminated and Gonzáles acting as secretary, Perales and Canales had the opportunity to further position themselves to define the new organization's tenets. Clemente Idar was absent from the founding meeting, and Eduardo Idar Sr. did not have delegate status. Individual LLAC chapters were not represented in this commission. Alice was the only OSA council in attendance. While this commission met for two hours, the audience listened to speeches at the general session.

The commission made seven recommendations. It urged the adoption of the name United Latin American Citizens (ULAC). This name mirrored Perales' and Canales' influence in the commission, though John C. Solís offered "United" to the name. It proposed that membership be confined to U.S. citizens, a reaffirmation of the Harlingen convention. It suggested that local councils represented at the meeting automatically become chapters. These included San Antonio (formerly OKA), Corpus Christi (formerly OSA), and Brownsville, McAllen, La Grulla, and Encino (former chapters of the LLAC). Councils would be organized in Alice and Laredo.

A constitutional convention would be held in Corpus Christi on May 19. English was recommended as the organization's official language. Twenty-five fundamental principles were accepted as the basis for the constitution.[81] Apparently originally written in Spanish, the principles were presented and accepted. They would later be translated to English, now ULAC's official language. Finally, the commission recommended that the foreword in the OKA constitution be accepted.[82] Canales suggested the motto "All for one and one for all," a befitting motto taken from the Three Musketeers (OSA, OKA, and LLAC).

Conventioneers selected the following temporary executive officers: Ben Garza, president; M. C. Gonzáles, secretary; and J. T. Canales and Prof. J. Luz Sáenz, trustees. They declared *El Paladín* the official organ and Corpus Christi as temporary headquarters.[83] Finally, they agreed that members should return to Corpus Christi on May 19 for the first annual convention, at which a constitution would be adopted. Members of ULAC left the meeting united at last.[84]

ULAC's founding pleased all concerned parties except Tafolla Sr. About a week later he wrote Castañeda expressing his discontent.[85] Tafolla Sr. remained active in the OSA in San Antonio; the OSA did not dissolve until 1934. Tafolla Sr. joined LULAC later, and his son became a national president in the 1930s.

Pérez of Alice was apparently upset that Tafolla had been marginalized, and he suggested that a coup had been organized against Tafolla. Pérez contended that Sáenz, who was originally from Alice, and Canales "influenced the Corpus Christi council of this good order to rebel and become part of this new order."[86] He asked, "Is this the way to unite our element?"[87] He asked Castañeda, "Don't you think that with this, our friends have implanted a precedent for disunity?"[88] Pérez referred to *caudillaje* (political chieftains), but there is no evidence that Sáenz and Canales played this role. Moreover, the Corpus OSA had cause to secede.

The reorganization of rural OSA councils into ULAC presented a problem especially for the chapters organized in Corpus Christi and Uvalde.[89] According to Pérez, the Alice OSA had not fully reorganized as ULAC, and only those members tricked into believing that Tafolla Sr. was a bad leader joined. So an OSA council continued to operate in Alice.[90] According to Tafolla Sr., Uvalde was active as an OSA council, and then

> some representatives of the LATIN-AMERICAN LEAGUE went over there and told them we had disbanded and that the Order Sons of America did not exist any longer and they organized a Council there with the very same element that we had—a work of tearing down and building up again, to suit their own ideas.[91]

Other localities readily embraced ULAC. By April thirteen councils had been established; among these were councils in Alice, Brownsville, Corpus Christi, Encino, La Grulla, San Antonio, and McAllen.[92] By May, Robstown, Falfurrias, and Edinburg had joined.[93]

LULAC'S CONSTITUTIONAL CONVENTION, MAY 1929

The convention to adopt the constitution was slated for May 1929. The convention committee included Garza, de Luna, and Joe Stillman of Corpus Christi.[94] They asked Castañeda to address the convention.[95]

On May 18 and 19, 1929, about one hundred fifty people gathered at Salón Ignacio Allende.[96] The business meeting apparently drew ninety-seven men: fifty-four delegates and forty-three visitors.[97] Delegates represented Corpus Christi, Robstown, Falfurrias, Edinburg, San Antonio, Brownsville, McAllen, Laredo, La Grulla, Encino, and Mission. Male and female visitors, some of whom were wives of delegates or visitors, came from Floresville, Sugarland, Gulf, Mission, and Laredo.[98]

The organizing committee planned the event as a family and community affair with a banquet and dance.[99] *La Prensa* and *El Paladín* reported the names of ladies (*damas*) and young ladies (*señoritas*) at the banquet.[100] The banquet and dance at Hotel Plaza drew three hundred. The evening's events were conducted in English.[101] The district attorney and a Chamber of Commerce representative, both European American men, gave speeches, as did several México Texanos.[102]

Men attending LULAC constitutional convention, Corpus Christi, May 1929. Left to right from bottom: row 1—J. T. Canales (1), Andrés De Luna (6), Ben Garza (9); row 3—Mauro Machado (11); row 4—M. C. Gonzáles (4), John Solís (5). Courtesy Nettie Lee Benson Latin American Collection, University of Texas.

On Sunday morning at nine-thirty, conventioneers met at Salón Ignacio Allende in a session conducted in Spanish.[103] Castañeda was to address the league but excused himself, saying, "I to this date am, in reality, a Mexican citizen and can't belong to the League."[104] Castañeda nevertheless sent his paper, "The Mexicans' Right to Public Education," written in English and delivered by attorney R. R. Lozano of San Antonio.[105] Castañeda wrote: "Our race, with beautiful and deep thoughts born of the warmth of our sacred and immense love for our fatherland [Mexico] absent from our eyes but alive and throbbing in our hearts."[106] Mexican nationalism would continue to be heard by ULAC circles, and some Mexicans would continue to play a role in the organization.

Garza opened the meeting, but the two o'clock session was suspended to allow the constitutional committee to conduct its work. The committee, apparently appointed in February, consisted of two representatives from each delegation present. Twenty-one delegates helped draft the constitution; among them were J. T. Canales, Gonzáles, Solís, Marín, Eduardo Idar Sr., de Luna Sr., Joe Stillman, and Sáenz. Reports fail to mention how nonmembers of the committee kept themselves occupied.

The convention changed the ULAC name to LULAC, League of United Latin American Citizens. The first LULAC officers were Ben Garza, president; M. C. Gonzáles, vice president; Andrés de Luna Sr., secretary; and Louis Wilmot, treasurer. As prescribed by the constitution, the secretary and treasurer automatically came from the president's hometown. Members named Perales, who was in Washington, D.C., and unable to attend the meeting, honorary president. Canales was also thanked for his work. Laredo was chosen as the 1930 convention site, and resolutions included a committee to devise rituals for local councils.[107] This last act was a continuation of the mutualista tradition, one that Perales would have rejected had he been there. With no further business, the meeting was adjourned.[108]

The Corpus Christi conventions were memorable events. The May convention moved Fernando de Peña of Alice to write,

It is seldom that you have the opportunity to hear men like this convention brought together, discuss [issues] as earnestly as they did Saturday and Sunday in Allende Hall. . . . These two days' experience will serve me all through life.[109]

On June 23, 1929, the Supreme Council met in McAllen to approve the bylaws. Twenty-six members representing thirteen councils were present. Canales explained the constitution and bylaws. President Garza appointed a committee to develop council bylaws and rituals. After eight years of splintering organizations and dueling egos, the League of United Latin-American Citizens was institutionalized; a new era was born.

LULAC CONSTITUTION

The constitution, which would prove a solid foundation, was largely written before the constitutional convention. The fourteen-page document consisted of a foreword and nine articles. Article 2 included the twenty-five aims and principles, the most important part. Twenty-one of these had first appeared in the LLAC manual. Principles 1, 2, 3, and 4 appeared in the LULAC constitution for the first time.

Just who wrote which part of the LULAC constitution is not clear, though Canales chaired the constitutional committee.[110] In 1953 Canales said he wrote the first four "aims and principles," which was true, and Eduardo

Idar Sr. the other twenty-one.[111] But in 1954 Canales' statement or memory changed. He said he wrote the entire 1929 constitution except for the aims and purposes, which he co-wrote with Idar.[112] However, there is evidence that Perales was also an author of the twenty-five aims and principles and the broader constitution as well; Canales probably excluded Perales by 1954 due to personal differences. Perales' handwriting, notations, and suggested revisions can be found on one version of the aims and principles. Perales may have translated them into English.[113]

In 1960 Canales changed his story again. He said Eduardo Idar provided valuable suggestions that he incorporated.[114] This time he said that he, Perales, Sáenz, and Eduardo Idar Sr. co-authored the aims but that he wrote the first four. These four men, then, were the authors of the aims and principles. I believe Canales wrote aims 1 thru 4 and Idar, Canales, Perales, and Sáenz wrote the twenty-one other aims and principles.

It is significant that the first aim referred to citizenship; the second, discrimination; the third, the law and equal rights; and the fourth, English as the "official language of our country." Central themes in the other aims included patriotism, "race" and "La Raza," politics, education, and workers' rights.

Patriotism to the United States was a theme in aims 1, 4, and 5. Aim 1 referred to persons of Mexican descent as a "race" and declared that the group's goal was to develop members (Mexican Americans) into "true citizens." LULAC did not accept the racialized notion of whites and "Mexicans" as members of two separate races. Also evident was its thinking about La Raza, an identity rooted in Mexican and Latin American nationalism.

The rhetoric of social citizenship emanating from the Americanization movement and Progressivism was evident. As in World War I, this group of México Texanos announced its devotion to the United States. This principle had little to do with encouraging Mexican immigrants to naturalize and become U.S. citizens. Moreover, it was a response to the Harlingen convention.

Aim 4 made English the official language of the organization and further established the association's intent to participate in U.S. society. Although English was not legally the official language of the United States, the dominant society certainly treated it as such. Moreover, Texas had officially re-adopted an English-only position in 1922. LULAC organizers believed that learning the language of the dominant society was a tool of defense.[115]

All LULAC members spoke Spanish; that was taken for granted, and Spanish remained their primary language. Yet aim 4 was written in Spanish before it was translated. Bilingualism was a political necessity. As colonized citizens concerned with survival, LULAC members recognized the importance of English, and members were to instruct their children in English.

Aims 2 and 9 addressed racism. Aim 2 made it clear that "discriminations against our people," which were viewed as undemocratic, would be abolished. Discrimination was plural because it was omnipresent and multiple in form. This principle was a statement in defense of all persons of Mexican origin in the United States, not just U.S. citizens. The U.S. Constitution served as the ideological basis for such protection.

LULAC founders anticipated racial repression. "Stigmas," a reference to racialization, would also be fought. Aim 23 denounced bossism and warned European Americans that LULAC would resist attempts to prevent México Texanos from organizing political associations.

Aim 7 stated that members were indeed proud of their "racial origin." It was a notice to Mexican citizens and a response to their criticism in post–Harlingen convention politics. Aim 8 announced that the organization existed for the goals of the Latin American community and would "defend their lives," a reference to racial violence and lynching.

Politics received the most attention. Aim 12 emphatically stated that the organization was not a political club, thereby acknowledging that politics in South Texas were corrupt. The principle sought to placate fears that members might operate as political bosses and sway elections. Aim 16 noted that members would participate in elections and pay the poll tax. It referred to paying the tax for family members, a reference to women and an assumption that men were the breadwinners.

Aim 13 hinted at the use of the ballot for "our people" and was therefore informed by political interests, race, and community. It made clear that racists would not be supported or elected. The LULAC constitution did not openly state that LULAC would strive to enlist Mexican American men to run for office, but this was its intent. Reference to "men" was specifically made here: LULAC founders failed to consider women as candidates, even though a woman had governed Texas just a few years earlier and other European American women held political office.

Aim 21 referred to the struggle to obtain the right for "our people" to serve on juries and other governmental functions. LULAC would fight for this right in the name of Mexican Americans; again Mexican American women were not identified in this aim.

The constitution also referred to education. Aims 6 and 7 stated that LULAC would take responsibility for La Raza's children. Aim 20 mentioned a plan to create educational institutions that supported private Mexican schools. Aim 24 expressed opposition to segregated public schools, although the word "segregated" was not used. LULAC organizers saw no contradiction in supporting private Raza-controlled schools and integrated public schools.

Aim 22 denounced peonage, worker abuse, and child labor. Principle 25 promised that LULAC would maintain statistics to aid workers. LULAC would protect Mexican-descent workers, especially in cases of wage discrimination or lack of mobility, but the constitution did not mention the working class or any class interests. Solidarity was primarily based on race.

The document delineated LULAC ideology on radicalism and religion in aims 18 and 19. Falling in accordance with antiradicalism in the post–World War I years, LULAC condemned radicalism as a means to an end. Likewise, Aim 19 called for the separation of religion and politics, leaving religion to the individual. This was a response to politics in Mexico, where a violent struggle between the Church and the state had occurred, yet the aim reflected the religiosity of LULAC founders.

LULAC leaders found it necessary to delineate some organizational concerns, informing outsiders of the plan of action in principles 3, 4, 11, 14, 15, and 17. Aim 3 stated that LULAC would use "legal means" as opposed to illegal means, violence, syndicalism, or radicalism.

Aim 11 stated that a defense fund would be established and that LULAC would take responsibility for its members' own education. Aim 14 made it known that the association would select good leaders; leadership was crucial in an organization, and the middle class was best suited for leading La Raza. In principle 15 LULAC claimed responsibility for its own strength, growth, and expansion. Principle 17 stated that the league would spread its ideology through newspapers, lectures, and pamphlets. Finally, aim 10 addressed the issue of organizational interests (and thus La Raza's interests) versus those of individual members of La Raza.

Absent in the league's aims was any mention of the particular subordination that Mexican-origin women faced such as México Texanas being prohibited from jury service. Within its middle-class and familial ideology, the league was not yet able to conceptualize equal opportunity for women.

The constitution contained several aims and articles written in male-specific language. The word "himself" was used in aim 10, while principle 13 declared that LULAC would place men in public office. Women were alluded to in aim 16 in the phrase "members of our families." Article 3, Section 1, on membership, made no reference to the inclusion or exclusion of men or women, only to citizenship.

LULAC permitted female honorary members, but they could not vote on LULAC decisions. Article 3, Section 2 provided that "any person who has distinguished himself or herself in science, arts, or letters or who has rendered some service to this organization in general or to any local council in particular may be elected an Honorary member by the Supreme Council or by the local councils."[116]

This article, then, failed to acknowledge the contributions that women could make as housewives, in organizations, or in other ways, and indeed, already had made. The work of wives, relatives, and allies was not equally valued. LULAC founders underestimated México Texanas' potential and undermined the league's own plan of Raza empowerment by excluding women.

OSA AND LULAC CONSTITUTIONS

A comparison of the LULAC and OSA constitutions suggests that the merger was not just a power struggle by jousting knights but the result of actual weaknesses in the OSA constitution, of which Perales was the major critic. He sought to omit provisions that protested against working on Sundays, finding employment for members, and offering assistance and protection to sick members; the latter two were mutualista tenets.

In addition, Perales hoped to delete the last three sentences on page 13 in the OSA constitution in Article 1, Section 1 on the OSA's purpose. This section provided that the OSA would function as "la Matriz" (the womb) in San Antonio, and that city's council would be Council No. 1. The LULAC constitution made all councils equally important and did not permit geographical or regional supremacy or centralization.

Perales also targeted Article 3, Section 10 which stipulated that the president of the United States and the governors of the states where the OSA existed would be ex-officio OSA presidents. Perales found this homage to be excessive, especially since they were political office holders. Article 3, on membership in the LULAC constitution, allowed them to be passive members without a vote but permitted them to speak at meetings.[117]

Perales called for revision of Section 1, Article 5, which named officers and permanent committees. He wanted to "make provision for a president general." The OSA constitution did not provide for state officers. Perales recognized this but also advocated the need for a president general. Article 4 of the LULAC constitution, on the Supreme Council, named a president general and a secretary and treasurer from the president's city of residence.[118]

In Section 1, Article 6 Perales wanted to "fix the duties of the president." The OSA constitution provided typical duties for the presidency and provided that the president would guard the passwords and change them every three months. Article 4, Section 5 of the LULAC constitution provided no password duties for the president.[119]

Perales requested that Section 14-a, Article 3 of the OSA constitution be revised or omitted entirely. This section dealt with the organizing committee of new councils and branches for men, local ladies auxiliary councils, and youth councils.[120] Local councils had to get Council No. 1's approval. Moreover, this subsection stated that the committee's work in reference to new councils was to be conducted in San Antonio and that the president or his representative had to attend these meetings. Under the LULAC constitution local ladies auxiliaries were abolished and committees were left to the discretion of the local council.

Perales asked for the revision of OSA's Article 4 on amendments and revocations. Proposed amendments were to be written and signed by three members. They would be reviewed in three consecutive meetings, and a two-thirds vote was required. Changes could only be made at the annual meeting. Article 4 stipulated the obligations of local officers to the mother council. Article 9 of the LULAC constitution provided that any council could offer an amendment at any annual or special convention. After it was accepted by the delegations present, a majority of councils had to ratify it. An entirely new constitution would have to go through the same procedure. The Supreme Council (board of directors) could act in a similar manner with regard to a resolution or general bylaw but not the entire constitution.[121]

Perales asked for the revision of OSA's Article 3, which stipulated quotas and dues. Article 6 of the LULAC constitution provided for dues assessed by the supreme or local councils.[122] Perales suggested adding six provisions:

1. There shall be a president general who shall be elected to office by a majority of votes of the delegates present at the annual convention.
2. Headquarters of the "Order Sons of America" shall be wherever the president general may happen to reside.
3. Each council shall appoint delegates who shall go to the annual convention with instructions to vote for whatever candidate is the

choice of said council for president general during the ensuing year.

4. Each council shall be entitled to two delegates for the first fifty members and one delegate for each additional fifty members; provided, however, that no council shall have less than two delegates.

5. No person shall be eligible for active membership who holds a public office. Such person, however, shall be eligible for honorary membership.

6. The entire membership shall consist wholly of American citizens of Mexican or Spanish descent.[123]

This last suggestion reflected both a Mexican American nationalist sentiment and an acknowledgment that racism separated the "races"; interracial cooperation with European Americans was unusual and was not anticipated. These then were the basic problems Perales had with the OSA constitution; the LULAC constitution incorporated his suggestions.

How did LULAC's aims and principles compare to the OSA's 1922 principles? Here we see the influence of the post–World War I era. Five ideological shifts were obvious: a shift from working-class ideology to a middle-class ideology with a casual concern for labor; a shift from a mutualista orientation with a broad definition of community that encompassed Mexicans to an organization of Mexican American professionals and businessmen; a shift from a subtle emphasis on U.S. citizenship to an organization stressing U.S. citizenship among Mexican Americans; a shift from a Mexican identity to an emerging Mexican American identity; and a shift from the conscious inclusion of women in community organization to their unconscious exclusion in political organization. While the OSA constitution largely reflected labor organizer Clemente Idar's ideology, the LULAC constitution reflected the predominant influence of Perales, Canales, and Eduardo Idar.

The 1922 OSA constitution referred to workers sixteen times. Principles 4, 5, 6, 8, 9, and 10 referred to workers and their oppression. The LULAC founders omitted any reference to "oppression" in that organization's constitution, and it excluded the principle that called for the investigation of working conditions and the condemnation of dual wages. LULAC would not find jobs for its members or "protect them from oppression"; it would keep statistics. A provision calling for the eradication of child labor, which for LULAC prevented the education of children and thus upward mobility, was retained in the LULAC constitution.

The LULAC constitution eliminated mutualista elements. Members did not join LULAC for personal or familial benefits. Principle 13 of the OSA constitution called for the aid to "our sick and distressed members," burial of the dead, and protection of members. References to "assisting one another" made apparent in aim 3 were deleted. Communitarianism was dealt a blow when the phrase about cooperation with Mexican organizations was deleted. The statement was deleted that would have committed LULAC to "use our influence with other organized bodies to assist us in accomplishing our object." LULAC would in fact do this anyway.

All references to Mexican citizens or residents were deleted. The LULAC constitution did not have principle 14, which addressed relations with organizations of citizens of the Republic of Mexico. OSA principle 16 concerned compiling data on all Mexican residents of the United States; this was changed in the LULAC constitution to compiling statistics for "our people." The term "Mexican" did not appear in the LULAC constitution. Nevertheless, LULAC founders recognized the contributions that members of the Mexican middle class could make and had made. Thus, a provision for their inclusion was made under the section in which membership was delineated: "Any person of distinction, or who has rendered distinguished service to the organization" could be an honorary member.[124]

Finally, in the transition from a mutualista and civil rights organization to a civil rights and civic organization, women lost their significance. Clemente Idar should be credited for intending their inclusion in 1922, but he did not attend the founding of LULAC, and the men who did failed to organize ladies auxiliaries since they did not see women as a necessity to LULAC's success. Eduardo Idar Sr. may have argued for women's inclusion, but Perales and Canales were the dominant figures, and Perales more readily discounted women as a political force. Moreover, women were victims of the transition from a broad communitarian philosophy so strongly advocated by Perales. With an emphasis on the middle class, the formally educated, and leaders, women lost their significance in the organization.

Although LULAC men were keen to pursue the new political opportunities afforded by the Progressive Era, such as the decline of bossism, they failed to recognize the significance of the vote as it applied to Mexican American women. Indeed, LULAC men largely defined women within the constraints of the family ideology. In his essays, Perales rarely mentioned women voters. When he did mention women, it was in reference to the family or domestic education.[125]

Nevertheless, LULAC organizers argued that LULAC would work for *nuestra Raza*, which included Mexican men, Mexican women, and México Texanas. Perales stated that LULAC was not a mutualista, secretive society, or political club, and members were free to join any of these.[126] Perales noted that LULAC was no more political than the American Legion, but he said this in front of European Americans.[127] And despite Perales' attempt to purge LULAC of its "secretive" and clublike nature, he was unable to do so completely, and several fraternal rituals were instituted by other leaders when Perales was absent.

LULAC RITUAL

After the LULAC constitutional convention in May, another meeting was held at which the local council bylaws and ritual were written; some members succeeded in adding a few mutualista practices. At the June 23, 1929, meeting Garza appointed a committee consisting of Canales, Sáenz, de Luna, Eulalio Marín of Corpus Christi, and Manuel B. Bravo of Edinburg.[128] According to a 1940 source, de Luna Sr., Sáenz, and Marín wrote the local rules of order, guidelines for councils.[129] Another source confirmed that Marín, de Luna Sr., and Sáenz wrote the ritual and that it was patterned after that of the Knights of America.[130]

The ritual included fraternal, Mexicanist, mutualista themes, influences that Perales tried to omit in the constitution. The ritual included sections on the opening of the meeting, closing of the meeting, initiation ceremony, installation of officers, funeral ceremony, and code. The entire ritual was written in Spanish; only Washington's Prayer and the code were included in English. All of the rituals were to be respected: "Nothing will more quickly destroy the beneficent influence of this organization than to have ritualistic ceremonies performed with meaningless effort. . . . And it is hereby recommended that the custom of singing patriotic songs in the gathering of this organization never be permitted to become extinct." The ritual rules were "not intended for public inspection." A quarterly password, a key to cipher confidential communications, and a code were included. One LULAC council apparently used the code "Be Loyal."[131]

The ritual reinscribed fraternity. References were made to Brother President, Brother Chaplain, and Brother Guide. Only one reference to women was made: "You also promise to be respectful in word and action to every woman; to be considerate to the widow and orphan." Mexican American men's chivalry survived. The ritual then added Mexicanist mutualista male clublike influences.

LULAC'S GROWTH AND RECEPTION

After the LULAC constitutional convention ended in May 1929, LULAC grew rapidly. The Supreme Council met on June 23 and appointed organizers. Sixteen councils existed by August 17, eighteen by November 5, and nineteen by January 1930; membership totaled two thousand.[132] In October 1929 Garza estimated one thousand members.[133] On the eve of 1930, Weeks concluded that LULAC "has made rather phenomenal progress in regard both to organization and growth."[134] Besides business owners, skilled laborers, and professionals, members included ranchers, independent farmers, and a few industrial foremen.[135]

Mexican-origin women received the league with open arms, though LULAC did not ask them to join. In June 1929 LULAC held a miniconvention in McAllen (probably the Supreme Council's meeting), and according to *El Paladín*, in attendance were "a large number of women for whom the convention was a matter of great interest."[136] In November 1929 the Alpha Club organized the Agrupación Filantrópica de Damas (Women's Philanthropic Group) to raise Christmas funds. The group held a joint meeting with LULAC Council No. 1 at the home of Ofelia and Louis Wilmot to plan Christmas fund-raising for Raza children. In late November the two groups co-sponsored a carnival, a dinner dance with a raffle on December 5, and a concert at the junior high school on December 15, raising more than four hundred dollars.[137]

A few European Americans heralded the league's founding. J. D. Autry of Falfurrias, a liberal European American, wrote a letter to the editor of the local newspaper *La Verdad* and commended LULAC as "the most worthy effort that has come under my observation." He noted that "when the general public comes to realize the splendid work your people are attempting there will be ample and substantial encouragement from every quarter where intelligent citizens are interested in the advancement of citizenship."[138] He saw "race pride" as "that most commendable characteristic" that "so deeply imbedded in the hearts of your people is actually one of the most important elements that go to make good citizenship."[139] Liberal educator J. O. Loftin praised LULAC and suggested that "every public school teacher . . . should assume as her primary objective, the eradication of racial prejudice."[140]

At least one European American political boss responded adversely to the founding. In March 1929 A. Y. Baker wrote to the *Hidalgo County Independent* of Edinburg:

My Mexican-Texan Friends . . . I have been and still consider myself
as your Leader or Superior Chief . . . I have always sheltered in my
soul the most pure tenderness for the Mexican-Texan race and
have watched over your interests to the best of my ability and knowledge. . . . Therefore I disapprove [of] the political activity of groups
which have no other object than to organize Mexican-Texan voters
into political groups for guidance by other leaders. . . . I have been
able to maintain the Democratic Party in power with the aid of my
Mexican-Texan friends, and in all the time that has passed we have
had no need for clubs or political organizations.[141]

Baker's was the most public opposition to LULAC's founding. According
to Weeks, others used "a less direct method of attack," though he did not
elaborate.[142] Cone Lozano of Jim Wells County, of which Alice was the seat
of county government, wrote that "the [LULAC] meeting was supposed to
be in Corpus Christi but the people were afraid to go there, so [we] met in
Alice instead on that day."[143] Actually, the 1930 convention was supposed
to occur in Laredo, but Laredo politics may have been too volatile, and it
sounds like politics in Corpus were, too.

Besides European Americans attacking the league, Mexican citizens in
Texas did too.[144] Economist Paul Taylor's interview with a Corpus Christi
LULAC member revealed the extent of such antagonism:

They tell us, who are trying to tell them [Mexicans in Texas] to
be more loyal to the United States. "But your forefathers are all of
Mexican origin and you should continue to be Mexican." We say he
is a visitor and [this is] none of his business.[145]

LULAC member Cástulo Gutiérrez of Del Rio responded to Mexican
criticism in an essay titled "Para los que no conocen nuestra institución,"
published in the local *El Popular:*

The objective of the American league is not to Americanize the
Mexican, much less to banish the Spanish language as has wrong-
fully been disclosed. The Mexican American who does not become a
citizen will remain the conquered one. I believe that after they have
children here they will be severed from the political machine of this
country, thinking they can unite in body and soul to Mexico.[146]

Masthead of *LULAC News*, 1931. Courtesy Center for American History, University of Texas.

He added, "It is precious [for Mexican Americans] to incorporate their soul and spirit in Mexican things, but not their body. This is impossible without living in Mexico or better said, ceasing to live in the United States."[147] He referred to Mexican Americans, Mexicans in the United States, and Mexicans in Mexico as a family.[148] What benefited the Mexican American "would also bring benefits to the Mexican citizen, who are our fathers, grandparents, and friends," he concluded.[149] Gutiérrez voiced LULAC thought.

Criticism led Perales to write the seven-part essay "La unificación de los méxico-americanos" (Mexican American Unification) that *La Prensa* published from September 4 through 10, 1929.[150] It is significant that Perales' essay title referred to the unity of Mexican Americans—not La Raza. He reiterated that LULAC was not founded to Americanize Mexican citizens in Texas. He stressed that its goal was not to separate itself from Mexicans. Moreover, the progress of Mexicans in the United States would occur when Mexican Americans were able to help newly arrived immigrants.[151] Regardless of criticism, the league prospered. The creation of the monthly news magazine *LULAC News* facilitated communications beginning in 1931.

SCHOLARS' COMMENTARIES

Scholars of the period commented on the league's founding. These included México Texana Jovita González, Carlos Castañeda, liberal Paul S. Taylor, and Oliver Douglas Weeks. In her master's thesis Jovita González expressed caution about "all these men" whom she characterized as politicians:

Border politics are just emerging from political bossism and rings. If the League tends to educate the Mexican-Americans for purely altruistic reasons, its labor is no doubt meritorious and praiseworthy. But should county bossism be superseded by an organized state-wide political machine, the results will be detrimental not only to the Mexican-American citizens but to the state at large.[152]

González had reason to be skeptical; she was critical of the Guerra political machine, Deodoro Guerra having taken a leadership role in the LLAC. Yet she gave LULAC the benefit of the doubt:

What these leaders propose to do is to arouse the political pride of these people by reminding them of their past traditions. The educated Mexican-American citizens realize the possibilities of their race and are fired by the desire to organize this element for the sole purpose of hastening the political development of their people.[153]

González did not criticize LULAC for excluding women, although she could not join LULAC, nor did LULAC invite her to speak at its functions in the 1930s.

Castañeda did not write about LULAC's founding but supported the league's work. He had expressed interest in the OSA's work as early as 1927 and had corresponded with Tafolla Sr., Francisco Pérez, Canales, and Perales. His professional stature and pro-Raza stance were appreciated, but until 1938 he was still a Mexican citizen.[154] However, he was either an official honorary member or an unofficial active member as of 1929. From 1929 on, Castañeda espoused transnational realities, espousing both Mexican nationalism and LULAC ideology.

Taylor commented on the league in *An American-Mexican Frontier:*

That an organized group of persons of Mexican ancestry in Texas has at last faced this situation with a combination of realism and idealism is a fact of great potential significance. If the leadership, which is mainly of the middle and professional classes, avoids the dissensions which are so common among Mexican societies in the United States, adheres to its program, and actually reaches the Mexican laborers, its influence can be immense.[155]

Taylor sympathized with the concerns of La Raza, especially the working class. Despite being an ally of La Raza, as a European American he could not join LULAC. In 1929 the league was unable to fathom white allies—they were too few.

The most significant commentary on LULAC's founding came from Oliver Douglas Weeks, the only European American at the founding conventions and a Progressive. The Department of Historical Investigation of the Government of Washington hired the University of Texas professor to conduct a study of Mexican Americans in politics.[156] The government funded him either because social scientists and the general public agreed that there was a "Mexican problem" or because he was investigating Mexican American *políticos*. On January 15 Castañeda wrote to Tafolla Sr., introducing Weeks and informing Tafolla of his study "The Mexican American in Politics."[157] Perales and Canales, both political elites, were involved in the founding, and this involvement may have elicited concern. Weeks' work, in fact, might have been the first evidence of government surveillance of LULAC.[158]

In 1930 Weeks published "The League of United Latin-American Citizens: A Texas-Mexican Civic Organization" in the *Southwestern Political and Social Science Quarterly*. He praised the association, but he held some racialized ideas about La Raza. First, he considered persons of Mexican origin passive. Thus he saw LULAC as a challenge to "hitherto existing lethargy."[159] Since he was unfamiliar with La Raza and its history of political activism, he assumed it had no tradition of self-help or resistance.

Second, he assumed La Raza had little organizing ability:

It is commonly thought to be a Latin, and particularly a Mexican, trait to make dramatic beginnings amidst a great show of idealism, enthusiasm, and unanimity and then to lie back and let the undertaking thus launched go on for itself. Old Mexico has shown aptitude in framing constitutions which are paragons of logic and construction, but constitutions which do not work.[160]

To Weeks, Anglo-Saxon civilization and government were superior. This was a subtle way of saying that LULAC members were still "Mexican," descendants of "Old Mexico."

Third, he considered most Mexicans inferior. They were "ignorant, slothful, unclean, dangerous, and incapable of assimilation or of good citizenship."[161] But he thought LULAC members might be different, not "Mexicans" or "aliens." He noted that "they are citizens and must be dealt with as such."[162] Finally, he blamed La Raza for its socioeconomic condition and its political subordination. He concluded that La Raza's problems were "created quite as much by their own deficiencies as by the deficiencies of the Anglo-American in his dealings with them."[163] He said that the Mexican American

> realizes full well that the greatest stumbling block in the way of accomplishing this end is the Mexican-American himself, who possesses no very clear conception of the significance of the privileges and duties of his American citizenship.[164]

Weeks added, "In order, therefore, that *these people* may be able to stand their ground, they must correct their own deficiencies, resulting from ignorance, docility, and prejudice against the Anglo-Saxon and his ways" (emphasis mine).[165] Weeks blamed the victim.

Despite these racist sentiments, Weeks praised LULAC, the general tone of his article was sympathetic, and his information was accurate. The group represented a new middle class, he observed. He noted, "He [the LULAC member] believes in his people; he believes that what he has accomplished for himself may be realized in part for his less fortunate brothers."[166] He saw LULAC members as "enlightened" men who would raise consciousness. He noted that Mexican Americans "must first be aroused to a consciousness of that citizenship and then must be educated as to what are his civil and political rights."[167]

Weeks, like LULAC, stressed leadership and considered middle-class males best able to lead their people to progress. He agreed with Perales that Mexican Americans must uplift Mexican residents of the United States. Weeks proved an ally, and he delivered an address titled "The Constitution" at the third annual convention, in Alice in 1931.[168] At that event he said the LULAC constitution was workable.

Weeks' article was the most important contribution by any scholar at the time. His ethnographic work is to be commended; he saved me hundreds of hours of work.

CONCLUSION

LULAC's amiable founding in February 1929 occurred without conflict or incident because México Texano activists had already ironed out differences among themselves at the Harlingen convention. Between 1927 and the founding, Tafolla Sr., Perales, and Canales wielded considerable influence. Perales played the largest role in rejecting the OSA as the major organizational force. Moreover, he and Canales conceptualized and pushed forward a substantially different constitution—a more democratic one.

The LULAC constitution reflected the influence of new leadership, with Canales, Perales, Eduardo Idar Sr., and Sáenz as its major authors. It embodied the ideas of the new middle class and lawyers Perales and Canales.

The constitution encompassed assimilationist perspectives but also an activist, progressive, and communitarian ethos.[169] Resistance to racism was a principal theme. And while Mexican nationalism was diffused and U.S. nationalism included, Raza nationalism of a hybrid people predominated.

The LULAC constitution, as opposed to the OSA's, reflected changes in the Mexican-origin community after World War I and before 1929. A comparison of the OSA and LULAC constitutions exhibited a new middle-class ethos. Little mention was made of the workplace as a site of struggle. Race and citizenship, not class or gender, became primary.

The LULAC constitution expressed a Mexican American consciousness that made clear distinctions between México Texanos and Mexicans. The LULAC constitution ignored Mexican immigration, and Mexican citizens were consciously excluded. U.S. citizenship was privileged. The constitution stressed the bicultural and bilingual realities of México Texanos. The constitution also represented the primacy of Mexican Americans versus the broader Raza community and a concern for individual rights and equal opportunities. Mutualism was rejected as political strategy; self-help was redefined to mean leadership by the male Mexican American middle class through an organization rather than a cooperative effort by all members of La Raza (including women) as envisioned by the Primer Congreso Mexicanista in 1911. Still, a few mutualista-like rituals were included.

Although no article in the LULAC constitution specifically excluded women, the political culture, organizing methods, and references to brotherhood did in practice. When mentioned, women were usually identified in the context of family. Moreover, the constitution ignored sexism.

While the Mexican community seems to have rejected the LULAC path, the México Texano community, especially its middle-class sector, embraced LULAC. Conservative white elements criticized LULAC, the European American community responded with indifference, and scholars responded favorably. The league was the first permanent and viable major organizational challenge to racism in Texas and the vanguard of an emerging Mexican American civil rights movement.

PART THREE

THEORY AND METHODOLOGY

The Mexican American
Civil Rights Movement

> *I have noticed that several persons have been named as*
> *"Father of L.U.L.A.C."; but I have kept silent because*
> *said organization did not have any Fathers. It was a*
> *movement which through the process of evolution devel-*
> *oped into LULAC.* —J. T. CANALES, 1960

Activism in the 1920s and the founding of LULAC signaled a Mexican American civil rights movement. J. T. Canales and Emma Tenayuca and her husband, Homer Brooks, though on opposite sides of the spectrum of capitalism and communism, thought so. In 1939 Tenayuca and Brooks wrote about what they called "the Significance of the Mexican Rights Movement."[1] Despite these references to a movement, historians have hesitated to refer to the Mexican American civil rights movement.

In this chapter I will ask whether activism heretofore described indeed constituted a civil rights movement. To answer, it is first necessary to survey social movement theory. I will assess the concept of a "Mexican American civil rights movement" and discuss why a prominent writer on the topic of LULAC, political scientist Benjamín Márquez, did not embrace the use of social movement theory until recently.[2] Finally, I explain how and why social movement theory should be applied to 1920s activism. In particular, I will address historical context, collective interests, mobilization, oratory and movement discourse.

SOCIAL MOVEMENTS

Simply put, a social movement is resistance to the status quo through collective claims, challenges, and actions. A movement can be radical, liberal, or conservative. Theorists have focused on participants, sources of conflict, resources, social structure, historical context, mobilization, ideology, and collective identity. Early social movement theory included the relative deprivation school of the 1960s and the resource mobilization school of the 1970s. Relative deprivation, as described by Mancur Olson and other scholars, centered on individuals and why they participate in a movement.[3] This school focused on class as the source of conflict.

The 1970s led to the resource mobilization school.[4] Its theorists considered social movements a challenge to the status quo and paid more attention to resources, social structure, and historical context. Anthony Oberschall defined mobilization as "the process of forming crowds, groups, associations, and organizing for the pursuit of collective goals" and argued that it must be taken into account.[5] Resource mobilization theorists identified race and gender as additional sources of conflict. Likewise, Charles Tilly argued that collective action results from a shifting combination of interests, organization, mobilization, and opportunity.[6]

In the 1980s "new social movement theorists" including Alain Touraine, Daniel Foss, and Ralph Larkin saw movements as a "natural" feature of daily life and argued that any group with a stake in social change could initiate a movement.[7] The source of conflict, they implied, could be class, race, gender, or sexuality. They defined collective action as action resulting from a group that has identified itself with the goal of empowerment during a specific time.

Foss and Larkin defined a social movement as the

> developing collective action of a significant portion of the members
> of a major social category, involving at some point the use of physical
> force or violence against members of other social categories, their
> possession, or their institutionalized instrumentalities, and interfer-
> ing at least temporarily whether by design or by unintended
> consequence—with the political and cultural reproduction of
> society.[8]

A movement exists, they argued, when "members of a social category usually excluded from history begin to assert themselves as historical actors."[9] They criticized the relative deprivation and resource mobilization schools because they saw movement participation as rational calculation by individuals or groups seeking to maximize psychological, social, or material profits. They contended that excessive attention had been given to whether a movement was successful; the fact that a challenge took place is more significant. Today's theorists, however, would argue that violence is not a necessary component. Likewise, Touraine saw a movement as an "expression of collective will" and as "the collective organized action through which a class actor battles for the social control of historicity in a given and identifiable context."[10]

Using these theories, I define a social movement as collective organized actions by a significant number of people with a shared identity and outside organizations representing a group (social category) with a collective identity seeking to assert its will as historical actors to challenge an existing situation or status for the purpose of a collective goal over a specific time or era.

In the 2000s literature on social movements continues to grow. Future analysis should consider the work of Aldon Morris, Doug McAdams, Suzanne Staggenborg, and M. Bahati Kuumba. However, in their 2006 survey of the literature, scholars Donatella Della Porta and Mario Diani suggest three key criteria in defining a social movement: Are actors involved in conflictual relations with identified opponents? Are actors linked by dense informal networks? Do actors share a distinct collective identity?[11]

MEXICAN AMERICAN CIVIL RIGHTS MOVEMENT

Applying my definition, one can ask whether there was a Mexican American civil rights movement. Several early scholars of Chicano history alluded to one. Only recently have Tenayuca and Brooks been treated as historians or intellectuals,[12] although they wrote of a "Mexican rights movement" in 1939:

> The Mexican people's movement in the Southwest will constitute
> one more important and powerful link in the growing movement for
> the democratic front in the United States. The achievement of its
> objectives will be a decisive step forward toward the national unifica-
> tion of the American people.[13]

Charles Chandler's 1968 dissertation referred to the "Mexican American protest movement," though he referred to the post–World War II era.[14] Carlos Larralde's *Mexican American Movements and Leaders* called various struggles "movements" and even called 1920s participants "activists" but still did not name the Mexican American civil rights movement.[15]

In fact, most historians before the mid-1990s did not refer to a "Mexican American civil rights movement." For instance, historian Mario García's *Mexican Americans: Leadership, Identity, and Ideology* focused on key organizations and activists from 1921 to 1965 without mentioning the movement. Ricardo Romo's essay on civil rights leader George I. Sánchez merely referred to "the" civil rights movement without calling it Mexican American.[16]

In 1992 I coined the phrase "Mexican American civil rights movement." Four years later, the four-part documentary series *Chicano! The Mexican American Civil Rights Movement* popularized the idea of the civil rights movement among persons of Mexican descent.[17] The film's intent was to focus on the Chicano movement of 1965–1978, not the Mexican American civil rights movement of earlier decades.

However, the series blurred the distinctions between the two movements. It focused on the Chicano movement of the post-1965 era, not the 1920–1965 era, and was therefore misnamed. The series was perhaps the last visual vestige of a Chicano movement nationalist politics, a politics that eschewed LULAC; it typified how Chicano-movement filmmakers viewed earlier generations.[18] Still, that film promoted the idea of a Mexican American civil rights movement. By 2000 it was commonplace for historians who were well read in Chicano history to refer to this movement before 1965.[19] But the mainstream has not yet caught up. For instance, Immanuel Ness' *Encyclopedia of American Social Movements* refers to the "Mutualista Movement" and "Mexican Americans and the Chicano Movement" but no Mexican American civil rights movement.[20]

So why, until recently, were the public and historians of Chicanos unable to fathom the Mexican American civil rights movement? For one reason, decades ago the dominant society considered La Raza incapable of initiating this effort. For another, historians have led many to believe that most Raza activism occurred in the post–World War II era, perhaps because most scholars living today did not participate in pre–World War II activism. Until recently, too, Chicano scholars had an ideological contempt for LULAC and those calling themselves Mexican American. Research on the topic also has been impeded in part because "the" civil rights movement has been theorized as African American.

Most pre-1960s scholars contended that La Raza was incapable of initiating a movement because of a tendency toward fatalism or docility. Scholars like Weeks, Taylor, and Jovita Gonzáles were the exception. Even Chandler wrote, "Until recently, they have accepted their condition with docility." Further, he argued,

> The members of a social movement must believe their actions can change the world. The Mexican-American, by virtue of his socialization and cultural training, often lacks this faith. Instead, he is influenced by some form of fatalism, either of an impersonal or divine nature.[21]

Scholars hesitated to refer to a movement or even extensive activism before World War II because, in their view, World War II was the watershed for La Raza. Chandler stated,

> During the last four decades [since 1948], however, Mexican Americans have increasingly been organizing and taking action against discrimination. The process has been slow; but after World War II it took on many of the characteristics of a regional minority group social movement.[22]

In Carl Allsup's study of the American GI Forum, a post–World War II Hispanic veterans association, he claimed that LULAC and pre-1945 activism were of little consequence. Before the GI Forum, Allsup argued, "political power was not accessible" because "the economic base was non-existent, experience was limited, voting was rare, and Anglo politicians chose to dominate Mexicans."[23] Numerous Chicano history texts in the 1980s and 1990s showed the pre–World War II era as rich in civil rights activism. But recent research on World War II, especially the United States Latinos and Latinas in World War II Oral History Project at the University of Texas in Austin, has added to the misconception of World War II as a marker for the origins of civil rights activism.[24]

Research on LULAC published in the 1990s and early 2000s, especially that of Benjamín Márquez during that period, has not paid enough attention to pre–World War II activism, either; this is especially apparent in research on the impact of World War I.[25] Consequently, while scholars now have an appropriate name for Mexican American activism, the scope of that movement had not been documented. Moreover, I refer to "the" Mexican American civil rights movement to give this broader movement over various regions across the decades before 1965 its proper due. I titled this chapter

"The" civil rights movement because I believe there was a broad movement between 1920 and 1965, though within this meta-movement were numerous movements across the decades in different states and regions. This book is about one regional effort in the 1920s.

BENJAMÍN MÁRQUEZ' RESEARCH ON LULAC

Chicano scholars' early ambivalence toward accepting the idea of the Mexican American civil rights movement is exemplified by Benjamín Márquez. In *LULAC: The Evolution of a Mexican American Political Organization*, he first studied the League as an organization and explicitly *not* as a social movement organization.[26] Nevertheless, his later work shows the influence of social movement theorists. Again, I examine his earlier work because this book has been influential.

Márquez' thesis was that

> LULAC's longevity was due to the organization's ability to effectively adjust its incentive structure during the late 1960s and early 1970s. . . .
>
> This change in the incentive structure transformed the organization from an activist civil rights group to a staff or elite-dominated group that would devote much of its energies to continuity and survival. . . .
>
> The incentive theory literature helps us understand LULAC's evolution as an organization because it analyzes the individual's reasons for participation in an organization and the relationship between leaders and followers.[27]

Márquez was influenced by relative deprivation theorist Olson, who argued that organizations "must provide rewards or incentives to its members in order to secure their commitment and participation."[28] According to Márquez, "Individually consumable rewards are still the strongest and most reliable incentive organizations can offer their members." He identified three incentives for joining LULAC: material, solidary (i.e., camaraderie, status), and purposive or expressive ("those derived from advocating a particular cause or ideological orientation").[29] Like scholars of the relative deprivation school, Márquez focused on individuals' motivations, psychology, and interests and not on collective interests.

In a book review of Márquez' *LULAC: The Evolution* historian David

Gutiérrez writes that the league was concerned with "not merely questions of status preservation, self-aggrandizement, or the consolidation and expansion of the political influence of a few individuals."[30] Touraine also reminds us that "an individual or a group is not determined by a single social situation" and that no social situation can be reduced to class relations.[31]

Márquez largely focused on class and discounted collective interests such as those of ethnicity or race as another reason people joined LULAC. He argued that "individual self-interest is at war with ethnic loyalty and that in the long run the latter will yield to the former." He agreed with Olson, arguing that there are "limits to solidarity." Márquez said ideological appeals to ethnic loyalty (or "purposive or expressive" incentives) were an insufficient reason to support an ideology or organization: "The logic of incentive theory suggests that even minority organizations cannot rely on the existence of racism or group subordination to maintain a viable and active group."[32]

The resource mobilization school also influenced Márquez. In attempting to address the question of changing membership, he argued that the league had two major mobilization periods—the late 1920s and the late 1940s, "times in which appeals were made to potential activists to work in the interests of mutual aid and protection."[33] Here I agree with Márquez. The late 1920s was indeed a period of mobilization and constituted a social movement. And it is true that mutual aid and protection were key.

Márquez conducted significant historical research on LULAC but still needed better historical context to place LULAC within the framework of a social movement.[34] Márquez recognized the importance of history but was unable to properly contextualize LULAC across time. The earlier Márquez had said, "The issue of race and racism, although the central political issue of LULAC, actually occupied a small part of its members' overall political philosophy."[35]

In a later work, revising his initial interpretation, Márquez and co-author Jack Jennings explicitly called LULAC "a social movement organization."[36] Márquez was influenced by the work of Aldon Morris and other theorists. In addition to his confirmation that indeed LULAC was part of a social movement, that is, the Mexican American civil rights movement, my research helps to properly situate 1920s activism and LULAC within a movement framework.

A SOCIAL MOVEMENT FRAMEWORK

Placing 1920s activism within this theoretical framework allows us to consider historical context, racism as a serious source of conflict, collective interests, and movement discourse.[37] Considering collective interests is crucial in understanding this social movement. La Raza has collective interests as a people of color in a society dominated by whites.[38] People joined LULAC for protection and the attainment of civil rights. Likewise, self-interest was often tied to collective interests since individuals could not escape ascriptive characteristics such as color, physical appearance, Spanish surnames, and accents.

Historian Robert Rosenbaum has addressed collective interests of La Raza. He suggests that "self-preservation of a group" is a historic goal of Chicanos as a colonized people and has distinguished three types of efforts at self-preservation: survival, preservation, and adaptation. Rosenbaum defines self-preservation as the

> active attempt by a subordinate group to maintain itself to preserve the qualities cherished by group members for cultural or ethnic self-identification—and to survive in a world dominated by the institutions and procedures and the standards and values of others.[39]

Rosenbaum adds, "Any process used by a group to make decisions that affect the group as a whole is a political process, and any process used by a group to deal with its subordinate position is an effort at self-preservation through politics." He also calls this "ethnic self-preservation."[40]

In Márquez' early work he says there are collective interests, but he stresses what Olson called "the limits of solidarity" and sees an individual's solidarity with La Raza as "altruism."[41] He cites the work of political scientist Mario Barrera and Aldon Morris' work on the African American civil rights movement as arguing that "the need to solve them [the limits of solidarity] is a pressing and lasting motivation to collective action," although again Márquez sees "individuals as economic maximizers."[42]

Activists in the 1920s were not simply concerned with individual interests or altruism—they were concerned with collective interests, the self-preservation of La Raza. In 1931 a LULAC member proclaimed that the organization's mission was "to claim that God-given right of self-preservation, equal education and to abolish once and for all illegal segregation."[43]

Sociologist William Gamson reminds us that collective interests alone do not create a social movement: "It cannot be taken for granted that it is natural that people come together for collective interest or action." And that "creation of commitment means a change from a low generalized readiness to act to a high generalized readiness to act collectively."[44] Thus, mobilization is also necessary. In this Mexican American civil rights movement, oratory played a key role in recruitment and mobilization.

MOBILIZATION AND ORATORY

Oratory prepared activists to stand ready. In the 1920s, there were no Spanish-language radio stations, and few members of La Raza owned telephones. Face-to-face contact was central; people gathered to listen to speakers in public spaces such as the San Antonio *mercado*, town *placitas* and parks, and mutualista halls. Community leaders spoke to working- and middle-class people.[45]

Tenayuca described the significance of oratory at the mercado in San Antonio.[46] My mother also listened to orators in the 1930s in Mercedes, in the Valley, and recalls:

> People got together to hear the Mexican consul, who would come to town to speak. There were lawyers and some societies that took part in these events. The people, with so much respect, would stand in the sun for hours hearing these men. The same thing happened during *las fiestas patrias*, which were celebrated the fifteenth and sixteenth of September. They still felt the love and respect for Mexico.[47]

Tenayuca and Orozco emphasized radical and "Mexicanist" orators, but there were also Mexican Americanist speakers. Adela Sloss-Vento, an activist in the post-1930 era, explained:

> We had the postwar depression [after WWI] on the one hand and the injustices on the other. Public spirit was daunted, dead, and in need of revival. Only three defenders [Perales, Sáenz, Canales] . . . raised themselves like three giants in defense of our problems. They were like three luminous beacons lighting the road and carrying hope to the Latin-American people.[48]

Defenders like Sáenz had to reckon with an arduous chore. It was necessary to organize meetings, to write and to speak to the people, and to give them inspiration, hope and optimism. They had to get the people out to fight and reclaim their rights. Sloss-Vento recalled Perales, Sáenz, and Canales as orators and spokesmen across the decades in indoor spaces and described the emotional appeal they evoked:

I can still hear their voices in the meetings and courtrooms, speaking to the people with all their heart and with the sincerity that characterized them. I seem to hear them urging the people to unite and protest the hate and injustice. Their sonorous voices were like those of a magic bell, reaching out to the heart of the Latin American people.[49]

Of Perales, Sáenz, and Canales she wrote: "These three leaders constantly made trips and worked among our people with regard to their rights. They held meetings, reunions, wrote to the different newspapers. They spoke before the law and defended our people from all kinds of injustices."[50] These three orators, among others, inspired and mobilized people. They appealed to reason, social justice, U.S. citizenship, patriotism, U.S., Raza, and Mexican nationalism, and emotion to foster action. Their appeals to morality, heritage, identity, and the Spanish language moved La Raza. These leaders and members of La Raza were not simply economic maximizers.

MOVEMENT DISCOURSE

Another essential component of a social movement is an ideological campaign. British historian George Rude has suggested that the full range of ideas underlying social and political action should be explored, that is, an "ideology of protest."[51] Key to this ideology is a discourse emphasizing self-preservation.

This "defense" discourse appeared in leaders' self-identity, organizational documents, and organizational symbols. Leaders made allusions to themselves as knights, defenders, warriors, and soldiers. For instance, Gonzáles used the language of a defense discourse to explain why he became an attorney:

There was no man of my race to defend them, who would fight for them, who would gain respect for them before the law and [therefore], in short, I always felt the desire to have an occupation that would allow me to channel my energies, my aspirations, my whole life to the defense of those [people] who changed countries [and became Americans].[52]

Similarly, J. Luz Sáenz saw himself as a defender: "My life problem has been working for the betterment of my race. I have done a great deal of news-

Medieval knight and shield of Order
Knights of America, representing
defense, *OKA News*, December 1927.
Courtesy Nettie Lee Benson Latin
American Collection, University of
Texas.

paper writing . . . in defense of our people; racial problem is my theme."[53]
This discourse appeared in organizational documents as well.[54] LULAC's
1929 principles referred to defense in at least five aims:

8. We shall protect and defend their lives and interest whenever
necessary.
9. We shall destroy any attempt to create racial prejudices against
our people.
11. We shall create a fund for our mutual protection, for the defense
of those of us who may be unjustly persecuted.
23. We shall resist and attack energetically all machinations tending
to prevent our social and political unification.
24. We shall oppose any tendency to separate our children in the
schools of this country.[55]

Emblema oficial de LULAC

LULAC emblem created by piano
instructor and artist Isaías Zepeda of San
Antonio, similar to shield symbol used
by J. Luz Sáenz during World War I.
Courtesy LULAC National.

Organizations used visual symbols connoting protection. Appealing to
the medieval world of Spain, England, and Europe, the OKA used knights—
military servants and mounted warriors—in its name. The OKA newsletter displayed a knight with armor, a shield, a sword, and a horse ready to
charge—guardians of La Raza.[56]

LULAC selected a shield as its emblem. It is not clear if the idea came
from J. Luz Sáenz, the OKA, or E. H. Marín of Corpus Christi. *LULAC
News* did not credit Sáenz with the image of a shield, but his World War I
scrapbook is full of postcards with illustrations he created, several with a
shield.[57] He named it "Memento from World War I," and he referred to the
"prestigious warrior tradition among La Raza."[58] Eulalio Marín of Corpus
Christi recommended the shield on a pin for a coat lapel, and in November
1931 *LULAC News* began using it as its symbol. In 1955 Dr. George J. Garza,
LULAC president, explained its significance:

The shield is LULAC's emblem and was adopted as being symbolic of
LULAC's protective principles. The shield has a background of stars

and stripes with a diagonal band of white stretching from upper left down to lower right and having the letters LULAC stamped on it.[59]

Symbols of defense proved central to the movement's goal of self-preservation.

Several newspapers besides *LULAC News* used allusions to defense. Among them was *El Paladin* (The Knight), an official LULAC newspaper in the 1930s. This discourse of defense seen in self-identity, organizational documents, organizational symbols, and newspapers proved a vital component of social movement behavior.

CONCLUSION

Civil rights activism of the 1920s should be understood in the context of a Mexican American civil rights movement. Recalling Foss and Larkin's definition of a social movement, we saw "developing collective action" in conferences, conventions, meetings, and oratorical gatherings. We saw a "significant portion" of La Raza involved. OSA organizational membership varied from 15 to 250 in cities and towns, and there was a dense network of organizations and collaborators. Nonmembers including Mexicans participated, and women also formed part of this effort.

Activists represented the "social category" of La Raza seeking to interrupt racial domination. They joined a movement, not just an organization. They fought for La Raza's collective interests. Expounding "defense and protection," a discourse was elaborated through oratory by self-identified defenders. Knights and shields symbolized this defense.

"Movement" connotes zealous efforts and the will of a people. Several activists themselves referred to their efforts as a "movement." The collective will and claims by La Raza demand that we refer to these struggles as a "Mexican American civil rights movement." The struggles of La Raza before the Chicano movement, and especially before World War II, need to be recognized.

Referring to a/the Mexican American civil rights movement is another device to distinguish Raza activism from African American efforts. It is time to stop naming "the" civil rights movement as solely one of African Americans; it is a tired hegemonic master narrative. "Mexican American civil rights movement" is a useful device to distinguish a political struggle waged by Mexican Americans and Mexicans between 1921 and 1965. It was Mexican and American. This movement is finally part of our historical discourse.

No Women Allowed?

EIGHT

> *The founding of LULAC constitutes one of the most*
> *transcendental phases in favor of the intellectual better-*
> *ment of Americans of Latin origin. . . . [A]s a native of*
> *this country and one who is proud of her origins, I have*
> *felt the enthusiasm.*   —ADELA SLOSS, 1932

When I began research on LULAC it never dawned on me that women might have been part of that movement. I was told that Ben Garza (or Alonso S. Perales) was the father of LULAC. I interviewed Manuel C. Gonzáles, John Solís, and several other men, along with some women, yet women and gender did not yet figure into my studies. So when historian Moisés Sandoval wrote that "all those that gathered to found LULAC were men," it seemed true.[1]

But while I was writing a senior honors thesis, two women entered the picture. Adela Sloss-Vento of Edinburg, Texas, active in civil rights struggles since 1927, let me use her archives, and Marta Engracia Pérez de Perales gave me access to the papers of her late husband, Alonso, that were kept in her home. I gained Pérez de Perales' trust, probably because Sloss-Vento wrote her comadre a letter of introduction on my behalf and because I was an energetic young woman. I failed to interview either since I did not see them as movement activists. Years later when I finally realized that Sloss-Vento was part of that movement, she did not want to be interviewed. Typical of many who rarely draw attention to themselves, she only hinted at her involvement by describing the participation of male leaders she knew. She talked about "them," not "we."[2] And Pérez de Perales talked mostly about her husband and other men.

Later as a graduate student I discovered women's history and realized Sloss was a participant in this Mexican American civil rights movement, mostly in the post-1929 era. I realized, too, that Pérez de Perales' work facilitated her husband's activism.

How, then, have women participated? Were they excluded? Did women have to be members of men's associations to participate in the Mexican American civil rights movement? How are we to account for their involvement if they were not members of organizations like the Order Sons of America? It is already clear that none were major founders of LULAC, but were they involved in some other way? Were they "political"? Leaders? Activists? Auxiliary members?

The study of men's organizations will not fully capture women's participation. Instead, only by using a social movement framework can we account for women's activism. A social movement consists of those inside and outside of organizations. How, then, do we study women and gender in social movements, particularly those that are male-dominated? How are we to understand women's exclusion, inclusion, and involvement in the Mexican American civil rights movement?

Exclusion would be a simple but erroneous response. The OSA's constitution actually permitted ladies auxiliaries, but none were organized. Overt evidence of most men's desire to keep women out of the organization does not exist. Yet, "No Women Allowed" was the policy and subtext of the LULAC constitution in 1929, and not until 1933 could women join. After 1933 men exerted little effort in organizing them and in fact discriminated against them.[3] Still, women's participation before 1933 was impressive. Interestingly enough, some of these women may not have been U.S. citizens.

In this chapter I will continue to gender LULAC and the Mexican American civil rights movement by paying attention to women.[4] Other chapters gendered the men, including how gender affected individual founders. I will address how scholars have explained women's lack of participation in political activism and assess how several women saw their own political involvement. Adela Sloss (not married at the time), Adelaida Garza (wife of Ben Garza), and Carolina B. de Luna (wife of Andrés de Luna Sr.) are highlighted. I discuss how women participated in this movement as individuals and family members. Then I look at kinds of organizations in which Mexican American women participated. These included women's clubs, women's auxiliaries, and Ladies LULAC chapters. I focus on whether women organized into separate associations because of male exclusion, difference, or feminist separatism. Finally, I consider women's inclusion as it related to LULAC's strategy for empowerment of La Raza. Here, I discuss Emma Tenayuca's and María L. de Hernández' thoughts on LULAC, gender, empowerment, and the Mexican American civil rights movement.

WOMEN'S NONPARTICIPATION?

Class, race, and gender explain México Texanas' lack of involvement in various organizations. Structural restraints such as education and occupational segregation prevented their participation. Few México Texanas graduated from high school. Only a small percentage of women were employed outside the home, and most of these held working-class jobs. Working women had less control over labor time; clerks, for instance, could not take time off from their workplace as easily as male business owners. There were no women lawyers.

Situational restraints such as marriage and motherhood also hindered involvement. Some women had husbands, children, and housework to tend. They were often less mobile than men—less likely to drive or own a car, less likely to have money, and less likely to spend it on themselves. Many no doubt had to fear sexual harassment, jealous husbands, and protective fathers or brothers.

Marriage, the division of labor, and reproduction could constrain women's participation. Husbands may not have wanted activist wives or may have disliked women's interaction with other men because of potential sexual relations. And they may have feared women's political education obtained through traveling and social interaction. Besides, women had to care for the family and home. Finally, political socialization prevented women from taking an active role. Religion and patriarchal family ideology kept politics a male domain. Prescriptive literature permeated the Spanish-language press and socialized women toward domesticity.[5]

As a result of all these subordinating factors, scholars have concluded that Mexican-descent women were subordinated and excluded from organizational life. In addition, machismo was allegedly predominant. Until recently, most scholars had rendered Mexican-origin women invisible in voluntary associations and social movements.[6] In 1922 scholar Thomas Rogers noted, "The Mexican women live in a cage of customs. Never, whether married or single, will they appear in public with a man to whom they are not related."[7] Charles August Arnold reported in his 1928 study, "The Mexican family is organized along patriarchal lines, with the father as the head, the ruler, and the arbiter of the destinies of his household."[8] Even Kathleen Gonzáles argued in her 1928 thesis that "the middle-aged women do not belong to any clubs. They are busy rearing a family and marrying it off but the older women whose families are well grown have church clubs which meet frequently and take very active part in church activities. Only among the upper class do afternoon gatherings of women exist."[9]

These interpretations lingered. Sister Frances Jerome Woods found in her 1949 study that the wife "must do his [the husband's] bidding without question, and prides herself on her submissiveness and subjection." Daughters "are taught absolute obedience not only to their fathers but to their brothers as well," she added.[10] Much later, in 1984, Julia Kirk Blackwelder contended in her research that "Mexican Americans preserved a culture that emphasized male authority and family loyalty above other values."[11] Early Chicano male political scientists added to the myth of women's submission. Ralph Guzmán wrote, "Women seldom appeared in the Anglo world alone or with their husbands to demand social change."[12]

Latina studies scholars have critiqued these male-centered analyses. Cultural studies critic Angie Chabram-Dernersesian analyzed the Chicano movement and concluded that Mexican American resistance to domination has been cast as male, and there is now "the necessity of altering the collective subject of Chicano movement discourse, of giving it a Chicana female presence."[13] Such is the case with both the Chicano and Mexican American civil rights movements.

Scholars speculated that if México Texanas did participate in politics before the 1970s, they did so in ladies auxiliaries. One researcher wrote that the auxiliary was "a social gathering for women to go drink coffee and get together."[14] Historian Martha Cotera reported that LULAC women had "a more subdued club woman reformist approach channeled through female auxiliary groups."[15] And theorist María Linda Apodaca argued that in organizations like LULAC, women "were only allowed to participate in an auxiliary capacity."[16] Even studies published in the 1990s and 2000s depict women in the 1920s and 1930s as either tokens or invisible.[17]

The construct of the apolitical Chicana has prevented scholars from seeing Chicanas as political actors. Political scientists Sierra and Sosa Riddell have pointed to the "narrow construction of analytical categories to explain political phenomena," and political scientist Carol Hardy-Fanta asks us to "challenge the invisibility of Latina women as political actors" and directs us to rethink their involvement.[18]

CONSTRUCTION OF THE SELF AS POLITICAL

In assessing the nature of México Texanas' participation in the 1920s and early 1930s it is important to see how women described their own involvement and contributions. Whether México Texanas saw themselves as part of the movement script and considered themselves "political," "activists," or "leaders" will be addressed.

Only Adela Sloss-Vento asserted herself as an "activist" of that era. At the age of seventy-five, she wrote *Alonso S. Perales, His Struggle for the Rights of Mexican Americans*. In 1927, as a recent high school graduate, she had read an essay in *El Fronterizo* of Rio Grande City by Alonso S. Perales and, as described earlier, was inspired to write him about her interest in the movement:

> I wrote immediately to Atty. Perales congratulating him for his efforts on our behalf. By return mail, I received a reply stating he wanted to meet me in his office . . . It was at this meeting that I became inspired to collaborate with our leaders in favor of our cause.[19]

Perales did not invite her to join his organization (League of Latin American Citizens) but may have encouraged her to take part in the movement.

We know of Sloss not because she left a collection in a library or wrote her memoirs, acts that suggest acknowledgment of self-importance; rather, we know of her because she wrote a book to honor a male leader. Her book is an effort to establish the lawyer's place in history as well as that of J. T. Canales and J. Luz Sáenz. Her intent was not, she wrote, "to develop extensive biographical data of other Mexican-Americans. Rather, it is my purpose to point out three early important and outstanding leaders who worked alone on behalf of our cause."[20] But they did not work alone. As early as 1931 Sloss promoted Perales and the cause.

Despite her intent to write about "our cause"—not "her" cause or "their" cause—she provided some information about herself though using an overt autobiographical voice only a few times. She recalled, "It was in 1927, when I became an enthusiastic collaborator on behalf of the cause of the Mexican American."[21] She offers a discourse of defense:

During the difficult days of 1927, I met Prof. J. Luz Sáenz through Lic. Alonso S. Perales. The Latin American people were victims of racial problems, exploitation, and other injustices. Long before they had already launched the difficult and noble struggle to defend justice and the rights for the Mexican American. Upon becoming acquainted with this noble cause it was evident that I should lend my help, along with many others of our cultural descent because this kind of help was necessary for the triumph of our progress and well-being.[22]

Sloss-Vento sought to "collaborate" and "lend" her "help" rather than lead. Collaborators and helpers are the majority in social movements. She called herself a "collaborator" and a "humble co-worker." Nor is she a self-conscious voice for women; she does not identify herself as a feminist, though her other writings and her life show otherwise.

While Sloss downplayed her own leadership, her contemporaries acknowledged it. As early as 1931, *La Prensa* called her "a well-known resident of the Rio Grande Valley in Texas." In the 1977 book Marta Pérez de Perales recognized Sloss' activism:

Mrs. Vento has been a collaborator since she was young. She's a brave woman and decided very early on to get to work. She too recognized that our community pleaded to bring forth justice. She did not hesitate to join the leaders [the men] so as to contribute to the monumental tasks at hand.[23]

And in 1977 activist Roberto Austin of Mission called Sloss-Vento a "Doña Josefa Ortiz de Domínguez of Texas," a reference to a heroine in México's struggle for independence. Sloss included these laudatory remarks in her book, perhaps as her subtle way of saying that she was indeed an activist and leader.[24]

Sloss was born on September 27, 1901, to Anselma Garza and David Sloss. Her mother was a midwife, *curandera* (medicinal healer), and "self-made woman who openly confronted men and difficult or dangerous situations."[25] A 1927 graduate of Pharr–San Juan–Alamo High School, her fellow graduates called her "brilliant" and "one of the smartest girls." Others said she was "willing to help everybody" and that she had "ambition and capacity for hard work."[26] She wanted to be a writer.[27] She worked as a secretary in the mayor's office, most likely in San Juan, Texas, around 1930, helping get rid

Adela Sloss-Vento, civil rights leader, San Juan, Texas, circa
1925. Courtesy Dr. Arnoldo Vento.

of the red-light district on the south side, the "Mexican" side of town. She
wrote letters to newspapers, gave speeches, and worked with the Good Government League to end corruption associated with the mayor's office. In
1931 she and Zacarías Gonzáles organized a benefit for the *Salvatierra v. Del
Rio Independent School District* lawsuit, LULAC's first desegregation case. In
1931 she wrote "L. Unida de Ciudadanos," for *El Paladín*, a LULAC newspaper. In 1932 for *LULAC News* she penned "Importancía de la Liga de
Ciudadanos Unidos Latino Americanos," which she wrote as a non-LULAC
member. In 1933 she founded or joined a ladies LULAC auxiliary in Alice.

In 1934 Sloss-Vento penned a feminist essay in *LULAC News*, "Porque
en muchos hogares latinos no existe verdadera felicidad" (Why No True
Happiness Exists in Many Latino Homes), a stinging critique of women's

subordination in the home.[28] She had no familial tie to any LULAC male member in the late 1920s and early 1930s. Later she married Pedro Vento and collaborated with her husband in political activism. All of these facts she omitted from her book.

Sloss' book should nonetheless be read as autobiography. Scholars Susan Groag Bell and Marilyn Yalom suggest that biographies can masquerade as autobiography.[29] Sloss' book is loosely ordered around a chronology of Texano activism in which she participated or about which she was well informed. She did not position herself as an actor in the movement script but did consider her contribution integral. She spoke of "we" and the collective La Raza.

Her movement discourse is similar to that of John Solís, who submerged himself to highlight the cause. Sloss' mention in her book that she had movement archives dated 1927 to 1960 signals her own involvement in La Raza's struggles. Like many women of her generation, she elaborated on the achievements and leadership of men but did not draw attention to herself, any individual women, or women as a group.[30] Sloss-Vento died on April 4, 1998, and the McAllen *Monitor* published a tribute to her,[31] apparently based on her son's essay, calling her "a founding member of LULAC." Although she was not a LULAC founder, she was a leader in this Mexican American civil rights movement.

Adelaida Garza and Carolina de Luna left evidence of their participation, although Garza left no papers and authored no memoirs or essays, other than a brief statement, describing her involvement in OSA or LULAC activities. In 1979, Texas LULAC director Rubén Bonilla asked her for a statement for a fiftieth-anniversary publication, and she wrote the following: "We as the wives of the members of LULAC were responsible for going to merchants and asking for donations of food and clothing for our needy people besides also helping our husbands when things weren't going right." She testified, "I have given the true history of the birth of LULAC, which I shared with my husband."[32] Besides these words we have no autobiographical voice from Garza.

University of Texas Mexican American studies librarian Elvira Chavira conducted an interview with Adelaida Garza but focused on Garza's husband, Ben. My interview with Adelaida, as well as scattered references in the LULAC archives, suggest that she did more than help her husband. She told me, "I was a witness to his suffering and disillusion," alluding to Ben's tribulations.[33]

But there is more to her story. She and the wife of José Stillman, also of Corpus Christi, solicited help from merchants to prepare baskets for 1,500 children. LULAC documents reveal that in 1931 the two women raised funds for the Salvatierra legal defense case. A 1931 photo of the annual LULAC convention shows Garza, Ofelia Wilmot, and other women attending an official meeting from which they, as women, were officially excluded. A 1947 *LULAC News* issue paid homage to Garza: "Mrs. Garza has always been a strong believer in the ideals of her husband and in the principles of LULAC. She has always been willing to contribute both time and money to the activities of Council No. 1." These activities occurred before and after her husband's death in 1937. Adelaida supported Ben, but the principles of LULAC were her own. She raised funds, gathered donations, organized, attended conventions, and supported desegregation.[34] When she died in 1987 she was not remembered as an activist but as a "wife."[35]

Carolina B. de Luna, the wife of Andrés de Luna Sr., left a similar self-construction. Her autobiographical voice was recorded in an oral history in 1973 by her nephew Richard Gutiérrez. She began, "My husband was always ready to fight high," and then she commented on his life and social conditions in Corpus Christi. She did not focus on her own involvement, and Gutiérrez did not ask her about it.[36] Nevertheless, his brother

Adelaida Carriles Garza (foreground) and family, 1941; photo of deceased husband, Ben, on mantle. Courtesy Ben Garza Jr.

Dr. Armando Gutiérrez told me that Carolina did much of Andrés' secretarial work. Whether she wrote his essays or speeches is not apparent in the Andrés de Luna Sr. Papers at the LULAC Archive.

These three self-constructions show that women may not fully reveal the nature or extent of their own activism. Latinas, single and married, have political ideologies and a corresponding praxis. Micaela Tafolla referred to "a willingness to serve."[37] Again, she asserted that her voluntarism was not abnegation but a readiness to help the collective of La Raza. Women were also particularly attentive to the social service needs of the community or benevolent politics. Adela Sloss-Vento, Adelaida Garza, and Carolina B. de Luna may not have called themselves political, activists, or leaders, but all advanced a movement.

WOMEN IN THE MEXICAN AMERICAN CIVIL RIGHTS MOVEMENT

Sociologist Joshua Gamson has explained inclusion and exclusion in social movements, noting that

> social movements depend on the active, ongoing construction of collective identity, and that deciding who we are requires deciding who we are not. All social movements, and identity movements in particular, are thus in the business, at least sometimes, of exclusion.[38]

Gamson contends that "identity required difference: building collective identities requires not simply pointing out commonalities but also marking who we are not."[39]

People—women as well as men—make social movements. Although many are unable or unwilling to join an organization, they are active in numerous ways. Women interfaced with the movement as individuals and as family members. Individuals who were single, married, or widowed connected to the movement because they supported movement ideology. Despite the male nature of the Mexican American civil rights movement, women struggled to forge their own identity around the movement. Women like Garza and de Luna interfaced with the movement through male family members and were drawn into a movement through personal connections.

Married women sustained the movement through the domestic or private front. Social scientist Linda Apodaca has referred to women "keeping the fire burning in the home and in the organization."[40] We must acknowledge the work that women performed in their homes that privileged men with leisure time to participate in politics. I asked Carolina Wilmot (married to Louis Wilmot) how she helped the OSA, and she responded, "We used to help our husbands." She added, "In those days we were busy with our children, the housework, and all of that."[41] Adelaida Garza told me, "I can hardly go with him [to organize] because when I wasn't expecting [a child], I was raising [children]. He went by himself."[42] Indeed, some women were in the midst of their child-bearing and child-rearing years. When the Alpha Club formed in Corpus Christi, five members were expecting children. "In that time, we was all with kids," Garza recalled. When the club was busy collecting Christmas donations, she continued, "I had to pay babysitters. And we started at one until five to have supper . . . to fix supper. And we [would] get some donations and go to the warehouses and ask if they could help us with apples, peanuts. We would do it." Likewise, the wife of Alonso S. Perales, Marta Engracia Pérez de Perales, was hardly seen on the public front of civil rights work. She belonged to the Pan American Round Table, a racially mixed club. But mostly she cared for Alonso and the home.[43] Women were responsible for children, men, meals, and the housework and still managed to contribute to the movement.

Women found ways to participate as nonmembers. They attended the 1929 constitutional convention, and the 1930 annual convention drew about one hundred men and twenty women including Adelaida Garza, Ofelia Wilmot, Manuelita Galván, Josefa Bravo, Celia Guerra, Lupita Barrera Guerra, and Hilda Guerra, the last four apparently single.[44] Were they there as individuals, as supportive wives, independent wives, family members, club women, or some combination of these identities? Were these women there

Women and men attending second LULAC convention, in Alice, Texas, 1930. Courtesy Carlota C. Ballí Collection, Hidalgo County Historical Museum.

as helpers, collaborators, or activists and how might we define these terms? While each individual's motivations and political consciousness needs to be understood, it is clear that women believed in, supported, and sustained a movement, even without membership in LULAC.

WOMEN'S PARTICIPATION IN ORGANIZATIONS

After 1929 there were still other ways women expressed concern for the movement. They took part in organizations such as women's clubs, ladies auxiliaries, and Ladies LULAC.[45] Women formed the Alpha Club of Corpus Christi around November 1929. Members included Adelaida Garza, Carolina de Luna, and Ofelia Wilmot. Garza insisted that the Alpha Club "had nothing to do with LULAC" (*No tenía nada que ver con LULAC*). Records reveal that in 1929 the Alpha Club formed a women's philanthropic group and held a joint meeting with LULAC Council No. 1 to plan Christmas fund-raising.[46]

In San Antonio, several women's clubs were active in the cause. A 1931 *LULAC News* issue referred to them as "helpers of our cause." In August, Club Talia was thanked for its "wholehearted co-operation in various events"; in November, Club Femenino Orquídea gave fifteen dollars of its dance proceeds to LULAC; and in December, the Modern Maids Social Club served as "ushers at the open house meeting of the Convention." In February 1932, *LULAC News* noted that "the 'Lucky Star' [women's club] is through her well timed leadership a strong, sincere and helpful friend of LULAC . . . We need helpers for our cause and these 'Lucky-Stars' have answered our call."[47]

In 1931 women formed ladies auxiliaries in LULAC that met for about a year in Texas. A *Feminist Dictionary* refers to "ladies" as "the well-adjusted woman in a patriarchal society," an "ideal of femininity," and "women who seem to stay in their male-defined place." "Ladies" was the English translation of *señoras* and *señoritas*, but American and Mexican culture and politics also designated women's place and behavior and feminine ideals.[48]

Ladies auxiliaries have been denigrated in history. Scholar and Catholic nun Jerome Woods, for instance, commented about them in the late 1940s: "Some ethnic associations have women's auxiliaries, but the accomplishments of these groups are meager in contrast with the men's groups." Ladies auxiliaries should not be judged by present standards. The inclusion of women in organizational life is political, even in ladies auxiliaries. As historical sociologist Mary Ann Clawson has shown, "the right of women to associate with each other" in public associations was a step in women's empowerment.[49] By the 1920s it was common for Mexican-origin women to join mutual aid associations, and by the 1930s separate women's clubs were typical.[50]

Ladies auxiliaries to LULAC follow traditions in Western civilization. In Rome under Emperor Augustus' rule after 27 BCE, there were three units of the army—the Praetorian guard (the elite corps), the Roman legions, and the third unit, the auxiliaries. Auxiliary members had to enlist in the army for twenty-five years before they could obtain the promise of Roman citizenship at the end of their service. Likewise, women joined ladies auxiliaries for a few years before becoming full members of LULAC.

San Antonio, Alice, and Kingsville women established auxiliaries. Corpus Christi women never organized one and continued to participate in the Alpha Club. The San Antonio auxiliary was formed in September 1931 with Spanish teacher Ester Pérez Carvajal presiding; members included Cornelia (Mrs. M. C.) Gonzáles, the wife of Frank Leytón, Susie Herrera, Bertha Cadena, and even the young Emma Tenayuca, later the famous pecan-shell strike labor organizer and communist. Scholars have been largely unaware of teenager Tenayuca's involvement in or with the auxiliary.[51]

This auxiliary sponsored a musical and literary event that two hundred people attended. Ester Pérez Carvajal gave an "interesting" address, touching upon the work that women must perform in carrying on the aims and principles of the league. In October 1931 *LULAC News* reported, "The ideas were clearly stated and denoted the clear conception that our sister organization has of the things that LULAC stands for." No further content was reported. Tenayuca addressed the event; her presentation was titled "I Am an American."[52] The content of the speech is not available. Young Tenayuca probably expressed LULAC ideology and was not yet a communist.

In M. C. Gonzáles' "major" address, he spoke of LULAC's significance, the auxiliary, and Parent-Teacher Associations. A month later, the auxiliary and LULAC Council No. 2 of San Antonio organized a parents advisory council at Sidney Lanier School in San Antonio. Council No. 2 men did not value the contribution of ladies auxiliaries enough to organize them. In an April 1933 speech before the Travis County Missionary Women, Gonzáles told the (presumably white) members, "In every place where we go, we organize the men into LULAC Councils and the women into a Parent-Teachers-Association in San Antonio, we have organized some 8 or 9 PTAs."[53] In the 1920s and 1930s, PTAs were women's domain. European American women, many who disliked "Mexicans," controlled the PTAs; meetings were held in English. But by the late 1920s, La Raza had begun founding Spanish-speaking PTAs that were recognized by the Texas Congress of Parents and Teachers in 1927, and Mexican-origin women predominated in these.

The Alice auxiliary appeared in April 1933 with twenty-two members, fourteen married and eight single women including Sloss. According to *LULAC News*, "Special Organizer" J. Luz Sáenz helped organize it, but perhaps Sloss was the real organizer. In May 1933 LULAC men in Kingsville established an auxiliary that was active until March 1934, when it merged with the Parent-Teacher Association, possibly the Spanish-speaking PTA. In 1933 the Stephen F. Austin PTA in Kingsville had thirty members, with Señora A. G. Treviño presiding, Mrs. J. Scarborough as secretary, and Mrs. E. Hernández as treasurer. The PTA bought trees; planted gardens; purchased a piano, a Victrola, and an encyclopedia set; and opened a cafeteria for poor children.[54]

A third way women organized was through Ladies LULAC chapters, official LULAC chapters for women, which replaced ladies auxiliaries after 1933. On May 7, 1933, Joe V. Alamia and J. M. Canales of Edinburg submitted a resolution "permitting Latin American women to organize on the same basis as men and to be known as Ladies LULAC Councils . . . [The women's chapters] are to have equal representation with men['s] councils at all conventions."[55] Alamia had been a member of the League of Latin American Citizens in 1927. It is unclear if women or men or both initiated the Ladies LULAC concept. What is clear is that men could not organize women without their consent, and women were already making contributions to the organizations and movement. From 1933 to the mid-1960s, women participated in LULAC largely through these women-only chapters.

It may not have even been women's voluntary association work that spurred the development of Ladies LULAC. In May 1932 a Latin American Democratic Women (LADW) organization took shape in the Valley. According to historian Gilberto Quezada, politician Manuel Bravo helped other prominent Texano party leaders organize the club. Yet, we should not doubt women's agency and should question whether it was Manuel Bravo who was organizing the club. His wife attended the 1930 LULAC convention in Alice and was LADW's reporter.[56] Thus, women already involved in LULAC circles may have initiated the LADW and Ladies LULAC. Through women's clubs, ladies auxiliaries, and Ladies LULAC, women advanced the movement.

WOMEN'S SEGREGATION AS EXCLUSION, DIFFERENCE, OR STRATEGY?

Now that it is clear that women were involved in civil rights work, let us focus on the issue of gender exclusion and segregation. Social movements are based on "the ongoing construction of collective identity" and thus on inclusion and exclusion.[57] As suggested earlier, male homosociality and fraternalism were central to this movement's formation. At the same time, male culture and the boundaries men constructed provided "messages of inclusion" for men and "messages of exclusion" for women. Yet, male leaders did not have a monolithic position on women's place and participation. Sociologist Joshua Gamson argues that "all social movements, and identity movements in particular, are thus in the business, at least sometimes, of exclusion." Group boundaries, he suggests, are constantly being negotiated.[58] So this exclusion was not fixed, permanent, or without resistance.

Women's clubs, ladies auxiliaries, and Ladies LULAC had independent agendas from those of men's organizations. Ladies auxiliaries were connected to men's groups, while Ladies LULAC signified a "significant reevaluation of women's capacity for self-government and public competence."[59]

An important question to ask is whether these women's groups existed simply because men excluded the women. They were an affirmation of LULAC's masculine character. The auxiliary reproduced male dominance but also was a step toward women's political empowerment.[60] Women simply wanted to be with their own kind, to be homosocial.[61] Women had a different approach to politics. Or was female segregation a strategy on the part of women to empower themselves, a kind of feminist separatism?

The issue of separate councils is a complex one. In assessing the issue, it is important to understand women's relations to one another and their relations to men. In "permitting" women to join in segregated chapters, men excluded women from their own chapters. In a conversation I had with Tenayuca in the 1980s, she asked me to "ask them [the men] why women weren't allowed in the organization."[62] Besides sexism, women's class status made them less desirable members. They were less educated. México Texanos commonly believed European American men in power would take Mexican American women less seriously.

Men also excluded women because they believed women's proper roles were as wives and mothers. In 1931 member J. Reynolds Flores wrote "How to Educate Our Girls" for *LULAC News*, in which he stated,

> The foundation of society rests on its homes. The success of our homes rests on the wives. Therefore, first of all, teach our girls how to be successful wives . . . Teach them the value of making themselves attractive by good health, physical development, neat dress, and perfect cleanliness.[63]

Sloss condemned this kind of thinking. In an essay on domestic life she commented that prescriptive behavior for women was "a perpetual chain of suffering" and that "Latino men have all the privileges and rights."[64]

Men and women may have recognized gendered differences in political activity. While women supported and participated in civil rights activism, they tended to be more active in beneficent politics. Historian Gabriela González has discussed this "politics of benevolence."[65] OSA and LULAC men were active in charity, but this was more a female endeavor. The Alpha Club focused on beneficent activism. Political scientist Hardy-Fanta might ask of this female involvement if it is volunteer work, social work, or politics and whether we should consider this activism a lesser form of politics.[66]

Historian Blanche Wiesen Cook has argued that women's groups are networks of support women needed to conduct political work,[67] and one might ask if that was the case in these organizations. Were they a strategy for female institution building and what historian Estelle Freedman called "separatism as strategy"?[68] Segregated chapters let women define their own politics, free of male domination and sexual harassment from men.

Ladies LULAC was not an attempt at "feminist separatism." Scholar Marilyn Frye has defined feminist separatism as

separatism of various modes from men and from institutions, relationships, roles, and activities which are male-defined, male-dominated, and operating for the benefit of males and the maintenance of male privilege—this separation being initiated or maintained at will by women.[69]

Separatism implies a feminist consciousness that the majority of LULAC women did not have. LULAC feminist Alice Dickerson Montemayor, active from 1938 to 1940, criticized machismo and sexist practices in LULAC in 1938 and said in 1984 that LULAC men "had no use for us."[70] But she never criticized the practice of segregated men's and women's councils. Acknowledging conflict between women and men, she did not argue for integration except for the youth councils she established in 1938.[71]

Most Mexican-descent women did not have feminist consciousness in these decades. Ladies LULAC as a separate institution was not a conscious plan or strategy for women's empowerment. Nonetheless, such organizations gave women political space and experience. They can be regarded as having permitted male authority and fraternalism to go unchallenged, leaving the "woman citizen" suspect, or they can be seen to have emerged because women had conflicts with men over their emerging participation.[72]

GENDER, CITIZENSHIP, NATION, EMPOWERMENT, AND LULAC

LULAC's initial method of mobilization was to organize Mexican American men to realize its goal, La Raza's political empowerment. Because of patriarchal thinking, most middle-class México Texanos were only able to think of organizing men. Most believed women should stay at home or join sister organizations such as women's clubs, ladies auxiliaries, Ladies LULAC, or Spanish-speaking PTAs. For instance, in 1931 Alonso S. Perales wrote,

> It is indispensable to undertake a formidable civic instruction campaign among the male element as among the female element. Also, we should impart civic instruction among the Mexican American female element. In this way we can considerably augment the number of Mexican American voters and consequently our political strength will be felt. In San Antonio there is already a League of Women Voters whose goal is to encourage women to exercise the privileges that have just taken effect in the body politic of this country [women's right to vote] and to show them how to vote intelligently. Mexican American women should join said League or form a society of Latin American women voters. Mexican American women's vote is indispensable if we want to improve our political situation in Texas.[73]

Perales did not argue for women's inclusion into LULAC and instead advocated that México Texanas join women's organizations. He mentioned how women might empower La Raza, but he did not work to include women in LULAC. Moreover, how women themselves might empower women or men he did not consider. He encouraged women to work with women and saw LULAC as the work of men. In 1982 Tenayuca told me, "So intense was this group's desire to achieve recognition as American citizens that they limited their membership to men and only men who were citizens."[74] Thus while Mexican American men were seeking to end their second-class citizenship, Mexican American women citizens were relegated to third-class citizenship.

Two women argued for women's inclusion as part of the goal of Raza empowerment. Before she became a communist, young Emma Tenayuca's vision of political empowerment was the LULAC path, a middle-class path.

Emma Tenayuca, ladies auxiliary member (as a teenager) and LULAC critic, August 1939. Courtesy San Antonio Light Collection, Institute of Texan Cultures, University of Texas, and donated by Hearst Corporation.

She was born on December 21, 1916, of the Cepeda family that settled during the Spanish colonial period. Her father was a Native American, but of which nation or tribe is unclear. Her grandparents raised her. When she was a teenager, family members, books, and oratory at the San Antonio mercado exposed her to politics,[75] and as a Mexican American teenager she was unable to resist the lure of LULAC. Her participation signifies how important LULAC was to Mexican American empowerment in Texas.[76]

Around the age of fifteen Tenayuca participated in or with the LULAC ladies auxiliary in San Antonio. Tenayuca said she was a member. As mentioned, the content of her public address "I Am an American" at the ladies' function is not available, and thus we could assume that she exhorted U.S. nationalist and assimilationist themes. Historians Richard García, Neil Foley, and Julia Kirk Blackwelder have used Tenayuca to create a binary political stance between working-class radicalism and middle-class conservativism.

According to Foley, she "resisted the lure of whiteness" (i.e., LULAC).[77] These scholars were not aware of her brief LULAC connection as a teenager.[78]

Before graduating high school in 1934, Tenayuca participated in a reading circle that must have radicalized her. In 1932–1933 she joined the Finck Cigar Company strikers and became a labor activist. In the post-1935 era as a young adult, Tenayuca adopted a strategy for the political empowerment of La Raza that was more working-class and pro-immigrant, with women playing a greater role. She became a leader in workers' struggles, a communist, and an internationalist. In 1939 she co-authored an essay with her husband, Homer Brooks, titled "The Mexican Question in the Southwest."

Presenting an analysis of race, class, citizenship, and nation, "The Mexican Question" raised questions about the path to empowerment for La Raza; however, Tenayuca and Brooks did not address women's gendered political empowerment. The essay alluded to whether La Raza constituted a nation. The authors paid significant attention to LULAC, particularly in a section titled "Sterile Paths." Even as communists they wrote,

> In the past, its [LULAC's] viewpoint was colored by the outlook of petit-bourgeois native-born, who seek escape from the general oppression that has been the lot of the Mexican people as a whole. It meant an attempt to achieve Americanization, while barring the still unnaturalized foreign-born from membership.[79]

But in the same essay they added,

> In Texas they have led successful struggles against segregation in public schools, parks, etc., not only in behalf of American citizens, but of all Mexicans. . . . [T]his important organization of the Mexican middle class will play an increasing role in the general movement for Mexican rights.[80]

A "sterile path"? No. Benefiting "all" Mexicans in the United States? Yes.

As a senior citizen in the 1980s Tenayuca, my friend, was still critical of LULAC and its vision of political empowerment. In 1982 Tenayuca argued that in excluding Mexicans LULAC "succeeded in dividing the Mexican population of Texas, leaving all who were residents without any representation . . . Few of the many who were citizens could afford the poll-tax, and many refused to deny their language and cultural heritage."[81] But the Mexican-descent people were already divided by national citizenship, and bilingualism was a political necessity. In 1982 Tenayuca was also more critical of LULAC for its lack of empowerment of the Mexican-origin women's community; it is then that she asked me to ask LULAC why it was segregated by gender. Still, in the 1980s she recognized LULAC's significance.

Another political activist, María Latigo de Hernández, also interfaced with LULAC and its plan of political empowerment for La Raza. She was born in Mexico in 1896. Her father was a professor of history and language, and her mother from a prominent military family. She was interning as a teacher in Monterrey, Mexico, when the Mexican Revolution began, and her family moved to Texas when she was seventeen. In 1915 she married Pedro Hernández of Hebbronville, Texas. They moved to San Antonio in 1918 and opened a grocery and bakery in 1928.[82]

Hernández gave birth to ten children and initiated her activism. In the early 1920s she had obtained a midwifery license and started a preschool for young children. In 1929 she and her husband, Pedro, founded the Orden Caballeros de América (not to be confused with the OKA founded in 1927), perhaps as an alternative to LULAC. This civic and "fraternal" organization of San Antonio included men and women and promoted civic activism and mutualista ethics among both Mexican Americans and Mexicans. The Hernándezes believed in La Raza and women's equality and leadership. Her husband, Pedro B. Hernández, said LULAC "didn't have what I mostly was interested in, fraternal and civic activity for both sexes. Other groups exclude their women or form auxiliary women's groups. In my view, the sexes are different but equal in their rights."[83]

At the same time Hernández was also involved in some seemingly women-only efforts in the 1930s. She joined male LULACers in giving speeches at community affairs. Hernández and Tenayuca both challenged the idea of Raza political empowerment through male homosocial organization.[84]

Hernández considered herself an *hija de México* (daughter of Mexico), although she became a U.S. citizen when she married Pedro. She maintained Mexicanist sentiments but was an active U.S. citizen. In 1945 she wrote, *Yo vivo la realidad de la vida de México y estoy orgullosa de ser Mexicano* (I live the reality of the life of Mexico and I'm proud of being Mexican). She promoted many of the same issues as LULAC; furthermore, she advocated social citizenship and activism by the woman citizen and the Mexican immigrant citizen.

In 1945 Perales recognized María and Pedro Hernández as *luchadores, siempre activos, honrados, entusiásticos y sinceros* (fighters, always active, honored, enthusiastic, and sincere).[85] In the 1930s and 1940s, she helped form

María L. de Hernández, LULAC ally and critic, circa 1970s.
Courtesy Nettie Lee Benson Latin American Collection,
University of Texas.

an organization for pregnant mothers, fought illiteracy, was the first Mexican woman radio commentator in Texas, and worked with the Liga Defensa
Pro-Escolar, a San Antonio pro-Raza school organization.

In 1945 Hernández published a booklet of more than thirty pages titled
"México y los cuatro poderes que dirigen el pueblo" (Mexico and the Four
Powers That Guide the People). Those four powers were politics, business,
religion, and society. She asked readers to take greater interest in politics
because the future civic, social, and material welfare of the community lay
there. She identified illiteracy as a particular problem. Regarding society as
a power, she pointed to mothers and the home as critical points of education.

She and her husband raised ten children. In the 1970s she campaigned for Raza Unida candidates.

Hernández became a U.S. citizen but still espoused Mexican nationalism:

> I have sustained a tireless civic-social fight for twenty years in this great nation, . . . [but] Mexico is my base of inspiration because I was born there, because I'm Mexican by blood, because a broad intuitive vision makes me live in Mexico.[86]

Hernández rejected both LULAC's and Tenayuca's agendas for political empowerment when she defined La Raza's "nation" as inclusive of Mexico. Her analysis was transnational because Mexico was her homeland. Her vision was called "Pan American" by one writer.[87] Tenayuca, on the other hand, was international in her class analysis but paid specific attention to La Raza in the United States. Both Hernández and Tenayuca contested how LULAC defined the Raza community and nation.[88] Still, neither fully addressed women's empowerment.

How would women have shaped the discourse about Raza empowerment, citizenship, and nation if they had been allowed in the 1920s? Would they have included themselves at the Harlingen convention? Sloss-Vento considered the exclusion of Mexican immigrants necessary.[89] Would Adelaida Garza and Carolina B. de Luna's Mexican American consciousness have led them to exclude Mexican immigrants? Probably. But their beneficent activism made no distinction between serving Mexican Americans and Mexicans.

Women and immigrants become "illegal aliens" on the grounds of participatory democracy and in the LULAC mind.[90] If Mexican American men were second-class citizens, then Mexican American women and Mexican immigrant men were third-class and Mexican immigrant women fourth-class citizens. How could Raza empowerment happen without their full inclusion? Despite the promptings by Sloss-Vento, Montemayor, Tenayuca, and Hernández, this question would not be fully addressed until the 1970s when a Chicana feminist movement emerged.

CONCLUSION

If LULAC had founding fathers, it also had mothers who engaged in resistance to racism. Scholars focusing on male leaders and politics have often rendered women invisible, creating the apolitical, submissive Chicana.

True, women's self-perceptions have at times misled researchers—it is not unusual for women of earlier generations to downplay their own activism as well as women's in general. They have instead advanced the collective and/ or men—not themselves or women.

Nevertheless, women participated in a social movement in various ways. Wives served the movement when they gave husbands the luxury of political activism. Few were woman warriors like Sloss; it was more typical for women to make punch than to throw a punch. Many participated in ladies auxiliaries. We need to pay attention to Emma Tenayuca when she was connected to the ladies auxiliary, not just to the Communist Party. Women's activism in all its facets must be respected.

As nonmembers of men's clubs such as the OSA, OKA, and LULAC, women began to contest membership requirements. They did so in individual and collective ways as collaborators, helpers, and leaders. They interfaced with the movement as individuals and family members. Women organized in women's clubs, ladies auxiliaries, and Ladies LULAC. Ladies auxiliaries were a female-defined political entity that did not simply meet the needs of men. Women recognized LULAC's worth even if men had not fully recognized women's worth. The auxiliary has typically been seen as a method for women to serve men. As auxiliary members, women too became soldier-citizens in the war against racism; they received partial citizenship within LULAC a year or two later when Ladies LULAC was created. Full citizenship in LULAC was still forthcoming.[91]

Women and men renegotiated gender boundaries in 1933 when they officially established Ladies LULAC. While *LULAC News* reported that women were "permitted," women had already contested membership. But both men and women wanted women to have a homosocial space. Men wanted fraternal clubs, and women enjoyed women-only company. Moreover, women's politics were different from men's, tending to include more beneficent politics.

Not all women of the 1920s and 1930s were happy with gender segregation. Emma Tenayuca and María L. de Hernández were critical of this separatism. For them, this segregation did not help empower La Raza, and they did not agree with LULAC men's strategy of political empowerment. Tenayuca thought of the working class and immigrants. And Hernández had a different notion of who constituted the nation of La Raza since she could not forget Mexico.

LULAC men, however, failed to recognize that women were half of La Raza and could organize and vote. Mexican American men contended that

Mexican American unity needed to be forged around brotherhood, middle-class status, and U.S. citizenship. It is unclear whether México Texanas, had they been present in Harlingen, would have permitted Mexican immigrants, including Mexican immigrant women.

My study concurs with M. Bahati Kuumba's research on gender and social movements. There were gendered structures, gender ideologies, gendered symbols, gendered divisions of labor, gender differentiated recruitment processes, gender parallel structures (versus integrated), and gender independent roles, all of which I discovered before reading Kuumba's excellent book.[92]

Today women constitute more than half the official LULAC membership.[93] Texas LULAC elected its first woman state LULAC director in 1969 and the second in 1988. LULAC selected its first national woman president in 1994 and the second in 2006. Whether or not women's empowerment is found in mixed-gender organizations is the subject of future research. Today we know that women also sought to remove "No Mexicans Allowed" signs. Women ignored the "No women allowed" messages and, like men, gave labor, thought, time, energy, and money; they too initiated a Mexican American civil rights movement in defense of La Raza.

CONCLUSION

The OSA and LULAC emerged in a society in flux and signaled the rise of the Mexican American civil rights movement in the 1920s. This movement resulted from the rise of the México Texano male middle class in San Antonio, Corpus Christi, Alice, and the Lower Rio Grande Valley. As twentieth-century society took shape amid urbanization and industrialization, a new identity and politics were being forged as early as the 1910s, especially in the 1920s, and less so in the 1930s.[1]

RACIAL FORMATION, HYBRIDITY, AND IDENTITY

Many members of La Raza had been citizens of the United States since 1848, but not until the twentieth century would a significant sector become true hybrids—Mexican and American. Citizen factories (public schools) and military service fostered a hybridity that now fostered more Americanness. The Mexican American male middle class of the 1920s was the first truly bilingual, bicultural sector, and its members consciously asserted citizenship in the United States.

The hybrid México Texano was constructed by European Americans, Mexican Americans, and Mexicans. The dominant society's evolving, shifting, and contradictory relationship with La Raza encompassed segregation and assimilation. European Americans fostered assimilation through the Americanization movement and English-only standards.

On the other hand, European Americans hindered incorporation of La

Raza. Whites made La Raza an "other" by institutionalizing racial segregation, constructing "the Mexican problem," and establishing the Border Patrol. They racialized La Raza by reemphasizing the construct called the "Mexican race." Likewise, they sought to homogenize La Raza by failing to acknowledge citizenship within the Mexican-origin community, calling all of La Raza "Mexican." "Mexican" was part of the dominant society's racial discourse used to disempower; it was synonymous with "alien," "noncitizen," and "un-American."

Racial formation was evolving in contradictory ways. While the dominant society fostered Mexican Americanization, European Americans also limited the meaning of "white" to themselves. The 1930 U.S. Census referred to a "Mexican race" for the first time, excluding La Raza from the category "white." At the same time, Mexican Americans took an active role in forming this "new race" as their own, not biologically but by constructing this identity and politics in a relational way with European Americans and Mexicans from Mexico as major points of reference. Both European Americans and Mexicans resisted change and were uncomfortable with this new construction. Mexican immigrants complained and protested when Mexican Americans began to emerge as a new sector within La Raza.

Mexican Americans embraced this new ethnic and national identity. "Mexican American" was not yet part of European American discourse; European Americans did not invent the term nor promote it. Middle-class México Texanos found that it accurately described their hybridity. Latino scholar Félix Padilla has noted, "Ethnic identity is not fixed and can constitute a strategy to attain the needs and wants of the group."[2] Indeed, México Texanos found it necessary to affirm their Americanness by acknowledging their U.S. citizenship to move European Americans away from their practices of racialization.

This new identity, proclaimed and acted out through the OSA and LULAC, challenged the binary, either/or identities of "Americans" versus "Mexicans." Activists sought to broaden and complicate these narrow categories so as to demand acceptance and respect for hybridity, and Mexican Americans more specifically sought to establish their difference from Mexicans in the United States. There was no one Mexican culture in the United States. Mexican Americans tried to convince Mexicans in the United States that the empowerment of La Raza was connected to citizenship, national and social. Both European Americans and Mexicanist Mexicans would be slow to accept plurality and difference.

The OSA and LULAC took pride in pointing to their Americanism. They claimed the privileges of U.S. citizenship and challenged the ways whites had appropriated the names "Americans" and "citizens" for themselves. In the public European American world, the OSA and LULAC abandoned an identity as Mexicans in order to pursue the benefits of identifying with "Americans."

Activists did not single out the term "Mexican American" only to identify themselves. Rather, they chose multiple identities, referring to themselves not only as Mexican Americans, but also as Mexicans, Americans, México Texanos, Spanish, Latin American, and La Raza. They did so because they had a hybrid, multicultural, multinational past and present. They saw themselves as both Americans and Mexicans. When they referred to themselves as "Americans," they acknowledged their place in U.S. society and their national origin and resisted European American racialization. When they referred to themselves as "Mexicans," they acknowledged their racial, ethnic, and national origin and identities.

The appearance of "Latin American" in LULAC's name reflected the influence of lawyer and diplomat Alonso S. Perales. It was a euphemism for "Mexican," but it was more than that. By selecting "Latin American," members did not simply attempt to "arrogate to themselves the privileges of whiteness."[3] In fact, the use of "Latin American" tied them to their *hispanidad* and Spanishness. Most México Texanos were Spanish-dominant and read Spanish-language newspapers.

Nor did the organizations deny their Mexican identity. "Mexican" was only one identity. Among friendly company, OSA and LULAC members continued to call themselves "Mexican."[4] But European Americans had stained the label. Moreover, Mexican Americans had to be true to their new identity. Both European Americans and Mexican immigrants in the United States sought to essentialize them. Mexican nationalists in the United States were hesitant to recognize new cultural and political realities, appealing instead to static and nostalgic ideas of Mexicanness and Mexican nationalism. OSA and LULAC members were pro-Raza. They did not respond to a fear that new immigrants would outnumber Mexican Americans, nor were they anti-Mexican.[5] And they did not see "Mexican immigrants as an obstacle to gaining 'Whiteness.'"[6]

México Texanos broke with Mexicans because they were different. The middle-class México Texanos were becoming more bilingual, while working-class México Texanas/os and recent immigrants were mostly Spanish monolinguals. Because the dominant society acknowledged only English, LULAC named English its official language. However, LULAC never engaged in an English-only campaign. LULAC recognized English as a tool of defense as well as a tool for individual and group empowerment. In the 1920s the promotion of English among La Raza was actually an argument for bilingualism.

The OSA and LULAC operated in a Spanish-dominant cultural milieu. The LULAC constitution was originally written in Spanish; the OSA, LACL, and LULAC constitutions were printed in Spanish, English, or some combination thereof. Moreover, LULAC reported its activities to the Spanish-language press.

CITIZENSHIP, NATIONALISM, AND TRANSNATIONALISM

The OSA and LULAC seemingly broke with ethnic and national solidarity and privileged their own citizenship status. The exclusion of Mexican immigrants was, in part, a class distinction. Yet, the organizations were pro-Raza. The OKA and the Alice OSA permitted Mexican immigrants. Again, the OSA was not a response to the fear that new immigrants would take over. LULAC even permitted a few Mexican citizens such as Dr. Carlos Castañeda to participate in its activities. LULAC undertook pro-Raza activism.

Citizenship became a foundation for a new Mexican American identity and politics. Mexican Americans were quick to note that European Americans appropriated the name "American citizen" and relegated México Texanos to a second class. Mexican Americans embraced their U.S. citizenship after World War I and the founding of the Border Patrol. Citizenship was part of their strategy to obtain rights, social justice, and empowerment for La Raza. They used national citizenship to point to their Americanness and social citizenship to advance their cause.

Using their U.S. citizenship, Mexican Americans had to construct a new nationalism—a hybrid nationalism—based on Mexican nationalism, U.S. nationalism, as well as a nationalism that concerned itself with the Raza nation in the United States. This nationalism had to compete with the dominant nationalism in the Mexican-origin community in the United States—Mexican nationalism.

European Americans questioned the loyalty of La Raza as U.S. citizens and could not comprehend the binational, transnational, or multinational context in which most of La Raza operated. When México Texano veterans returned from the war, they were confronted by the contradictions of fighting for a "democracy" that discriminated against them at home.[7] This contradiction in U.S. citizenship led them to action. Ex-servicemen, among others, formed civil rights organizations. Rejecting the mutual aid society as the organizational prototype to battle racial oppression, México Texanos initiated a civil rights movement in the midst of a repressive racial order.

At the same time, México Texanos recognized their unique nationalism. Not only were they citizens of the United States, they were also citizens of the Raza nation. Consequently, they could move between the nations of the United States and La Raza. Mexico was part of their nation, not as a state or government but because La Raza moved back and forth culturally between Mexico and the United States.

CLASS

This movement reflected the politics of the México Texano male middle class. This middle class differed from that of European Americans. Professionals in most cities or towns could be counted on a hand or two. It is misleading to refer to this middle class as "educated Mexicans."[8] Only some of the leaders had attended college; most did not complete high school. Secretaries of the Corpus Christi and Alice OSA councils, for instance, revealed limited writing proficiency in English or Spanish.

Despite the organizations' class composition, members were not alienated from working-class interests and needs. The OSA's and LULAC's strategy went beyond calling for an expanded middle class.[9] The OSA addressed issues that cut across class lines and affected all persons of Mexican origin. It did not take up "class-specific" protests per se.[10] Contrary to one assessment that "many of the successes achieved by these middle-class efforts did not challenge the rule of discrimination," the OSA's and LULAC's objective was to battle racism.[11] Collective interests, not self-interest, ruled their actions.

The OSA was sensitive to working-class interests because most of its leadership constituted a first-generation middle class. Most grew up working-class. The OSA collaborated with mutual aid societies, to which many working-class members belonged, and some OSA members belonged to mutualistas. The OSA sympathized with the working poor but fell short of solidarity with unions or the working class itself. The OSA constitution voiced numerous working-class interests, and middle-class members pledged to abide by this constitution.

The OSA and LULAC acted on issues important to the Raza working class. The OSA's constitution referred to child labor and exploitative wages but did not focus on these issues. Nevertheless, the Corpus Christi OSA took up the case of an exploited tenant, and the San Antonio chapter paid for legal defense. The councils, the OKA, and women also got involved in benevolence toward the poor.

The OSA was more concerned with the majority than its own class privilege, as shown by its focus on education. The OSA sought to improve the lot of the working class by desegregating schools at the primary grades in local school districts where the majority of Raza children were. The OSA and LULAC did not identify student recruitment at Texas colleges as an issue, nor did they place their efforts there.[12] Later, in the 1930s, they created a college scholarship. Both groups were born into a Mexicanist culture fostering mutuality, social responsibility, and defense of their "race."

Nor was this middle class exempt from racism because of class privilege.[13] Biographies reveal that all the leaders, even wealthy J. T. Canales, were personally affected by discrimination.

POLITICS

The Mexican American middle class organized a new politics in the Raza community in the 1910–1930 era. This new organizational type shifted away from the mutualista and toward leadership by the male middle class. This shift also meant a different emphasis on community that hindered the inclusion of Mexicans and women. Even by 2007 historian Rodolfo Acuña conceded, "In fairness to LULAC founders, they were expressing the common sense of the era of the time."[14]

The new politics sought independence from the Mexican consulate. México Texanos acknowledged the consulate's limited ability to protect either Mexicans or Mexican Americans, although some still argued that the consul did offer immigrants limited protection. The civil rights associations collaborated with the consuls. The OSA and LULAC sought to harness the emerging political power of the Mexican American electorate. They sought to wrest the "Mexican" vote from bosses and machines, and they battled Progressives who launched campaigns on independent México Texano voters by racializing the vote. The organizations sponsored lectures promoting the vote, poll tax, and civic duty.

Intellectuals like Alonso S. Perales outlined the vote as a cornerstone of the new politics. Mexicans could no longer vote in Texas after 1927. And while the electorate included women, the OSA's and LULAC's patriarchal ideology prevented them from mobilizing México Texana voters. Class barriers such as the poll tax, education, proficiency in English, and residency requirements limited the franchise. But over time the vote would prove a vehicle for reform.

RESISTANCE, ADAPTATION, AND WHITENESS

The new organizations would not acquiesce to the subordination of La Raza and criticized La Raza's colonized status. They questioned white privilege, rejected second-class citizenship, asserted first-class citizenship, and denounced the appropriation of the term "American" by European Americans. Moreover, comfortable in their new hybrid identity, members fought against the dominant discourse about La Raza, the racialization of La Raza, and "the Mexican problem."

The OSA and LULAC resisted racial oppression. The OSA fought jury exclusion, the institutionalization of segregated schools, segregated public accommodations, and the racist misadministration of justice. The OSA in Alice expressed concern over the lack of Spanish-speaking teachers and of the teaching of Spanish. Both organizations emerged from a Mexicanist tradition, a heritage of "protection" and "defense" of La Raza.

Their strategy was also to appeal to European American elected officials and individual citizens on the basis of a shared U.S. national citizenship, social citizenship, middle-class status, and English language. Many European Americans viewed Mexicans as "aliens," considered U.S. citizens superior to citizens of Mexico, did not understand Spanish, and acknowledged only English. The European American middle class had disdain toward the working class. Finally, since OSA and LULAC members were men, as were most of the authorities in U.S. society, they appealed to a shared male political culture. In this sense, activists were involved in the politics of accommodation and adaptation.

The OSA and LULAC operated as mediators or brokers working for pro-Raza interests as interpreted through a male, middle-class, Mexican American perspective. Their issues did not always consider the interests of women, immigrants, and workers. Nevertheless, La Raza benefited from their pro-Raza activism. After 1929 LULAC was institutionalized, as were its efforts to defend La Raza and struggle for civil rights and self-preservation.

As the OSA and LULAC were involved in both resistance and adaptation, we should avoid simplifying their racial ideology. The race ideas of European Americans did constitute much of the cultural ground on which segregationist policies were discussed and debated.[15] But whites were in most positions of power, and La Raza had to negotiate its interests on those grounds. Likewise, La Raza had attended the colonizers' schools; LULACers, like Chicano movement activists, had "internalized racism." Thus their protest partly conformed to the dominant ideas of the time. But México Texanos did not fully accept the notion that they were inferior, dirty, and alien.

Nor did LULAC seek to arrogate the privileges of whiteness. LULAC did not have access to these privileges. During the Chicano movement, it was popular to say that LULAC "wanted to be white." In the wake of whiteness studies, neo-Chicano scholars have equated LULAC with whiteness. LULAC sought the privileges whites had and could only imagine whiteness.

GENDER, HOMOSOCIALITY, AND POLITICAL CULTURE

While the OSA and LULAC challenged white privilege, they did not challenge male privilege. In fact, the organizations were crafted like fraternities. The purpose of this male solidarity was to benefit La Raza, but women still received messages of exclusion.

Women circumvented the OSA's "No women allowed" signs and acted politically in public and private spheres. Some single women proved allies. They were independent and had no familial or sexual connection to OSA or LULAC members. Some married women acted through their relationship to an OSA or LULAC member. They raised funds and acted on behalf of the men's associations. Married women privileged husbands with the leisure of politicking while the wives tended to the home.

A third group of women, which included wives of OSA members as well as single women and widows, was active in women's clubs such as the Alpha Club in Corpus Christi. In San Antonio numerous independent women's clubs collaborated with LULAC.

Women defined their own political participation and their own brand of citizenship. They determined whether or not to form an auxiliary or a club. Their actions were not a result of some dictated order from OSA men. In Corpus Christi women decided not to organize an official auxiliary. The Alpha Club did not engage in direct desegregationist activism and instead chose a benevolent politics of providing food and clothing—concerns perhaps performed less often by men. Women organized on a different basis than men did. The Alpha Club met on an informal basis in private homes rather than in a clubroom. Moreover, women met locally and did not form a statewide organization like the OSA in the 1920s.[16] In the 1930s women founded Ladies LULAC, which became a statewide network under the LULAC banner. Homosociality defined how women and men organized.

These benevolent politics and acts of citizenship did not involve feminist consciousness. But women's consciousness involved a concern for civic duty. There was a México Texana woman citizen in the 1920s,[17] though there was no ideology for México Texanas that designated them as social housekeepers or citizens. Women's consciousness, which was subject to domesticity, patriarchal ideology, and benevolence, determined that they were willing to serve the collective of the personal family and the family of La Raza. Nonetheless, like the men, they opposed racism and racial segregation.

At the same time, from 1929 to 1933 México Texanas defined a more public role as citizens. They established their right to associate with other women in public organizations. They initiated women's auxiliaries that questioned the right of men only to conduct affairs on behalf of La Raza. Separate Ladies LULAC chapters were a second indicator of women's empowerment as a sign of women's capacity for self-governance and public competence. For all of these activities, men expressed indifference and overt opposition.[18]

In addition to these public political acts, women contributed to the men's organizations and the movement through their domestic labor. They permitted husbands and fathers to attend meetings and conventions; they raised children, prepared meals, and did housework. More importantly, they contested men's patriarchal ideology of empowerment, social citizenship, and organizational membership. Lacking feminist ideology, they could not assert more for women's gendered interests.

THE MEXICAN AMERICAN CIVIL RIGHTS MOVEMENT

Within U.S. history, the phenomenon of the Mexican American civil rights movement has been reduced to an uncomfortable fit within the hegemonic entity called "the" civil rights movement, usually colored black and white. Within Chicano history this phenomenon previously was cast within the context of a "generation" or "mind," and the significance of the activism itself has been lost. I use "Mexican American civil rights movement" to conceptualize activism from 1921 to 1965 that preceded the Chicano movement and used citizenship and rights rhetoric as part of a strategy of empowerment. All these conceptual tools (movement, generation, and mind) are complicated by class, gender, citizenship, ideology, nation, and region.

LULAC would eventually become a major force in the Mexican American civil rights movement in the United States. Raza civil rights organizations emerged beyond Texas' borders in other states in the 1930s. These included the Congreso de Pueblos de Habla Español (1938, California); Community Service Organization (CSO, 1947, California, Arizona); American GI Forum (1947, Texas); American Council of Spanish Speaking Persons (1951, Texas); Asociación Nacional México Americana (1951, New Mexico); Mexican American Political Association (MAPA, 1959, California, Texas);

and Political Association of Spanish-Speaking Associations (PASSO, 1961, Arizona, California, Texas).[19] These were the major Mexican American national associations before 1965, but only LULAC, the American GI Forum (a LULAC derivative), and MAPA survived.

The OSA and LULAC protected and served. In the post-2000 era, messages of exclusion—"No Mexicans Allowed," "No Women Allowed"—are still present, but my generation never encountered a single sign bearing the words "No Mexicans Allowed." For that we can thank the men and women who fought in defense of La Raza. Those struggles must not be underestimated, belittled, taken for granted, or forgotten.

Appendix 1

*Order Sons of America Declaration
of Principles, 1922*

First—We declare it the duty of citizens of the United States of Mexican or Spanish extraction to use their influence in all the fields of social, economic and political action to secure the fullest possible enjoyment of all rights, privileges and prerogatives granted to them under the American Constitution and to accomplish this we believe that a national organization should exist, whereby all organized citizens of the United States of Mexican or Spanish extraction may be represented, and matters pertaining to their condition be discussed and improved.

Second—While we are opposed to entering any political party as a body, we declare it our duty to use our influence with the law-making powers of our country to secure laws, whenever deemed necessary, beneficial to our interest and we further believe that as citizens of the United States, we, and all qualified persons of our families, should have a poll tax receipt that we may at all times properly exercise our political rights, ever endeavoring to see that our activities shall be confined to fundamental, constitutional and legal rights of citizens in political matters, and in politics as well as in religion we shall be non-partisan and non-sectarian.

Third—We hereby pledge ourselves to assist one another in and under all possible circumstances tending to bring about the advancement, progress and prosperity of the people of our extraction in general, regardless of citizenship, and to use our influence with other organized bodies to assist us in accomplishing our object.

Fourth—We especially denounce the system of peonage, slavery or maltreatment perpetrated upon persons of Mexican blood by being compelled to labor in the farming districts of some of our States for a number of hours daily that go beyond human endurance, for wages that keep then [them] undernourished and under most abominable housing and living conditions.

Fifth—We pledge ourselves to investigate the conditions under which farm laborers and tenants of our race work and operate in Texas and in other States of the Union.

Sixth—We recognize it a duty to our country, ourselves, and our American civilization, to evolutionize and establish in our households the principle that we must adopt in their entirety the standard living conditions of the American people and that in all our occupations and places of employment we must seek to obtain for ourselves the same rates of pay, salaries or wages paid citizens of any and all other racial extractions.

Seventh—To endeavor, to the best of our ability, to disseminate useful information by means of lectures, pamphlets, literature and general publicity.

Eighth—To secure and retain employment for our members, to protect them from oppression, and to place ourselves on a foundation sufficiently strong to resist any encroachments on their rights.

Ninth—We denounce the desecration of Sunday wherever our members are compelled to forfeit their freedom by working on that day, and we declare that this abuse shall be abolished. Where laws exist pertaining to said desecration they should be rigidly enforced, and where they do not exist they should be framed at once and put in effect, and we pledge ourselves to do all in our power to have them enforced.

Tenth—We declare it our duty to abolish child labor in the retail stores and workshops; the school house and not the workshop being the proper place for children.

Eleventh—We firmly pronounce ourselves in favor of bringing about a better feeling, relationship and understanding wherever necessary, between our beloved children of school age and the children of all other extractions in all the States where we may have occasion to establish branches of our Order, to the end that passion, racial prejudice or discrimination may not bar our children from the privilege of co-mingling in the school room with all other classes of American children, inasmuch as Almighty God has given us our Country, our Civilization, and the American Constitution for our common heritage.

Twelfth—We solemnly advocate and declare ourselves now and forever defenders of the principle that through the moral and mental training of the people of our race we shall be in the pathway of an onward and forward march substantially beneficial to society and the Civilization of our great and beloved American Republic—Arts, Letters, Science, Professions, Honorable Industry, Thrift, Progress, and Social Evolution must be, and shall be moral foundations upon which our Order shall stand.

Thirteenth—To provide aid to our sick and distressed members, to bury the dead and to provide such other protection as we may be able to give our members.

Fourteenth—We shall strive to establish cordial relations with all the social organizations now existing in the United States composed of citizens of the United States of Mexican or Spanish extraction and citizens of the Republic of Mexico.

Fifteenth—We are decidedly in favor of establishing in all sections of the United States wherever there may be need of it, Local Councils (for men), Local Ladies Auxiliary Councils, and Juvenile Branches, chartered by our Order.

Sixteenth—It shall be one of our most earnest endeavors to form statistical information relative to general conditions surrounding citizens of the United States of Mexican or Spanish extraction and we shall also strive to compile data concerning all Mexican residents of the United States.

Appendix 2

*Objectives and Aims of the Latin
American Citizens League, circa 1927*

1. To define with clarity, and absolute and unequivocal precision our indisputable loyalty to the ideals, principles, and citizenship of the U.S.

2. To assume complete responsibility of educating our children in the knowledge of all their duties and rights, language and customs of this country as far as there is good in them.

3. We declare for once and forever that we will maintain a respectful and sincere worship for our racial origin and be proud of it.

4. Secretly and openly, by all right means, we will aid the culture and orientation of Mexican-Americans and we will govern our life as a citizen to protect and defend their life and interests in so far as is necessary.

5. We will destroy every impulse put forward to create racial prejudices against our people, we will combat the infamous stigmas which are imposed upon them, and we will claim for them the respect of the [U.S.] Constitution and the prerogatives which belong to us all.

6. Each of us considers himself with equal responsibility in our institution to which we voluntarily swear subordination and obedience.

7. We will create funds for mutual protection, for defense in the courts, for the education and culture of our people.

8. This organization is no political club, but as citizens we will participate in the local, state, and national political campaigns from the point of view of collective interests, paying no attention to and abjuring for once and all any compromise of personal character not in harmony with our principles.

9. We will aid with our vote and influence the election of individuals who by their acts show respect and consideration for our people.

10. We will elevate as our leaders those among us who by their integrity and culture show themselves capable of guiding and directing us aright.

11. We will maintain means of publicity to define these principles, to extend the ramifications of our organization, and to consolidate it.

12. We will pay our poll tax and that of our households in order to fully enjoy our rights.

13. We will spread our ideals by means of the press, lectures, and pamphlets.

14. We will oppose all violent, radical manifestations which tend to create conflicts and violate the peace and tranquility of the country.

15. We will respect the religious ideas of everyone and we will never refer to them in our institutions.

16. We will encourage the creation of educational institutions for Mexican-Americans, and we lend our aid to those already in existence.

17. We will [work] toward the end that our people have more representation in the juries and the public administration in general.

18. We will denounce every act of peonage or mistreatment as well as work of our minor children.

19. We will resist and attack with energy all machinations tending to prevent our social and political unification.

20. We will combat every tendency towards putting our children in separate schools in the towns of this country.

21. We will establish statistics which will inform our people with regards to the conditions of work, life and agricultural and commercial activity in various parts of this country.

Appendix 3

*Constitution, League of United
Latin American Citizens, 1929*

Article 2, Aims and Purposes

1. To develop within the members of our race the best, purest and most perfect type of a true and loyal citizen of the United States of America.

2. To eradicate from our body politic all intents and tendencies to establish discriminations among our fellow-citizens on account of race, religion or social position as being contrary to the true spirit of Democracy, our [U.S.] Constitution and Laws.

3. To use all the legal means at our command to the end that all citizens in our country may enjoy equal rights, the equal protection of the laws of the land and equal opportunities and privileges.

4. The acquisition of the English language, which is the official language of our country, being necessary for the enjoyment of our rights and privileges, we declare it to be the official language of this Organization, and we pledge ourselves to learn and speak and teach the same to our children.

5. To define with absolute and unmistakable clearness our unquestionable loyalty to the ideals, principles and citizenship of the United States of America.

6. To assume complete responsibility for the education of our children as to their rights and duties and the language and customs of this country; the latter, in so far as they may be good customs.

7. We solemnly declare once and for all to maintain a sincere and respectful reverence for our racial origin of which we are proud.

8. Secretly and openly, by all lawful means at our command, we shall assist in the education and guidance of Latin-Americans and we shall protect and defend their lives and interest whenever necessary.

9. We shall destroy any attempt to create racial prejudices against our people, and any infamous stigma which may be cast upon them, and we shall demand for them the respect and prerogatives which the Constitution grants to us all.

10. Each of us considers himself with equal responsibilities in our organization, to which we voluntarily swear subordination and obedience.

11. We shall create a fund for our mutual protection, for the defense of those of us who may be unjustly persecuted and for the education and culture of our people.

12. This Organization is not a political club, but as citizens we shall participate in all local, state and national political contests. However, in doing so we shall ever bear in mind the general welfare of our people, and we disregard and abjure once for all any personal obligation which is not in harmony with these principles.

13. With our vote and influence we shall endeavor to place in public office men who show by their deeds, respect and consideration for our people.

14. We shall select as our leaders those among us who demonstrate, by their integrity and culture, that they are capable of guiding and directing us properly.

15. We shall maintain publicity means for the diffusion of these principles and for the expansion and consolidation of this organization.

16. We shall pay our poll tax as well as that of members of our families in order that we may enjoy our rights fully.

17. We shall diffuse our ideals by means of the press, lectures and pamphlets.

18. We shall oppose any radical and violent demonstration which may tend to create conflicts and disturb the peace and tranquility of our country.

19. We shall have mutual respect for our religious views and we shall never refer to them in our institutions.

20. We shall encourage the creation of educational institutions for Latin-Americans and we shall lend our support to those already in existence.

21. We shall endeavor to secure equal representation for our people on juries and in the administration of Governmental affairs.

22. We shall denounce every act of peonage and mistreatment as well as the employment of our minor children, of scholastic age.

23. We shall resist and attack energetically all machinations tending to prevent our social and political unification.

24. We shall oppose any tendency to separate our children in the schools of this country.

25. We shall maintain statistics which will guide our people with respect to working and living conditions and agricultural and commercial activities in the various parts of our country.

NOTES

INTRODUCTION

Eusebio "Chevo" Morales, "L.U.L.A.C. Te Felicito," *Latino Magazine* (May–June, 1989), 12. The original Spanish epigraph follows. Unless otherwise noted, translations throughout are my own, with assistance from Irma Orozco. Morales passed away in 2008.

> *Amigo quiero contarles*
> *Lo que en Corpus sucedió*
> *Unos hombres se juntaron*
> *Y L.U.L.A.C. allí se formó.*
> *Ellos eran muy poquitos*
> *Pero de mucho valor.*
> *Cansados de ver a su gente*
> *Sufriendo tanto dolor.*
> *Garza y otros amigos*
> *Hombres de devoción.*
> *Pero en sus corazones*
> *Sentían revolución.*

1. LULAC is not the oldest Mexican American organization in the nation. The Penitentes, a religious fraternity, holds that distinction, though the Alianza Hispano Americano was the first secular organization. See Kaye Lynn Briegel, "Alianza Hispano Americano, 1894–1965: A Mexican-American Fraternal Insurance Society," Ph.D. diss., University of Southern California, 1974; Kaye Lynn Briegel, "Alianza Hispano Americano and Some Civil Rights Cases in the 1950s," in *An Awakened Minority: the Mexican Americans*, ed. Manuel P. Servín (Beverly Hills, CA: Glencoe

Press, 1970), 174–187; José Amaro Hernández, *Mutual Aid for Survival* (Malabar, FL: Krieger, 1983).

2. The Orden Hijos de América, or Order Sons of America, as they were known in English, and the Order Knights of America, or Orden Caballeros de America in Spanish, did not use the preposition "of" or "de" in their names in English or Spanish.

3. Constitution of the League of United Latin American Citizens, 1929 (hereinafter LULAC constitution), 2, Oliver Douglas Weeks Papers (hereinafter ODWP), Nettie Lee Benson Latin American Collection, University of Texas at Austin (hereinafter BLAC).

4. Alfredo Cuellar, "Perspective on Politics," in *Mexican Americans*, Joan W. Moore with Alfredo Cuellar (Englewood Cliffs, NJ: Prentice-Hall, 1970) 137–158; Miguel D. Tirado, "Mexican American Community Political Organization: The Key to Chicano Political Power," *Aztlán* 1, no. 1 (Spring 1970): 53–78; Juan Gómez-Quiñones, "Notes on Periodization," *Aztlán* 1, no. 1 (Spring 1970): 115–118; Armando Navarro, "The Evolution of Chicano Politics," *Aztlán* 5, no. 1 (1974): 57–84.

5. Julie Leininger Pycior, "La Raza Organizes: Mexican American Life in San Antonio 1915–1930, as Reflected in Mutualista Activities," Ph.D. diss., University of Notre Dame, 1979.

6. Constitution and By-Laws of Order Sons of America, Council No. 1, San Antonio, Texas, adopted June 25, 1922 (hereinafter OSA constitution), ODWP.

7. Mario Barrera, "The Historical Evolution of Chicano Ethnic Goals: A Bibliographic Essay," *Sage Race Relations Abstract* 10, no. 1 (February 1985): 1; Alfredo Cuellar, "Perspective on Politics"; R. C. Rodríguez, "A Measurement of Political Attitudes in Mexican American Civic Organizations," master's thesis, University of Texas at El Paso, 1972.

8. William Gamson argues for the need to understand "the historical context of challenges" waged by organizations and social movements; William A. Gamson, *The Strategy of Social Protest* (Homewood, IL: Dorsey Press, 1975).

9. See Nelson A. Pichardo, "The Role of Community in Social Protest: Chicano Working Class Protest, 1848–1933," Ph.D. diss., University of Michigan, 1990.

10. See Carlos Muñoz Jr., *Youth, Identity, and Power* (London: Verso, 1989).

11. O. Douglas Weeks, "The League of United Latin-American Citizens: A Texas-Mexican Civic Organization," *Southwestern Political and Social Science Quarterly* 10, no. 3 (December 1929): 265–266. To understand Chicano movement politics see the works of Muñoz Jr. as well as Ernesto Chávez, *¡Mi Raza Primero! (My People First!): Nationalism, Identity, and Insurgency in the Chicano Movement in Los Angeles, 1966–1978* (Berkeley: University of California Press, 2002); Ignacio M. García, *Chicanismo: The Forging of a Militant Ethos among Mexican Americans* (Tucson: University of Arizona Press, 1997); and George Mariscal, *Brown-Eyed Children of the Sun: Lessons from the Chicano Movement, 1965–1975* (Albuquerque: University of New Mexico Press, 2005).

12. Preceding the scholars of the 1970s were John Burma, *Spanish-Speaking Groups in the United States* (Durham, NC: Duke University Press, 1954); Ralph Guzmán, "Politics and Policies of the Mexican-American Community," *California Politics and Policies*, ed. Eugene P. Dvorin and Arthur J. Misner (Palo Alto, CA: Addison-

Wesley, 1966), 350–385; and Robert A. Cuellar, "The Social and Political History of the Mexicans in Texas, 1929–1963," master's thesis, North Texas State College, 1969.

13. Navarro, "Evolution of Chicano Politics," 62.

14. Alfredo Cuellar, "Perspective on Politics," 142, 145.

15. See Robert R. Brischetto, *The Political Power of Texas Mexicans, 1974–1988* (San Antonio: Southwest Voter Research Institute, 1988); Roberto E. Villarreal, Norma G. Hernández, and Howard D. Neighbor, eds., *Latino Empowerment: Problems and Prospects* (New York: Greenwood Press, 1988); Karen O'Connor and Lee Epstein, "A Legal Voice for the Chicano Community: The Activities of the Mexican American Legal Defense and Educational Fund, 1968–1982," in *The Mexican American Experience: An Interdisciplinary Anthology*, ed. Rodolfo O. de la Garza (Austin: University of Texas Press, 1985): 281–292.

16. Muñoz Jr., *Youth, Identity, and Power*, 175. A barometer of changing interpretations of LULAC can be seen in Rodolfo Acuña, *Occupied America; the Chicano's Struggle Toward Liberation*, 1st edition (San Francisco: Canfield Press, 1972), 189–190, 210, 223, and in the five subsequent editions listed in the bibliography. Acuña, like most scholars today, understood LULAC better than many in the 1970s.

17. John C. Hammerback, Richard J. Jensen, and José Ángel Gutiérrez, *A War of Words: Chicano Protest in the 1960s and 1970s* (Westport, CT: Greenwood Press, 1985), 141.

18. Armando Navarro, *Mexicano Political Experience in Occupied Aztlán, Struggles and Change* (Los Angeles: Altamira Press, 2005).

19. Neil Foley, "Becoming Hispanic: Mexican Americans and the Faustian Pact with Whiteness," *Reflexiones: New Directions in Mexican American Studies*, ed. Neil Foley (Austin: Center for Mexican American Studies, University of Texas at Austin, 1997), 53–70; Katsuyuki Murata, "The (Re)Shaping of Latino/Chicano Ethnicity," *American Studies International* 39, no. 2 (June 2001): 4–33.

20. Craig A. Kaplowitz, *LULAC, Mexican Americans, and National Policy* (College Station: Texas A&M University, 2005).

21. Benjamín Márquez, *LULAC: The Evolution of a Mexican American Political Organization* (Austin: University of Texas, 1993); Benjamín Márquez, "The Politics of Race and Class: The League of United Latin American Citizens," *Social Science Quarterly* 68, no. 1 (March 1987): 84–101; Benjamín Márquez, "The League of United Latin American Citizens and the Politics of Ethnicity," in *Latino Empowerment*, ed. Villarreal, Hernández, and Neighbor, 11–24; Benjamin Márquez, "The Problems of Organizational Maintenance and the League of United Latin American Citizens," *Social Science Journal* 28, no. 2 (1991), 203–222; and Benjamín Márquez and James Jennings, "Representation by Other Means: Mexican American and Puerto Rican Social Movement Organizations," *Political Science and Politics* 33, no. 3 (September 2000), 541–546. Márquez' shift is most apparent in his *Constructing Identities in Mexican American Political Organizations: Choosing Issues, Taking Sides* (Austin: University of Texas Press, 2003).

22. Weeks, "League of United Latin American Citizens," 257–278. Histories of the American West, most written by European American historians, do not mention LULAC. Gerald Nash was an exception; see Nash, *The American West in the Twentieth Century: A Short History of an Urban Oasis* (Albuquerque: University of New

Mexico Press, 1977). More typical is Donald Worcester, who argued that "it was not until the 1950s that Mexican American political and social organizations began to question the effectiveness of educational practices by public schools"; Worcester, "The Significance of the Spanish Borderlands to the United States," in *New Spain's Far Northern Frontier: Essays on Spain in the American West, 1540–1821* (Albuquerque: University of New Mexico Press, 1979), 39. See also James R. Lawrence, "A Study of the Latin American Problem and the Growth of the LULAC Organization," master's thesis, Texas College of Arts and Industry, 1966.

23. Mario T. García, *Mexican Americans: Leadership, Ideology, and Identity* (New Haven, CT: Yale University Press, 1989), 3. See also Rodolfo Álvarez, "The Psycho-Historical and Socio-Economic Development of the Chicano Community in the United States," *Social Science Quarterly* 52 (March 1973), 920–942. Other works that have a generational approach include Mario T. García, "Americans All: The Mexican American Generation and the Politics of Wartime Los Angeles, 1941–1945," *Social Science Quarterly* 65 (June 1984), 278–289; Guadalupe San Miguel Jr., "Social and Educational Influences Shaping the Mexican-American Mind: Some Tentative Thoughts," *Journal of the Midwest History of Education Society* 14 (1986): 57–66; Arnoldo De León, *Ethnicity in the Sunbelt: A History of Mexican Americans in Houston* (Houston: Mexican American Studies Monograph Series, 1989); and Muñoz Jr., *Youth, Identity, and Power.*

24. See Jesús Martínez Saldaña, "At the Periphery of Democracy: The Binational Politics of Mexican Immigrants in Silicon Valley," Ph.D. diss., University of California at Berkeley, 1993; Gilbert G. González, *Labor and Community: Mexican Citrus Worker Villages in a Southern California County, 1900–1950* (Urbana: University of Illinois Press, 1994); and F. Arturo Rosales, *¡Pobre Raza!: Violence, Justice, and Mobilization Among Mexico Lindo Immigrants, 1900–1936* (Austin: University of Texas Press, 1999).

25. Richard A. García, "The Making of the Mexican-American Mind, San Antonio, Texas, 1929–1941: A Social and Intellectual History of an Ethnic Community," Ph.D. diss., University of California at Irvine, 1980, 10.

26. Ibid. Richard A. García, "The Mexican American Mind: A Product of the 1930s," in *History, Culture, and Society: Chicano Studies in the 1980s*, ed. Mario T. García and Bert Corona (Ypsilanti, MI: Bilingual Press/Editorial Bilingüe, 1983), 67–94. Richard A. García, *Rise of the Mexican American Middle Class* (College Station: Texas A&M Press, 1991); see my review of García's *Rise of the Mexican American Middle Class* in *Southwestern Historical Quarterly* 96, no. 4 (October 1992): 296–297.

27. Foley, "Becoming Hispanic," 62–63.

28. Ibid., 55.

29. Mario Barrera, "Chicano Class Structure," in *Chicano Studies: A Multidisciplinary Approach*, ed. Eugene E. García, Francisco A. Lomeli, and Isidro D. Ortiz (New York: Teachers College Press, 1984), 40–55.

30. Ramón Gutiérrez, "Unraveling America's Hispanic Past: Internal Stratification and Class Boundaries," *Aztlán* 17, no. 1 (Spring 1986): 79–101.

31. Revisionist work correcting this misrepresentation includes Guadalupe San Miguel Jr., *"Let Them All Take Heed": Mexican Americans' Campaign for Educational Equality in Texas, 1910–1981* (Austin: University of Texas, 1987); Mario T. García,

Mexican Americans; Richard A. García, *Rise of the Mexican American Middle Class*; and Arnoldo De León, *Ethnicity in the Sunbelt*.

32. F. Arturo Rosales, "Shifting Ethnic Consciousness in Houston," *Aztlán* 16, nos. 1–2 (1985), 71–91.

33. Félix Padilla, *Latino Ethnic Consciousness: The Case of Mexican Americans and Puerto Ricans in Chicago* (Notre Dame, IN: University of Notre Dame Press, 1985).

34. George J. Sánchez, *Becoming Mexican American* (New York: Oxford University Press, 1995).

35. Nelson A. Pichardo, "The Establishment and Development of Chicano Voluntary Associations in California, 1910–1930," *Aztlán* 19, no. 2 (1992): 93–155. Pichardo showed that the majority of Mexican-descent organizations maintained a dominant Mexican identity. In Los Angeles, the assimilation process was slower than it was in San Antonio, and thus it took longer for a Mexican American identity to take shape there.

36. Emilio Zamora, *The World of the Mexican Worker* (College Station: Texas A&M University Press, 1995).

37. David Gregory Gutiérrez, *Walls and Mirrors: Mexican Americans, Mexican Immigrants, and the Politics of Ethnicity* (Berkeley: University of California Press, 1995); David Gregory Gutiérrez, "Ethnicity, Ideology, and Political Development: Mexican Immigration as a Political Issue in the Chicano Community, 1910–1977," Ph.D. diss., Stanford University, 1988. See also Katsuyuki Murata, "(Re)Shaping of Latino/Chicano Ethnicity."

38. Anthony Quiroz, *Claiming Citizenship: Mexican Americans in Victoria, Texas* (College Station: Texas A&M University Press, 2005).

39. Ronald Beiner, ed., *Theorizing Citizenship* (Albany: State University of New York Press, 1995); Linda K. Kerber, "The Meanings of Citizenship," *Journal of American History* 84, no. 3 (December 1997): 833–854; Linda K. Kerber, *No Constitutional Right to Be Ladies: The Obligations of Citizenship* (New York: Hill and Wang, 1998).

40. See Raymond Rocco, "Transforming Citizenship: Membership, Strategies of Containment, and the Public Sphere in Latino Communities," in *Latinos and Citizenship: The Dilemma of Belonging*, ed. Suzanne Oboler (New York: Palgrave MacMillan, 2006), 301–328. In Latina/o studies see Carlos G. Vélez-Ibáñez and Anna Sampaio, eds., with Manolo González-Estay, *Transnational Latina/o Communities, Politics, Processes, and Cultures* (Lanham, MD: Rowman and Littlefield, 2002); and Adelaida R. del Castillo, "Illegal Status and Social Citizenship: Thoughts on Mexican Immigration in a Post-Modern World," *Aztlán* 27, no. 2 (Fall 2002): 11–32.

41. Amanda Gouws, ed., *(Un)thinking Citizenship: Feminist Debates in Contemporary South Africa* (Aldershot, England: Ashgate, 2005).

42. Márquez' post-2000 publications are an exception.

43. David Montejano, *Anglos and Mexicans in the Making of Texas, 1836–1986* (Austin: University of Texas, 1987), 244; David Montejano, "The Demise of 'Jim Crow' for Texas Mexicans, 1940–1970," *Aztlán* 16, nos. 1–2 (1985): 27–70.

44. Pycior, "La Raza Organizes."

45. See Charles Ray Chandler, "The Mexican American Protest Movement," Ph.D. diss., Tulane University, 1968; Ricardo Romo, "George I. Sánchez and the

Civil Rights Movement, 1940–1960," *La Raza Law Journal* 1, no. 3 (Fall 1986): 342–362; Ricardo Romo, "Southern California and the Origins of Latino Civil Rights Activism," *Western Legal History* 3 (Summer/Fall 1990): 379–406; Carl Allsup, "Education Is Our Freedom: The American GI Forum and the Mexican American School Segregation in Texas, 1948–1957," *Aztlán* 8 (Fall 1977): 27–50; Carl Allsup, *The American GI Forum: Origins and Evolution* (Austin: Center for Mexican American Studies, University of Texas, 1982); San Miguel Jr., *"Let Them All Take Heed"*; Arnoldo De León, *Ethnicity in the Sunbelt*; Mario T. García, *Mexican Americans*; Thomas Kreneck, "The Letter from Chapultepec," *Houston Review* 3, no. 2 (Summer 1981): 268–271; Thomas Kreneck, *Del Pueblo: A Pictorial History of Houston's Hispanic Community* (Houston: Houston International University, 1989); Patrick Carroll, *Felix Longoria's Wake: Bereavement, Racism, and the Rise of Mexican American Activism* (Austin: University of Texas Press, 2003); and Michael Olivas, ed., *Colored Men and Hombres Aquí: Hernandez v. Texas and the Rise of Mexican American Lawyering* (Houston: Arte Público Press, 2006).

46. *Chicano! The Mexican American Civil Rights Movement*, film produced by National Latino Communications Center, 1997.

47. F. Arturo Rosales, *Chicano!: The Mexican American Civil Rights Movement* (Houston: Arte Público Press, 1997). Surprisingly, most early studies paid little attention to individual civil rights activists and biography and instead offered sociological descriptions. The most notable exceptions are those written by Mario T. García; see his *Mexican Americans* and writings on Bert Corona, Ruben Salazar, César Chávez, and Dolores Huerta. See Thomas Kreneck, *Mexican American Odyssey: Felix Tijerina, Entrepreneur and Civic Leader, 1905–1965* (College Station: Texas A&M University, 2002), about Felix Tijerina; Michelle Hall Kells, *Hector P. García: Everyday Rhetoric and Mexican American Civil Rights* (Carbondale: Southern Illinois University, 2006); and Felix Almaraz, *Knight Without Honor* (College Station: Texas A&M University Press, 2000), on Carlos Castañeda.

48. My gendered work includes Cynthia E. Orozco, "Alice Dickerson Montemayor: Feminism and Mexican American Politics in the 1930s," in *Writing the Range: Race, Class, and Culture in the Women's West*, ed. Elizabeth Jameson and Susan Armitage (Norman: University of Oklahoma Press, 1997), 435–456; Orozco, "Ladies LULAC," in *New Handbook of Texas*, ed. Ronnie Tyler, Douglas Barnett, and Roy Barkley, 4:1–2 (Austin: Texas State Historical Association, 1996); Orozco, "League of United Latin American Citizens," in *New Handbook* 4:129–131; Orozco, "League of United Latin American Citizens," in *Reader's Companion to U.S. Women's History*, ed. Wilma Mankiller, Gwendolyn Mink, Marysa Navarro, Barbara Smith, and Gloria Steinem (Boston: Houghton Mifflin, 1998), 378; Orozco, "Regionalism, Politics, and Gender in Southwestern History: The League of United Latin American Citizens' (LULAC) Expansion into New Mexico from Texas, 1929–1945," *Western Historical Quarterly* 29, no. 4 (November 1998), 459–483.

49. Chicana voluntary association literature is vast. Cynthia E. Orozco, "Beyond Machismo, La Familia, and Ladies Auxiliaries: A Historiography of Mexican-Origin Women's Participation in Voluntary Associations and Politics in the United States, 1870–1990," *Renato Rosaldo Lecture Series* 10, 1992–1993 (Tucson: Mexican American Studies and Research Center, University of Arizona, 1994), 1–34. Chicanas

are underrepresented in most mainstream women's studies literature, such as Anne Firor Scott, *Natural Allies: Women's Associations in American History* (Urbana: University of Illinois, 1991); Karen J. Blair, *The History of American Women's Voluntary Organizations, 1810–1960: A Guide to Sources* (Boston: G. K. Hall, 1989); Ester Stineman, *American Political Women, Contemporary and Historical Profiles* (Littleton, CO: Libraries Unlimited, 1980); and Gayle J. Hardy, ed., *American Women Civil Rights Activists: Bio-bibliographies of 68 Leaders, 1825–1992,* (Jefferson, NC: McFarland, 1993).

50. Carroll Smith-Rosenberg, "The Female World of Love and Ritual," *Signs* 1, no. 1 (Autumn 1975), 1–19.

51. Alfredo Mirandé, *Hombres y Machos: Masculinity and Latino Culture* (Boulder: University of Colorado Press, 1997); Ray González, *Muy Macho: Latino Men Confront Their Manhood* (New York: Anchor Books, 1996). Also see the writings of Ramón Gutiérrez, José Limón, Manuel Peña, and a newer generation that includes Eric Christopher García and Raúl Coronado.

52. Richard A. García, *Rise of the Mexican American Middle Class;* Richard A. García, "Class, Consciousness, and Ideology—The Mexican Community in San Antonio, Texas: 1930–1940," *Aztlán* 9 (Fall 1978): 23–70; Richard A. García, "Making of the Mexican American Mind"; Richard A. García, "The Mexican American Mind: A Product of the 1930s"; Mario T. García, "Mexican Americans and the Politics of Citizenship: The Case of El Paso, 1936," *New Mexico Historical Review* 59 (April 1984): 187–204; San Miguel Jr., "Social and Educational Influences"; Arnoldo De León, *Ethnicity in the Sunbelt;* Mario T. García, *Mexican Americans.*

53. Benjamin Heber Johnson, *Revolution in Texas: How a Forgotten Rebellion and Its Bloody Suppression Turned Mexicans into Americans* (New Haven, CT: Yale, 2003).

54. See Carole E. Christian, "Joining the American Mainstream: Texas's Mexican Americans During World War I," *Southwestern Historical Quarterly* 92, no. 4 (April 1989): 550–598.

55. Mae M. Ngai, *Impossible Subjects: Illegal Aliens and the Making of Modern America* (Princeton, NJ: Princeton University Press, 2004).

56. Briegel, "Alianza Hispano Americano, 1894–1965"; Pycior, "La Raza Organizes"; Allsup, *American GI Forum;* Mario T. García, *Mexican Americans;* Richard A. García, *Rise of the Mexican American Middle Class;* and Márquez, *LULAC.*

57. For instance, LULAC founder Alonso S. Perales wrote, "Are we going to continue our backward state of the past, or are we going to get out of the rut, forge ahead, and keep abreast of the hardworking Anglo-Saxon?"; quoted in Rodolfo Acuña, *Occupied America,* 6th edition (New York: Pearson Longman, 2007), 151.

58. Michael Omi and Howard Winant, *Racial Formation in the United States: From the 1960s to the 1980s* (New York: Routledge and Kegan Paul, 1987), 64.

59. Ibid.

60. See Juan Gómez-Quiñones, *Chicano Politics, Promise, and Reality, 1940–1980* (Albuquerque: University of New Mexico Press, 1990).

61. The first scholarly discussion of México Texano identity is in Richard Flores' "The Corrido and the Emergence of Texas-Mexican Social Identity," *Journal of American Folklore* 105, no. 4 (Spring 1992): 166–182. "México Texano" was spelled with an *x* and not a *j.* The term "México Texana" was not located in any document, but it is used in this study to refer to women.

62. Elliot Young, "Deconstructing La Raza: Identifying the Gente Decente of Laredo, 1904–1994," *Southwestern Historical Quarterly* 98 (October 1994): 227–259. On nations and imagined communities see Benedict Anderson, *Imagined Communities: Reflections on the Origin and Spread of Nationalism* (London: Verso, 1983).

CHAPTER 1: THE "MEXICAN" COLONY OF SOUTH TEXAS

1. Daniel D. Arreola, *Tejano South Texas: A Mexican American Cultural Province* (Austin: University of Texas, 2001), 9–22.

2. See Armando C. Alonzo, *Tejano Legacy: Rancheros and Settlers in South Texas, 1734–1900* (Albuquerque: University of New Mexico Press, 1998).

3. Montejano, *Anglos and Mexicans*, 31.

4. Gilberto Miguel Hinojosa, *A Borderlands Town in Transition, Laredo, 1755–1870* (College Station: Texas A&M University Press, 1983).

5. Camilo Amado Martínez, "The Mexican and Mexican American Laborers in the Lower Rio Grande Valley of Texas, 1870–1930," Ph.D. diss., Texas Tech University, 1987, 22.

6. Américo Paredes, *With His Pistol in His Hands* (Austin: University of Texas Press, 1958); Jovita González, "Social Life in Cameron, Starr, and Zapata Counties," master's thesis, University of Texas, 1930.

7. Catarino E. Garza addresses the topic of how residents referred to themselves in his manuscript (circa 1890) " 'La lógica de los hechos,' O sean observaciones sobre las circumstancias de los mexicanos en Tejas, desde el año 1877 hasta 1889," 9, Corpus Christi (BLAC). See entry on Catarino E. Garza in *Mexican American Archives at the Benson Collection: A Guide for Users*, comp. María G. Flores, ed. Laura Gutiérrez-Witt (Austin: University of Texas General Libraries, 1981); Gilbert M. Cuthbertson, "Catarino Erasmo Garza," *New Handbook*, 3:106–107; Elliot Young, *Catarino Garza's Revolution on the Texas-Mexico Border* (Durham, NC: Duke University Press, 2004).

8. Américo Paredes, *With His Pistol*; David G. Gutiérrez, "Migration, Emergent Ethnicity, and the 'Third Space': The Shifting Politics of Nationalism in Greater Mexico," *Journal of American History* 91, no. 3 (September 1999): 906–931.

9. Paul S. Taylor, *An American-Mexican Frontier: Nueces County, Texas* (Chapel Hill: University of North Carolina Press, 1934): 68, 78–79, 92.

10. Taylor, *American-Mexican Frontier*, 189. A 1914 study showed that half of all tenants borrowed on 100 percent of their gross incomes; Robert Calvert and Arnoldo De León, *The History of Texas* (Arlington Heights, IL: Harley Davidson, 1990), 226.

11. Montejano, *Anglos and Mexicans*, 151, 170, 172. In the 1880s, Nueces County encompassed land in present-day Jim Wells County.

12. Taylor, *American-Mexican Frontier*, 188.

13. Emilio Zamora, "Mexican Labor Activity in South Texas, 1900–1920," Ph.D. diss., University of Texas at Austin, 1983, 33–34n15; Dellos Urban Buckner, "Study of the Lower Rio Grande Valley as a Culture Area," master's thesis, University of Texas, 1929, 87.

14. Ibid.

15. Montejano, *Anglos and Mexicans*, 172; notes, conversations with F. W. Hoepf-

ner, County Agent, Nueces County, Texas, Paul S. Taylor Papers (hereinafter PSTP), Bancroft Library, Berkeley.

16. Guadalupe San Miguel Jr., "Endless Pursuits: The Chicano Educational Experience in Corpus Christi, Texas, 1880–1969," Ph.D. diss., Stanford University, 1979, 30; Montejano, *Anglos and Mexicans*, 172; Dan E. Kilgore, "Corpus Christi: A Quarter Century of Development, 1900–1925," *Southwestern Historical Quarterly* 75, no. 4 (April 1972): 443; Eleazar Paredes, "The Role of Mexican Americans in Kleberg County, 1915–1970," master's thesis, Texas A&I University, 1973, 9.

17. Taylor, *American-Mexican Frontier*.

18. Ricardo Romo, "The Urbanization of Southwestern Chicanos in the Early Twentieth Century," in *New Directions in Chicano Scholarship*, ed. Ricardo Romo and Raymund Paredes (La Jolla, CA: Chicano Studies Monograph Series, University of California at San Diego, 1978), 184–187; Richard A. García, "Making of the Mexican-American Mind," 10, 27; William John Knox, "The Economic Status of the Mexican Immigrant in San Antonio, Texas," master's thesis, University of Texas, 1927 (reprint, San Francisco: R and E Research Associates, 1971), 63; James K. Harris, "A Sociological Study of a Mexican School in San Antonio, Texas," master's thesis, University of Texas, 1927, 39–40.

19. *1904 Texas Almanac*, (Dallas: Dallas Morning News, 1904), 215, Center for American History (hereinafter CAH), University of Texas at Austin; *1929 Texas Agricultural and State Industrial Guide* (Dallas: Dallas News, 1929), 211, CAH; June Rayfield Welch, *Texas: New Perspectives* (Austin: Steck-Vaughn, 1972), 218, 285; Calvert and De León, *History of Texas*, 269; *1924 Texas Almanac and State Industrial Guide* (Dallas: Dallas Morning News, 1925), 249, CAH; Buckner, "Study of the Lower Rio Grande," 98.

20. Robert Garland Landolt, "The Mexican American Workers of San Antonio," Ph.D. diss., University of Texas at Austin, 1965, 41; George A. Schreiner, "San Antonio, Metropolis of Southwest Texas," *Texas Magazine*, May 1910, 69, CAH; Richard A. García, "Making of the Mexican-American Mind," Table 1, 30, 37, 81; Romo, "Urbanization," 185–186. LULAC member Alonso S. Perales estimated there were 85,000 persons of Mexican descent in San Antonio; Perales, *El México americano y la política del sur de Texas: Comentarios* (San Antonio: Artes Gráficas, 1931), 6, BLAC. This is a translation of and commentary on O. Douglas Weeks' "The Texas-Mexican and the Politics of South Texas," *American Political Science Review* 24 (August 1930), 606–627.

21. Lillian J. Stambaugh and J. Lee Stambaugh, *The Lower Rio Grande Valley of Texas* (San Antonio: Naylor, 1954), 171; Jovita González, "Social Life," 45–46.

22. Zamora, "Mexican Labor Activity," 53.

23. Jovita González, "America Invades the Border Towns," *Southwest Review* 15, no. 4 (Summer 1930): 467–477.

24. Jovita González, "Social Life," 101.

25. Ibid., 102.

26. Buckner, "Study of the Lower Rio Grande," 66, Figure 2. See also J. T. Canales, "Personal Recollections of J. T. Canales Written at the Request of and for Use by the Honorable Harbert Davenport in Preparing a Historical Sketch of the Lower Rio Grande Valley for the Soil Conservation District" (Brownsville, Texas, 1945), 21–22, CAH.

27. Terry G. Jordan, "A Century and a Half of Ethnic Change in Texas, 1836–1986," *Southwestern Historical Quarterly* 79, no. 4 (April 1986): 398.

28. George C. Rehmet, "Alice, Sweetheart of South Texas," in *New Encyclopedia of Texas*, comp. and ed. Ellis A. Davis and Edwin H. Grobe (Dallas: Texas Development Bureau, 1929), 120; Pope A. Presnall, "Alice and Jim Wells County," *New Encyclopedia*, 120–121; "Alice, Texas," *Handbook of Texas*, 1952, 1:28; Alicia Salinas, "Alice, Texas," *New Handbook*, 1:105–106.

29. Salinas, "Alice, Texas," *New Handbook*; Arreola, *Tejano South Texas*, 177.

30. Alonzo, *Tejano Legacy*; Buckner, "Study of the Lower Rio Grande," 45, Table 1; Zamora, "Mexican Labor Activity."

31. Julian Samora, *Los Mojados* (Notre Dame, IN: University of Notre Dame Press, 1971), 36. Linda B. Hall and Don M. Coerver, *Revolution on the Border: The U.S. and Mexico, 1910–1920* (Albuquerque: University of New Mexico Press, 1988), 128–129, Table 8.3.

32. Ngai, *Impossible Subjects*, 3.

33. Richard A. García, "Making of the Mexican-American Mind," 84; James K. Harris, "Sociological Study," 90. Mark Reisler, *By the Sweat of Their Brow, Mexican Labor 1900–1940* (Westport, CT: Greenwood Press, 1976), 209–210.

34. Buckner, "Study of the Lower Rio Grande," 88. See also Kelly Lytle Hernandez, "Entangling Bodies and Borders: Racial Profiling and the History of U.S. Border Patrol," Ph.D. diss., University of California at Los Angeles (UCLA), 2002.

35. James K. Harris, "Sociological Study," 47, 71. In his survey of one-eighth of San Antonio's Mexican-descent community in 1927, William John Knox estimates that 10,000 Mexican-origin male laborers had no union affiliations; Knox, "Economic Status of the Mexican Immigrant," 34–35.

36. Calvert and De León, *History of Texas*, 222, 228. For national figures on the occupational distribution of Mexicans in the Southwest of 1930–1980 see Vicki L. Ruiz, "'Working for Wages': Mexican Women in the Southwest, 1930–1980," Working Paper No. 19 (Tucson: Southwest Institute for Research on Women, 1984).

37. Mario T. García, "Racial Dualism in the El Paso Labor Market," *Aztlán* 6, no. 2 (Summer 1975): 197–218.

38. Knox, "Economic Status of the Mexican Immigrant," 46–48.

39. Manuel Gamio, *Mexican Immigration to the United States* (New York: Dover, 1971), 37.

40. Buckner, "Study of the Lower Rio Grande," 69.

41. Knox, "Economic Status of the Mexican Immigrant," 40, 42. Kenneth L. Stewart and Arnoldo De León, "Work Force Participation Among Mexican Immigrant Women in Texas, 1900," *Borderlands* 9, no. 1 (Spring 1986): 70.

42. Knox, "Economic Status of the Mexican Immigrant," 40. Vicki L. Ruiz, "Mexican Women," in *Encyclopedia of Southern Culture*, ed. Charles Reagan Wilson and William Ferris (Chapel Hill: University of North Carolina Press, 1989), 1559–1660; Kathleen May Gonzáles, "The Mexican Family in San Antonio, Texas," master's thesis, University of Texas, 1928, 65.

43. Calvert and De León, *History of Texas*, 222, 228; Richard A. García, "Making of the Mexican-American Mind," 298; Knox, "Economic Status of the Mexican Immigrant," 27; Julia Kirk Blackwelder, "Women in the Work Force: Atlanta, New

Orleans, and San Antonio, 1930–1940," *Journal of Urban History* 4, no. 3 (1978): 351; Taylor, *American-Mexican Frontier,* 161, 177; "Corpus Christi—'Where Texas Meets the Sea,'" *Texas Municipalities* 12, no. 6 (November–December 1925): 177, CAH; Knox, "Economic Status of the Mexican Immigrant," 20.

44. Max S. Handman, "The Mexican Immigrant in Texas," *Southwestern Political and Social Science Quarterly* 7 (1926): 336–337; this was an address before the National Conference of Social Work.

45. Knox, "Economic Status of the Mexican Immigrant," 27; James K. Harris, "Sociological Study," 40–41, 46; Calvert and De León, *History of Texas,* 223; Victor Nelson Cisneros, "La clase trabajadora en Tejas, 1920–1940," *Aztlán* 6, no. 2 (Summer 1975): 239–266.

46. "Directorio mexicano de negocios," in *Guía general y directorio mexicano de San Antonio, Texas,* ed. J. C. Sologaistoa, (San Antonio: N.p., 1924), 191–194, CAH.

47. Frank Stricker, "Affluence for Whom?—Another Look at Prosperity and the Working Classes in the 1920s," *Labor History* 24, no. 1 (Winter 1983): 23.

48. Edgar Greer Shelton Jr., *Political Conditions Among Texas Mexicans Along the Rio Grande,* master's thesis, University of Texas, 1946 (reprint, San Francisco: R and E Associates, 1974), 7.

49. Jovita González, "Social Life," 30.

50. Richard A. García, "Making of the Mexican-American Mind," 117, 317; Knox, "Economic Status of the Mexican Immigrant," 46–48, James K. Harris, "Sociological Study," 64–65.

51. Richard A. García claims that this group filled a leadership vacuum, but he does not pay attention to La Raza's native leadership as does Julie Leininger Pycior: García, *Rise of the Mexican American Middle Class,* 21; Pycior, "La Raza Organizes."

52. On *La Prensa* see Onofre di Stefano, "'Venimos a Luchar': A Brief History of *La Prensa's* Founding," *Aztlán* 16, nos. 1–2 (1985): 94–118; Onofre di Stefano, "*La Prensa* of San Antonio and Its Literary Page, 1913 to 1915," Ph.D. diss., UCLA, 1983. On Alicia Lozano see "Alicia Elizondo Lozano, Widow Of Paper Founder," *San Antonio Light,* December 4, 1984, and "Alicia Lozano Ran *La Prensa,*" *San Antonio Express,* December 4, 1984, vertical files, San Antonio Public Library, San Antonio, TX (hereinafter SAPL); and Cynthia E. Orozco, "Alicia Lozano," *New Handbook* 4:318.

53. Richard A. García, "Making of the Mexican-American Mind," 204.

54. *Guía general,* 215. *San Antonio Telephone Directory,* July 1928, CAH; this directory included attorneys Anacleto Martínez, Leonard Garza Jr., M. C. Gonzáles, and Rubén R. Lozano. A "Martínez" was listed with "Davis & Martínez" but is considered here as the same person. A few of the two hundred may have been African American.

55. Olivas, *Colored Men,* 221.

56. *Guía general,* 211–222.

57. San Miguel Jr., "Endless Pursuits," 39–40, 55n40; Taylor, *American-Mexican Frontier,* 177; Eleazar Paredes, "Role of Mexican Americans," 34. *C. R. Wallin's Corpus Christi City Directory, 1915–1916* (Corpus Christi: C. R. Wallin, 1915), CAH; Moisés Sandoval, *Our Legacy: The First Fifty Years* (Washington, DC: LULAC, 1979), 30.

58. Knox, "Economic Status of the Mexican Immigrant," 42.

59. S. J. Montiel Olvera, *Primer anuario de la habitantes hispano-americanos de Texas* (San Antonio: Mexican Chamber of Commerce?, 1939), 29, SAPL. Original text: *No es común que las mujeres de nuestra raza se pongan al frente de empresas industriales, aunque su competencia es indudable y sus tamaños para sacar avante una empresa mercantil son de la misma magnitud que la de los varones. Sin embargo, es habitual verlas enroladas en negociaciones de índole tal, que los servicios prestados o los artículos elaborados, tienen directa relación o son consumidos por miembros de su sexo* (It is not common for the women of our race to run industrial companies, although their competence is unquestionable and their [capacities] to get ahead in a mercantile firm are of the same magnitude as men's. Nevertheless, it is common to see them taking part in negotiations such that the services rendered or goods made have a direct relationship to or are consumed by members of their gender).

60. Blackwelder, "Women in the Work Force," 346–347; Sandoval, *Our Legacy*, 6.

61. *C. R. Wallin's Corpus Christi City Directory* lists the last name and a first initial; however, it distinguishes women as "Mrs." or "Miss." Conclusion based on San Miguel Jr., "Endless Pursuits," 55n40; Taylor, *American-Mexican Frontier*, 161.

62. *Corpus Christi City Directory*, 1923–1924, comp. Ernest Miller (Asheville, NC: Miller Press, 1924?), 267, 270; copy at Lorenzo De Zavala Texas State Library, Austin.

63. Knox, "Economic Status of the Mexican Immigrant," 63; Stricker, "Affluence," 23.

64. Américo Paredes, *With His Pistol*, 40; *San Antonio Daily Express*, "Mexicans Discovered at Gonzales" and "Account of the Killing from Luling," June 16, 1901; Rodolfo Rocha, "The Influence of the Mexican Revolution on the Mexico-Texas Border, 1910–1916," Ph.D. diss., Texas Tech University, 1981, 37; Cynthia E. Orozco, "Gregorio Cortéz," *New Handbook* 1:342–343.

65. Américo Paredes, *With His Pistol*, 40, 78; Richard J. Mertz, "'No One Can Arrest Me': The Story of Gregorio Cortéz," *Journal of South Texas* 1, no. 1 (1974), 1; Arnoldo De León, "The Tejano Experience in Six Texas Regions," *West Texas Historical Association Year Book* 65 (1989): 36–43; Rocha, "Influence of the Mexican Revolution," 28.

66. Pichardo, "Role of Community," 35.

67. Manuel Gamio, *Mexican Immigration to the United States* (Chicago: University of Chicago Press, 1930), 130.

68. Mario T. García, "Mexican Americans and the Politics of Citizenship."

69. Emory S. Bogardus, *The Mexican in the United States* (1934; reprint, San Francisco: R and E Research Associates, 1970), 9.

70. U.S. Congress, House Committee on Immigration and Naturalization, Hearings on Western Hemisphere Immigration, 71st Congress, 2d Session, 1930 (hereinafter U.S. Congress, House Immigration Committee Hearings).

71. In Richard A. García, "Making of the Mexican-American Mind," 325.

72. Buckner, "Study of the Lower Rio Grande," 85.

73. Questionnaire by O. Douglas Weeks answered by Bexar County LULAC member, 1929, ODWP, BLAC.

74. Buckner, "Study of the Lower Rio Grande," 85.

75. Charles Harris III and Louis Sadler, *The Texas Rangers and the Mexican Revolution: Their Bloodiest Decade* (Albuquerque: University of New Mexico Press, 2004).

76. Montejano, *Anglos and Mexicans*, 154, illustration. Original text: *Los crímenes y atropellos que a diario se están cometiendo en indefensas mujeres, ancianos y niños de nuestra raza, por los bandidos y miserables rangers que vigilan las riberas del Río Bravo.* See Johnson, *Revolution in Texas*, and Richard Henry Ribb, "Jose T. Canales and the Texas Rangers: Myth, Identity, and Power in South Texas, 1900–1920," Ph.D. diss., University of Texas at Austin, 2001.

77. Julian Samora, Joe Bernal, and Albert Peña, *Gunpowder Justice* (Notre Dame, IN: University of Notre Dame Press, 1979), 66–67; Evan Anders, *Boss Rule in South Texas* (Austin: University of Texas, 1982), 267; U.S. Congress, Proceedings of the Joint Committee of the Senate and the House in the Investigation of the Texas State Ranger Force, 1919, Lorenzo De Zavala Library, Austin; Robert Utley, *Lone Star Lawmen: The Second Century of the Texas Rangers* (New York: Oxford University Press, 2007).

78. Charles C. Alexander, "Crusades for Conformity: The Ku Klux Klan in Texas, 1920–1930," *Texas Gulf Historical Association* 6, no. 1 (August 1962): v, 77; June Rayfield Welch, *Texas: New Perspectives*, 276; Pycior, "La Raza Organizes," 96; *Austin American-Statesman*, "Lessons from the Past," May 5, 1991. Research on the Klan and La Raza is limited; on California see Martha Menchaca, *Mexican Outsiders: A History of Marginalization and Discrimination in California* (Austin: University of Texas, 1995).

79. Alexander, "Crusades for Conformity," 6; Enrique Santibáñez, *Ensayo acerca de la inmigración mexicana en los Estados Unidos* (San Antonio: Clegg, 1930), 90–91, BLAC; Shelton Jr., *Political Conditions*, 21; Kilgore, "Corpus Christi," 442.

80. Rosales, *¡Pobre Raza!*, 119.

81. Walter Prescott Webb, *The Texas Rangers* (Cambridge, MA: Riverside Press, 1935), 41.

82. In Reisler, *By the Sweat of Their Brow*, 143.

83. José E. Limón, "El Primer Congreso Mexicanista de 1911: A Precursor to Contemporary Chicanismo," *Aztlán* 5, nos. 1–2 (1974): 88.

84. Alonso S. Perales, *En defensa de mi raza* (San Antonio: Artes Gráficas, 1937), 1:6–7.

85. Jovita González, "Social Life," 105.

86. Richard A. García, "Making of the Mexican-American Mind," 32 (quote), 108; Arreola, *Tejano South Texas*, 142; Gussie Scott Chaney, "The Mexican Element in San Antonio," *The Passing Show* 3, no. 5 (June 13, 1908): 78, CAH.

87. Richard A. García, "Making of the Mexican-American Mind," 107.

88. In Perales, *En defensa de mi raza*, 1:6–7. See also "The Ghost of Goliad," *Ferguson Forum* (Temple, TX), December 15, 1920, CAH; Alonso S. Perales, "Réplica a Mr. James E. Ferguson," letter to editor of *El Latino Americano*, January 14, 1920, and "A los votantes de origen mexicano, en el Distrito Número [no number], del Estado de Texas," October 1924 (broadside), Casamiro Pérez Alvarez Papers, CAH. James Ferguson and Miriam Amanda Ferguson governed Texas during terms in 1914–1917, 1924–1926, and 1932–1934. See "James Edward Ferguson" and "Ferguson Forum," *Handbook of Texas* (Austin: Texas State Historical Association, 1952), 590–592; "Mir-

iam Amanda Ferguson," *Handbook of Texas* (Austin: Texas State Historical Association, 1976), 293–294.

89. Hall and Coerver, *Revolution on the Border*, 140; Jovita González, "Social Life," 109.

90. Interview with Mr. [M. C.?] Gonzáles, September 1967, Transcription Notes, vertical file "Mexicans Organizations," Institute of Texan Cultures, University of Texas at San Antonio.

91. San Miguel Jr., "Endless Pursuits," 62.

92. Limón, "El Primer Congreso Mexicanista," 124. See also Anders, *Boss Rule*, 267, 271–272.

93. Carlos M. Álcala and Jorge C. Rangel, "Project Report: De Jure Segregation in Texas Schools," *Harvard Civil Rights–Civil Liberties Law Review* 7, no. 2 (March 1972): 312.

94. Taylor, *American-Mexican Frontier*, 191–192.

95. Montejano, *Anglos and Mexicans*, 160, 169; Alcalá and Rangel, "Project Report," 313–314; Thomas Edward Simmons, "The Citizen Factories: The Americanization of Mexican Students in Texas Public Schools, 1920–1945," Ph.D. diss., Texas A&M University, 1976, 137.

96. Notes on *The Argus*, Mid-April, No. 1927, Transcript of John Box immigration files, 91, ODWP.

97. Richard A. García, "Making of the Mexican-American Mind," 420; Alvin S. Johnson, "Mexico in San Antonio," *New Republic*, June 24, 1916, 16, in *Teaching Foreigners*, CAH; *El Paladín*, "Se combatirá la segregación de los niños mexicanos en las escuelas," December 12, 1930, and "El regreso del Lic. Perales y la segregación de niños mexicanos en las escuelas de Texas," December 19, 1930, ODWP.

98. San Miguel Jr., "Endless Pursuits," 61.

99. In ibid., 78; *Corpus Christi Caller*, "More Early History of City Schools," March 24, 1921, "Corpus Christi," vertical files, Corpus Christi Public Library (hereinafter CCPL); *Corpus Christi Caller*, "Clark Recalls Days When Top Salary was $1200 a Year," April 30, 1948; *Corpus Christi Times*, advertisement by Citizens State Bank and "Stories of Corpus Christi," April 4 and 5, 1962, "Corpus Christi," vertical files, CCPL.

100. Taylor, *American-Mexican Frontier*, 200.

101. H. T. Manuel, "The Mexican Child," *Southwest Review* (April 1932): 26–27. Original text: *En algunos casos las diferencias son muy marcadas: la escuela para los niños mexicanos es un cobertizo cualquier en malas condiciones, sin cortinas para el sol, con un mobilario viejo e insuficiente, sin biblioteca y sin equipo educativo, fuera de libros de texto viejos, sin instalación de agua, instalaciónes sanitarias primitivas, profesores mal preparados y mal remunerados y periodos escolares muy cortos, contraslando con las otras escuelas en el mismo distrito, que cuentan con buenos edificios modernos, convenientemente equipados y con toda clase de facilidades educativas. Esta no es una situación excepcional.*

102. In H. T. Manuel, *The Education of Mexican and Spanish-Speaking Children in Texas* (Austin: Fund for Research in the Social Sciences, 1930), 61–62.

103. Ibid., 65.

104. San Miguel Jr., "Endless Pursuits," 150; Harris, "Sociological Study," 35–37; Montejano, *Anglos and Mexicans*, 193; Taylor, *American-Mexican Frontier*, 201.

105. Eleuterio Escobar Jr., Autobiography, final draft, Eleuterio Escobar Jr. Papers, BLAC (hereinafter EEJP), n.p.

106. *1929 Texas Agricultural and State Industrial Guide*, "Scholastic Population, Counties and Districts, 1928–1929," 230, 236, CAH. Taylor, *American-Mexican Frontier*, 191; Richard A. García, "Making of the Mexican-American Mind," Table 9, 415, 420.

107. Jovita González, "Social Life," 104.

108. Simmons, "Citizen Factories," 60.

109. Ibid., 55.

110. Jovita González, "Social Life," 113.

111. Gilbert G. Gonzáles, *Chicano Education in the Era of Segregation*, (Philadelphia: Balch Institute Press, 1990), 89–90.

112. San Miguel Jr., "Endless Pursuits," 197. He notes that in 1942 Alicia Alemán was one of the first Chicanas to graduate from high school.

113. *Corpus Christi Caller*, "And the battles are still not over . . . ," February 11, 1979, CCPL; Jovita González, "Social Life," 81; Taylor, *American-Mexican Frontier*, 202; Eleazar Paredes, "Role of Mexican Americans," 13; San Miguel Jr., "Endless Pursuits," 139n62; Michael V. Miller and Robert Lee Maril, "Poverty in the Lower Rio Grande Valley of Texas: Historical and Contemporary Dimensions," Departmental Technical Report No. 78–2 (College Station: Texas Agricultural Experiment Station, Texas A&M University System, 1979), 117. In 1918 in Brownsville there were no Mexican-descent administrators, faculty members, or high school seniors.

114. Richard A. García, "Making of the Mexican-American Mind," 212; Manuel, *Education*, 106; *LULAC News*, "Contact with Your Legislators," March 1933, 8.

115. H. T. Manuel, *Spanish-Speaking Children of the Southwest: Their Education and The Public Welfare* (Austin: University of Texas Press, 1965), 61; Weeks, "Texas-Mexican," 10; *Daily Texan*, "Gets Citizenship after 30 Years in Texas," June 11, 1936, CAH.

116. San Miguel Jr., "Endless Pursuits," 116; Knox, "Economic Status of the Mexican Immigrant," 64–65; Taylor, *American-Mexican Frontier*, 191. According to the 1930 Census, 7.7 percent of all persons in San Antonio over ten years of age were illiterate, nine-tenths of whom were of Mexican descent; this figure is an underestimate. See Richard A. García, "Making of the Mexican-American Mind," 432.

117. Francisco Javier Hernández, "Schools for Mexicans: A Case Study of a Chicano School," Ph.D. diss., Stanford University, 1982, 48; *C. R. Wallin's Corpus Christi City Directory*; Taylor, *American-Mexican Frontier*, 191. See also Pycior, "La Raza Organizes," and Zamora, "Mexican Labor Activity."

118. Roberto R. Calderón, "Tejano Politics," *New Handbook* 6:239–242.

119. Richard A. García, *Rise of the Mexican American Middle Class*, 22, 25; Arnoldo De León, *The Tejano Community, 1836–1900* (Albuquerque: University of New Mexico Press, 1982), 103; Shelton Jr., *Political Conditions*, 82; Questionnaire by O. Douglas Weeks answered by Bexar County LULAC member, 1929, ODWP, BLAC; *1929 Texas Agricultural and State Industrial Guide*, 273–289, CAH.

120. Norman Binder and Frank J. García, "Winning Political Office in Cameron County, 1876–1988: The Mexican-American Case," in *More Studies in Brownsville History*, ed. Milo Kearney (Brownsville: Pan American University, 1989), 423–438.

121. Shelton Jr., *Political Conditions*, 35.

122. Jovita González, "Social Life," 87–89; Shelton Jr., *Political Conditions*, 29, 65.

123. *D. W. Glasscock, Contestant, vs. A. Parr, Contestee,* Supplement to the Senate Journal, Regular Session of the 36th Legislature, 1919, CAH (hereinafter *Glasscock* Supplement), 848.

124. Ibid., 847; Jovita González, "Social Life," 78; Perales, *El México americano*, 6.

125. Questionnaire by O. Douglas Weeks to Bexar County LULAC member, 1929, ODWP.

126. In Shelton Jr., *Political Conditions*, 76. In Kenedy County voters received ice cream as a bribe. *Glasscock* Supplement, 86.

127. Escobar Jr., Autobiography, final draft, 20.

128. Joe B. Franz, *Texas: A Bicentennial History* (New York: W. W. Norton, 1976), 171.

129. *Glasscock* Supplement, 1003–1005; Shelton Jr., *Political Conditions*, 82.

130. *Glasscock* Supplement, 36–37.

131. In *Copies of Affidavits Showing Corruption in the 1914 Congressional Election at San Antonio, Bexar City* (Cooperstown, NY: Crist, n.d.), CAH.

132. John A. Booth and David R. Johnson, "Power and Progress in San Antonio Politics, 1836–1970," in *The Politics of San Antonio, Community, Progress, and Power,* ed. David R. Johnson, John A. Booth, and Richard J. Harris (Lincoln: University of Nebraska Press, 1983), 15–17.

133. *Guía general,* "Los mexicanos y el 'Poll Tax,'" 107. Original text: *En primer lugar, debemos decir que a sabiendo de que muchos mexicanos residentes en la ciudad, en el condado y en el estado en general, no saben exactamente si tienen que pagar o no el impuesto de referencia.*

134. In Perales, *El México americano*, 5. Original text: *La amistad y el temor los influye grandemente cuando intentan sufragar. Para ellos el votar tiene muy poco o ningun significado fuera de volverle un favor a alguien de mayor herarquía a quien le deben empleo, dinero, atención personal o alguna otra cosa. Ellos reconocen como su cabecilla político local. Cuando se llega el tiempo de las elecciones en muchos casos reciben comprobantes del "poll-tax" por correo o algun otro modo. Algun benefactor amable ha pagado el "poll-tax" por ellos.*

135. In Taylor, *American-Mexican Frontier*, 237–238.

136. Perales, *El México americano*, 6.

137. Letter to Jas. [*sic*], February 16, 1928, transcript, John Box immigration files, ODWP.

138. In Montejano, *Anglos and Mexicans*, 131.

139. Jovita González, "Social Life," 93–94.

140. Shelton, *Political Conditions*, 114. J. T. Canales, "A los votantes Méxicotexanos," *La Crónica* (Laredo), July 16, 1910, 2; Hall and Coerver, *Revolution on the Border*, 18.

141. Taylor, *American-Mexican Frontier*, 235.

142. Shelton Jr., *Political Conditions*, 82; *1929 Texas Agricultural and Industrial Guide*, 262, CAH; Questionnaire by O. D. Weeks answered by Bexar County LULAC member, 1929, ODWP.

143. Montejano, *Anglos and Mexicans*, 135; Shelton Jr., *Political Conditions*, 7; An-

ders, *Boss Rule*, x, xi; *1914 Texas Almanac and State Industrial Guide*, (Dallas: A. H. Belo, 1914), 217, CAH.

144. In Taylor, *American-Mexican Frontier*, 238.

145. "Ejemplo de la boleta apoyada por la Asociación de Votantes Independientes." Association of Independent Voters folder, EEJP, BLAC.

146. *1929 Texas Agricultural and State Industrial Guide*, 262–289; *Members of the Texas Legislature, 1846–1962* (Austin: Texas Legislature, 1962), CAH.

147. John C. Solís, interview by Angie del Cueto Quirós, San Antonio, Texas, circa 1977, cassette 13, BLAC; Petition to Judge Hopkins, December 1, 1925, from the Order Sons of America, PSTP; De León, *Tejano Community*, 34; Questionnaire by O. D. Weeks, answered by Bexar County LULAC member, 1929, ODWP. In 1910 in Brownsville, only two Mexican Americans served as members of the grand jury, and one served on the petit jury; see Rocha, "Influence of the Mexican Revolution," 27.

CHAPTER 2: IDEOLOGICAL ORIGINS OF THE MOVEMENT

1. Montejano, *Anglos and Mexicans*; Richard A. García, *Rise of the Mexican American Middle Class*; Mario T. García, *Mexican Americans*; Benjamín Márquez, *LULAC*. See also Márquez, "League of United Latin American Citizens"; Márquez, "Politics of Race and Class"; and Márquez, "Problems of Organizational Maintenance."

2. See F. Arturo Rosales, "Shifting Ethnic Consciousness." Also on identity politics see Ramón A. Gutiérrez, "Unraveling America's Hispanic Past: Internal Stratification and Class Boundaries," *Aztlán* 17, no. 1 (Spring 1986): 79–101.

3. De León, *Tejano Community*; "Esperamos," *El Voluntario* (Rio Grande City, TX), October 16, 1892, 3, Casimiro Pérez Álvarez Papers, CAH. The newspaper's subtitle read, "Independent Newspaper, Organ of the Mexico-Texano Element."

4. Rodolfo Rocha, "Influence of the Mexican Revolution," 47.

5. Limón, "El Primer Congreso Mexicanista"; Limón paid attention to the "Mexican" identity there, but during the Chicano movement Mexicans and Mexican Americans were often cast as the same group.

6. Constitution and By-Laws of Order Sons of America, Council No. 1, San Antonio, Texas, adopted June 15, 1922 (hereinafter OSA constitution), José Limón Papers, Austin, private collection (hereinafter JLP). I thank Limón for sharing this source. Self-referents can be studied also by looking at the names of organizations; see Pycior, "La Raza Organizes."

7. Peter V. N. Henderson, *Mexican Exiles in the Borderlands, 1910–1913* (El Paso: Texas Western University Press, 1979), 212, 218; Rocha, "Influence of the Mexican Revolution," 90–91.

8. Charles H. Harris III and Louis R. Sadler, "The 1911 Reyes Conspiracy: A View From Texas," in Charles H. Harris III and Louis R. Sadler, *The Border and the Revolution* (Las Cruces: Center for Latin American Studies, New Mexico State University, Joint Border Research Institute, 1988): 27–52.

9. Rocha, "Influence of the Mexican Revolution," 116, 251; Richard J. Mertz, "'No One Can Arrest Me,' The Story of Gregorio Cortez," *Journal of South Texas* 1 (1974): 14; Nancy Baker Jones, "Jovita Idar," *New Handbook*, 3:814–815.

10. John Busby McClury, "The Texas Rangers Along the Rio Grande," Ph.D. diss., Texas Tech University, 1981, 57.

11. Rocha, "Influence of the Mexican Revolution," 162.

12. Paul J. Vanderwood and Frank N. Samponara, *Border Fury: A Picture Postcard Record of Mexico's Revolution and U.S. War Preparedness, 1910–1917* (Albuquerque: University of New Mexico Press, 1988), 122. Governor Oscar Colquitt wrote President Woodrow Wilson in 1913 that "Mexicans make no hesitancy in expressing their intentions to fight for Mexico . . . Their minds embrace loyalty to the Patria only"; in Rocha, "Influence of the Mexican Revolution," 22–23.

13. James Leroy Evans, "The Indian Savage, the Mexican Bandit, the Chinese Heathen—Three Popular Stereotypes," Ph.D. diss., University of Texas at Austin, 1967, 72. U.S. Congress, House Immigration Committee Hearings, 171; Rocha, "Influence of the Mexican Revolution," 140; McClury, "Texas Rangers," 67.

14. McClury, "Texas Rangers," 67.

15. Ibid., 59.

16. Ibid., 61. Vanderwood and Samponara, *Border Fury*.

17. Anders, *Boss Rule*, 215.

18. Ibid., 219. Rocha, "Influence of the Mexican Revolution," 140.

19. Anders, *Boss Rule*, 215–220, 232; Rocha, "Influence of the Mexican Revolution," 76; *Weslaco 1919–1969 Official Historical Booklet*, December 4–7, 1969, 6, Mercedes, TX, Public Library; Kilgore, "Corpus Christi," 439; Samora, Bernal, and Peña, *Gunpowder Justice*, 66; Howard C. Smith, "The Legion Comes Home," *Bunker's Monthly: The Magazine of Texas*, August 1925, 176, CAH.

20. J. Luz Sáenz, "Racial Discrimination," in *Are We Good Neighbors?*, ed. Alonso S. Perales (San Antonio: Artes Gráficas, 1948): 32–33.

21. Webb, *Texas Rangers*, 476. See also Johnson, *Revolution in Texas*; Utley, *Lone Star Lawmen*; McClury, "Texas Rangers," 61; Rocha, "Influence of the Mexican Revolution," 140.

22. Anders, *Boss Rule*, 221; Samora, Bernal, and Peña, *Gunpowder Justice*, 64; Vanderwood and Samponara, *Border Fury*, 122.

23. Hall and Coerver, *Revolution on the Border*, 24.

24. In Simmons, "Citizen Factories," 14.

25. Rocha, "Influence of the Mexican Revolution," 272; Anders, *Boss Rule*, 223; Samora, Bernal, and Peña, *Gunpowder Justice*, 64.

26. Anders, *Boss Rule*, 224; McClury, "Texas Rangers," 92.

27. Dorothy Lee Pope, *Rainbow Era on the Rio Grande* (Brownsville, TX: Springman-King, 1971), 121.

28. Ibid., 67.

29. In Anders, *Boss Rule*, 218.

30. In U.S. Congress, Proceedings of the Joint Committee, 324.

31. Anders, *Boss Rule*, 221.

32. U.S. Congress, Proceedings of the Joint Committee, 17, 1071. Anders, *Boss Rule*; Harris and Sadler, *Texas Rangers*; Ribb, "José T. Canales."

33. Vanderwood and Samponara, *Border Fury*, 122.

34. Ibid., 7, 37, 113. Eighty Rangers were authorized, but the budget allowed only for twenty-seven; Hall and Coerver, *Revolution on the Border*, 21.

35. Webb, *Texas Rangers*, 478.

36. U.S. Congress, Proceedings of the Joint Committee, Testimonies of Virginia Yeager and J. T. Canales, 6, 870.

37. Oscar J. Martínez, *Fragments of the Revolution* (Albuquerque: University of New Mexico Press, 1983), 171.

38. Anders, *Boss Rule*, 266; McClury, "Texas Rangers," 111.

39. U.S. Congress, Proceedings of the Joint Committee, 49.

40. Rocha, "Influence of the Mexican Revolution," 316.

41. J. Luz Sáenz, "Racial Discrimination," 33.

42. U.S. Congress, House Immigration Committee Hearings, 186.

43. Robert H. Wiebe, *A Search for Order* (New York: Hill and Wang, 1967); Paula S. Fass, *Outside In: Minorities and the Transformation of American Education* (New York: Oxford University Press, 1989).

44. George J. Sánchez, "'Go After the Women': Americanization and the Mexican Immigrant Woman, 1915–1929," working paper (Stanford, CA: Stanford University Center for Chicano Research, 1983).

45. Richard A. García, "Making of the Mexican-American Mind," 416.

46. *San Antonio Express-Light*, "Mexican Voters Being Stirred to Support 'Better Governmenters' by Former Interpreter at Embassy," July 18, 1924, M. C. Gonzáles Collection, BLAC.

47. Cynthia E. Orozco, "Hidalgo County Rebellion," *New Handbook*, 3:593; Montejano, *Anglos and Mexicans*, 147; J. Gilberto Quezada, *Border Boss, Manuel B. Bravo and Zapata County* (College Station: Texas A&M University Press, 1999), 18–19.

48. Emory S. Bogardus, *The Essentials of Americanization* (Los Angeles: University of Southern California Press, 1919), 12; Stanley Feldstein and Lawrence Costello, eds., *The Ordeal of Assimilation: A Documentary History of the White Working Class* (Garden City, NY: Anchor Press, 1974), 357–358.

49. Alfred Eugene White, "The Apperceptive Mass of Foreigners as Applied to Americanization: The Mexican Group," master's thesis, University of California at Berkeley, 1923 (reprint, San Francisco: R and E Research Associates, 1971), 3–4; Mario T. García, "Americanization and the Mexican Immigrant, 1880–1930," *Journal of Ethnic Studies* 6, no. 2 (1978–1979): 19–34.

50. Theodore Roosevelt, *Fear God and Take Your Own Part* (New York: George H. Doran, 1916), 370.

51. White, "Apperceptive Mass," 4.

52. Allen F. Davis, *Spearheads of Reform: The Social Settlements and the Progressive Movement, 1890–1914* (New York: Oxford University Press, 1967); "Mexican Christian Institute," 1, vertical files, "Mexican Americans," CAH; Colby D. Hall, *Texas Disciples: A Study of the Rise and Progress of that Protestant Movement Known as Disciples of Christ or Christians* (Fort Worth: Texas Christian University Press, 1953), 221; María Cristina García, "Agents of Americanization: Rusk Settlement and the Houston Mexicano Community, 1907–1950," in *Mexican Americans in Texas History*, ed. Emilio Zamora, Cynthia Orozco, and Rodolfo Rocha (Austin: Texas State Historical Association, 2000): 121–138.

53. Bogardus, *Essentials of Americanization*, 12, 21; White, "Apperceptive Mass," 2.

54. Supplement to the Texas Senate Journal, Regular Session of the 36th Legislature, 1919, Testimony of Captain Hansen, 177, CAH.

55. William E. Leuchtenberg, *The Perils of Prosperity, 1914–1932* (Chicago: University of Chicago Press, 1958), 45; Simmons, "Citizen Factories," 68. Emphasizing patriotism, the movement led to the suppression of radicalism. See Zamora, "Mexican Labor Activity," 180; Emilio Zamora Jr., "Chicano Socialist Labor Activity in Texas, 1900–1920," *Aztlán* 6, no. 2 (Summer 1975): 221–236; and Neil Foley, *The White Scourge: Mexicans, Blacks, and Poor Whites in the Texas Cotton Culture* (Berkeley: University of California Press, 1997).

56. Joe B. Franz, *Texas, A Bicentennial History* (New York: W. W. Norton, 1976), 171. J. T. Canales favored the ban against German in public schools; Anders, *Boss Rule*, 236. Thomas F. Gosset, *Race: the History of an Idea in America* (Dallas: Southern Methodist University Press, 1963), 371; John J. Mahoney, "Training Teachers for Americanization," *Bulletin* 1–2, Department of the Interior, Bureau of Education (Washington, DC: Government Printing Office, 1920), 42.

57. In San Miguel Jr., *"Let Them All Take Heed,"* 65.

58. Published in *San Antonio Express*, "Sowing Americanism to Raise Better Citizens," November 2, 1919, 17, CAH.

59. Charles August Arnold, "The Folklore, Manners, and Customs of Mexicans in San Antonio," master's thesis, University of Texas, 1928, 68. In 1934 in Harlingen, the English Club promoted the English language and penalized its members for speaking Spanish. If a child spoke Spanish during the group's activities, he or she was assigned to another room to study; see Gilbert G. González, *Chicano Education*.

60. Simmons, "Citizen Factories."

61. Works that mention World War I include George C. Kiser and Martha Woody Kiser, eds., *Mexican Workers in the United States: Historical and Political Perspectives* (Albuquerque: University of New Mexico Press, 1979), and Sarah Deutsch, *No Separate Refuge: Culture, Class, and Gender on an Anglo-Hispanic Frontier in the American Southwest, 1880–1940* (New York: Oxford University Press, 1987). Phillip Gonzales and Ann Massman, "Loyalty Questioned: Nuevomexicans in the Great War," *Pacific Historical Review* 75, no. 4 (November 2006): 629–666. On World War II see Carl Allsup, *American GI Forum*; Henry A. J. Ramos, *A People Forgotten, A Dream Pursued: The History of the American GI Forum* (Corpus Christi, TX: American GI Forum, 1982); Manuel P. Servín, "The Post–World War II Mexican-Americans, 1925–1965: A Nonachieving Minority," in *An Awakened Minority: The Mexican Americans*, 2d edition (Beverly Hills: Glencoe Press, 1970); Alberto M. Camarillo, "Research Note on Chicano Community Leaders: The GI Generation," *Aztlán* 2, no. 2 (Fall 1971): 145–150; Maggie Rivas-Rodriguez, *A Legacy Greater than Words* (Austin: University of Texas Press, 2004); Maggie Rivas-Rodriguez, ed., *Mexican Americans and World War II* (Austin: University of Texas Press, 2005); and Richard Griswold del Castillo, *World War II and Mexican American Civil Rights* (Austin: University of Texas Press, 2008).

62. Christian, "Joining the American Mainstream," 559.

63. T. R. Fehrenbach, *Lone Star: A History of Texas and the Texans* (New York: Macmillan, 1968), 643; Lawrence A. Cardoso, "Labor Emigration to the Southwest, 1916 to 1920: Mexican Attitudes and Policy," in *Mexican Workers*, ed. Kiser and Kiser,

27. Texans responded in large numbers, in part as a reaction to German influence in Mexico.

64. U.S. Congress, House Immigration Committee Hearings, Testimony of J. T. Canales, 171.

65. *Demócrata Fronterizo* (Laredo), August 24, 1918, 2, CAH. Original text: *Los hijos de ciudadanos mexicanos nacidos en los Estados Unidos son Americanos.*

66. *El Popular* (Del Rio, TX), "Para los que no conocen nuestra institución," circa 1930, Ben Garza Collection (hereinafter BGC), Album 2, BLAC. Original text: *Uno de los errores más grandes de algunos padres mexicanos es creer que cuando su hijo cumple los 21 años, va al consulado y saca su carta de ciudadano americano automáticamente ni obstante haber nacido en Estados Unidos.*

67. U.S. Congress, Proceedings of the Joint Committee, Testimony of Ventura Sánchez, 347.

68. Letter to John C. Box from H. W. Bayor, March 23, 1928, ODWP, BLAC.

69. Cardoso, "Labor Emigration," 27.

70. Taylor, Field notes, Texas, notes 1–127, *Nueces Study*, no. 26, PSTP.

71. Hall and Coerver, *Revolution on the Border*, 132–133.

72. Cardoso, "Labor Emigration," 27–28; Manuel Gamio, *Quantitative Estimate of Sources and Distribution of Mexican Immigration into the United States* (Mexico City: Talleres Gráficas, 1930), Table 1.

73. In U.S. Congress, Proceedings of the Joint Committee, 316 (first Yeager quote), 318 (second Yeager quote), 324; McClury, "Texas Rangers," 100; Anders, *Boss Rule*, 266.

74. Anders, *Boss Rule*, 235.

75. Cardoso, "Labor Emigration," 28; Taylor, Field notes; Guillermo Hernández, *Canciones de la raza* (Berkeley: El Fuego de Aztlán, 1978), 37.

76. U.S. Congress, Proceedings of the Joint Committee, Testimony of J. T. Canales, 870.

77. In U.S. Congress, House Immigration Committee Hearings, Testimony of Alonso S. Perales, 187.

78. Craig Phelon, "The Hero Who Hid His Heritage," *San Antonio Express-News*, May 21, 1989.

79. U.S. Congress, Proceedings of the Joint Committee, 347.

80. Ibid., 615.

81. "La Guerra," Manuel Gamio Papers (hereinafter MGP), Bancroft Library. Original text: *Los Texanos también sabemos morir con una nación tan grande.* See also the song "Registro de 1918" in Guillermo Hernández, *Canciones de la Raza: Songs of the Chicano Experience* (Berkeley, CA: El Fuego de Aztlán, 1978), 37.

82. In Jovita González, "Social Life," 106.

83. *Corpus Christi Times*, "Years of Segregation are Recalled," January 23, 1970, vertical files, "Mexican Americans," CCPL.

84. J. Luz Sáenz, *Los méxico-americanos en la Gran Guerra contingente en pro de la democracia, la humanidad y la justicia* (San Antonio: Artes Gráficas, 1933), SAPL.

85. *LULAC News*, "Are Texas-Mexicans 'Americans'?" April 1932, 8, LULAC Archive, BLAC. This issue mentions that the Sons of America would be given two plaques bearing the names of San Antonio Mexican American soldiers and their

mothers; "Soldier Dead Are Honored," 8. See also Welch, *Texas: New Perspectives*, 266; and *Standard Blue Book*, Texas Edition (San Antonio: Standard Blue Book, 1921), "Roll of Honor, Texans Who Made the Supreme Sacrifice," 13, 61–77, and Charles W. Scruggs, "Texas' Part in the World War," 14, 97.

86. Christian, "Joining the American Mainstream," 559.

87. J. Luz Sáenz, "Racial Discrimination," 33.

88. Alonso S. Perales, "Principios contraproducentes para la americanización en Estados Unidos," in his *En defensa de mi raza*, 1937), 1:1–2. Original text: *Pero el propietario de dicho hotel se rehusó a aceptarlo exponiendo como razón que en su hotel no se admitían mexicanos, fueran or no ciudadanos americanos. Unos cuantos meses después que regresaron de Francia varios méxico-americanos después de haber participado en todos los combates librados por la famosa División 90.*

89. In Jovita González, "Social Life," 106.

90. Ibid., 108–109.

91. Manuel Gamio, "Relaciones entre mexicanos, méxico-texanos y americanos," manuscript, MGP. Original text: *Numerosos méxico-texanos fueron a la guerra europea formando parte del ejército americano, y ésto lo echan en cara o lo sacan a relucir cada vez que se les humilla o se pretende desconocer sus derechos por autoridades o por la sociedad en general. ¡Fuimos a la guerra[!], dicen, dimos nuestra sangre por los Estados Unidos y tenemos derecho a que se nos trate igual a los americanos.*

92. Taylor, *American-Mexican Frontier*, 245.

93. Ibid.

94. M. C. Gonzáles, "Echoes of the Kingsville Convention," *LULAC News*, September 1931, 8, PSTP.

95. Ibid.

96. Pycior, "La Raza Organizes," 98. LULAC established a fund for this monument under the administration of M. C. Gonzáles, then diverted the fund to desegregation efforts.

97. Guillermo Hernández, *Canciones de la Raza*, 12; Pycior, "La Raza Organizes," 98; Henry Hutchings, "Texas in the World's War," *Standard Blue Book*, Texas Edition 13 (San Antonio: Standard Blue Book, 1921), 30.

98. David Gregory Gutiérrez, "Ethnicity, Ideology," 60, 64.

99. Ibid., 60.

100. Richard A. García, "Making of the Mexican-American Mind," 415.

101. Ibid.

102. di Stefano, "'Venimos a luchar.'"

103. Rodolfo Acuña, *Occupied America*, 6th edition (New York: Pearson Longman, 2007), 151.

104. Will Kymlicka, *Theorizing Citizenship*, ed. Ronald Beiner (New York: State University of New York Press, 1995), 283.

105. Ngai, *Impossible Subjects*, 67.

106. Gloría Anzaldúa, *Borderlands/La Frontera: The New Mestiza* (San Francisco: Aunt Lute Books, 1987).

107. John Martínez, *Mexican Emigration to the United States, 1910–1930*, Ph.D. diss., University of California at Berkeley, 1957 (reprint, San Francisco: R and E. Research Associates, 1971), 17.

108. Clifford Alan Perkins, *Border Patrol: With the U.S. Immigration Service on the Mexican Boundary, 1910–1954* (El Paso: Texas Western University Press, 1978), 115.

109. Jerome Dowd, "Race Segregation in a World of Democracy," in *Fourteenth Annual Proceedings of the American Sociological Society* (Chicago: University of Chicago Press, 1920), 199–200.

110. Leuchtenberg, *Perils of Prosperity*, 207.

111. Letter to John C. Box from Arthur E. Knolle, February 4, 1928, ODWP.

112. Simmons, "Citizen Factories," 113.

113. Perales, *En defensa de mi raza*, 1:85; Weeks, 257. Montejano offers the best treatment of "the Mexican problem" in his *Anglos and Mexicans*. Also on "the Mexican problem" see Ray Padilla, "Apuntes para la documentación de la Cultura Chicana," *El Grito* 5, no. 2 (Winter 1971–1972): 3–46.

114. Letter to John C. Box from Roddis Lumber and Veneer Company of Missouri in San Antonio, February 22, 1928, ODWP.

115. Juanita Luna Lawhn, "The Making of Cultural Values: La sección del hogar in La Prensa," paper delivered at the Mexican Americans and Texas History conference of the Texas State Historical Association, San Antonio, May 4, 1991. According to Lawhn, typical headings in the women's section included "La educación de los hijos" (The education of children), "Sobre el casamiento" (About marriage), and "El hogar y la belleza" (Home and beauty).

CHAPTER 3: RISE OF A MOVEMENT

1. Montejano, *Anglos and Mexicans*, 244. David Montejano, "The Demise of 'Jim Crow' for Texas Mexicans, 1940–1970," *Aztlán* 16, nos. 1–2 (Spring 1987). Donald E. Worcester has dated the origins of these efforts in the 1950s; Worcester, "Significance of the Spanish Borderlands," 11.

2. Eleazar Paredes, "Role of the Mexican American," 4.

3. María Eva Flores, "What a Difference a War Makes!" *Mexican Americans and World War II*, ed. Maggie Rivas-Rodríguez (Austin: University of Texas Press, 2005), 178.

4. San Miguel Jr., *"Let Them All Take Heed"*; Thomas Kreneck, *Del Pueblo*; Mario T. García, *Mexican Americans*; Richard A. García, *Rise of the Mexican American Middle Class*; Arnoldo De León, *Ethnicity in the Sunbelt*.

5. Pycior, "La Raza Organizes."

6. Adriana Ayala, "Negotiating Race Relations Through Activism: Women Activists and Women's Organizing in San Antonio, Texas during the 1920s," Ph.D. diss., University of Texas at Austin, 2005, 98; Gilbert González, *Mexican Consuls and Labor Organizing: Imperial Politics in the American Southwest* (Austin: University of Texas Press, 1999), 42.

7. Juan Gómez-Quiñones, "Piedras contra la luna, México en Aztlán y Aztlán en México: Chicano-Mexicano Relations and the Mexican Consulates, 1900–1920," in *Contemporary Mexico: Papers at the IV International Congress of Mexican History*, ed. James W. Wilkie, Michael C. Meyer, and Edna Morgan de Wilkie (Berkeley: University of California Press, 1976), 496–497. The Reglamento del Cuerpo Consular

reads, *Les está absolutamente prohibido mezclarse en la política del país en que residen* (Involvement in the politics of the resident country is strictly prohibited).

8. Reisler, *By the Sweat of Their Brow*, 142–143.

9. In Pycior, "La Raza Organizes," 98n25.

10. In Gómez-Quiñones, "Piedras contra la luna," 523.

11. Limón, "El Primer Congreso Mexicanista," 91, 94; Zamora, *World of the Mexican Worker*, 97; Pycior, "La Raza Organizes," 156–169, 215; and LRR, "Observaciones," section on "Vida social de los mexicanos," Manuel Gamio Papers (hereinafter MGP), BLAC.

12. Barrera, "Historical Evolution," 5; José Amaro Hernández, *Mutual Aid for Survival*; Zamora, *World of the Mexican Worker*, 86.

13. José Rivera, *Mutual Aid Societies in the Hispanic Southwest: Alternative Sources of Community Empowerment*, research report submitted to Alternative Financing Project, Office of Assistant Secretary for Planning and Evaluation (Washington, DC: U.S. Department of Health and Human Services, October 1984), v, 29–30; Pycior, "La Raza Organizes," 73, 97, 121.

14. Zamora, *World of the Mexican Worker*, 5, 86, 236n2.

15. David Gregory Gutiérrez, "Ethnicity, Ideology," 77.

16. Pycior, "La Raza Organizes," 26, 42, 46–50, 213; Kathleen May Gonzáles, "Mexican Family in San Antonio," 1–2.

17. *Primer Congreso Mexicanista verificado en Laredo, Texas, EE.UU. de A. Discursos y conferencias, por La Raza* (Laredo: Tipografía de N. Idar, 1912), 20. On organizational life in Laredo see Simón G. Domínguez Letterbooks, 1904–1920, CAH.

18. De León, *Tejano Community*, 195; *C. R. Wallin's Corpus Christi Directory, 1915–1916*, 348, CAH.

19. Pycior, "La Raza Organizes," 35, 77.

20. Rosenberg, "Female World," 1–2.

21. Pycior, "La Raza Organizes," 77–80. See also *Guía general*, which documents the lack of female professionals, and Teresa Acosta Palomo, "Cruz Azul," *New Handbook*, 1:101.

22. Julie Leininger Pycior, "Tejanas Navigating the 1920s," in *Tejano Epic: Essays in Honor of Felix D. Almaraz*, ed. Arnoldo De León (Austin: Texas State Historical Association, 2005), 74.

23. LRR, "Observaciones," section on "Vida social de los mexicanos"; *La Vanguardia* (Austin), April 28, 1921, 1, Martha X. García Personal Papers, Lago Vista, Texas; Pycior, "La Raza Organizes," 158–194; Ayala, "Negotiating Race Relations," 104, 109.

24. Pycior, "La Raza Organizes," 173.

25. *La Prensa*, "Importantes acuerdos de los Hijos de México," July 3, 1927, 3; Kathleen May Gonzáles, "The Mexican Family in San Antonio," 3; Pycior, "La Raza Organizes," 177, 183–184.

26. Américo Paredes, *With His Pistol*; Mertz, "'No One Can Arrest Me,'" 10. Zamora called the Cortéz campaign "political mobilization, although admittedly rudimentary at this stage"; Zamora, *World of the Mexican Worker*, 65. See also Cynthia E. Orozco, "Gregorio Lira Cortéz," *New Handbook*, 2:89.

27. Mertz, "'No One Can Arrest Me,'" 10–12; Américo Paredes, *With His Pistol*,

87–88, 100. On Cruz see also *El Regidor,* "Rasgos biográficos de Pablo Cruz, extinto fundador de 'El Regidor,'" August 18, 1910, 1.

28. J. Luz Sáenz, "Al derredor de una profecía maliciosa," *Diógenes* (McAllen) April 1931, 3, Adela Sloss-Vento Papers (hereinafter ASVP), Edinburg, TX. Original text: *En nuestro mundo social hemos visto nacer movimientos cada vez que alguna catastrofe fatal se nos viene encima. A raíz de muchos abusos injustificados, de linchamientos bárbaros y bestiales perpetrados en las personas de indefensos desamparados es cuando hemos visto a nuestro pueblo exitarse pero solamente por el instinto de la propia conservación. Hemos visto nacer muchas organizaciones: El caso de Gregorio Cortez, en 1906, nos aceleró la circulación sanguínea, pero todo quedó en componer y cantar corridos.*

29. Ibid. Original text: *Movidos por dos linchamientos brutales, uno en Stockdale y otro en Rocksprings, nació en los altos del mercado de San Antonio la "Agrupación Protectora Mexicana."*

30. *The Tejano Yearbook 1519–1978,* comp. and ed. Philip Ortego y Gasca and Arnoldo De León (San Antonio: Caravel Press, 1978), 65.

31. *Primer Congreso Mexicanista verificado,* "Felicitación a la Srita. Hortencia Moncayo," 27, and "Temas para el Congreso Mexicanista," 31; Limón, "El Primer Congreso Mexicanista," 92–93; Zamora, *World of the Mexican Worker,* 29–30, 73; J. Luz Sáenz, "En la convención de Alice," *Revista Latino-Americana,* circa 1951, Enrique Sáenz Papers, Austin.

32. Limón, "El Primer Congreso Mexicanista," 87; *Primer Congreso Mexicanista verificado,* "Introducción," 1; Gómez-Quiñones, "Piedras contra la luna," 503.

33. Limón, "El Primer Congreso Mexicanista," 91.

34. *Primer Congreso Mexicanista verificado:* "Circular," 2–3; Lisandro Peña, "Introducción," 1, 6; F. E. Rendón, "Conferencia," 5, 8, 15. Limón, "El Primer Congreso Mexicanista," 87, 95.

35. Limón, "El Primer Congreso Mexicanista," 98.

36. *Primer Congreso Mexicanista verificado,* "Constitución de la Gran Liga Mexicanista de Beneficencia y Protección," 39.

37. Limón, "El Primer Congreso Mexicanista," 98.

38. *Primer Congreso Mexicanista verificado,* "Discurso pronunciado por la Srita. Hortencia Moncayo en la Conferencia del Congreso Mexicanista," 15.

39. *Primer Congreso Mexicanista verificado,* "Discurso pronunciado por el Sr. Gregorio E. González, Delgado por Nuevo Laredo, Tamaulipas" and "A La Patria, poesía leída por el joven Francisco Armendáriz," 8–11.

40. *Primer Congreso Mexicanista verificado,* "Discurso pronunciado por el Sr. Gregorio E. González," 9. Verb conjugation unclear.

41. Limón, "El Primer Congreso Mexicanista," 99.

42. Ibid., 43.

43. Ibid., 97–98.

44. Montejano says the Gran Liga Mexicanista's "resolutions" proved "ineffectual rhetoric," but the problem was an organizational one; Montejano, *Anglos and Mexicans,* 117.

45. Gonzáles then founded the Asociación Jurídica Mexicana "to familiarize mexicanos with the origin, goals, substance, and social effect of the laws and customs

of the State of Texas." He made it known that "if required [he] will give personal attention to cases"; Pycior, "La Raza Organizes," 114, 172n108.

46. Zamora, *World of the Mexican Worker*, 74n2; LRR, "Observaciones," section on "Vida social de los mexicanos"; Pycior, "La Raza Organizes," 217.

47. Américo Paredes, *With His Pistol*, 105–106.

48. Barrera, "Historical Evolution."

49. John Solís, "LULAC Milestones," *LULAC News*, February 1961, n.p., William Flores Collection, BLAC; Moisés Sandoval, *Our Legacy*, 7. In 1961 Solís wrote that he and his friends talked for "about a year" before acting to form the organization; in 1979 he told Sandoval they met every weekend throughout 1920.

50. Solís, "LULAC Milestones"; Sandoval, *Our Legacy*, 7. With the exception of Longoria, Solís gave these names to Sandoval. Leyton was thirty, the oldest of the group, and Solís the youngest at twenty; author interview with John C. Solís, January 18, 1980.

51. Author interview with John C. Solís, January 18, 1980.

52. Solís, "LULAC Milestones."

53. In Sandoval, *Our Legacy*, 5.

54. Ibid., 7.

55. Solís, "LULAC Milestones."

56. "Entrevista Sr. Tafolla" by E. Landaquin, MGP. Tafolla Sr. would later be a district clerk in the county attorney's office. O. D. Weeks, "League of United Latin American Citizens"; Weeks wrote that the OSA "seems to have been the brain child of two or three Mexican-Americans of influence in the Mexican quarter of that city" (260). Three men, one of whom was Clemente Idar of Laredo, wrote the OSA constitution, but the idea for the organization came from Solís and the original eight young men early in their careers in various trades, not yet men of influence or professionals.

57. Solís, "LULAC Milestones"; Sandoval, *Our Legacy*, 8; interview with John C. Solís by Nacho Campos and Emilio Zamora, September 1972, author's files. It is unclear if the founding date was October 12 or 13, 1921. Solís cited October 13, 1921, in his 1961 article "LULAC Milestones": "On October 13, 1921, the first organization, or mother organization, was formed . . . the Order Sons of America." But he told Sandoval in 1979 that they had a meeting and "that same night, Tafolla drafted an application for a charter and the next morning, October 13, 1921, he went to the Secretary of State's office and obtained the first charter ever issued to a Mexican American organization." *La Prensa* cited the first meeting date as November 4, 1921; *La Prensa*, "La sociedad 'Hijos de América,'" November 7, 1921, 1. Officers obtained the charter on January 4, 1922. M. C. Gonzáles had a printing shop nearby at 1506 South Flores Street; see Ritual of Order Sons of America, Council No. 1, San Antonio, adopted June 25, 1922, which he published (Box 1, Folder 3, ODWP, BLAC).

58. Solís, "LULAC Milestones"; Eleuterio Escobar Jr., Autobiography, 1e, n.p.; letter of recommendation, May 21, 1921, Box I, EEJP.

59. Escobar Jr., Autobiography, 1e, 10, EEJP.

60. Ibid.

61. Ibid.

62. Sandoval, *Our Legacy*, 8; Escobar Jr., Autobiography, 1e, 10, EEJP. According

to Solís, Tafolla Sr. was selected because of his education; author interview with John C. Solís, January 19, 1980. Another reason Tafolla Sr. may have been selected was because of his ability to speak fluent English; see LRR, "Observaciones," section on "Vida política e intelectual," MGP.

63. Pycior, "La Raza Organizes," 173–174; *La Prensa*, November 7, 1921. The meeting address comes from *John F. Worley's City Directory, San Antonio, 1927–1928*, 49.

64. Order Sons of America was the official name of the organization in English; Weeks, "League of United Latin American Citizens," 260n2. City directories reveal that the name "Order Sons of" was commonplace among ethnic and patriotic groups at the time. There seem to have been several European American organizations with similar names and that were opposed to Mexican immigration. See Testimony of James H. Patten of the Order Sons of America, U.S. House, Commission on Immigration and Naturalization, Hearings on the Temporary Admission of Illiterate Mexican Laborers, 66th Congress, 2d Session (on HJ Res. 271), January and February 1920. This OSA was a secret fraternal club originating in 1840 that maintained a strong antiradical nativist stance; John Higham, *Strangers in the Land* (New York: Athenaeum, 1966), 57, 367.

65. *La Prensa*, "La Sociedad 'Hijos de América,'" November 7, 1921, 1.

66. Texas Secretary of State, Articles of Incorporation, Order Sons of America, January 4, 1922.

67. Pycior, "La Raza Organizes," v, 184.

68. Membership card, San Antonio, Box 1, Folder 3, ODWP, BLAC.

69. Ritual of Order Sons of America, ODWP, BLAC.

70. OSA constitution, 45. A 1922 constitution in Spanish has not been located.

71. Constitución y Leyes de la Orden Hijos de América, San Antonio, Texas, 1927, Box 1, Folder 3, ODWP, BLAC. A 1927 constitution in English has not been located.

72. Pycior, "La Raza Organizes," 34.

73. OSA constitution, 11.

74. Ibid., 11–12.

75. Application card, Box 1, Folder 3, ODWP, BLAC; Pycior, "La Raza Organizes," 210; OSA Constitution, Article 3, Membership, 14.

76. Application card, Box 1, Folder 1, ODWP, BLAC.

77. Pycior, "La Raza Organizes," 185.

78. Notes to interview with Micaela Tafolla by E. Landázini, MGP; Tafolla family tree by Carmen Tafolla, 1980, Tafolla Family Papers, BLAC; "Short History of the Idar Family," Idar Family Reunion, May 30, 1981, Ed Idar Jr. Personal Papers, San Antonio; Pycior, "La Raza Organizes," 176.

79. Escobar Jr., Autobiography, 1c (thirteen typewritten pages), EEJP, 3. Escobar Jr. mentions members Mauro Machado and Antonio Herrera.

80. *La Prensa*, "La Orden 'Hijos de América' ayudará a Juan Morales," November 7, 1923, 8; author interview with M. C. Gonzáles, June 14, 1979.

81. Pycior, "La Raza Organizes," 176, 183; OSA Constitution, 27; Escobar Jr., Autobiography, 1c, 13, EEJP, BLAC; Weeks, "League of United Latin-American Citizens," 261; *John F. Worley's City Directory, San Antonio, 1927–1928*, 46. Escobar Jr. wrote in his autobiography that they met at Adelman Hall at 501 West Commerce, which intersected with Main Street. From 1925 to 1927 the group maintained a room

in the basement at 120 or 127 Main Street. The city directory reported that the group met on the first and third Wednesdays of the month.

82. Pycior, "La Raza Organizes," 175–176, 184, 190, 218; *John F. Worley's City Directory, San Antonio, 1927–1928; La Prensa*, February 21, 1924, 6, and June 13, 1926, 4. Tafolla Sr. served as secretary or president of the Alianza de Sociedades Mutualistas de San Antonio and later served as Cruz Azul's first vice president.

83. Pycior, "La Raza Organizes," 182. *La Prensa*, "La Orden 'Hijos de América' ayudará a Juan Morales," November 7, 1923, 8; "Sigue el jurado por la muerte de F. Roberts," November 8, 1923, 10; "Una sesión pública de la Orden 'Hijos de América,'" January 11, 1924, 10; and "Morales y Fuentes volverán pronto a San Antonio," December 8, 1923, 1. La Logia América de AL y AM, probably a mutualista, of Corpus Christi took up the case. *La Prensa*, "La gobernadora está perdonando a mexicanos," July 3, 1925, 1.

84. Kathleen May Gonzáles, "Mexican Family in San Antonio," 11–12; author interview with John C. Solís, January 19, 1980; author interview with M. C. Gonzáles, June 14, 1979. M. C. Gonzáles printed the Ritual of Order Sons of America.

85. Pycior, "La Raza Organizes," 177, 180, 185, 218, 220.

86. *La Prensa*, "Una sesión pública de la Orden 'Hijos de América,'" January 11, 1924. Original text: *Tenemos patria y no la tenemos . . . de acuerdo con las leyes tenemos derechos, en igualdad de circunstancias con cualesquiera otros hijos del país, pero lo cierto es que de hecho, no los tenemos: hace falta que surja entre nosotros el Moisés que redimió a los oprimidos israelitas de Egipto.*

87. Texas Secretary of State, Articles of Incorporation, Club Protectora México-Texano, November 3, 1921.

88. *LULAC News*, "Do You Know?" February 1933, 17.

89. Texas Secretary of State, Articles of Incorporation, Order Sons of Texas, June 15, 1923. Pycior, "La Raza Organizes," 175–176. An undated issue of *El Nacional* of San Antonio cites the founding date as July 11, 1923; Alonso S. Perales Papers (hereinafter ASPP), San Antonio, TX. Also see *La Prensa*, "Abogarán por sus derechos los méxico texanos," July 10, 1923, 1; *John Worley's City Directory, San Antonio, 1927–1928*, 49; Escobar Jr., Autobiography, 1e, 10–11, EEJP.

90. *El Nacional* (San Antonio), "Hoy hace un año," July 11, 1924, ASPP; Pycior, "La Raza Organizes," 143.

91. Pycior, "La Raza Organizes," 181.

92. *La Prensa*, "Abogarán por sus derechos."

93. Ibid. Original text: *Que esos hombres de raza mexicana se marcharon un día a los campos de batalla y expusieron sus vidas en defensa de la bandera de las barras y estrellas y que aquellos hermanos que tuvieron la suerte de regresar con vida se entristecen ahora que ven que la antipatía que les tenían los americanos desde hace casi un siglo continúa y aumenta de día en día pero que ya estaban dispuestos a "Ser a Ser."*

94. *La Prensa*, "Abogarán por sus derechos."

95. *La Prensa*, "Los 'Hijos de Texas' visitan al cónsul," July 26, 1923, 10. *La Prensa* did not report on the case again.

96. *La Prensa*, "Solo la mitad de los niños mexicanos que deben ir a las escuelas rurales del condado, están yendo a ellas," January 11, 1924, 10, and "Una protesta por la separación de unos escolares mexicanos," February 8, 1924, 1.

97. *La Prensa*, "La 'Order of the Sons of Texas' en defensa de la raza," February 29, 1924, 10, and "El caso del joven texano insultado en Devine," March 2, 1924, 4.

98. Pycior, "La Raza Organizes," 180.

99. OSA Constitution, preamble.

100. *La Prensa*, "La Orden 'Hijos de América' ayudará a Juan Morales," November 7, 1923, 8; Weeks, "League of United Latin-American Citizens," 261n5; letter to Oliver Douglas Weeks from James Tafolla, October 1929, Carlos E. Castañeda Papers (hereinafter CECP), BLAC.

101. Author interview with John C. Solís, January 18, 1980.

102. In *LULAC, 50 Years of Serving Hispanics, Golden Anniversary, 1929–1979* (Corpus Christi: Texas State LULAC, 1979), n.p., BLAC.

103. Minutes, 1924–1929, OSA, Corpus Christi. On August 1924 the council rented the hall for four dollars, and the March 2, 1927 meeting was held at the Lozano Woodmen of the World Hall. See minutes also for April 6, 1927, May 18, 1927, and July 27, 1927. Various halls in Corpus Christi are listed in the *Corpus Christi City Directory, 1923–1924* under "Mexican Societies and Fraternal Organizations," 310.

104. In Sandoval, *Our Legacy*, 8.

105. In ibid., 16.

106. Minutes, July 24, 1924, OSA, Corpus Christi, 1–6. Solís identified the key organizers as Wilmot, Joe Stillman, Dave Barrera, Al Cano, Desi Luna, and the three "Meza boys" (perhaps brothers). See also Sandoval, *Our Legacy*, 8.

107. Minutes, 1924–1929, OSA, Corpus Christi. "Ben Garza Named Head of Order of Sons of America," December 30, 1926, Album 1, BGC, BLAC.

108. Minutes, August 24, 1927, OSA, Corpus Christi, 27.

109. Minutes, July 25, 1924, OSA, Corpus Christi, 2, 6; *Corpus Christi City Directory 1923–1924*. Sixty-six names were listed in the minutes dated July 25, 1924. These names were compared with the directory, and those with identical names are cited.

110. Minutes, October 12, 1927, OSA, Corpus Christi, 56.

111. Author interview with Ofelia Wilmot and Louis Wilmot, August 27, 1981; author interview with Adelaida Garza, August 28, 1981.

112. Author interview with John C. Solís, January 18, 1980.

113. Adelaida Garza and family interview with Elvira Chavira, Corpus Christi, March 8, 1981, LULAC Archive, BLAC.

114. Minutes, August 10, 1927, OSA, Corpus Christi, 45.

115. Adelaida Garza mentioned several members in our interview: Mrs. Wilmot, Mrs. Daulet, Mrs. Campbell, Mrs. Anita García, Mrs. Josephine Truches, and Mrs. Germina Sáenz. She mentioned two as widows, Mrs. Rodríguez and Mrs. Sáenz.

116. Author interview with Adelaida Garza.

117. *Miller's Corpus Christi, Texas, City Directory, 1929*, CAH.

118. Author interview with Adelaida Garza.

119. Minutes, 1924–1929, OSA, Corpus Christi, 1–4. The first set of minutes with a date is July 24, 1924.

120. Minutes, May 18, 1927, OSA, Corpus Christi, 32; February 16, 1927, 21; September 27, 1927, October 5, 1927, 54–55.

121. Minutes, circa March 1927, OSA, Corpus Christi, 26.

122. In Montejano, *Anglos and Mexicans*, 243; Montejano did not include the full quote. The proprietor did not budge until protesters threatened legal action to remove a sign, presumably one that said "No Mexicans Allowed."

123. Minutes, May 21, 1926, OSA, Corpus Christi, 97.

124. Minutes, September 7, 1927, OSA, Corpus Christi, 51.

125. Petition, December 1, 1925, OSA, Corpus Christi, MGP, Bancroft.

126. Minutes, February 16, 1927, OSA, Corpus Christi, 21.

127. Petition, December 1, 1925, OSA, Corpus Christi, MGP, Bancroft.

128. Ibid.

129. Angie del Cueto Quirós interview with John C. Solís, circa 1977, cassette 13, LULAC Archive, BLAC.

130. Author interview with John C. Solís, January 18, 1980.

131. *Corpus Christi Times Caller*, March 24, 1921, and April 4, 1962, "Corpus Christi," vertical files, CCPL.

132. Ibid., April 30, 1948.

133. Program, Dedication of the Chester L. Heath School by the Sons of America, September 13, 1925, Corpus Christi, Andrés de Luna Sr. Collection, BLAC.

134. John C. Solís interview with the author, January 18, 1980. Minutes, May 21, 1926, OSA, Corpus Christi, 97; the graduates who received watches were Elisa Espinosa and Margarita Perales.

135. John C. Solís interview with Angie del Cueto Quirós.

136. Minutes, June 1, 1927, OSA, Corpus Christi.

137. Citing Paul S. Taylor's work, David Montejano mentions a LULAC chapter in Robstown in 1923–1924 and its informal boycott of racist real estate practices. This was probably an OSA chapter or a LULAC chapter at a later date; Montejano, *Anglos and Mexicans*, 243. Letter from James Tafolla to Prof. O. Douglas Weeks, October 25, 1929, ODWP, BLAC.

138. Minutes, November 9, 1927, OSA, Corpus Christi, 61.

139. Letter from James Tafolla to Prof. O. Douglas Weeks, October 25, 1929, ODWP, BLAC.

140. Minutes, August 3, 1927, OSA, Corpus Christi, 44.

141. Montejano, *Anglos and Mexicans*, 242.

142. José T. Canales interview with Taylor, folder titled "Along the Rio Grande El Paso to Brownsville," PSTP.

143. Minutes, July 27, 1927, OSA, Corpus Christi, 43. Some Corpus OSA minutes have information about Alice.

144. Minutes, February 3, 1927, OSA, Alice, Order Sons of America Records, BLAC; these records are dated February 3 to September 20, 1927.

145. Minutes, August 10, 1927, OSA, Alice, 45.

146. Minutes, circa February 1927, OSA, Alice, 23; minutes, November 9, 1927, OSA, Alice, 61. The latter minutes read "call president to invite the Mex. council," probably meaning "consulate."

147. Minutes, OSA, Alice, 1927.

148. Minutes, September 20, 1927, OSA, Alice. Original text: *pidiendo a los hermanos que se hiciera una propaganda en forma para traer nuevos miembros que si posible fuera que hicieramos una viaje a Palo Blanco, Orange Grove y demás Lugares.*

149. Perales, in a section titled "El verdadero origen de la Liga de Ciudadanos Unidos Latinoamericanos," says the OKA formed in February 1927; Perales, *En defensa de mi raza*, 2:102. On the OKA see "Velada de la Orden Hijos de América," *La Prensa*, July 11, 1927, 4; and "OKA Notes," *OKA News* 1, no. 2 (December 1927), n.p., ODWP, BLAC.

150. Mark C. Carnes, *Secret Ritual and Manhood in Victorian America* (New Haven, CT: Yale University Press, 1989), 5.

151. Taylor, *American-Mexican Frontier*, 241.

152. Sandoval, *Our Legacy*, 8.

153. Texas Secretary of State, Articles of Incorporation, Order Knights of America, October 22, 1927. The OKA constitution has not been located.

154. "Objects and Principles," *OKA News* 1, no. 2 (December 1927), n.p., ODWP, BLAC.

155. Articles of Incorporation, OKA.

156. OKA newsletters, ODWP, BLAC. M. C. Gonzáles interview with the author, June 14, 1979. Escobar Jr., Autobiography, 1c, 3, EEJP.

157. "Xmas Tree Drive" and "El Árbol de Navidad," *OKA News* 1, no. 2 (December 1927), n.p.; M. C. Gonzáles, "It Was a Merry Christmas, and a Happy New Year" and "Banquete," *OKA News* 1, no. 3 (January 1928), n.p., ODWP, BLAC.

158. M. C. Gonzáles, "It Was a Merry Christmas."

159. Pycior, "La Raza Organizes," 97.

160. *LULAC News*, "Henry Cañamar, Our New Editor," February 1933, 6.

161. *OKA News* 1, no. 2 (December 1927), n.p. Also see *OKA News* 1, no. 3 (January 1928), ODWP, BLAC.

162. Mauro M. Machado, "An Answer to Our Critics," OKA News 1, no. 3 (January 1928): n.p.

163. Perales, *En defensa de mi raza*, 2:101.

164. Ibid., 102; "Conferencia," *El Monitor* (Falfurrias), July 10, 1924; *Corpus Christi Caller*, "Will Lecture to New Club at Theater," July 12, 1924; *La Prensa*, "Exito de una conferencia en Kingsville," July 22, 1924, and "Conferencias en pro del mejoramiento de los mexicanos," August 2, 1924; *El Fronterizo* (Rio Grande City), "Se encuentra de paso en esta el Sr. Lic. Alonso S. Perales, en gira de propaganda pro-raza," August 9, 1924; *El Independiente* (Rio Grande City), "Grata visita," September 6, 1924; all at ASPP.

165. *La Prensa*, "Éxito de una conferencia."

166. Rivera, *Mutual Aid Societies*, 81.

167. Montejano, *Anglos and Mexicans*, 234.

CHAPTER 4: FOUNDING FATHERS

1. Márquez, *LULAC*.

2. Anthony Oberschall, *Social Conflict and Social Movements* (Englewood Cliffs, NJ: Prentice-Hall, 1973), 146.

3. Richard A. García, *Rise of the Mexican American Middle Class*; Emilio Zamora, "Fighting on Two Fronts: The WWI Diary of José de la Luz Sáenz and the Language of the Mexican American Civil Rights Movement," http://www. lulac.org./

about/diary.html; Ribb, "José T. Canales." Benjamin Heber Johnson, "Sedition and Citizenship in South Texas, 1900–1930," Ph.D. diss., Yale University, 2000. Taking my dissertation lead, Benjamin Heber Johnson has considered Sáenz and Clemente Idar as cohorts; Johnson, *Revolution in Texas.*

4. "Es encomiada labor del Lic. Perales," *La Prensa,* May 20, 1931, 2. She recalled this article as titled "Alonso Perales: Founder of LULAC." Adela Sloss-Vento, *Alonso S. Perales: His Struggle for the Rights of the Mexican American* (San Antonio: Artes Gráficas, 1978), 101.

5. Letter to Mauro Machado from Andrés de Luna Sr., September 23, 1939, Andrés de Luna Sr. Papers (hereinafter ADLP).

6. *LULAC News,* "History of LULAC," February 1940, 5–8. Canales served as associate editor at the time.

7. Perales, "El verdadero origen"; photocopy of letter to Mauro Machado from Andrés de Luna Sr., September 23, 1929, ADLP, BLAC; *LULAC News,* "History of LULAC"; *LULAC News,* "LULAC Milestones," February 1940, 34; Sandoval, *Our Legacy; LULAC, 50 Years;* Amy Waters Yarsinke, *All for One and One for All: A Celebration of 75 Years of the League of United Latin American Citizens (LULAC)* (Virginia Beach, VA: Donning, 2004). Sandoval interviewed several founders, but Yarsinke used only Sandoval, Márquez, and websites, conducted no original research, and ignored the writings of professionally trained historians.

8. For more detailed notes on some of these leaders see *New Handbook of Texas* archives at North Texas University in Denton.

9. My interviews and those conducted by other historians and librarians permitted identification of these eleven men, and my review of 1920s documents aided me in this endeavor as well. Audio tapes of John Solís, M. C. Gonzáles, Louis Wilmot, and Eleuterio Escobar Jr. are available at BLAC.

10. I have left out key activists like barber Ramón Carvajal, Francisco and Melchor Leytón, and Henry Cañamar of San Antonio; José Stillman, Pablo Cano, Ezequiel Meza, Ernesto Meza, Dave Barrera, and E. H. Marín of Corpus Christi; and Fortino Treviño of Alice. This is because they were not available for oral histories or I could not find documents by or about them, and I had to end my work. Of these, Carvajal deserves special attention. Several leaders mentioned him as significant, and future works should highlight him as well; "Frank Leytón," LULAC Golden Years Appreciation Banquet program, September 16, 1974, n.p., author's files. Leytón was a soldier in World War I, finished the fourth grade, worked as a saddle maker, and then established a tire-vulcanizing business. He reported, "I was a soldier; I did not even make it to Sergeant." The banquet program noted, "Soldiers do the major part of the work to build the best armies."

11. See Orozco, "Beyond Machismo."

12. Evan Anders, "José Tomás Canales," *New Handbook* 1:953–954. I added information about Canales' family life and LULAC to this article while a research associate at the *Handbook.* I used "Personal Recollections of J. T. Canales Written at the Request of and for Use by the Honorable Harbert Davenport in Preparing a Historical Sketch of the Lower Rio Grande Valley for the Soil Conservation District," manuscript, Brownsville, TX, 1945, CAH. The best work on Canales is Ribb.

See also Anders, *Boss Rule*, Jerry David Frasier, "A Political Biography of José Tomás Canales," master's thesis, Corpus Christi State University, 1992; and Michael John Lynch II, "South Texas Renaissance Man: The Humanitarian, Political, and Philanthropic Activities of Judge J. T. Canales," master's thesis, Texas A&M University at Kingsville, 1996.

13. U.S. Congress, House Committee on Immigration Hearings, Testimony of J. T. Canales, 171.

14. Frank Haron Weiner and Navarro Attorneys at Law, "FHWN Partner Receives University of Michigan Law School Distinguished Alumni Award," www.fhwnlaw.com/lawyer-attorney-1177750.html.

15. Johnson, "Sedition and Citizenship," 230.

16. Limón, "El Primer Congreso Mexicanista," 124; Américo Paredes, *With His Pistol*, 138.

17. Interview by Taylor with J. T. Canales, in folder "Along the Rio Grande, El Paso to Brownsville," PSTP.

18. J. T. Canales, "Get Acquainted," *LULAC News*, November 1931, 4.

19. Cecilia Aros Hunter and Leslie Gene Hunter, "'My Dear Friend': The J. T. Canales–Lyndon B. Johnson Correspondence," *Journal of South Texas* 5 (Spring 1992): 28. The footnotes list seven books Canales wrote after 1930. The Canales Papers were established in 1991 at the South Texas Archives, Jernigan Library, Texas A&M University at Kingsville.

20. Ibid., 27.

21. Canales, "Get Acquainted," 10.

22. Author interview with Enrique Sáenz, August 3, 1989. I wrote a brief biography of Sáenz intended for the *New Handbook*, but it was inadvertently omitted. Professor Juan Rodríguez of Texas Lutheran College presented a paper on Sáenz, but it remains unpublished. Some of Sáenz' essays used here include "Alocución en el Salón San José, Alice, Texas," *Revista Latino-Americano;* "En la convención de Alice," *Revista Latino-Americana*, circa 1951, Enrique Sáenz Papers, Austin; and *Texas Outlook*, "On Patriotism," October 1943. See also *Texas Outlook*, "Spanish from Another Angle," August 1939, 11, and "Has Time Come?" April 1942, 44.

23. Emilio Zamora, "José de la Luz Sáenz," *El Mesteño* 3, no. 31 (April 2000), 4.

24. "Standard Record of Teacher Qualifications." J. Luz Sáenz Collection, BLAC, Box 1, Folder 1.

25. Zamora, "Fighting on Two Fronts," n.p.

26. Adela Sloss-Vento, *Alonso S. Perales, His Struggle for the Rights of Mexican-Americans* (San Antonio: Artes Gráficas, 1977), 40.

27. Eleazar M. Paredes, "The Role of the Mexican American in Kleberg, County, Texas, 1915–1970," master's thesis, Texas Arts and Industrial College, 1973, 13.

28. J. Luz Sáenz, "Racial Discrimination," in Alonso S. Perales, *Are We Good Neighbors?* (San Antonio: Artes Gráficas, 1948), 29–33.

29. Zamora, "José de la Luz Sáenz," 5.

30. In Zamora, "Fighting on Two Fronts," n.p.

31. Ibid. J. Luz Sáenz letter to G. P. Putnam's Sons, June 21, 1943, J. Luz Sáenz Collection, BLAC, Box 2, Folder 21.

32. "Publicity Questionnaire," answered by J. Luz Sáenz, February 1950, J. Luz Sáenz Collection, Box 2, Folder 13.

33. Zamora, "Fighting on Two Fronts," n.p.

34. Sloss-Vento, *Alonso S. Perales*, 7, 61–62. Her coverage of Sáenz is the best secondary source about him. Zamora's forthcoming book will be the most thorough.

35. Perales, "El verdadero origen," 101.

36. Zamora, *World of the Mexican Worker*, 89, 92, 208–209; Christian, "Joining the American Mainstream," 581; Pycior, "La Raza Organizes," 98.

37. "5th Annual Statewide LULAC Founders and Pioneers and Awards Banquet (Honoring Prof. J. Luz Sáenz)," November 23, 1968, San Antonio, author's files; Gilberto Díaz, "Muere un professor ejemplar," *Revista Latino-Americana*, 1953, ESP; *American Council of Spanish Speaking Persons Newsletter*, "Prof. J. Luz Sáenz Dies in Corpus Christi Hospital," May 1953, George I. Sánchez Papers, BLAC.

38. Henry Cañamar, "Mauro M. Machado of San Antonio," *LULAC News*, May 1933, 12.

39. Ibid.

40. In Moisés Sandoval, *Our Legacy* (Washington, DC: LULAC, 1979), 80.

41. *LULAC News*, "Minutes of the Eleventh Annual Convention of League of United Latin American Citizens," July 1939, 21.

42. Also on Machado see "Do You Know," *LULAC News*, February 1933; *LULAC News*, June 1937; *LULAC, 50 Years*.

43. Cynthia E. Orozco, "Clemente Idar," *New Handbook*, 3:813–814.

44. In Zamora, *World of the Mexican Worker*, 97.

45. Johnson, *Revolution in Texas*, 230.

46. Clara Lomas, ed., *The Rebel* (Houston: Arte Público Press, 1994), 263.

47. Zamora, "The Texas-Mexican Worker and the American Federation of Labor," unpublished paper. *The Rebel*, edited by Lomas, includes a brief biography.

48. Lomas, *The Rebel*, 174.

49. Cynthia E. Orozco, "Eduardo Idar Sr.," *New Handbook*, 3:814.

50. Simón Domínguez Letterbook, January 10, 1922, CAH.

51. Letter to Luis Alvarado from J. T. Canales, September 7, 1960, J. T. Canales Estate Collection (hereinafter JTCEC), South Texas Archives, James C. Jernigan Library, Texas A&M University at Kingsville.

52. "José María Jesús Carbajal," *New Handbook*, 1:971.

53. Cynthia E. Orozco, "Manuel C. Gonzáles," *New Handbook*, 3:227. See also "M. C. Gonzáles" in Verónica Salazar's *Dedication Rewarded: Prominent Mexican Americans* (San Antonio: Mexican American Cultural Center, 1976), 49.

54. Pycior, "La Raza Organizes," 145–155.

55. "Un joven méxico-texano que ha sabido triunfar honrando a su estado natal," M. C. Gonzáles Collection, BLAC.

56. Richard A García, *Rise of the Mexican American Middle Class*, 291.

57. Ibid., 290.

58. Author conversation with Emma Tenayuca, circa 1984.

59. In Resume of Proceedings at San Diego, Texas, by LULAC, February 16, 1930, PSTP.

60. In Richard A. García, *Rise of the Mexican American Middle Class*, 262.

61. Cynthia Morales, "Todo por La Raza: Community Activism Among Mexican-American Women in San Antonio, 1920–1940," master's thesis, Texas A&M University at Kingsville, 2001, 27.

62. Gonzáles gave interviews to the following: Institute of Texan Cultures, San Antonio (1968); Richard García (1978); Moisés Sandoval (1979); Orozco (1979, 1980); and Benjamín Márquez (1986).

63. Cynthia E. Orozco, "John C. Solís," *New Handbook*, 5:1140–1141. See also Verónica Salazar, "John Solís, a Founder of LULAC," *San Antonio Express*, August 18, 1974; "John Solís," Golden Years Appreciation Banquet program, September 16, 1974, author's files.

64. Cynthia E. Orozco, "A Tribute to John Solís and Louis Wilmot: LULAC Pioneers," paper presented at the Past Presidents Luncheon at the 56th Annual National LULAC Conference, June 28, 1985, Anaheim, California.

65. In Taylor, *An American Mexican Frontier*, as cited in Zamora, *World of the Mexican Worker*, 88.

66. John C. Solís, "LULAC Milestones." This is the only article written by Solís that I found.

67. Ibid.

68. Ibid.

69. Solís gave interviews to the following: Nacho Pérez and Emilio Zamora (1972), Richard Erickson (1976), Pycior (1976), Angie del Cueto Quirós (1977), Richard García (1978), Sandoval (1978), and Orozco (1980).

70. Santiago Tafolla Sr., "Nearing the End of the Trail: The Autobiography of Rev. James [Santiago] Tafolla Sr.—a Texas Pioneer, 1837–1911," trans. Fidel C. Tafolla, Tafolla Family Papers, BLAC. This collection includes none of the OSA president's papers, which have been lost to time and the elements. Dr. Carmen Tafolla acts as a family historian and has a few documents. There is no published biography of James Tafolla Sr.

71. Weeks, "League of United Latin-American Citizens," 260.

72. Pycior, "La Raza Organizes," 190.

73. "Entrevista Sr. Tafolla by E. Landázini," October 5, 192?, MGP. Original text: *Dice sentirse Mexicano; pero es ciudadano americano. Respeta a este país pero dice que las leyes de los hombres han decretado que su nacionalidad sea americana, no sus sentimientos. Hay mala voluntad del Mexicano para el tejano, últimamente ha disminuido algo y hay mejor entendimiento. Los Americanos se sienten mas inclinados a reconocer los méritos del tejano.* The archive also has a Landázini interview with Micaela Tafolla. Landázini apparently was an assistant to Gamio.

74. James Tafolla Sr., "Motherhood," *LULAC News*, January 1939, 10.

75. "Tafolla Rites Set Tuesday," *San Antonio Express and News*, 1947, Dr. Carmen Tafolla Papers, San Antonio.

76. Cynthia E. Orozco, "Alonso S. Perales," *New Handbook*, 5:148–149. Lorenzo Cano of the University of Houston presented a paper on Perales, but it remains unpublished.

77. Araceli Pérez Davis, "Marta Pérez de Perales," *El Mesteño* 4, no. 37 (October 2000), 16.

78. Perales, *En defensa de mi raza*, 1:9. Original text: *Insultó a los representantes*

oficiales del Gobierno Mexicano y a todas los demás funcionarios diplomáticos hispanoameri-
canos que residen en Washington, quienes aunque no son mexicanos, resienten tanto como
nosotros los ultrajes inferidos a nuestra raza por virtud de los vínculos de sangre e idioma que
nos ligan.

79. Perales, "El verdadero origen," 2:116.

80. U.S. Congress, House Immigration Committee Hearings, Testimony of Alonso S. Perales, 180.

81. Ibid., 179–182.

82. Ibid., 180.

83. Perales, *En defensa de mi raza*, 50.

84. Richard A. García, *Rise of the Mexican American Middle Class*, 284, 16.

85. Sloss-Vento, *Alonso S. Perales*, 7. His oratory has been included in Josh Gottheimer's *Ripples of Hope: Great American Civil Rights Speeches* (New York: Basic Civitas Books, 2003).

86. *La Calavera*, anonymous, November 2, 1942, Alonso S. Perales Collection (hereinafter ASPC), San Antonio. Original poem:

> *Símbolo de corrección*
> *lo fue desde sus auroras*
> *tuvo palabras sonoras*
> *dichas con la devoción*
> *de un buen patriota tejano*
> *que defendió al mexicano*
> *en cualquier dado momento*
> *fue de empuje y fue de idea*
> *machote ciento por ciento*
> *de la corte en la pelea*

87. Letter to author from Gilbert R. Cruz, August 9, 1999.

88. Rebecca Martínez, "Alonso S. Perales," dedication ceremony at Alonso Perales Elementary, Edgewood School District, circa 1977.

89. Morales, "Todo por La Raza," 27.

90. "Unsung Hero of Civil Rights 'Father of LULAC' a Fading Memory," *San Antonio Express*, September 14, 2003; this article's author evidently did not access my *Handbook* article online.

91. Minutes, 1924–1929, OSA, Corpus Christi, ADLP. The de Luna papers include little personal information about him. Rubén Bonilla and other Corpus Christi LULAC members are responsible for getting this collection into the library.

92. Carolina B. de Luna interview with Richard Gutiérrez, December 9, 1973, South Texas Oral History and Folklore collection, South Texas Archives, James C. Jernigan Library, Texas A&M University at Kingsville.

93. In Taylor as quoted in Montejano, *Anglos and Mexicans*, 243.

94. Information on de Luna Sr. is scattered. Information on his education came from Letter to R. B. Fischer from Andrés de Luna Sr., May 4, 1939, ADLP. On his notary job see *El Paladín*, "Registro de *El Paladín*," April 11, 1930, 3, ADLC. On his presidency of the OSA see "Sons of America Elect Officers," Ben Garza Album 1,

and "Dedication of the Chester R. Heath School by the OSA, 1925" program, BGC, BLAC. A citation to his Woodmen involvement came from *El Paladín*, "Aviso," May 23, 1930, 4, ADLC. His obituary is in the *Corpus Christi Caller*, December 13, 1956, and Texas Death Index. Carolina B. de Luna also addresses his life in her interview with Richard Gutiérrez.

95. Cynthia E. Orozco, "Bernardo F. Garza," *New Handbook*, 3:105. See Ben Garza Papers, BLAC.

96. San Miguel Jr., *"Let Them All Take Heed,"* 68–69; his is the only secondary source on Garza.

97. U.S. Congress, House Immigration Committee Hearings, Testimony of Ben Garza.

98. Perales, "El verdadero origen," 106–107.

99. *LULAC News*, "Ben Garza Spent Life in Hard Work and Activity for Civic Betterment," March 1937, 4–5; Sandoval, *Our Legacy*, 76.

100. In *LULAC, 50 Years*, n.p.

101. Adelaida Garza and family granted an interview with Elvira Chavira, March 8, 1981; LULAC Archive, BLAC. I interviewed Adelaida Garza on August 28, 1981.

102. Leopoldo Castañon, "A Word from a LULACker," *LULAC News*, December 1931, 8.

103. Montejano, *Anglos and Mexicans*, 232.

104. Montejano argues that "invariably only 'qualified' Mexicans—that is, the middle-class Mexicans themselves—were exempted from social discrimination"; *Anglos and Mexicans*, 243–244.

CHAPTER 5: THE HARLINGEN CONVENTION OF 1927: *NO MEXICANS ALLOWED*

1. *El Cronista del Valle* (Brownsville), "Una gran convención de mexicanos en Harlingen, Texas," August 12, 1927, 1, 4, CAH; *La Avispa* (Del Rio), "Se organiza una importante asociación de méxico-americanos y mexicanos," August 6, 1927, ASVP. Perales and Sáenz lectured for El Comité Pro-Raza. A flyer titled "Conferencias Culturales Pro-Raza" announced that they would lecture on "the evolution of Mexican Americans and Mexican citizens"; ASPP.

2. *La Prensa*, "La Asociación Pro-Patria inicia sus labores," July 27, 1927.

3. *El Cronista del Valle*, "Una gran convención." Original text: *personalidades de alto relieve en la política y en las esferas comerciales de esta región.*

4. *La Prensa*, "Importante asamblea en Harlingen," August 5, 1927, 2, CAH. Representatives included Felipe Herrera, P. Carreño, M. Flores Villar, Juan B. Lozano, A. M. González (Harlingen); Antonio G. García, Federico Johnson (Mercedes); Benicio Salinas, M. S. Domínguez (Weslaco); J. T. Canales, Ismael Zárate (Brownsville); Pedro Montalvo, Ed J. Corral (Edinburg); Hilario Gómez, Eligio de la Garza (Mission); Víctor Gómez, Porfirio Treviño (San Benito); P. Avila (Donna); L. Puente, Leonardo G. Serna (Raymondville).

5. Perales, "La evolución de la raza mexicana," *La Prensa*, September 13, 1927.

6. George Garza, "History of LULAC," *LULAC News*, December 1945, 20.

7. Minutes, 1924–1929, OSA, Corpus Christi, 42, ADLP.

8. Ibid., 43. Other committee members included Louis Wilmot, Joe Stillman,

(Lee?) Campbell, Dave Barrera, T. (Teodoro?) Góngora, Fred Barrera, and Ernest Meza.

9. Garza, "History of LULAC."

10. Ibid. Perales, "El verdadero origen."

11. Garza, "History of LULAC," 20–21.

12. Ibid. *La Prensa*, "Importante asamblea en Harlingen."

13. *Houston Chronicle*, August 8, 1927; *Brownville Herald*, August 7, 1927; *McAllen Daily Press*, August 11, 1927; *San Antonio Express*, August 7 and 10, 1927, ASPP.

14. *La Prensa*, "Importante asamblea en Harlingen."

15. M. F. V. (Manuel Flores Villar), "Alerta Sres. Convencionistas," *El Comercio*, August 12, 1927, 5, ASPP.

16. Eleuterio Escobar Jr., Autobiography, final draft, EEJP, Box 2, 12, BLAC.

17. *La Prensa*, "Importante asamblea en Harlingen."

18. Z. Vela Ramírez, "Bienvenidos los Sres. Delegados de la Convención 'Pro-Raza' de Harlingen, Texas," *El Comercio*, August 12, 1927, 3; M. F. V., "Alertes Sres. Convencionistas," ASPP.

19. *El Cronista del Valle*, "Una gran convención." The program included: formation of the board of directors to function during the convention, writing of the constitution, discussion of the inclusion of Mexican Americans or Mexican Americans and Mexicans, location of the central office, nature of the Supreme Council, the organization with which to merge, and dues.

20. *La Avispa*, "Se organiza una importante asociación," ASVP.

21. Letter to Alonso Perales from Carlos Basañez Rocha, August 10, 1927, ASPP.

22. Copy of letter to Don C. B. Rocha from Alonso S. Perales, August 11, 1927, ASPP.

23. Ramírez, "Bienvenidos los Sres. Delegados."

24. M. F. V., "Alerta Sres. Convencionistas."

25. *El Comercio*, "Sugestiones," August 12, 1927, 1, 8, ASPP.

26. Author interview with M. C. Gonzáles, June 14, 1979.

27. Letter to C. B. Rocha from Alonso S. Perales, August 29, 1927, ASPP.

28. *La Prensa*, "Resultado de la convención de Harlingen," August 17, 1927, 2.

29. Carol Hardy-Fanta, *Latina Politics, Latino Politics: Gender, Culture, and Political Participation in Boston* (Philadelphia: Temple University Press, 1993), 83.

30. Escobar Jr., Autobiography, final draft, EEJP, Box 2, 12.

31. *La Prensa*, "Resultado de la convención." Author interview with M. C. Gonzáles, June 14, 1979; Gonzáles estimated that 75 percent walked out, while George Garza, who was not present, and a LULAC president later reported 90 percent. See George Garza, "History of LULAC."

32. *La Prensa*, "Importante asamblea en Harlingen."

33. J. Luz Sáenz, "Al derredor," 3.

34. Author interview with M. C. Gonzáles, June 14, 1979.

35. *Mission Enterprise*, "Mexicans Form Organization at Harlingen," August 18, 1927, ASPP.

36. Ibid.

37. *La Prensa*, "Resultado de la convención."

38. Copy of letter to J. T. Canales from Alonso Perales, September 1, 1927, ASPP.

39. *La Prensa*, "Importante asamblea en Harlingen."

40. Quoted in a copy of letter to J. T. Canales from Alonso S. Perales, September 1, 1927, ASPP.

41. Copy of letter to J. T. Canales from Alonso S. Perales, September 1, 1927, ASPP.

42. Hunter and Hunter, "J. T. Canales–Lyndon B. Johnson Correspondence."

43. M. C. Gonzáles, "Echoes of the Kingsville Convention," *LULAC News*, September 1931, 7.

44. Ibid.

45. Phil (?) and Nancy (?) interview with M. C. Gonzáles, 1967, vertical files, "Mexican Organizations," Institute of Texan Cultures, University of Texas at San Antonio.

46. Ibid.

47. Author interview with M. C. Gonzáles, June 14, 1979.

48. Ibid.

49. Ibid.

50. Ibid. Gonzáles said English was used at the meeting, but he might have confused the Harlingen meeting with LULAC meetings in general.

51. Phil (?) and Nancy (?) interview with M. C. Gonzáles, 1967, vertical files, "Mexican Organizations," Institute of Texan Cultures, University of Texas at San Antonio.

52. J. T. Canales letter to Luis Alvarado, September 6, 1960, J. T. Canales Estate Collection (hereinafter JTCEC), James C. Jernigan Library, South Texas Archives, Texas A&M University at Kingsville.

53. Escobar Jr., Autobiography, final draft, EEJP, Box 2, 12.

54. M. Flores Villar, *México en el Valle*, September 10, 1927, ASVP.

55. As quoted in a copy of letter to C. B. Rocha from Alonso S. Perales, August 24, 1927, ASPP.

56. Ibid.

57. Copy of letter to C. B. Rocha from Alonso S. Perales, August 29, 1927, ASPP.

58. Copy of letter to J. Luz Sáenz from Alonso S. Perales, September 1, 1927, ASPP.

59. Ibid.

60. Copy of letter to J. T. Canales from Alonso S. Perales, September 1, 1927, ASPP.

61. Ibid.

62. M. Flores Villar, "Raza o nacionalidad," *México en el Valle*, September 10, 1927 ASPP. Only this paragraph, translated in English, is available.

63. Copy of Carlos Basañez Rocha, "Falsos apóstoles y malos políticos," *México en el Valle*, September 17, 1927, ASPP.

64. Perales, "La evolución de la raza mexicana en Texas" series, September 7–13, 1927.

65. Ibid., September 13, 1927, 5.

66. Ibid.

67. Ibid. Original text: *Entonces yo, no queriendo me tildara de egoísta, dictador o imperialista, les propuse que convocásemos a los líderes de nuestra raza y que discutiésemos allí la cuestión.*

68. Ibid., 3. Original text: *Han dicho, por ejemplo, que la cuestión de ciudadanía fue*

sometida a votación dos veces; que la primera vez ganaron por "aplastante mayoría" los que deseaban que compuesta por ambos elementos.

69. Letter to J. Luz Sáenz from Alonso S. Perales, August 29, 1927, ASPP. See *McAllen Monitor*, "McAllen Americans of Mexican Descent Unite," September 9, 1927, ASPP.

70. Copy of letter to D. W. Brewster, U.S. Immigration Office, Brownsville, Texas, and Special Agent in charge of the Bureau of Investigation, Department of Justice, Federal Building, San Antonio, Texas, from Deodoro Guerra, President of the Mexican League of McAllen, September 27, 1927, ASPP.

71. Copy of letter to Deodora Guerra from Andrés de Luna, October 1, 1927, ASPP.

72. Copy of letter to D. W. Brewster, U.S. Immigration Office, Brownsville, Texas, from A. de Luna, October 1, 1927, ASPP.

73. Paul S. Taylor, Field notes, n.p., PSTP, Bancroft.

74. Eduardo Idar, "Editorial," *Las Noticias* (Laredo), October 10, 1927, ASVP.

75. Ibid.

76. Copies of letters to Mauro Machado, Rubén Lozano, and Clemente Idar from Alonso S. Perales, September 10, 1927, ASPP.

77. Western Union telegram to Alonso S. Perales from C. N. Idar, September 12, 1927. Letter to Eduardo Idar from Alonso S. Perales, September 23, 1927, ASPP.

78. Eduardo Idar, "Editorial," *Las Noticias*, October 1, 1927.

79. Author interview with M. C. Gonzáles, June 14, 1979.

80. Alonso S. Perales, "La unificación de los méxico americanos," *La Prensa*, September 4, 1929, 3. Original text: *Nuestro bienestar y nuestro progreso, serían iguales a los de los europeos que también emigran a este país, si nosotros, como ellos recibiéramos la ayuda y protección de los que son de nuestra raza. Desafortunadamente, los mexicanos que han nacido y vivido bajo el poderío norteamericano se hallan colocados en un bajo nivel político, social y económico . . . No nos guían, no tratan de inculcarnos el lenguaje, esas leyes y esas costumbres. Si ellos no tienen oportunidades en la política, en el comercio y en el trabajo, nosotros, naturalmente, tampoco las tendremos. Si a ellos se les insulta, se les segrega y se les ultraja, también a nosotros, lo que emigramos de México, se no vejara y se nos negará el contacto social con las otras razas.*

81. Ibid., September 6, 1929, 3. Original text: *En primer lugar, la tendencia de los México-americanos es americanista. Es decir, aún cuando no se proponen americanizar a los ciudadanos mexicanos, si piensen desarrollar dentro de aquellos miembros de nuestra raza que ya son ciudadanos americano por nacimiento o naturalización. El ciudadano mexicano no tiene a americanizarse. Las razones son varios. Por una parte existe su sentimiento nacionalista y por otra parte existe la falta de ambiente propicio, como acertadamente lo han declarado los señores Vásquez, Maus y Handman.*

82. Ibid.

83. Ibid. Original text: *¿Por qué se intenta americanizar a los niños de padres mexicanos, cuando que ningún esfuerzo se hace en México para mexicanizar a los americanos? El Padre mexicano no mandará a sus hijos a una escuela en que la americanización sea compulsoria. Él sabe que aunque sea ciudadano americano de nombre no es aceptado como tal de hecho por el pueblo americano.*

84. Ibid. Original text: *El mexicano no se americanizará. Ha vivido mucho tiempo en México y se le han inculcado pensamiento e ideales mexicanos, así es que difícilmente se le*

podria en americanizarse sabiendo que no es el tipo americano. Su sangre, sus ideales y sus pensamientos son diferentes, y por último, cuando ve que el pueblo no la acepta completamente como americano. Por lo que se refiera a americanizar a los adultos, esa es una bobería, pués casi todos han vivido demasiado tiempo en México y sus sentimientos son tan nacionalistas que la educación americana no los cambiaría.

85. Ibid.

86. Perales, "La unificación de los méxico americanos," September 9, 1929, 3. Original text: *Cuando nosotros, los ciudadanos americanos de algún Estado, condado o municipalidad, tenemos razones para creer que nos gobiernan funcionarios que abrigan prejuicios raciales, que son incompetentes, deshonestos, injustos, y buenos para nada, no tenemos a nadie a quien culpar más que a nosotros mismos. El remedio efectivamente es la casilla electoral.*

87. Eduardo Idar, "Editorial," *La Noticias*, October 10, 1927, n.p. Original text: *Si Mexicanos de prestigio, personalidades verdaderamente respetables, de antecedentes puros que hubiera vivido entre nosotros muchos años y estuvieran con nosotros identificados, por el cariño que les inspiramos nos hicieron sugestiones inteligentes y constructivas, bien justificados dentro de la más estricta lealtad, naturalmente que nosotros no la despreciaríamos, nos gustaría tener su concurso y obtener su consejo, aún, lo pedimos, pero cuando viene de individuos sin personalidad alguna entre nosotros, que ayer llegaron a este país, no podemos tolerar asociarnos con ellos siquiera.*

88. Ibid. Original text: *Allí hubo personalidades respetabilísimas por todos conceptos . . . esas personalidades no se han dada a la tarea de atacarnos, nos han dejado que laboraremos por ideales comunes de raza y aspiraciones legitimas de verdadera orientación general.*

89. Ibid.

90. José Limón, "El Primer Congreso Mexicanista," 89.

91. Eduardo Idar, "Editorial," *Las Noticias*, October 10, 1927.

92. Ibid. Original text: *Si hay extranjeros que indirectamente participan en las contienda[s] electorales corrompiendo el voto de los México-americanos para ganar ellos influencia y dinero, inequivocamente llegará la ocasión en que habremos de ir contra ellos, como iremos sin duda contra los políticos que siendo ciudadanos de este pais utilizan nuestro voto sin respetar nuestros intereses morales y sociales.*

93. Ibid.

94. J. Luz Sáenz, "Al derredor." Original text: *la facilidad con que se escandalizaron muchos de nuestros conraciales al ser testigos de nuestros primeros choques de opiniones en la primera batalla campal de nuestra evolución social.*

95. Adolph A. Garza, "Citizenship," *LULAC News*, September 1931, 8.

96. Ibid., 9.

97. Manuel Gamio, "Relaciones entre mexicanos, méxico-texanos y americanos," circa 1930, MGP. Original text: *El méxico-texano, que tiene sangre mexicana y sentimientos americanos, es en mi concepto un producto híbrido; ama a los Estados Unidos, pero más especialmente a Texas, por que nació aquí, rinde culto a la bandera americana porque se lo enseñaron en la escuela, se siente parte integrante de este gran pueblo y por lo tanto, se cree superior a hombres de su misma raza que viene de México.*

98. Manuel Gamio, "Entrevista Sr. Tafolla," n.p., circa 1930, MGP.

99. In Limón, "El Primer Congreso Mexicanista," 90. Original text: *Con profunda pena hemos visto a maestros mexicanos enseñando inglés a ninos de su raza, sin tomar*

para nada en cuenta el idioma materno que cada día se va olvidando más y cada día van sufriendo adulteraciones y cambios que hieren materialmente al oído de cualquier mexicano por poco versado que esté en la idioma de Cervantes. . . . si en la escuela americana a que concurren nuestros niños se les enseña la Biografía de Washington y no la de Hidalgo y en vez de hechas gloriosas, de Juárez se le refieren las hazañas de Lincoln, por más que estas sean nobles y justas, no conocerá ese niño las glorias de su Patria, no la amará y hasta verá con indiferencia a los coterráneos de sus padres.

100. Knox, "Economic Status of the Mexican Immigrant," 23–24.

101. See Jesús Martínez Saldaña, "On the Periphery of Democracy: Mexican Nationals and the Silicon Valley," 1993; and David Gregory Gutiérrez, *Walls and Mirrors.*

102. Beiner, *Theorizing Citizenship.*

103. Renato Rosaldo, "Cultural Citizenship, Inequality, and Multiculturalism," in *Latino Cultural Citizenship: Claiming Identity, Space, and Rights* (Boston: Beacon Press, 1997), 37. Ray Rocco makes a similar argument for the reconfiguration of citizenship as regionally based in "Citizenship, Civil Society, and the Latina/o City: Claiming Subaltern Spaces, Reframing the Public Sphere," in *Transnational Latina/o Communities,* ed. Vélez-Ibañez and Sampaio, with González-Estay, 273–292.

104. Nacho Campos and Emilio Zamora interview with John C. Solís, September 1972, author's files.

105. Emma Tenayuca and Homer Brooks, "The Mexican Question in the Southwest," *The Communist,* March 1939, 260.

106. Ibid., 262.

107. Ibid., 266.

108. Ibid., 262.

109. Letter to Cynthia Orozco from Emma Tenayuca, October 5, 1981.

110. *La Prensa,* "Una sesión pública de la Orden 'Hijos de América,'" January 11, 1924, 10.

111. In Johnson, "Sedition and Citizenship," 69.

112. Hardy-Fanta, *Latina Politics,* 11.

113. Gamio, "Relaciones."

CHAPTER 6: *LULAC'S FOUNDING*

1. *LULAC News,* "History of LULAC," December 1945, 20, Library of Congress, Washington, DC. Alonso S. Perales, *En defensa de mi raza,* 2:102; see the section "El verdadero origen," Perales' version of the founding of LULAC. It was a response to the death of Ben Garza and subsequent interest in the league's founding.

2. *La Avispa,* "Se organiza una importante asociación."

3. Escobar Jr., *Autobiography,* 15.

4. Ibid., 12.

5. Ibid.

6. Ibid.

7. Letter to Eduardo N. Idar from James Tafolla, December 16, 1927, ADLP. Tafolla Sr. "told the story about the Greeks, the Chinamen [Chinese] and the Mexicans—the two forer [*sic*] races always getting together and establishing some sort

of profitable business and the Mexicans always getting together and establish[ing] a real, sure enough fight."

8. Copy of letter to Eduardo N. Idar from James Tafolla, December 16, 1927, ADLP.

9. Escobar Jr., Autobiography, 11. Escobar said that in the early morning hours "the majority, but not all, agreed on the title of the new organization, League of United Latin American Citizens, known as LULAC." But he confused the Harlingen meeting with the founding of LULAC, which he did not attend.

10. *La Prensa*, "Resultado de la convención." Perales, *En defensa de me raza*, 2:101. Perales accomplished his original intent—to found a different group. Later in 1937, he wrote that the OSA, OST, and OKA *NO CORRESPONDÍAN CON EL IDEAL QUE NOSOTROS NOS HABÍAMOS FORMADO* (emphasis his). Translation: "They didn't correspond to the ideal we had." *Nosotros* here refers to Perales, Sáenz, and Filberto Galván.

11. Letter from Alonso S. Perales(?) to J. Luz Sáenz, August 29, 1927, ASPP.

12. Copy of letter to D. W. Brewster and Special Agent from Deodoro Guerra ASPP.

13. Letter to Adela Sloss from Alonso S. Perales, November 7, 1927, ASVP.

14. LLAC, "Manual for Use by the League of Latin American Citizens," circa 1928, ODWP, BLAC.

15. Jackson J. Spielvogel, *Selected Chapters from Western Civilization* (Belmont, CA: Wadsworth, 2000), 122–123.

16. "Record of negotiations with the Order Sons of America with a view to consolidating the Order Sons of America and the League of Latin American Citizens," transcribed by Andrés de Luna Sr. as Custodian of Records, circa 1937, Folder 1, ADLP, BLAC. This record consists of typed notes of key documents and correspondence from 1927 to 1929 that led to the founding of LULAC. Andrés de Luna was LULAC's historian in 1937.

17. *McAllen Daily Press*, "Perales Chairman of Committee," August 19, 1927, ASPP; Perales, *En defensa de mi raza*, 2:104. Committee members included Felipe A. Herrera, Clemente Idar, and Juan B. Lozano (Harlingen); Ismael Zárate (Brownsville); Arturo Torres (Mercedes); J. González Jr. (Weslaco); Eligio de la Garza (Mission); José Guerra Barrera (Edinburg); and Eduardo Idar Sr. (Laredo). Canales reported chapters in Cameron and Hidalgo counties. See letter to Luis Alvarado from J. T. Canales, September 6, 1960, JTCEC.

18. Letter from Alonso S. Perales(?) to J. Luz Sáenz, August 29, 1927, ASPP; *La Prensa*, "Se instaló solemnemente el Concilio de la Liga de Ciudadanos Latino-Americanos," November 16, 1927, ASPP; *OKA News*, "Inside Information," December 1927, n.p., ODWP. The date here is January 1927, but this is probably a typographical mistake. See also Perales, *En defensa de mi raza*, 2:104. Councils had been planned or short-lived in Edinburg and Weslaco. *El Fronterizo* (Río Grande), "Se instalará un concilio en Brownsville, Texas," n.d., circa December 19, 1927(?), ASPP. In his interview with Sandoval, Gonzáles mentioned the Loyal Mexican American Citizens of Brownsville and that Perales was president. This was an incorrect reference to the LLAC. See Moisés Sandoval, *Our Legacy*, 9.

19. Copy of letter from Eduardo Idar to Alonso Perales, March 20, 1928, ASVP.

20. Ibid.

21. Quezada, *Border Boss*, 20.

22. Letter from Adela Sloss to Alonso S. Perales, November 7, 1927, ASVP.

23. LLAC, "Manual for Use by the League." An LLAC constitution has not been found. Weeks made reference to this manual as the constitution. Since consolidation with the OSA was planned, a constitution was probably never written; Weeks, "League of United Latin-American Citizens," 261n6.

24. Transcript, translations of articles in *El Paladín*, February 22, 1929, ODWP; letter from Alonso S. Perales to Ben Garza, September 13, 1928, in Perales, *En defensa de mi raza*, 2:109. Someone besides Weeks probably translated some important issues of *El Paladín*, Corpus Christi.

25. Letter from Eduardo Idar to James Tafolla, December 14, 1927; letters from Alonso Perales to James Tafolla, September 23 and October 12, 1927; "Record of negotiations," ADLP. Committee members included Perales (McAllen); J. T. Canales (Brownsville); Arturo Torres (Mercedes); Jacinto Gonzáles Jr. (Weslaco); José Barrera Guerra (Edinburg); Eligio de la Garza (Mission); and Eduardo Idar (Laredo). Modesto Guerra (McAllen) and L. Puente (Raymondville) were added to the group later.

26. Minutes, September 27, 1927, OSA, Corpus Christi, 54, ADLP. The Corpus Christi committee members who worked on this were Andrés de Luna, Góngora, Dave (Barrera?), Ben (Garza?), and (Joe?) Stillman.

27. Minutes, August 17, 1927, OSA, Corpus Christi, 46, BLAC.

28. Letter from James Tafolla to Alonso Perales, October 10, 1927, "Record of negotiations," ADLP.

29. Minutes, November 2, 1927, OSA, Corpus Christi, 60, ADLP.

30. Ibid.

31. Copy of letter from Eduardo Idar to Canales, Perales, Tafolla, and Garza, November 19, 1927, ADLP.

32. Letter to J. T. Canales, Alonso S. Perales, Santiago Tafolla, Bernardo de la Garza (Ben Garza) from Eduardo Idar, November 19, 1927, ADLP.

33. Perales, *En defensa de mi raza*, 2:101–116. This is the best summary and evidence of Perales' problems with the OSA.

34. Ibid., 103, 111.

35. Ibid., 102. Original text: *Y no una que concretará a tratar de "IMPRESIONAR" a los jefes políticos y a los funcionarios públicos con el único objeto de conseguir favores, y colocaciónes en el palacio municipal y la casa cortés.*

36. OSA Constitution, JLP; "Constitución y Leyes de la 'Orden Hijos de América'" San Antonio, 1927, ODWP.

37. Suggestions made by Alonso S. Perales, Folder 1, ADLP.

38. Copy of letter from Eduardo Idar to James Tafolla, December 14, 1927, ADLP.

39. Copy of letter from James Tafolla to Eduardo Idar, December 16, 1927, ADLP.

40. Ibid.

41. Perales, *En defensa de mi raza*, 2:103–104, 109.

42. Letter to Oliver Douglas Weeks from James Tafolla, October 25, 1929, ODWP.

43. Perales, *En defensa de mi raza*, 2:104.

44. Ibid., 105–106.

45. Ibid., 105.

46. Ibid., 106.

47. Ibid., 105.

48. Copy of letter from Alonso Perales to Ben Garza, June 22, 1928, ADLP, BLAC.

49. Perales, *En defensa de mi raza*, 2:108.

50. Ibid., 109, 111. Sandoval cites the date as August 4, 1928; Sandoval, *Our Legacy*, 10.

51. *El Paladín*, "Iniciativa," n.d., circa August 1928, Folder 1, ADLP. Original text: *Una sola grande y fuerte [organización], ya es tiempo de que sacrifiquemos parte de nuestras ideas, todo nuestro egoísmo, y admitemos nuestros errores. . . . vamos formando una raza nueva al margen de dos naciones poderosos y grandes y seguimos siendo americanos para cumplir religiosamente con todo lo que sea nuestro dever y mexicanos cuando se trata de repartir los derechos muy en particular en el Sur de Texas.*

52. In Perales, *En defensa de mi raza*, 2:109.

53. Ibid.

54. Letter to C. E. Castañeda from James Tafolla, February 7, 1929, ODWP.

55. In Perales, *En defensa de mi raza*, 2:112.

56. Ibid.

57. Ibid.

58. Letter from Franco Pérez to Carlos Castañeda, January 10, 1929, CECP, BLAC. Original text: *Sociedades pretenden tener una convención con el propósito de ver si les es posible consolidar éstas en una sola.*

59. Perales, *En defensa de mi raza*, 2:113.

60. Letter to C. E. Castañeda from James Tafolla, February 7, 1929, ODWP, BLAC.

61. Translation notes of *El Paladín*, February 22, 1929, 3–4, ODWP, BLAC.

62. Perales, *En defensa de mi raza*, 2:113.

63. Edward D. Garza, "League of United Latin-American Citizens," master's thesis, Southwest Texas State Teachers College, 1951, 6. He used the February 7, 1929, minutes.

64. Letter to Carlos E. Castañeda from Franco Pérez, February 11, 1929, CECP, BLAC.

65. Perales, *En defensa de mi raza*, 2:115.

66. *LULAC, 50 Years*; "Three Mexican Organizations to Meet Here" (*Corpus Christi Caller Times*, February 18, 1929?), n.p., BLAC.

67. Weeks referred to the Salón as Salón Obreros; Weeks, "League of United Latin-American Citizens," 263. Solís recalled the day as cold and rainy; in Sandoval, *Our Legacy*, 11; LULAC: *50 Years*, "Three Mexican Organizations to Meet Here," n.p.

68. Weeks said delegates represented the three organizations, but the Alice OSA and former Corpus Christi group were represented also; "League of United Latin-American Citizens," 263.

69. Ibid., 262.

70. Ibid., 263.

71. Transcript, translations of articles in *El Paladín*, February 22, 1929, ODWP, BLAC.

72. Weeks, "League of United Latin-American Citizens," 263.

73. Transcript, translation, *El Paladín*, February 22, 1929, n.p., ODWP, BLAC.

74. Weeks, "League of United Latin-American Citizens," 263.

75. Transcript, translation, *El Paladín*, February 22, 1929, ODWP, BLAC.

76. Ibid.

77. Ibid.

78. Ibid.

79. Weeks, "League of United Latin-American Citizens," 263.

80. Ibid.

81. Ibid.

82. Letter to Dr. O. D. Weeks from M. C. Gonzáles, February 21, 1929, with Report Made by Committee on Organization, Box 1, Folder 6, ODWP, BLAC.

83. Transcript, translation, *El Paladín*, February 22, 1929, ODWP; *LULAC: 50 Years*, "Federation of Three Groups Is Organized."

84. Minutes of founding convention by Andrés de Luna, February 17, 1929, Folder 1, ADLP, BLAC.

85. Copy of letter from Carlos Castañeda to Francisco Pérez, February 25, 1929, CECP, BLAC.

86. Ibid. Original text: *Influenciaron al concilio de Corpus Christi de esta buen orden para rebelarse y formar parte de esta nueva orden.*

87. Ibid. Original text: *¿Esto sea el modo de unir a nuestro elemento más bien creo que con estos procedimientos se desanima y pierde la confianza?*

88. Letter to Carlos E. Castañeda from Franco Pérez, April 30, 1929, CECP, BLAC. Original text: *¿No cree Ud. que con esto[,] estos amigos han implantado entre nuestro elemento un precedente de desunión?*

89. Letter to Weeks from James Tafolla, October 25, 1929, ODWP, BLAC.

90. Ibid.

91. Ibid.

92. Letter from Andrés de Luna Sr. to Carlos Castañeda, April 13, 1929, CECP, BLAC.

93. Weeks, "League of United Latin-American Citizens," 264.

94. Letter to Carlos E. Castañeda from Andrés de Luna, April 13, 1929, CECP, BLAC.

95. Ibid.

96. Transcript, translation, *El Paladín*, May 10, 1929, ODWP, BLAC.

97. *La Prensa*, "Fueron numerosos los delegados que asistieron a la convención verificada en Corpus Christi, Tex.," May 20(?), 1929, BGC, BLAC. Delegates are listed here. The photo included ninety-seven men at the event.

98. Transcript, translation, *El Paladín*, May 24, 1929, ODWP; *La Prensa*, "Fueron numerosos los delegados."

99. Among the men whose wives accompanied them from San Antonio to Corpus Christi were M. C. Gonzáles, John C. Solís, R. R. Lozano, Vicente Rocha, and Frank Leytón; see *La Prensa*, "Fueron numerosos los delegados."

100. Corpus Christi women at the banquet included Adelaida Garza (wife of Ben Garza), Ofelia Wilmot (wife of Louis Wilmot), Luisa Solís, Jacinta M. Rodríguez, Enriqueta R. de Rodríguez, Estela Acuña, and Sabina Rodríguez. These women, especially the last five named, may have been widows or unmarried women. They may also have been present as members of the Alpha Club. Other *señoras*, mostly

from Corpus Christi, included the wives of G. G. de Rodríguez, Joe Stillman, J. G. Barrera, Fred Barrera, D. Barrera, Joe Treviño, G. Serna, M. Martínez, F. Canales, A. de Luna, J. A. Gude, Tom Dunlap, Willie Benson, J. Galván, Lee Campbell, B. González, Gil Zepeda, and Ezequiel Mesa. See Transcript, translation, *El Paladín*, May 24, 1920, 3–4, ODWP.

101. *La Prensa*, "Fue un grandioso éxito"; letter to Carlos Eduardo Castañeda from Andrés de Luna, April 1929, CECP, BLAC.

102. Weeks, "League of United Latin-American Citizens," 264.

103. Letter to Carlos E. Castañeda from Andrés de Luna, May 4, 1929, CECP. He noted that the opening meeting on Sunday was to be in Spanish. *La Prensa*, "Fue un grandioso éxito." Weeks reported the meeting starting at 10 A.M. and did not provide the complete name of Ignacio Allende.

104. Letter to Francisco Pérez from Carlos E. Castañeda, May 7, 1929, CECP, BLAC. Original text: *Aunque yo en verdad soy hasta la fecha ciudadado [sic] mexicano y no puedo en realidad pertenecer a la Liga.* It is unclear if Castañeda was unable to attend or simply preferred to stay out of the battles between the OSA and ULAC of which Pérez had informed him.

105. Copy of letter from Carlos Castañeda to Andrés de Luna, April 16, 1929, CECP, BLAC; copy of letter to Andrés de Luna from Carlos Castañeda, May 10, 1929; letter to Carlos Castañeda from R. R. Lozano, May 21, 1929; and copy of letter to R. R. Lozano from Carlos Castañeda, May 22, 1929, CECP, BLAC.

106. *La Prensa*, "Fue un grandioso éxito." Original text: *Nuestra raza, bellos y profundos pensamientos nacidos al calor del santo e inmenso cariño a nuestra Patria ausente de nuestra vista, pero que vive y palpita en nuestro corazón.*

107. Weeks, "League of United Latin-American Citizens," 264.

108. Transcript, translation, *El Paladín*, May 24, 1929, ODWP, BLAC.

109. "United Latin Americans Name Officers," in *LULAC: 50 Years*, n.p., LULAC Archive, BLAC. This article lists his residence as San Diego, although he is listed in *La Prensa* as an Alice delegate.

110. J. T. Canales letter to Luis Alvarado, September 6, 1960, JTCEC.

111. J. T. Canales letter to Luciano Santoscoy, September 29, 1953, JTCEC.

112. "In Our Mailbox," letter from J. T. Canales to Mr. Armendáriz, *LULAC News*, April 1954, 2, William Flores Papers, BLAC; Draft, United Latin American Citizens Constitution, circa March 1929, ASVP. Canales probably wrote the first six aims because these all, with the exception of aim 4, begin with "To." Those following, with the exception of aim 10, 12, and 13, begin with "We." See LULAC Constitution, Article 2, ODWP, BLAC.

113. Minutes of founding convention by Andrés de Luna Sr., February 17, 1929, Folder 1, ADLP, BLAC; Draft, "Aims and Purposes of This Organization," and Draft, United Latin American Citizens Constitution, circa March 1929, ASVP.

114. J. T. Canales letter to Luis Alvarado, September 7, 1960, JTCEC.

115. Jovita González, "America Invades the Border Town," *Southwest Review* 15, no. 4 (Summer 1930): 469–477.

116. LULAC Constitution, 1929, 4–5, ODWP, BLAC.

117. Ibid., 5.

118. Ibid., 7–8.

119. Ibid., 8.

120. Ibid., 8.

121. Ibid., 13.

122. Ibid., 10.

123. Suggestions made by Alonso S. Perales, Folder 1, ADLP, BLAC.

124. Weeks, "League of United Latin-American Citizens," 264.

125. Alonso S. Perales, "Unificación de los méxico americanos."

126. Ibid., September 10, 1929, 3, CAH.

127. Ibid., September 9, 1929, 3, CAH.

128. "Special Meeting of the LULAC, at McAllen, Texas," Box 1, Folder 6, ODWP, BLAC.

129. "LULAC Milestones," *LULAC News*, February, 1940.

130. Edward D. Garza, "League of United Latin-American Citizens," 9. The committee prepared local council bylaws.

131. Ritual, League of United Latin American Citizens, circa 1929, ODWP, BLAC. This code was written on the document.

132. Letter to Carlos Castañeda from Andrés de Luna, August 17, 1929, CECP, BLAC; Weeks, "League of United Latin-American Citizens," 267; U.S. Congress, House Immigration Committee hearings, 263; *Corpus Christi Caller*(?), "Ben Garza Goes to Washington to Aid in Fight on Immigration Bills," circa 1930, BGC, BLAC.

133. "Ben Garza Enthusiastic Supporter of 'LULAC News,'" *LULAC News*, February 1940, 15.

134. Weeks, "League of United Latin-American Citizens," 267.

135. Ibid., 269.

136. Transcript, translation, *El Paladín*, "The Convention of the L. of U.L.A.C. Which Met in McAllen Sunday Was Great Success," June 28, 1929, ODWP, BLAC; Weeks, "League of United Latin-American Citizens," 267.

137. *El Paladín*, November 1, 22, and 29, 1929; December 13, 1929; and January 3, 1930, ODWP, BLAC.

138. J. D. Autry, letter to the editor, *La Verdad*, August 23, 1929, BGC, BLAC.

139. Ibid.

140. J. O. Loftin, "Our Mexicans," *Texas Outlook*, April 1931, 29.

141. In Weeks, "League of United Latin-American Citizens," 276.

142. Ibid., 277.

143. Note accompanying accession record of photo of 1930 Alice LULAC convention, comment written on March 16, 1972, Carlota C. Balli Collection, Hidalgo County Historical Museum.

144. Weeks, "League of United Latin-American Citizens," 270.

145. In Taylor, *American-Mexican Frontier*, 315.

146. Cástulo Gutiérrez, "Para los que no conocen nuestra institución," LULAC Council 16 section, *El Popular* (Del Río), circa 1930, BGC, BLAC. Original text: *No son los fines de esta Liga americanizar a los mexicanos, ni mucho menos para relegar al olvido el idioma español, como maliciosamente se propia. Porque los méxico-americanos, mientras no nos elevemos al nivel de ciudadanos, no seremos más que conquistados.* He added, *Pero cuando que estos mismos, una vez teniendo hijos aquí les eviten tomar parte en la maquinaria política de esta tierra, creyendo que pueden incorporarlos en cuerpo y alma la patria mexicana.*

147. Ibid. Original text: *Podrán y es muy precioso incorporar su alma y espíritu en las cosas mexicanas, pero su cuerpo no, es imposible prácticamente, sin vivir en México, o mejor dicho, sin dejar de vivir en Estados Unidos.*

148. Ibid. Original text: *Sino toda la familia mexicana, aún hasta la de México.*

149. Ibid. Original text: *Traerán también beneficios para los ciudadanos mexicanos, quienes son nuestros padres, abuelos y amigos.*

150. Alonso S. Perales, "Unificación de los méxico-americanos," *La Prensa*, September 4–10, 1929.

151. Ibid., 9.

152. Jovita González, "Social Life," 128.

153. Ibid., 95.

154. *Daily Texan*, "Gets Citizenship After 30 Years in Texas," June 11, 1936.

155. Taylor, *American-Mexican Frontier*, 249. Herschel T. Manuel, a Jewish professor of education at the University of Texas at Austin, proved an ally. In 1928, Manuel received a grant to study the education of Spanish-speaking children, this becoming a lifelong research interest. He addressed the 1930 LULAC convention and cooperated with the organization thereafter.

156. Transcript, translation, *El Paladín*, February 22, 1929, ODWP, BLAC.

157. Copy of letter to James Tafolla Sr. from Carlos E. Castañeda, January 15, 1929, CECP. Letters were also written to Ben Garza and J. T. Canales. See letter from Carlos E. Castañeda to Francisco Pérez, February 25, 1929, CECP, BLAC.

158. José Angel Gutiérrez, "Chicanos and Mexicans Under Surveillance, 1940–1980," Renato Rosaldo Lecture Series Monograph 2, Series 1984–1985 (Tucson: Mexican American Studies and Research Center, University of Arizona, 1986).

159. Weeks, "League of United Latin-American Citizens," 267.

160. Ibid., 268.

161. Ibid., 257.

162. Ibid., 258.

163. Ibid., 277–278.

164. Ibid., 259.

165. Ibid., 278.

166. Ibid., 259.

167. Ibid., 259.

168. Oliver Douglas Weeks, "The Constitution," address delivered before the LULAC Convention, ODWP, BLAC.

169. Richard A. García, *Rise of the Mexican American Middle Class*.

CHAPTER 7: THE MEXICAN AMERICAN CIVIL RIGHTS MOVEMENT

1. Tenayuca and Brooks, "Mexican Question," 265–266.

2. Márquez, *LULAC: The Evolution*.

3. Mancur Olson, *The Logic of Collective Action, Public Goods, and the Theory of Groups* (Cambridge: Harvard University Press, 1971).

4. Anthony Oberschall, *Social Conflict and Social Movements* (Englewood Cliffs, NJ: Prentice-Hall, 1973); Charles Tilly, *From Mobilization to Revolution* (Reading, MA: Addison-Wesley, 1978).

5. Oberschall, *Social Conflict*, 102.

6. Tilly, *From Mobilization to Revolution*, 29.

7. Alain Touraine, *The Voice and the Eye: An Analysis of Social Movements* (Cambridge, England: Cambridge University Press, 1981); Daniel Foss and Ralph Larkin, *Beyond Revolution: A New Theory of Social Movements* (South Hadley, MA: Bergin and Garvey, 1986).

8. Foss and Larkin, *Beyond Revolution*, 2.

9. Ibid.

10. Touraine, *Voice and the Eye*, x.

11. Donatella Della Porta and Mario Diani, *Social Movements: An Introduction*, 2d edition (Malden, MA: Blackwell, 2006).

12. Gabriela González, "Carolina Munguía and Emma Tenayuca: The Politics of Benevolence and Radical Reform," *Frontiers* 24, nos. 2–3 (2003): 200–229.

13. Tenayuca and Brooks, "Mexican Question," 268.

14. Chandler, "Mexican American Protest Movement," 19.

15. Carlos Larralde, *Mexican American Movements and Leaders* (Los Alamitos, CA: Hwong, 1976). See also the slightly earlier Lois B. Jordan, *Mexican Americans: Resources to Build Cultural Understanding* (Littleton, CO: Libraries Unlimited, 1973), which included a list of "Leaders of Social Movements."

16. Mario T. García, *Mexican Americans*; Romo, "George I. Sánchez" and "Southern California"; and Acuña, *Occupied America*. Some works displaying ambivalence in using the phrase "Mexican American civil rights movement" include Rubén Donato, *The Other Struggle for Equal Schools, Mexican Americans During the Civil Rights Era* (New York: State University of New York, 1996); Zaragosa Vargas, "In the Years of Darkness and Torment: The Early Mexican American Struggle for Civil Rights, 1945–1963," *New Mexico Historical Review* 76, no. 3 (October 2001): 382–413; and Carroll, *Félix Longoria's Wake*.

17. Rosales' book of the same name accompanied the film series.

18. See especially episode 4, "Fighting for Political Power," produced by Robert Cozens; the associate producer was Ray Santiesteban.

19. Matt S. Meier and Margo Gutiérrez, eds., *Encyclopedia of the Mexican American Civil Rights Movement* (Westport, CT: Greenwood Press, 2000); and F. Arturo Rosales, *Dictionary of Latino Civil Rights History* (Houston: Arte Público Press, 2006).

20. Immanuel Ness, ed., *Encyclopedia of American Social Movements* (Armonk, NY: Sharpe Reference, 2003).

21. Chandler, "Mexican American Protest Movement," 2, 67.

22. Ibid., 2.

23. Allsup, *American GI Forum*, 10. See also Camarillo, "Research Note," and Montejano, *Anglos and Mexicans*, 244.

24. See Rivas-Rodríguez, *Legacy Greater Than Words* and *Mexican Americans in World War II*, and Griswold del Castillo, *World War II*.

25. Márquez, *LULAC: The Evolution*.

26. Ibid. Kaplowitz, *LULAC, Mexican Americans, and National Policy*.

27. Márquez, *LULAC: The Evolution*, 4.

28. Ibid.

29. Ibid., 5.

30. David G. Gutiérrez, *Walls and Mirrors*, 82.

31. Touraine, *Voice and the Eye*, x.

32. Márquez, *LULAC: The Evolution*, 5.

33. Ibid., 3.

34. In particular *LULAC: The Evolution* provided a cursory survey of selected collections and selected *LULAC News* issues between 1929 and 1965. It lacked focus at a local, district, state, regional, or national level and ignored gender.

35. Márquez, "Politics of Race and Class," 2.

36. Márquez and Jennings, "Representation by Other Means."

37. William Gamson, *Strategy of Social Protest*; see the chapter on "The Historical Context of Challenges," 110–129.

38. Rodolfo D. Torres and George Katsiaficas, eds., *Latino Social Movements: Historical and Thematical Perspectives* (New York: Routledge, 1999); the volume offers case studies but little theoretical discussion.

39. Robert J. Rosenbaum, *Mexicano Resistance in the Southwest: The Right of Self-Preservation* (Austin: University of Texas Press, 1981), 141.

40. Ibid.

41. Márquez, *LULAC: The Evolution*, 4. Janet J. Mansridge, ed., *Beyond Self-Interest* (Chicago: University of Chicago Press, 1990); see Christopher Jencks, "Varieties of Altruism," and Robert H. Frank, "A Theory of Moral Sentiments," chapters in *Beyond Self-Interest*. These scholars address how the individual identifies with the collective; they reject self-interest as an explanation of political life.

42. Márquez, *LULAC: The Evolution*, 5. Mario Barrera, *Race and Class in the Southwest: A Theory of Race Inequality* (Notre Dame, IN: University of Notre Dame Press, 1979); Aldon Morris, *The Origins of the Civil Rights Movement* (New York: Free Press, 1984).

43. Quoted in Márquez, *LULAC: The Evolution*, 17–18.

44. William Gamson, *Strategy of Social Protest*, 20.

45. Research on oratory in the Chicano and Chicana community is limited. See Hammerback, Jensen, and Gutiérrez, *War of Words*.

46. Roberto R. Calderón and Emilio Zamora, "Manuela Solís Sager and Emma Tenayuca: A Tribute," in *Chicana Voices: Intersections of Class, Race, and Gender*, ed. Teresa Córdova, Norma Cantú, Gilberto Cardenas, Juan García, and Christine M. Sierra (Austin: Center for Mexican American Studies, University of Texas, 1986): 38–39.

47. Aurora Orozco, "Mexican Blood Runs Through My Veins," in *Speaking Chicana: Voice, Power, and Identity*, ed. Letticia Galindo and María Dolores Velásquez González (Tucson: University of Arizona, 1999), 109.

48. Adela Sloss-Vento, *Alonso S. Perales*, 62.

49. Ibid., 62–63.

50. Ibid., 18.

51. George Rude, *Ideology and Popular Protest* (New York: Pantheon Books, 1980).

52. "Un joven méxico-texano que ha sabido triunfar honrado a su estado natal," newspaper article, M. C. Gonzáles Collection.

53. "Publicity Questionnaire," February 1950, Box 2, Folder 13, JLSC, BLAC.

54. Zamora, *World of the Mexican Worker*, 86.

55. LULAC constitution, 1929, ODWP.

56. *OKA News* 1, no. 2 (December 1927), and 1, no. 3 (January 1928), ODWP.

57. J. Luz Sáenz scrapbook, No. 12232, J. Luz Sáenz Collection, BLAC.

58. Ibid.

59. George J. Garza, "Founding and History of LULAC," *LULAC News*, May 13, 1955, 5.

CHAPTER 8: NO WOMEN ALLOWED?

1. Sandoval, *Our Legacy*, 70.

2. Author's conversations with Adela Sloss-Vento, 1978–1980.

3. See Cynthia E. Orozco, "Alice Dickerson Montemayor," *New Handbook*, 4:798; Cynthia E. Orozco, "Alice Dickerson Montemayor's Feminist Challenge to LULAC in the 1930s," Intercultural Development Research Association newsletter, March 1996; Cynthia E. Orozco, "Alice Dickerson Montemayor," in *Writing the Range;* Cynthia E. Orozco, "Alice Dickerson Montemayor," in *Latinas in the United States,* ed. Vicki L. Ruíz and Virginia Sánchez Korrol (Bloomington: Indiana University Press, 2006), 483–484.

4. See Albert J. Mills and Peta Tancred, eds., *Gendering Organizational Analysis* (Newbury Park, CA: Sage, 1992).

5. Juanita Lawhn, "Victorian Attitudes Affecting the Mexican Women Writing in *La Prensa* During the Early 1900s and the Chicana of the 1980s," in *Missions in Conflict, Essays on U.S. Mexican Relations and Chicano Culture,* ed. Renate von Bardeleben, Dietrich Briesemeister, and Juan Bruce Novoa (Tubingen: Gunter Narr Verlag, 1986), 65–74.

6. Anne Firor Scott, *Natural Allies;* Blair, *History of American Women's Voluntary Organizations;* Nancy Cott, *The Grounding of Modern Feminism* (New Haven, CT: Yale University Press, 1987); Elisabeth Israels Perry, *Women in Action: Rebels and Reformers 1920–1980* (Washington DC: League of Women Voters Education Fund, 1995); Gayle J. Hardy, *American Women Civil Rights Activists;* Sara Evans, *Personal Politics: The Roots of Women's Liberation in the Civil Rights Movement and the New Left* (New York: Knopf, 1974); Mary Rothschild, *A Case of Black and White: Northern Volunteers and the Southern Freedom Summers, 1964–1965* (Westport, CT: Greenwood Press, 1982); Vicki L. Crawford, Jacqueline Anne Rouse, and Barbara Woods, *Women in the Civil Rights Movement: Trailblazers and Torchbearers, 1941–1965* (Brooklyn, NY: Carlson, 1990); Lois Scharf and Joan M. Jensen, eds., *Decades of Discontent: The Women's Movement, 1920–1940* (Westport, CT: Greenwood Press, 1983); and Stanley J. Lemons, *The Woman Citizen: Social Feminism in the 1920s* (Urbana, IL: University of Illinois, 1975).

7. Thomas G. Rogers, "The Housing Situation of the Mexicans in San Antonio, Texas," master's thesis, University of Texas at Austin, 1926, 6.

8. Charles August Arnold, "The Folklore, Manners, and Customs of the Mexicans in San Antonio, Texas," master's thesis, University of Texas at Austin, 1928, 4.

9. Kathleen May Gonzáles, "Mexican Family," 4.

10. Frances Jerome Woods, "Mexican Ethnic Leadership in San Antonio, Texas," Catholic University of America, Ph.D.diss., 1949, 25.

11. Julia Kirk Blackwelder, *Women in the Depression: Caste and Culture in San Antonio, 1929–1939* (College Station: Texas A&M Press, 1984), 36.

12. Ralph Guzmán, *The Political Socialization of Mexican American People* (New York: Arno Press, 1976), 232.

13. Angie Chabram-Dernersesian, "I Throw Punches for My Race, but I Don't Want to Be a Man: Writing Us-Chica-nos (Girl, Us)/Chican*as*—into the Movement Script," in *Cultural Studies*, ed. and with introduction by Cary Nelson, Paula A. Treichler, and Lawrence Grossberg (New York: Routledge, 1992), 84; Lily Castillo-Speed, "Who Will Gather Us?, The Chicano Studies Library," *Chispas* 3 (Spring 1990): 6.

14. José A. Estrada interview with Belen B. Robles, oral history transcript, University of Texas at El Paso, Institute of Oral History, April 26–27, 1976, 9.

15. Martha P. Cotera, "Brief Analysis of the Political Role of Hispanas in the United States," paper presented at the Women of Color Institute, Washington, DC, November 1983, BLAC.

16. María Linda Apodaca, "They Kept the Home Fire Burning: Mexican American Women and Social Change," Ph.D. diss., University of California at Irvine, 1994, 79; Mario T. García, *Mexican Americans*, 29; Benjamín Márquez, *LULAC: The Evolution.*

17. Mario T. García, *Mexican Americans*; Benjamín Márquez, *LULAC: The Evolution*; Richard A. García, "Making of the Mexican-American Mind," 322; Richard A. García, *Rise of the Mexican American Middle Class*, 261; Johnson, *Revolution in Texas*; Kaplowitz, *LULAC, Mexican Americans, and National Policy.*

18. Christine Sierra and Adalijza Sosa Riddell, "Chicanas as Political Actors: Rare Literature, Complex Practice," *National Political Science Review* 4 (1994): 301–302. Carol Hardy-Fanta, *Latina Politics*, 131.

19. Sloss-Vento, *Alonso S. Perales*, 6–7.

20. Ibid., 2.

21. Ibid., 1.

22. Ibid., 61.

23. Marta Pérez de Perales, "Carta para el libro de Mrs. Adela Sloss Vento," in Adela Sloss-Vento, *Alonso S. Perales*, 80. Original text: *La Señora de Vento, fue una coloboradora desde muy joven. Valiente mujer y decidida se adherió a la obra. Pues, ella también sabía que el pueblo nuestro clamaba por que se la brindaba justicia y no vaciló en unirse a los líderes para contribuir con su grano de arena a la monumental obra.*

24. Sloss-Vento, *Alonso S. Perales*, 23, 80–82.

25. *The Monitor*, "LULAC to Honor the Late Adela Sloss-Vento," February 28, 1999. This was probably written by Dr. Arnoldo Vento, Adela's son.

26. Address by Dr. Arnoldo Vento, LULAC Scholarship fund-raiser honoring Adela Sloss-Vento, April 30, 1999, McAllen, TX. I also spoke about her at this event. See Cynthia E. Orozco, "Adela Sloss-Vento," in *Latinas in the United States*, ed. Ruiz and Sánchez Korrol, 686–687.

27. Arnoldo Carlos Vento, "Adela Sloss-Vento," Second Annual LULAC Scholarship fund-raiser, LULAC Council No. 4591, April 30, 1999.

28. Author interview with Arnoldo Vento, April 10, 1991; Adela Sloss, "Importancia de la Liga"; *LULAC News*, "Se instaló otro concilio auxiliar LULAC de Damas

en Alice, Texas," April 1933, 18–19. Original text: *Yo, como nativa de este país pero orgulloso de mi origen mexicano, he sentido el entusiasmo que animara al Licenciado Perales al fundar la Liga y me he dedicado con ahínco a secundar dentro de mis posibilidades la obra cultural y cívica que está siendo desarrollado por la Liga en general*; Adela Sloss, "Por que en muchos hogares," 31–32.

29. Susan Groag Bell and Marilyn Yalom, eds., *Revealing Lives: Autobiography, Biography, and Gender* (New York: State University of New York Press, 1990), 4.

30. Adela Sloss-Vento, "A la memoria del gran patriota y defensor del pueblo latino-americano, El Profesor J. Luz Sáenz," November 20, 1966, Author's files, newspaper article sent to author by Eva Sáenz Alvarado, Saenz' daughter.

31. *The Monitor*, "LULAC to Hold Scholarship Fund-Raiser," February 28, 1999.

32. Mrs. Ben Garza Sr., "A Message from the Founder's Wife . . . Mrs. Ben Garza Sr.," in *LULAC, 50 Years*.

33. Author interview with Adelaida Garza, August 28, 1981. See also Elvira Chavira interview with Adelaida Garza and family, March 8, 1981, LULAC Archive; and Cynthia E. Orozco, "Ben Garza and Adelaida Fought for Equality," *Corpus Christi Caller*, July 2, 1999.

34. Sandoval, *Our Legacy*, 77; *El Paladín*, "Lista de colecta para las escuelas de Del Río, Texas," September 17, 1931; Cynthia E. Orozco, "Del Río v. Salvatierra," *New Handbook*, 2:578–579. Accession record, panoramic photograph, LULAC Convention, Alice, 1930, Hidalgo County Historical Museum, Edinburg, TX; names identified by Carlota Ballí.

35. Rose Garza letter to author, October 3, 1999.

36. Richard Gutiérrez interview with Carolina B. de Luna, December 9, 1973, South Texas Oral History and Folklore Collection, South Texas Archives, Jernigan Library, Texas A&M University at Kingsville. I thank Dr. Armando Gutiérrez for bringing this oral history to my attention.

37. E. Landázini, interview with Micaela Tafolla, October 5, 192?, MGP.

38. Joshua Gamson, "Messages of Exclusion: Gender, Movements, and Symbolic Boundaries," *Gender and Society* 11, no. 2 (April 1997): 179.

39. Ibid., 181.

40. Apodaca, "They Kept the Home Fire Burning," 72.

41. Author interview with Louis and Carolina Wilmot, August 27, 1981.

42. Author interview with Adelaida Garza, August 28, 1981.

43. Araceli Pérez Davis, "Marta Pérez de Perales." The nature of her role still needs research. Pérez Davis reports on her "activist years" when she traveled with Alonso on thirteen diplomatic missions and attended the founding of the United Nations. They married in 1922.

44. Accession record, panoramic photograph, LULAC convention, Alice, 1930, Hidalgo County Historical Museum, Edinburg, TX.

45. Cynthia E. Orozco, "Ladies LULAC," in *New Handbook*.

46. Author interview with Adelaida Garza; author interview with Ofelia and Louis Wilmot, August 27, 1981. *El Paladín*, "El árbol de Navidad," November 22, 1929, 1.

47. *LULAC News:* "Delightful Dance Given," August 1931, 14; "Honorable Mention, Club Femenino Orquídea," November 1931, 15; "Honorable Mention, Modern Maids Social Club," December 1931, 7; Lucky Star article, February 1932, 4.

48. Cheris Kramarae and Paula A. Tricher, eds., "Ladies," in *A Feminist Dictionary* (Boston: Pandora Press, 1985), 222–223.

49. Mary Ann Clawson, *Constructing Brotherhood: Class, Gender, and Fraternalism* (Princeton, NJ: Princeton University Press, 1989), 196. In her research on César Chávez' wife, Helen, Margaret Rose found, "As was customary for *this generation of women,* [emphasis mine] her activities were essentially auxiliary, she helped in the office, mimeographing fliers or sorting the mail," 27. Rose used categories that made women "auxiliary" and men "activists"; Margaret Rose, "Traditional and Nontraditional Patterns of Female Activism in the United Farm Workers of America, 1962–1980," *Frontiers* 11, no. 2 (1990): 26–32.

50. Cynthia E. Orozco, "Beyond Machismo"; Ayala, "Negotiating Race Relations."

51. *LULAC News*, "Ladies Auxiliary," October 1931; telephone conversation with Emma Tenayuca, October 24, 1981.

52. *LULAC News*, "Ladies Auxiliary," October 1931.

53. *LULAC News*, "An Address Delivered at the Wesley House Before the Travis Missionary Women's Association," April 1933, 5; "Ladies Auxiliary"; "Sidney Lanier School Organizes Parents Advisory Council," November 1932, 13. See also Cynthia E. Orozco, "Spanish-Speaking PTA," *New Handbook*, 6:13–14.

54. *LULAC News*, "Se instaló otro concilio"; A. G. de la Rosa, "Annual Report of the Kingsville LULAC Council No. 24," *LULAC News*, March 1934.

55. *LULAC News*, "Brief Resume of the Work Accomplished at the Del Rio Annual Convention," May 1933, 13; see also Cynthia E. Orozco, "League of United Latin-American Citizens," in *Reader's Companion to U.S. Women's History*, ed. Wilma Mankiller, Gwendolyn Mink, Marysa Navarro, Barbara Smith, and Gloria Steinem (Boston: Houghton Mifflin, 1998), 378; and Cynthia E. Orozco, "LULAC," in *Latinas*, 378–380.

56. Quezada, *Border Boss*, 24.

57. Joshua Gamson, "Messages of Exclusion," 179.

58. Ibid., 179–180.

59. Clawson, *Constructing Brotherhood*, 203.

60. Orozco, "Ladies LULAC," in *New Handbook*.

61. Smith-Rosenberg, "Female World of Love and Ritual"; Jean Lipman-Blumen, "Toward a Homosocial Theory of Sex Roles: An Explanation of the Sex Segregation of Social Institutions," *Signs* 1, no. 3, part 2 (Spring 1976): 15–31.

62. Author interview with Emma Tenayuca, July 1981, handwritten notes.

63. J. Reynolds Flores, "How to Educate Our Girls," *LULAC News*, December 1931, 6.

64. Sloss, "Por que en muchos hogares," 31–32.

65. Gabriela González, "Carolina Munguía and Emma Tenayuca."

66. Carol Hardy-Fanta, *Latina Politics*, 64, 131.

67. Blanche Wiesen Cook, "Female Support Networks and Political Activism: Lillian Wald, Crystal Eastman, Emma Goldman," *Chrysalis* 3 (1977): 43–61.

68. Estelle Freedman, "Separatism as Strategy: Female Institution Building and American Feminism, 1870–1930," *Feminist Studies* 5, no. 3 (Fall 1979): 512–529.

69. Marilyn Frye, "Separatism," in *A Feminist Dictionary*, 407–408.

70. Norma Cantú interview with Alice Dickerson Montemayor, with questions prepared by the author, 1984, author's personal files.

71. Mrs. F. I. Montemayor, "Let's Organize Junior Councils," *LULAC News,* August 1938.

72. Suzanne Staggenborg, *Gender, Family, and Social Movements* (Thousand Oaks, CA: Pine Forge Press, 1998), 47.

73. Alonso S. Perales, "El méxico americano y la política del sur de Texas: Commentarios," (San Antonio: N.p., 1931): 11, LULAC Archive, BLAC. Original text: *Es indispensable emprender una campaña de instrucción cívica formidable tanto entre el elemento masculino como entre el feminino. También al elemento femenino méxicoamericano debemos impartirle instrucción cívica. De esta manera aumentará considerablemente el número de votantes méxico-americanos y, en consecuencia, nuestra fuerza política se hará sentir. Ya hay en San Antonio una Liga de Mujeres Votantes que tiene por objecto exhortar a la mujer que ejerza los privilegios que acaba de obtener en el cuerpo política de este país y enseñarle a votar inteligentemente. La mujer méxico-americana debe incorporarse a dicha Liga o formar una sociedad de damas votantes latinoamericanas. El voto de la mujer méxicoamericana es indispensale si queremos mejorar nuestra situación política en Texas.*

74. Letter from Emma Tenayuca to author, September 10, 1982, author's files.

75. Roberto R. Calderón and Emilio Zamora, "Manuela Solís Sager and Emma Tenayuca: A Tribute," *Chicana Voices: Intersections of Class, Race, and Gender,* ed. Teresa Córdova, Norma Elia Cantú, Gilberto Cardenas, Juan García, and Christine M. Sierra (Austin: Mexican American Studies, 1986):30–41; "Emma Tenayuca," *Notable Latino Americans: A Biographical Dictionary,* ed. Matt S. Meier, Conchita Franco Serri, and Richard A. García (Westport, Conn.: Greenwood Press, 1997): 368–371. To hear her voice or read an interview access Texan.cultures.utsa.edu/ memories/ htms/tenayuca_transcript.htm, an interview conducted by Gerry Poyo February 21, 1987.

76. Neil Foley, *The White Scourge: Mexicans, Blacks, and Poor Whites in Texas Cotton Culture* (Berkeley: University of California Press, 1997), 211. Foley mistakenly identified Tenayuca as "working class" and argued that she "resisted the lure of whiteness," which he erroneously associated with LULAC.

77. Neil Foley, "Becoming Hispanic: Mexican Americans and the Faustian Pact with Whiteness," *Reflexiones* (Austin: Center for Mexican American Studies, University of Texas at Austin, 1997), 64; Julia Kirk Blackwelder, "Emma Tenayuca, Vision and Courage," in *The Human Tradition,* ed. Ty Cashion and Jesús de la Teja (Wilmington, DE: Scholarly Resources, 2001), 191–208.

78. Zaragosa Vargas, "Tejana Radical: Emma Tenayuca and the San Antonio Labor Movement During the Great Depression," *Pacific Historical Review* 66 (November 1997): 553–580; Gabriela González, "Carolina Munguía and Emma Tenayuca"; Gabriela González, "Emma Tenayuca," in *Latinas in the United States,* 743–744.

79. Tenayuca and Brooks, "Mexican Question," 265–266.

80. Ibid., 266.

81. Emma Tenayuca letter to author, September 10, 1982, author's files. Other thoughts on LULAC can be found in letter to author, October 5, 1981. Aurora Orozco, my mother, wrote of LULAC in the 1930s, "A lot was said about the organization . . . that it was only for Mexicans born in Texas to try to better their lives

and educate them. This was something good, but it left the Mexican from Mexico isolated and caused resentment"; Aurora Orozco, "Mexican Blood," 112.

82. Cynthia E. Orozco, "María L. de Hernández," in *New Handbook*, 3:572–573; author interview with María L. de Hernández, September 8, 1981; Cynthia E. Orozco, "María L. de Hernández," in *Latinas in the United States*, 319–320.

83. In Hammerback, Jensen, and Gutiérrez, *War of Words*, 141.

84. Cynthia E. Orozco, "María L. de Hernández."

85. In María L. de Hernández, *México y las cuatro poderes que dirigen al pueblo* (San Antonio: Artes Gráficas, 1945), BLAC.

86. Ibid., 9. Original text: *La incansable lucha cívico-social que por más de 20 años he sostenido en este gran país, . . . el México que es la base de mi inspiración, porque en él nací, porque soy mexicana de sangre, porque una amplia visión intuitiva me hace vivir en el México.*

87. Sally Foster, "María Latigo Hernández," in *Dictionary of Hispanic Biography*, ed. Joseph C. Tardiff and L. Mpho Mabunda, 421–423.

88. Pedro Hernández argued that European Americans in the United States had appropriated the term "American": *La palabra 'Americano,' el verdadero Americanismo es de todos los hijos de América, no importa su color, mi nacionalidad, o raza. Yo siempre que hablo digo Mexicano o Estudianse [Estadunidense] en lugar de México Americano. La palabra que viene primero es "American."* Translation: "The term 'American,' real Americanism includes all the citizens of America without regard to color, nationality, or race. When I speak, I use Mexican or United States citizen, instead of Mexican American. The word that comes first is 'American'"; in Hammerback, Jensen, and Gutiérrez, *War of Words*, 141.

89. Sloss-Vento, *Alonso S. Perales*, 38–49.

90. Carol Hardy-Fanta, *Latina Politics*, 3.

91. On women and citizenship see Kerber, *No Constitutional Right*.

92. M. Bahati Kuumba, *Gender and Social Movements* (Walnut Creek, CA: Altamira Press, 2001). This is the most important book on women and social movements.

93. To understand the significance of LULAC on El Paso women at the local and national level see Ernestina Muñoz, Alisandra Mancera, Alma Fajardo, Mayra García, and Adriana Alatorre, "El Paso Women Gained Power in LULAC," *Borderlands* 25 (El Paso: El Paso Community College, 2006–2007), 7.

CONCLUSION

1. I disagree with Mario T. García and Richard A. García that the 1930s witnessed the rise of this Mexican American civil rights movement. Benjamin Heber Johnson agreed with my 1992 analysis that the 1910s proved key to developments in the 1920s; see Johnson, *Revolution in Texas*.

2. Félix Padilla, *Latino Ethnic Consciousness*, 4–5.

3. Foley, *White Scourge*, 209. He stated, "LULAC members constructed new identities as Latin Americans in order to arrogate to themselves the privilege of whiteness routinely denied to immigrant Mexicans, blacks, Chinese, and Indians." Nor did they seek "acceptance as white Americans."

4. Ramón A. Gutiérrez, "Unraveling America's Hispanic Past."

5. Benjamín Márquez, "League of United Latin American Citizens and the Politics of Ethnicity," 13.

6. Katsuyuki Murata, "(Re)Shaping of Latino/Chicano Ethnicity," 7.

7. Christian, "Joining the American Mainstream."

8. Montejano, *Anglos and Mexicans*, 232.

9. Ibid., 285.

10. Ibid., 243.

11. Ibid.

12. Ibid., 285.

13. Montejano argues that "invariably only 'qualified' Mexicans—that is, the middle-class Mexicans themselves—were exempted from social discrimination"; Montejano, *Anglos and Mexicans*, 233–234.

14. Acuña, *Occupied America*, 6th edition, 151.

15. Montejano, *Anglos and Mexicans*, 232.

16. Ibid., 137.

17. Lemons, *Woman Citizen*.

18. Clawson, *Constructing Brotherhood*.

19. F. Arturo Rosales, *Dictionary of Latino Civil Rights History*, Houston: Arte Público, 2006.

APPENDIX 1: ORDER SONS OF AMERICA DECLARATION OF PRINCIPLES, 1922

Constitution and By-Laws of Order Sons of America, Council No. 1, San Antonio, Texas, adopted June 25, 1922, José Limón Papers, Austin, Texas.

APPENDIX 2: OBJECTIVES AND AIMS OF THE LATIN AMERICAN CITIZENS LEAGUE, CIRCA 1927

"Objectivos y fines de la 'Latin American Citizens League,' " in *Manual for Use by the League of Latin American Citizens*, circa 1927, ODWP, BLAC; translated as "Objectives and Aimf [*sic*] of the United Latin American Citizens," circa February 1929, ODWP, BLAC.

APPENDIX 3: CONSTITUTION, LEAGUE OF UNITED LATIN AMERICAN CITIZENS, 1929

Constitution, League of United Latin American Citizens, 1929, 2–4, ODWP, BLAC.

SELECTED BIBLIOGRAPHY

ARCHIVAL AND PRIMARY SOURCES

The most important collections of the Order Sons of America and League of United Latin American Citizens are located in the LULAC Archive in the Nettie Lee Benson Latin American Collection at the University of Texas at Austin. Constitutions, minutes, and membership lists can be found there. Key collections of the 1920s include Andrés de Luna Sr., Oliver Douglas Weeks, and Ben Garza. The Order Knights of America newsletters are in Weeks. The most important collection of *LULAC News*, the official LULAC newsmagazine, can be found at the Benson Latin American Collection, as can interviews with several LULAC founders. The statewide Spanish-language newspaper *La Prensa* is located at the Center for American History at the University of Texas at Austin. The Alonso S. Perales and Adela Sloss-Vento collections are in the possession of family members; both contain essential documents on the Harlingen convention.

Books, Articles, Government Documents

Hernández, María L. de. *México y los cuatro poderes que dirijan al pueblo*. San Antonio: Artes Gráficas, 1945.

Perales, Alonso S. *El méxico americano y la política del sur de Texas: Comentarios*. Pamphlet. San Antonio: Artes Gráficas, 1931. Translation of and commentary on Oliver Douglas Weeks' "The Texas-Mexican and the Politics of South Texas," *American Political Science Review* 24 (August 1930): 606–627.

———. *En defensa de mi raza*. 2 vols. San Antonio: Artes Gráficas, 1937.

Sáenz, J. Luz. *Los méxico-americanos en la Gran Guerra y su contingente en pro de la democracia, la humanidad y la justicia*. San Antonio: Artes Gráficas, 1934.

Sloss-Vento, Adela. *Alonso S. Perales: His Struggle for the Rights of the Mexican American*. San Antonio: Artes Gráficas, 1977.

Sologaistoa, J. C., ed. *Guía general y directorio mexicano de San Antonio, Texas.* San Antonio: N.p., 1924.

Tenayuca, Emma, and Homer Brooks. "The Mexican Question in the Southwest." *The Communist* (March 1939): 257–268.

Texas Secretary of State. Articles of Incorporation: Club Protector Mexico-Texano, November 3, 1921; Order Knights of America, October 22, 1927; Order Sons of America, January 4, 1922; Order Sons of Texas, June 15, 1923.

U.S. Congress. House Committee on Immigration. Hearings on Western Hemisphere Immigration. 71st Congress, 2nd Session, 1930.

Weeks, O. Douglas. "The League of United Latin-American Citizens: A Texas-Mexican Civic Organization." *Southwestern Political and Social Science Quarterly* 10, no. 3 (December 1929): 257–278.

Collections

Bancroft Library, University of California at Berkeley

Gamio, Manuel, Papers (MGP)
LULAC News, September 1931, April 1932
Taylor, Paul S., Papers (PSTP)

Benson Latin American Collection, University of Texas at Austin (BLAC)

Castañeda, Carlos E., Papers (CECP)
de Luna, Andrés Sr., Papers (ADLP)
Escobar, Eleuterio Jr., Papers (EEJP)
Garza, Ben, Collection (BGC)
Gonzáles, Manuel C., Collection
League of United Latin American Citizens (LULAC) Archive
LULAC, 50 Years of Serving Hispanics, Golden Anniversary, 1929–1979. Corpus Christi: Texas State LULAC, 1979.
LULAC News, various dates, December 1931–February 1961
Order Sons of America (OSA), Council 5, Records
Sáenz, José de la Luz, Collection
Solís, Juan, Collection
Tafolla Family Collection
Texas LULAC News, November 1974–December 1979
Weeks, Oliver Douglas, Papers (ODWP)
Wilmot, Louis, Collection

Center for American History, University of Texas at Austin (CAH)

Canales, J. T. "Personal Recollections of J. T. Canales Written at the Request of and for Use by the Honorable Harbert Davenport in Preparing a Historical Sketch of the Lower Rio Grande Valley for the Soil Conservation District." Brownsville, TX, 1945.
Domínguez, Simon C., Letterbooks
LULAC News, various dates, August 1931–May 1933

Pérez Álvarez, Casimiro, Papers
Primer Congreso Mexicanista verificado en Laredo, Texas, EE.UU. de A. los días 14 al 22 de septiembre de 1911, discursos y conferencias, por La Raza. Laredo, TX: Tipografía de N. Idar, 1912.

Hidalgo County Historical Museum, Edinburg, TX
Balli, Carlota C., Collection

James C. Jernigan Library, South Texas Archives, Texas A&M University at Kingsville
Canales, J. T., Estate Collection (JTCEC)

Private Collections
García, Martha X. Lago Vista, TX
Idar, Ed Jr. San Antonio
Limón, José. Austin
Orozco, Cynthia E., files. Arnoldo Vento address, LULAC scholarship fund-raiser honoring Adela Sloss-Vento, April 30, 1999.
Perales, Alonso S., Papers (ASPP). San Antonio
Sáenz, Enrique. Austin
Sloss-Vento, Adela, Papers (ASVP). Edinburg, TX
Tafolla, Dr. Carmen. San Antonio

Interviews

de Luna, Carolina B., with Richard Gutiérrez. Corpus Christi, December 9, 1973. James C. Jernigan Library, South Texas Archives, Texas A&M University at Kingsville.
Garza, Adelaida, with author. Corpus Christi, August 28, 1981.
Garza, Adelaida, and family, with Elvira Chavira. Corpus Christi, March 8, 1981. LULAC Archive, BLAC.
Gonzáles, Manuel C., with author. San Antonio, June 14, 1979, and January 19, 1980.
Gonzáles, Manuel C., with Institute of Texan Cultures. Transcription notes, 1967, "Mexican organizations." Vertical files, San Antonio.
Idar, Ed Jr., with author about Eduardo Idar Sr. Austin, January 7, 1991.
Sáenz, Enrique, with author about J. Luz Sáenz. Austin, August 3, 1989.
Sloss-Vento, Adela. Correspondence and conversations with the author, 1978–1980.
Solís, John C., with Nacho Campos and Emilio Zamora. Austin, September 1972. In author's files.
Solís, John C., with Angie del Cueto Quirós. San Antonio, circa 1977. Cassette 13, LULAC Archive, BLAC.
Solís, John C., with author. San Antonio, January 18, 1980.
Tenayuca, Emma. Correspondence and conversations with author, 1980–1984.
Vento, Arnoldo, with author about Adela Sloss-Vento. Austin, April 10, 1991.
Wilmot, Ofelia, and Louis Wilmot, with author. Corpus Christi, August 27, 1981.

Periodicals

Corpus Christi Caller. 1979
Demócrata Fronterizo. Laredo. 1918
El Cronista del Valle. Brownsville. 1927
El Paladín. Corpus Christi. 1929
Ferguson Forum. Temple. 1920
La Crónica. Laredo. 1910–1911
La Prensa. San Antonio. 1921–1929
San Antonio Daily Express. 1901
San Antonio Express. 1919, 1964

SECONDARY SOURCES

Acuña, Rodolfo. *Occupied America: The Chicanos' Struggle Toward Liberation.* 1st edition, San Francisco: Canfield Press, 1972. 2nd edition, New York: Harper and Row, 1981. 3rd edition, New York: Harpercollins College Division, 1988; 4th edition, New York: Pearson Education, 1999. 5th edition, New York: Pearson Longman, 2000. 6th edition, New York: Pearson Longman, 2007.

Anderson, Benedict. *Imagined Communities: Reflections on the Origin and Spread of Nationalism.* London: Verso, 1983.

Barrera, Mario. "Chicano Class Structure." In *Chicano Studies: A Multidisciplinary Approach*, ed. Eugene P. García, Francisco A. Lomelí, and Isidro D. Ortíz, 40–55. New York: Teachers College Press, 1984.

———. "The Historical Evolution of Chicano Ethnic Goals: A Bibliographic Essay." *Sage Race Relations Abstract* 10, no. 1 (February 1985): 1–48.

Beiner, Ronald, ed. *Theorizing Citizenship.* Albany: State University of New York Press, 1995.

Brah, Avtar, and Annie E. Coombes, eds. *Hybridity and Its Discontents, Politics, Science, and Culture.* London: Routledge, 2000.

Carnes, Mark C. *Secret Ritual and Manhood in Victorian America.* New Haven, CT: Yale University Press, 1989.

Chandler, Charles Ray. "The Mexican American Protest Movement." Ph.D. diss., Tulane University, 1968.

Christian, Carole E. "Joining the American Mainstream: Texas's Mexican Americans During World War I." *Southwestern Historical Quarterly* 92, no. 4 (April 1989): 559–598.

Clawson, Mary Ann. *Constructing Brotherhood: Class, Gender, and Fraternalism.* Princeton, NJ: Princeton University Press, 1989.

Collier-Thomas, Betty, and V. P. Franklin, eds. *Sisters in Struggle, African American Women in the Civil Rights and Black Power Movements.* New York: New York University Press, 2001.

Flores, Richard. "The Corrido and the Emergence of Texas-Mexican Social Identity." *Journal of American Folklore* 105, no. 4 (Spring 1992): 166–182.

Flores, William, and Rita Benamoyer, eds. *Latino Cultural Citizenship: Claiming Identity, Space, and Rights.* Boston: Beacon Press, 1998.

Foley, Neil. "Becoming Hispanic: Mexican Americans and the Faustian Pact with Whiteness." In *Reflexiones: New Directions in Mexican American Studies,* ed. Neil Foley, 53–70. Austin: Center for Mexican American Studies, University of Texas at Austin, 1997.

———. "Partly Colored or Other White." In *Beyond Black and White: Race, Ethnicity and Gender in the U.S. South and Southwest* ed. Stephanie Cole and Alison M. Park, 341–355. College Station: Texas A&M University Press, 2004.

———. *The White Scourge: Mexicans, Blacks, and Poor Whites in the Texas Cotton Culture.* Berkeley: University of California Press, 1997.

Foss, Daniel, and Ralph Larkin. *Beyond Revolution: A New Theory of Social Movements.* South Hadley, MA: Bergin and Garvey, 1986.

Freedman, Estelle. "Separatism as Strategy: Female Institution Building and American Feminism, 1870–1930." *Feminist Studies* 5, no. 3 (Fall 1979): 512–529.

Gamson, Joshua. "Messages of Exclusion: Gender, Movements, and Symbolic Boundaries." *Gender and Society* 11, no. 2 (April 1997): 178–199.

Gamson, William A. *The Strategy of Social Protest.* Homewood, IL: Dorsey Press, 1975.

García, Mario T. "Mexican Americans and the Politics of Citizenship: The Case of El Paso, 1936." *New Mexico Historical Review* 59 (April 1984): 187–204.

———. *Mexican Americans: Leadership, Ideology, and Identity.* New Haven, CT: Yale University Press, 1989.

García, Richard A. "Class, Consciousness, and Ideology—The Mexican Community in San Antonio, Texas: 1930–1940." *Aztlán* 9 (Fall 1978): 23–70.

———. "The Making of the Mexican-American Mind, San Antonio, Texas, 1929–1941: A Social and Intellectual History of an Ethnic Community," Ph.D. diss., University of California at Irvine, 1980.

———. "The Mexican-American Mind: A Product of the 1930s." In *History, Culture, and Society: Chicano Studies in the 1980s,* ed. Mario T. García and Bert Corona, 67–94. Ypsilanti, MI: Bilingual Press/Editorial Bilingue, 1983.

———. *Rise of the Mexican American Middle Class.* College Station: Texas A&M University Press, 1991.

Gómez, Laura E. *Manifest Destinies: The Making of the Mexican American Race.* New York: New York University Press, 2007.

González, Gabriela. "Carolina Munguía and Emma Tenayuca: The Politics of Benevolence and Radical Reform." *Frontiers: A Journal of Women Studies* 24, nos. 2–3 (2003): 200–229.

———. "Two Flags Intertwined: Transborder Activists and the Politics of Gender, Class, and Race in South Texas, 1910–1960." Ph.D. diss., Stanford University, 2004.

González, Gilbert G. *Mexican Consuls and Labor Organizing: Imperial Politics in the American Southwest.* Austin: University of Texas Press, 1999.

Griswold del Castillo, Richard. *World War II and Mexican American Civil Rights.* Austin: University of Texas Press, 2008.

Gutiérrez, David G. (Gregory). "Ethnicity, Ideology, and Political Development: Mexican Immigration as a Political Issue in the Chicano Community, 1910–1977." Ph.D. diss., Stanford University, 1988.

———. "Migration, Emergent Ethnicity, and the 'Third Space': The Shifting Politics of Nationalism in Greater Mexico." *Journal of American History* 91, no. 3 (September 1999): 906–931.

———. *Walls and Mirrors: Mexican Americans, Mexican Immigrants, and the Politics of Ethnicity*. Berkeley: University of California Press, 1995.

Hernández, José Amaro. *Mutual Aid for Survival: The Case of the Mexican American.* Malabar, FL: Krieger, 1983.

Johnson, Benjamin Heber. *Revolution in Texas: How a Forgotten Rebellion and Its Bloody Suppression Turned Mexicans into Americans.* New Haven, CT: Yale, 2003.

———. "Sedition and Citizenship in South Texas, 1900–1930." Ph.D. diss., Yale University, 2000.

Kaplowitz, Craig A. *LULAC, Mexican Americans, and National Policy.* College Station: Texas A&M University, 2005.

———. "Mexicans, Ethnicity, and Federal Policy: The LULAC and the Politics of Cultural Disadvantage, 1942–1975." Ph.D. diss., Vanderbilt University, 1997.

Kuumba, M. Bahati. *Gender and Social Movements.* Walnut Creek, CA: Altamira Press, 2001.

Limón, José E. "El Primer Congreso Mexicanista de 1911: A Precursor to Contemporary Chicanismo." *Aztlán* 5, nos. 1–2 (1974): 85–115.

Lowery, Charles D., and John F. Marszalek, eds. *The Greenwood Encyclopedia of African American Civil Rights.* 2 vols. Westport, CT: Greenwood Press, 2003.

Mansbridge, Jane J., ed. *Beyond Self-Interest.* Chicago: University of Chicago, 1990.

Mansbridge, Jane, and Aldon Morris. *Oppositional Consciousness, The Subjective Roots of Social Protest.* Chicago: University of Chicago, 2001.

Márquez, Benjamín. *Constructing Identities in Mexican American Political Organizations: Choosing Issues, Taking Sides.* Austin: University of Texas Press, 2003.

———. "The League of United Latin American Citizens and the Politics of Ethnicity." In *Latino Empowerment: Problems and Prospects*, ed. Roberto B. Villarreal, Norma G. Hernández, and Howard D. Neighbor, 11–24. New York: Oceanwood Press, 1988.

———. *LULAC: The Evolution of a Mexican American Political Organization.* Austin: University of Texas Press, 1993.

———. "The Politics of Race and Class: The League of United Latin American Citizens." *Social Science Quarterly* 68, no. 1 (March 1987): 84–101.

———. "The Problems of Organizational Maintenance and the League of United Latin American Citizens." *Social Science Journal* 28, no. 2 (1991): 203–226.

Márquez, Benjamín, and James Jennings. "Representation by Other Means: Mexican American and Puerto Rican Social Movement Organizations." *Political Science and Politics* 33, no. 3 (September 2000): 541–546.

McAdams, Doug, and David A. Snow, eds. *Social Movements: Readings on Their Emergence, Mobilization, and Dynamics.* Los Angeles: Roxbury, 1997.

Meier, Matt, and Margo Gutiérrez, eds. *Encyclopedia of Mexican American Civil Rights Movement.* Westport, CT: Greenwood Press, 2000.

Montejano, David. *Anglos and Mexicans in the Making of Texas 1836–1986.* Austin: University of Texas, 1987.

———. "The Demise of 'Jim Crow' for Texas Mexicans, 1940–1970." *Aztlán* 16, nos. 1–2 (1985): 27–70.

Morris, Aldon. *The Origins of the Civil Rights Movement.* New York: Free Press, 1984.

Morris, Aldon D., and Carol McClung Mueller. *Frontiers in Social Movement Theory.* New Haven, CT: Yale, 1992.

Murata, Katsuyuki. "The (Re)Shaping of Latino/Chicano Ethnicity Through the Inclusion/Exclusion of Undocumented Immigrants: The Case of LULAC's Ethno-Politics." *American Studies International* 39, no. 2 (June 2001): 4–34.

Navarro, Armando. *Mexicano Political Experience in Occupied Aztlán, Struggles and Change.* Los Angeles: Altamira Press, 2005.

Ngai, Mae M. *Impossible Subjects: Illegal Aliens and the Making of Modern America.* Princeton, NJ: Princeton University Press, 2004.

Oberschall, Anthony. *Social Conflict and Social Movements.* Englewood Cliffs, NJ: Prentice-Hall, 1973.

Oboler, Suzanne, ed. *Latinos and Citizenship: The Dilemma of Belonging.* New York: Palgrave Macmillan, 2006.

Olivas, Michael, ed. *Colored Men and Hombres Aquí:* Hernández v. Texas *and the Rise of Mexican American Lawyering.* Houston: Arte Público Press, 2006.

Olson, Mancur. *The Logic of Collective Action, Public Goods, and the Theory of Groups.* Cambridge: Harvard University Press, 1971.

Omi, Michael, and Howard Winant. *Racial Formation in the United States: From the 1960s to the 1980s.* New York: Routledge and Kegan Paul, 1987.

Orozco, Cynthia E. "Alice Dickerson Montemayor: Feminism and Mexican American Politics in the 1930s." In *Writing the Range: Race, Class, and Culture in the Women's West,* ed. Elizabeth Jameson and Susan Armitage, 434–456. Norman: University of Oklahoma Press, 1997.

———. "Beyond Machismo, La Familia, and Ladies Auxiliaries: A Historiography of Mexican-Origin Women's Participation in Voluntary Associations and Politics in the U.S., 1870–1990." *Perspectives in Mexican American Studies* 5 (1995):1–34. Tucson: Mexican American Studies and Research Center, University of Arizona.

———. "League of United Latin American Citizens." In *Reader's Companion to U.S. Women's History,* ed. Wilma Mankiller, Gwendolyn Mink, Marysa Navarro, Barbara Smith, and Gloria Steinem, 378. Boston: Houghton Mifflin, 1998.

———. "The Origins of the League of United Latin American Citizens (LULAC) and the Mexican American Civil Rights Movement with an Analysis of Women's Political Participation in a Gendered Conext, 1910–1929." Ph.D. diss., UCLA, 1992.

———. "Regionalism, Politics, and Gender in Southwestern History: The League of United Latin American Citizens' (LULAC) Expansion into New Mexico from Texas 1929–1945." *Western Historical Quarterly* 29, no. 4 (November 1998): 459–483.

———. Various entries in *Latinas in the United States: A Historical Encyclopedia,* ed. Vicki L. Ruiz and Virginia Sánchez Korrol, 3 vols. (Bloomington: Indiana University Press, 2006). Entries by author: "Hernández, María Latigo"; "League of

United Latin-American Citizens"; "Montemayor, Alice Dickerson"; "Orozco, Aurora Estrada"; "Sloss-Vento, Adela."

———. Various entries in *New Handbook of Texas*, ed. Ronnie C. Tyler, Douglas E. Barnett, and Roy R. Barkley, 6 vols. Austin: Texas State Historical Association, 1996. Entries by author: "Gregorio Lira Cortéz"; "*Del Rio v. Salvatierra*"; "Eleuterio Escobar Jr."; "Bernardo F. Garza"; "Manuel C. Gonzáles"; "Harlingen Convention"; "María L. Hernández"; "Hidalgo County Rebellion"; "Clemente N. Idar"; "Eduardo Idar Sr."; "Ladies LULAC"; "League of United Latin American Citizens"; "Alicia Guadalupe Elizondo de Lozano"; "Mexican American Women"; "Alice Dickerson Montemayor"; "Carolina Munguía"; "Order Knights of America"; "Order Sons of America"; "Alonso S. Perales"; "School Improvement League"; "John C. Solís"; "Spanish Speaking PTA."

Padilla, Félix. *Latino Ethnic Consciousness: The Case of Mexican Americans and Puerto Ricans in Chicago.* Notre Dame, IN: University of Notre Dame Press, 1985.

Porta, Donatella Della, and Mario Diani. *Social Movements: An Introduction.* Malden, MA: Blackwell, 2006.

Pycior, Julie Leininger. "La Raza Organizes: Mexican American Life in San Antonio 1915–1930, as Reflected in Mutualista Activities." Ph.D. diss., University of Notre Dame, 1979.

Ribb, Richard Henry. "José T. Canales and the Texas Rangers: Myth, Identity, and Power in South Texas, 1900–1920." Ph.D. diss., University of Texas at Austin, 2001.

Rivas-Rodríguez, Maggie. *A Legacy Greater Than Words.* Austin: University of Texas Press, 2003.

———, ed. *Mexican Americans and World War II.* Austin: University of Texas Press, 2005.

Robnett, Belinda. *How Long? How Long? African-American Women in the Struggle for Civil Rights.* New York: Oxford University Press, 1997.

Rosales, F. Arturo. *Chicano!: The Mexican American Civil Rights Movement.* Houston: Arte Público Press, 1997.

———. *Dictionary of Latino Civil Rights History.* Houston: Arte Público Press, 2007.

———. *¡Pobre Raza!: Violence, Justice, and Mobilization Among México Lindo Immigrants, 1900–1936.* Austin: University of Texas Press, 1999.

———. "Shifting Ethnic Consciousness in Houston." *Aztlán* 16, nos. 1–2 (1985): 71–91.

Rosales, Francisco, ed. *Testimonio: A Documentary History of the Mexican American Struggle for Civil Rights.* Houston: Arte Público Press, 2000.

Ruiz, Vicki, and Virginia Sánchez Korrol, eds. *Latinas in the United States, A Historical Encyclopedia.* Bloomington: University of Indiana Press, 2006.

Sánchez, George J. *Becoming Mexican American.* New York: Oxford University Press, 1995.

Sandoval, Moisés. *Our Legacy: The First Fifty Years.* Washington, DC: LULAC, 1979.

San Miguel, Guadalupe Jr. "Endless Pursuits, The Chicano Educational Experience in Corpus Christi, Texas, 1880–1960." Ph.D. diss., Stanford University, 1979.

Staggenborg, Suzanne. *Gender, Family, and Social Movements.* Thousand Oaks, CA: Pine Forge Press, 1998.

Taylor, Paul S. *An American-Mexican Frontier: Nueces County, Texas.* Chapel Hill: University of North Carolina Press, 1934.

Tilly, Charles. *From Mobilization to Revolution.* Reading, MA: Addison-Wesley, 1978.

Touraine, Alain. *The Voice and the Eye, an Analysis of Social Movements.* Cambridge, England: Cambridge University Press, 1981.

Tyler, Ronnie C., Douglas E. Barnett, and Roy R. Barkley. *New Handbook of Texas.* Austin: Texas State Historical Association, 1996.

Vélez-Ibáñez, Carlos G., and Anna Sampaio, eds., with Manolo González-Estay. *Transnational Latina/o Communities, Politics, Processes, and Cultures.* Lanham, MD: Rowman and Littlefield, 2002.

Yarsinke, Amy Waters. *All for One and One for All: A Celebration of 75 Years of the League of United Latin American Citizens (LULAC).* Virginia Beach, VA: Donning, 2004.

Zamora, Emilio. "Fighting on Two Fronts: The WWI Diary of José de la Luz Sáenz and the Language of the Mexican American Civil Rights Movement." www.lulac. org/about/diary.html.

———. "José de la Luz Sáenz." *El Mesteño*, April 2000, 4–5.

———. *The World of the Mexican Worker.* College Station: Texas A&M University Press, 1995.

INDEX

Page numbers in *italics* indicate images.

African Americans, 20, 23, 26, 29, 33, 35, 190
Agrupación Filantrópica de Damas, 174
Agrupación Protectora Mexicana, 66, 69–70, 97, 100
Alice, Texas, 22, 84–86
Alpha Club, 79–81, 174
American Federation of Labor (AFL), 58, 75, 102–103
Americanization movement, 48–50, 52, 58, 139–140, 221
Asian Americans, 60

Baker, A.Y., 174–175
Barrera, Dave, 272n10
Bonilla, Rubén, 3, 203
bossism, 42, 86–87, 95–96, 106, 167, 172, 174–175, 177; and the Mexican vote, 34–37, 47, 61, 226
Box, John, 22, 40, 51, 59, 60
Bravo, Josefa, 206, 209
Bravo, Manuel B., 173, 206, 209
Brigadas Cruzes Azules, 68, 90, 109, 142, 143
Brooks, Homer, 148–149, 183, 185, 214

Canales, J.T., 27, 87, 93, 96, 104, 106, 118, 121, 132, 134, 136–137, 164, 177, 183, 191, 200, 226; account of Harlingen, 130–131; biography of, 94–97; and class, 118, 128; and education equality, 82, 84; and LLAC, 152, 155–157, 160–161; and LULAC constitution, 163–166, 171, 180; LULAC formation, 93–94, 112, 160–163, 171, 173, 179–180; and Mexican American civil rights, 73; and Mexican citizens, 126–128, 130–131; oratory qualities of, 118, 191–192; and OSA, 78, 82, 83–84, 155–157, 161; in politics, 28, 30, 37, 119; and race, 27; and Texas Rangers, 28, 46, 50–51; and women's participation, 172; and World War I patriotism, 50, 52
Cano, Pablo, 272n10
Cantú, Clara, 48–49
Cañamar, Henry, 87, 88, 272n10
Carvajal, Ramón H., Jr., 74, 75, 86, 87–88, 122, 123